JUDGING STUDENT PROGRESS

R. MURRAY THOMAS
STATE UNIVERSITY OF NEW YORK, COLLEGE OF EDUCATION AT BROCKPORT

JUDGING STUDENT PROGRESS

SECOND EDITION

1960
LONGMANS, GREEN AND CO.
NEW YORK LONDON TORONTO

LONGMANS, GREEN AND CO., INC.
119 WEST 40TH STREET, NEW YORK 18

LONGMANS, GREEN AND CO. LTD.
6 & 7 CLIFFORD STREET, LONDON W 1

LONGMANS, GREEN AND CO.
20 CRANFIELD ROAD, TORONTO 16

THOMAS

JUDGING STUDENT PROGRESS

PUBLISHED SIMULTANEOUSLY IN THE DOMINION OF CANADA
BY LONGMANS, GREEN AND CO., TORONTO

FIRST EDITION FEBRUARY 1954
REPRINTED SEPTEMBER 1954
AUGUST 1955
JULY 1957
SECOND EDITION SEPTEMBER 1960

Library of Congress 60-13576
Printed in the United States of America

VAN REES PRESS • NEW YORK

Preface

JUDGING STUDENT PROGRESS introduces the prospective or the in-service elementary or junior high teacher to ways of evaluating children's growth in the classroom.

The principal differences between the original edition of the book and this revised edition are these:

1. Two new chapters have been developed: Chapter 13, treating Marking Student Progress, and Chapter 16, treating ways of Developing Students' Evaluation Skills.

2. A new appendix has been added to furnish sources of standardized tests.

3. Numbers of other chapters have been revised in detail to bring to the teacher recent developments in evaluation and to furnish additional examples of uses for evaluation techniques in classrooms.

As in the first edition, each chapter except the final one begins with an actual classroom or school incident. The incident pictures teachers talking and acting as they do in their daily tasks of judging students' progress. These incidents, based on true situations, are generally set in a typical American school, Central Elementary and Junior High. The inclusion of such introductory incidents is not an attempt to appear "folksy." Rather, it is an effort to show in their real settings some problems which the evaluation techniques discussed in this book will help teachers solve. It is also an attempt to bring to life evaluation practices which sometimes appear to be merely remote and unrealistic theory to the prospective teacher who reads educational textbooks.

In addition to including introductory scenes the writer has tried to present the material in a direct style, unencumbered by unnecessary technical language which sometimes beclouds meaning in professional literature.

The content of this volume differs in focus from that of some other evaluation books. The evaluation techniques included here are ones that appear most useful for classroom appraisal needs. Ones most appropriate for research or for use in high schools, colleges, and industry are not included, as they are in more general evaluation texts.

Some evaluation books are composed chiefly of descriptions of standardized achievement and intelligence tests and attitude and interest scales. Their authors have treated thoroughly the standardization procedures and types of reliability and validity. As references for the teacher or administrator, these books are valuable sources of specific test descriptions. However, a typical elementary-school teacher does not need such complete knowledge of standardized tests, because these tests play a relatively small role in effective day-by-day judgments of students' growth. The present volume, therefore, presents general descriptions of types of achievement, aptitude, and personality tests as well as practical criteria by which teachers can judge them. It does not include definitive descriptions of many tests. For such descriptions the reader is referred to the bibliographical references at the ends of the chapters on these topics.

Some volumes on evaluation include numerous statistical procedures for analyzing and reporting test and measurement data. However, an inspection of the elementary or junior high teacher's job shows that a few simple statistics are useful but that more complex ones are a luxury. The time a prospective teacher might spend learning complex statistics can be better spent gaining skill with appraisal techniques that will actually be used in the classroom. Consequently, the present volume contains a simplified description of basic statistical procedures. For those interested in more sophisticated statistical methods, the references at the end of Chapter 7 are recommended.

After an extended and careful inspection of the elementary or junior high teacher's daily tasks and teaching goals, the writer has concluded that the prospective teacher at these levels needs skills in constructing effective classroom tests, administering and interpreting results from standardized achievement and aptitude scales, observing and recording children's behavior accurately, judging children's social relationships, judging their participation in class, organizing records, talking effectively with students and parents, and marking and reporting pupils' progress. Teachers should also be able to organize an over-all evaluation program and stimulate students in efficient self-evaluation. The major portion of *Judging Student Progress* is dedicated to a discussion of ways these tasks can be carried out efficiently by elementary and junior-high teachers.

No book is the result of only one person's work or thought. Helpful concepts in the present volume are the result of the teaching of Professors Lucien B. Kinney, H. B. McDaniel, Maude Merrill, Lois Meek Stolz, and Quinn McNemar, all of Stanford University, and of William Wrinkle, formerly of Colorado State College, and Maurice Freehill, Western Washington College of Education.

The writer is also grateful to three of his fellow staff members, Albert deGroat, Howard Kiefer, and Edward Stephany, who tested out the material with their classes and made worth-while suggestions. Other Brockport professors who aided were Gordon Allen, George Anselm, Raye Conrad, Richard Elton, Frank Lane, Herman Lybarger, and William Stebbins.

Acknowledgment is gratefully extended to the many school systems throughout the United States that responded so generously to a survey of current marking and reporting practices. A similar acknowledgment is due the teachers who provided specific examples of effective evaluation techniques they are using.

Note on references: Throughout this volume the italicized numbers in parentheses refer to the suggested readings at the end of the chapter. When two numbers appear in the parentheses, i.e. (*3:57*), the first indicates the particular reference and the one following the colon indicates the page number in that reference.

R. MURRAY THOMAS

To

LUCIEN B. KINNEY

Contents

PART I

Understanding the Place of Evaluation

WHEN TEACHERS EVALUATE STUDENT PROGRESS THEY ARE TRYING TO answer the question: "How well have students learned?" or "How closely have they approached the goals?" or "How well have my teaching methods helped the pupils pursue the goals?"

To answer these questions accurately, the teacher cannot focus only on the *evaluation phase* of the teaching and learning process, he must also understand the phases of *goal setting* and *choice of methods and materials,* for all these aspects are interrelated.

It is the purpose of Part I to show the relationship of the evaluation phase to these other aspects of the educational process.

CHAPTER

I

Analyzing the Teaching-Learning Process

JOHN LEONARD, a university junior, had just completed his first two weeks as a student teacher in the sixth-grade class of Miss June Kennedy. Most of the two weeks he had concentrated on getting acquainted with the pupils and observing the way Miss Kennedy conducted classwork.

The part of the class that had interested him most was the work organized around a study of industrial change in the community. These are the aspects of this study that particularly caught his attention:

The first day Miss Kennedy projected some colored photographic slides she had taken of different industrial establishments in the community, and she asked the students what they knew about each place. This precipitated a discussion of industries that resulted in a number of differences of opinion about what certain plants manufactured, how long they had been operating, and where the products were sold. The teacher said these arguments would be settled within the next few weeks as the class studied local industrial development and its effect on their own lives. She asked what things the students thought would be important and interesting to learn during this study. As pupils offered ideas, she wrote them on the blackboard. She also added her own ideas in order to develop an extensive list of questions about *Industry in Our Community.*

Then, with the teacher's guidance, the class discussed methods of finding answers to their questions. They finally decided to work together part of the time as an entire class and part of the time in small committees. They thought that by using the smaller groups they could learn about a greater variety of industries, and later each group could share its findings with the rest of the class. They thought they might collect information by interviewing representatives of businesses, by visiting some plants, by collecting brochures, by talking with parents and friends who worked in local industries, by reading newspapers on file in the library, and by consulting the Chamber of Commerce.

Following this planning, the teacher led a discussion about the techniques they might use throughout the study to judge how well they were learning answers to the questions they had posed. They decided that, before each group gave its report to the rest of the class, the questions the group was assigned to answer should be written on the board. Then, as the class listened to the report, each student could write in his notebook the answers to the questions. It was also agreed that every committee should prepare an illustrated booklet about its particular industry to serve as a record which other members of the class could consult. The teacher suggested that a final method of judging how much each pupil had learned about local industry would be a test composed of questions created by the teacher and, in some cases, by the committees.

During the two weeks following this first day's planning session the class carried forward this variety of activities:

1. Searched through the telephone book and city directory for names and addresses of industries.

2. Decided how many committees would be needed and what types of industries each group would study. At the teacher's suggestion, every pupil wrote down the names of three classmates he would like to work with on a committee. The teacher considered these preferences in forming the work groups.

3. Met in the small committees to decide how best to learn about each organization assigned to the group. Just prior to these meetings the teacher led a discussion about efficient ways of working in a group, the responsibilities of group leaders and members, and ways for each student to judge whether he was doing his part. After the group meetings, each committee reported its progress to the class, and the teacher asked every student to use a rating scale she had prepared for estimating his own effectiveness as a participant in the group.

4. Practiced in class the way they would later talk on the telephone while arranging to interview industrial representatives and to visit selected businesses.

5. Practiced in class the way they would interview industrial representatives and the way they would record the information.

6. Wrote letters to industries requesting brochures and information. After students composed first drafts of their letters, Miss Kennedy and John Leonard inspected them, gave suggestions for improvements, and asked the pupils to make final copies which would be mailed.

7. After school and on Saturday interviewed industrial representatives at their places of business.

8. Began organizing their reports in consultation with Miss Kennedy and John Leonard. Before they planned the types of reports they would give, Miss Kennedy led a class discussion during which they established criteria for oral reports and for the final illustrated written records. The teacher wrote the criteria on the board and indicated that the work of each committee would be judged according to these standards (such as, standards of accuracy, holding class interest, completeness in answering the questions originally posed, clarity of oral and written expression, and neatness and artistic design of the booklet).

John Leonard was much impressed by the variety of activities, by the way Miss Kennedy included the students in the planning yet always kept activities carefully directed, and by the ways the students continually analyzed their own progress under the teacher's direction. When he asked Miss Kennedy how she had learned to plan this somewhat complex group of activities so that she always knew what she was doing, she answered by explaining a framework for the teaching-learning process that underlies sound planning at any educational level. This is the framework:

THE EDUCATOR'S TASKS

Any educator, whether he is a classroom teacher planning one day's work or the state curriculum director helping to outline twelve years of schooling, faces three basic tasks. These tasks may be stated as three questions that must be answered by the teacher or administrator:

1. What is worth teaching?
2. How can it best be taught?
3. How can we find out how well we succeeded in teaching it?

Some people prefer to have the questions stated in terms of the learner instead of the teacher. They then become: *What is worth learning? How can we best learn it? How can we judge how well we learned it?* Whether stated as the teacher's questions or the learner's, the three basic tasks are the same.

EDUCATIONAL OBJECTIVES

When the educator has answered the question, *What is worth teaching?* he has stated the *objectives* (sometimes called *aims, ends, desired outcomes,* or *goals*) of the school. Some teachers say that outlining objectives is no concern of theirs, but is the job of the educational philosophers, the school board, the curriculum committee, the textbook writer, the county superintendent of schools, or the principal. It is true that these theorists and administrators often organize and write out what they deem is worth while to teach. As a result the course of study in a school, the textbooks, or the state education department syllabi reflect their beliefs. However, the fact remains that even in the most *administrator-dominated* or *course-of-study-dominated* schoolroom the individual teacher has to make decisions about what is worth teaching. In most schools the classroom teacher has much to say about the objectives of specific lessons and units. The conscientious teacher, therefore, cannot excuse himself from the responsibility of examining critically what he teaches merely by saying, "Objectives are the theorists' concern, not mine."

The teacher's task of establishing aims for his classes is simplified considerably by the fact that many aims of the school for some time have been widely accepted in our society, and the teacher has been hired by the community to carry them out.

Among the oldest and most generally accepted goals of the American school is the teaching of the fundamental skills of reading, writing, and computing. In addition to the three R's, other widely accepted aims have evolved in more recent years. Among them are promoting physical health, developing special vocational skills (typing, auto mechanics, farming), improving ability to work with other people, and using leisure time in a profitable and pleasant manner. Stated differently in various communities, these goals exhibit their widespread acceptance by the increasing place of health and physical education courses, vocational classes, group and committee work, and the arts and literature in the school curriculum during the past fifty years. As with the three R's, the teacher does not have to decide whether or not to teach for these additional goals, because they already have been established as proper by the faculty and the people of the community. Therefore, we see that many of the decisions about *what is worth teaching* have already been made for the classroom instructor.

If the goals of the school have basically been established, why should a teacher be concerned about objectives? There are two principal reasons. One has to do with the teacher's role as a policy maker on the school-wide level. The other has to do with his job of selecting activities and materials each day for his students.

On the school-wide level we should note that teachers can be strong influences in establishing new objectives in the schools. Although most teachers do not accept this role in any active way, still the opportunity exists and is grasped by some. By studying the children in their classes and by seeing what the children need to learn in order to grow up successful and happy, teachers hope to see new ways to help them. For example, today there is considerable debate in hundreds of communities about whether sex education should be taught in the schools. In the past the school has not been given the responsibility of instructing children in the facts of how the human race perpetuates itself. This type of education has been left primarily to the home. However, evidence in recent years has indicated that the home in a large number of cases has done a poor job of sex education, with the result that much unhappiness, worry, guilt, physical disease, and emotional shock have marred young people's lives. Many communities are now trying to answer such questions as: "Should children receive sex education in school? If so, at what ages and in what grades? Who should teach it? What methods should be used—films, discussions, booklets?" The central issue here is one of *beliefs* concerning what is true and proper in life and *objectives* which arise from these beliefs. This issue—should sex education become a goal of the school?—must be decided jointly by parents, religious groups, school administrators, and teachers.

In addition to such major issues of objectives as this, minor issues arise from year to year in any community where the school has not completely stagnated. The alert classroom teacher holds the responsibility for helping determine what new objectives are established, for it is often because the parents are impressed by the teacher's sincerity and ability that the community allows new types of subject matter and activities to enter the curriculum.

However, even if the teacher does not take part in formulating some of the broader objectives of the school, he still has responsibilities for deciding upon goals in his own classroom. Even when the objectives of the school seem to have been set by the curriculum builders, the teacher has great influence on them in his daily classwork. When we analyze the study of industries in Miss Kennedy's class we see how this is true.

In the Central School system each grade is assigned particular objectives to work toward. These objectives, which are written into the curriculum plan, were drawn from various sources: state department of education recommendations, the city-wide curriculum committee, and the staff of the school. It is each teacher's responsibility to plan activities that carry the students as far as possible toward these goals. Some of the goals are stated as types of knowledge pupils should gain, such as information about scientific phenomena around them or about the way their society operates. (For the sixth grade this knowledge is to include an understanding of the industries in the community, the reasons these particular industries were established, and the reasons changes have occurred in them during past years.) Other goals are stated as skills the pupils should develop, such as skills in reading, speaking, writing, organizing information, working well with other people on committees, and making a plan for finding answers to questions they face.

It is in implementing these goals that we see how Miss Kennedy makes decisions about objectives each day as she plans class activities. The curriculum plan sets forth local industries as one part of sixth-grade study, but the teacher has not been told by the school's curriculum organizers how much time she is to spend on this area. It has been Miss Kennedy's decision to spend several weeks on the study and to pursue the topic to some depth. Another sixth-grade teacher in this same Central School has used a different procedure which has involved only two days of class discussion about industries and one day of interviewing in class a Chamber of Commerce representative. Miss Kennedy chose to stress the goal of understanding industry, whereas the other teacher has given it only brief treatment so that his class could immediately move into a two-week study of current city election issues and a one-week study of recreation facilities in the county. Later these election and recreation topics were touched only very briefly by Miss Kennedy's class. Thus by emphasizing different goals, these two teachers have caused the specific objectives of the two classes to be somewhat different in practice.

And so it is with the skills goals pursued during the study of industries. According to the school's curriculum plan, sixth graders should improve in oral and written expression—specifically in writing letters, presenting oral reports, and developing written outlines and reports. While studying industries, the pupils worked toward all these skills objectives in Miss Kennedy's class. But, in addition, she developed two more specific aims under the broader category of "effective oral expression," namely, the objectives of improving students' telephoning and interviewing techniques. These telephoning and interviewing skills were objectives unique to Miss Kennedy's class and were not systematically pursued by the other sixth-grade classes.

It should also be noted that Miss Kennedy's pupils played a role in setting their goals. The teaching method she used for initiating this study involved discussing with the class what things they thought important and interesting to learn about local industries. Thus she defined the area of study, local industries, and the students were asked to offer questions (which implied goals) they wished to answer through the study. In this way some student-suggested aims were added to those offered by the teacher. Although students sometimes are not mature enough nor yet familiar enough with an area of study to offer very useful ideas about desirable goals, often it is advantageous to have them included in the planning. Miss Kennedy's procedure has two principal purposes: (1) to capture students' interest in the area about to be investigated and (2) to gather from the pupils good ideas about specific goals which might not have occurred to the teacher.

In this section, then, we have seen the teacher's first important job: to help decide *what is worth learning*. In such ways as Miss Kennedy's, the teacher daily revises, expands, eliminates, or adds to the objectives outlined by the school curriculum plan.

EDUCATIONAL METHODS AND MATERIALS

After deciding what is worth teaching, the educator must inquire, *How can it best be taught?* This is the problem of selecting appropriate *methods* and *materials*. (Sometimes other words are used to describe this phase of the teaching process, such as *teaching procedures, techniques, tactics, approaches,* or *learning activities.*)

For the classroom teacher this step usually assumes more importance than the first one. The average teacher follows established objectives and makes only minor decisions about them from day to day. However, the task of selecting the best methods for reaching the goals is a major one faced daily in the classroom.

In past centuries a typical teacher's repertoire of methods was meager. It usually consisted of (1) lecturing, (2) assigning reading in a text and expecting an oral recitation or the writing of memorized portions, and (3) drilling the class through such means as having the group chorus the answers or having students compete in spelling bees and arithmetic matches.

During the present century the acceptable methods available to teachers have expanded greatly. Some of these techniques depend *only on the teacher* and his personal skills, as when he lectures or interviews pupils or when he directs students' discussion sessions, oral reports, excursions, group work, certain kinds of games and dances, sociodramas and role playing, and the creation of stories and poems.

Other modern methods, however, depend also on the teacher's *skillful use of materials.* These materials and related media include such things as reading sources (textbooks, periodicals, encyclopedias, pamphlets), drawing and painting equipment, modeling equipment, radio and television programs, motion pictures, slides, film strips, cameras and photographs, charts, posters, maps, models, displays, bulletin boards, classroom radio productions, puppet shows, exhibits, tape and disc recordings, and equipment for conducting experiments and demonstrations.

To make the wisest selection of methods and materials, the teacher should know:

1. *The characteristics of his pupils*—their skills, background information, interests, and attitudes.

2. *A learning pattern* or principles of learning that will be most efficient to apply to students of this type who are pursuing these particular goals.

3. *The methods and materials* available and how well they are suited to these students and these kinds of goals.

For example, if one of the school's aims is to have children speak clearly and be able to convey their ideas readily to a group, what is the best method for a particular seventh-grade teacher to use? And what is best for a first-grade teacher? Should the teacher have students read the biographies of great orators? Have them learn the phonetic alphabet? Have them put pebbles in their mouths and try to talk, as the Greek orator, Demosthenes, is said to have done? Have them give informal talks in class? Have them practice conversing with the teacher? Have them take part in formal debates? Have them imitate the speech they hear on the radio or on special recordings? Have them listen to the teacher talk about effective speech? Have them read material aloud to be recorded on tape, and then listen critically to the tape recording? Varieties of all these methods have been used at some time by teachers to help students pursue the goal of effective speech. Which method a teacher chooses should be based on his understanding of children's characteristics, his knowledge of learning principles, and on his skill in using methods and materials.

The methods used by Miss Kennedy's class included: class discussion, small-group work, role playing to practice telephoning and interviewing, actual interviewing of industrial representatives, letter writing, oral reports, written reports, reading in newspapers and brochures, taking notes on reading and on oral reports, designing and illustrating booklets. She selected these methods because she felt they would stimulate the class to work hard to attain a wide variety of goals.

It should be noted that Miss Kennedy tried to make efficient use of school time by pursuing both the knowledge and the skills goals through the same activities. Hence, the students learned skills of talking on the telephone, interviewing, and letter writing as they located information about industries. They learned better ways to work in groups as they organized their reports about industries.

EDUCATIONAL EVALUATION

The third phase of the teaching process involves answering the question: *How well did we teach?* or *How closely did we approach the objectives?* In today's school this third task of the educator is commonly termed *evaluation,* or sometimes *appraisal.* It is with this phase of the teacher's job that this textbook will be primarily concerned.

Many people in the past have thought that evaluation meant only giving students tests. And they have thought that the sole reason for this testing was to assign marks in a course and thus determine who passed and who failed.

Today, however, evaluation is viewed in a much broader manner. For instance, in addition to using objective and essay tests for gathering evidence about students' progress, teachers also garner much data from rating scales, check lists, anecdotal records, unrecorded observation, sociograms, situation tests, charts of student participation, interviews, and student projects or samples of work products.

The modern teacher also has more uses for these data than only that of assigning a final mark. For example, at the beginning of the semester he can test the students to judge their past progress and to estimate at what point he should start teaching them new material. Then, as he provides learning experiences, he observes and tests the pupils to determine how well each one is progressing.

The evaluation data can help the teacher in two principal ways:

First, he can focus on the individual student. That is, he can determine the rate of progress, strengths, and weaknesses of each pupil. With evaluation data the teacher can judge how well a student is working up to his ability, how well he understands current work, what quality of work should be expected of him in the future, and what kind of report of progress should be given to the pupil, to his parents, and to the school administration.

Second, the teacher can focus on himself and his own teaching procedures. That is, he can use evaluation data to judge the effectiveness of the learning activities and materials the class is using. For instance, if with a test or a rating scale the instructor discovers that the entire class has failed miserably to reach the goals, then apparently the methods and materials the teacher has used have been inappropriate for all students. If, on the other hand, tests or ratings show that most students have reached the goals, we conclude that the teaching methods were apparently appropriate for the majority. But for the few students who failed to reach them the methods and materials were inappropriate. (Or it is possible, of course, that the objectives were unreasonable ones for the slower learners. We should recognize that the teacher who is trying to judge his own effectiveness should consider two questions when interpreting test and observation data. He should not only ask, "What do these results show about my methods and materials?" but he should also ask, "Did some students fail—not because my teaching methods were poor—but because I expected too much of them?")

Let us return now to Miss Kennedy's class to review the techniques of evaluation that she was using during the first two weeks of the study of local industry. The techniques can be listed as follows:

1. *Class discussion.* During the discussion precipitated by showing colored slides the first day, the teacher could make some tentative estimates about the class's present knowledge of local industries. By hearing the pupils' comments she was able to improve her guess about which students already had a fair knowledge of different manufacturing firms. We should stress that she made only "tentative" estimates and did not draw any firm conclusions. She realized, as many teachers apparently do not, that oral question-answer sessions in class or general class discussions do not adequately sample each student's knowledge. This is because the more apt or more verbal students often answer all the questions or carry out all the discussion. In addition, just because one student can answer a question correctly, the teacher cannot conclude that all the others also know the answer. Hence, Miss Kennedy used class discussion as both a method of stimulating student interest in the topic and as a technique for making a rough appraisal of the class's present knowledge. This appraisal helped guide her planning the following days.

2. *Observation of pupils' skimming skills.* As a committee of pupils searched through such sources as the city directory and the telephone book for names of industries, the teacher observed them in order to judge their skills. The observing enabled her to see which students were already skillful and it also gave her an immediate opportunity to teach the ones who needed to improve their skimming techniques.

3. *Sociograms.* Before being assigned to a group, each student wrote the names of classmates he would prefer as fellow committee members. Miss Kennedy first created a sociogram, that is, she mapped the social relationships in the class as they were reflected by the student choices. The sociogram helped her learn which students were especially sought by classmates and which were neglected or rejected. It helped her see more clearly the types of cliques within the class. This information, combined with her own observations of student relationships and personality characteristics, enabled the teacher to form groups which might work well on the project and at the same time might improve the social acceptability and social skills of pupils.

4. *Observations recorded as anecdotes.* During the student committee meetings the teacher moved from one group to another,

watching their progress. Occasionally as she passed her desk she stopped to jot down a note on a slip of paper which she then put in a drawer. Each note contained a brief observation about an individual student's contribution to the group or his behavior in it. She had jotted these observations down because she considered them important and did not want to risk forgetting them. Later she slipped each note into the manila record folder which she kept for the particular pupil.

5. *Committee progress reports.* As each committee reported on its work, Miss Kennedy was able to judge how well the students were advancing toward the goal and how much help they would need from her at this point. Without constant progress reports the groups might well have become confused or irresponsible or have wandered off the track.

6. *Rating scales.* Each student was stimulated to inspect his own skills in working with others as he used a rating scale to judge his role in the group work. In addition to encouraging self-appraisal, the rating-scale activity focused pupil attention more clearly on the goals of group work and also enabled the teacher to see how objectively students could view their own behavior.

7. *Observations of telephoning and interviewing skills.* The simulated telephone conversations and interviews gave the teacher and students opportunities to inspect their skills critically and to correct errors before they could occur later in the real-life situations.

8. *Student work products.* Several types of student work products resulted from the study of industries. They included business letters, outlines for oral reports, and illustrated written reports. Before students embarked on these projects, the teacher in discussion sessions clearly outlined the criteria that would be used for evaluating them. Later she, along with the students, used these criteria for appraising and marking these products.

9. *Written test items.* By using a written test later in the study the teacher secured a sample of each pupil's knowledge of facts about local industry and his knowledge of the probable future prospects for industrial development.

These nine types of evaluation devices or sources suggest the principal ways in which Miss Kennedy secured information about student progress. It is important to note that she did not evaluate only at the end of the study. Instead she constantly gathered data. As a teacher, you should remember that when you plan a particular ac-

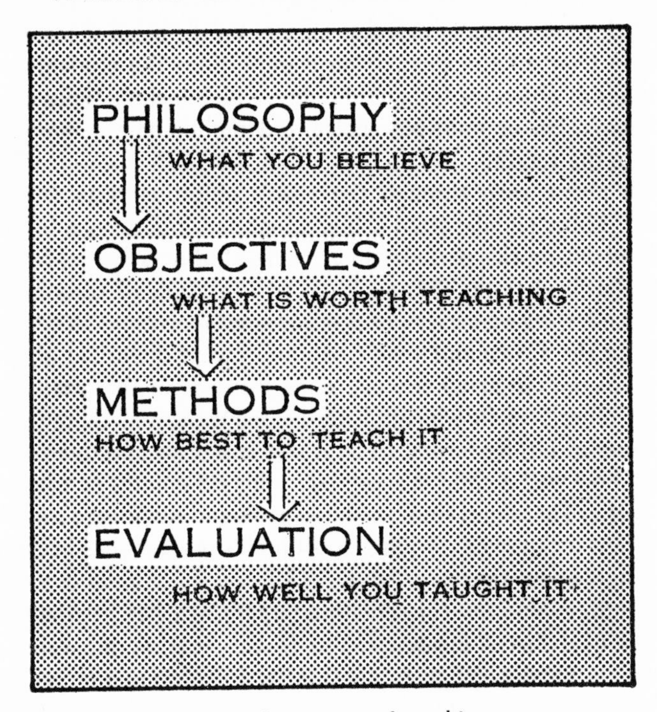

Fig. 1. The process of teaching

tivity for the class you are never completely sure ahead of time that it will work. That is, when you plan to show a film or take a field trip you are only estimating (or hypothesizing) that it will succeed as planned. Only after you have used the method and have in some way judged the students' progress toward the goal can you appraise how appropriate the method was. As with Miss Kennedy's class, it is important for the teacher to use methods that provide for as much evaluation of student learning as possible as you go along. Only when the teacher has this constant *feedback* of information about pupils' successes and failures can he properly adjust the pacing of classwork and the selection of methods.

THE GROWTH OF EVALUATION IN EDUCATION

The term *evaluation* and the tools that it includes are relatively new in education. Before 1900 teachers had very limited methods for determining how well children were succeeding. Instructors apparently judged students' progress primarily on the basis of formal recitation in front of the class or on compositions the students wrote. The kinds of objective tests used today, which include types of items like completion or multiple choice, did not become common until well into the 1900's.

From about 1910 through the 1920's objective tests were very popular. Many standardized achievement and intelligence tests were produced during this period, which has been termed the *gold-rush era* of standardized tests. This rapid growth in kinds of tests has been called the *testing movement* or *measurement movement* in education.

During the 1930's and 1940's educators were disturbed about the overuse of tests in many schools. They pointed out that many of the modern objectives in education cannot be measured thoroughly, or sometimes at all, by formal tests. A test is not an effective means of judging how well a child is accepted by his classmates or whether he likes music. Therefore, since the late 1920's and early 1930's a variety of different techniques for judging children's progress has been evolving to supplement the use of tests.

The term *evaluation* (or sometimes *appraisal*) has been used with numbers of different meanings. But in this text we are using it in perhaps its most popular form, that is, to refer to *the process of determining how effectively students are advancing toward learning objectives.* This process involves the use of many techniques in addition to formal testing to present a many-sided picture of pupil progress.

These techniques form the subject matter of this book. The chief concern in this volume is to help elementary and junior high teachers use evaluation procedures effectively in *judging the progress of individual children* and in *improving the teacher's appraisal of his instructional methods.*

SUGGESTED READINGS

1. FURST, EDWARD J. *Constructing Evaluation Instruments.* New York: Longmans, Green and Co., 1958. Chapters 1 and 2 treat purposes of evaluation.
2. GREENE, HARRY A.; JORGENSEN, ALBERT N.; and GERBERICH, J. RAYMOND. *Measurement and Evaluation in the Elementary School.* New York: Longmans, Green and Co., 1953. Chapter 1: measurement's place in the classroom. Chapter 2: history of measurement.

3. ROSS, C. C., and STANLEY, J. C. *Measurement in Today's Schools* (Third Edition). New York: Prentice-Hall, Inc., 1954. Early chapters treat history and purposes of measurement.
4. SCHWARTZ, ALFRED, and TIEDEMAN, STUART C. *Evaluating Student Progress in the Secondary School.* New York: Longmans, Green and Co., 1957. Chapter 2: the when, what, who, where, and how of evaluation.
5. THORNDIKE, ROBERT L., and HAGEN, ELIZABETH. *Measurement and Evaluation in Psychology and Education.* New York: Wiley and Sons, 1955. Chapters 1 and 2: historical-philosophical orientation and overview of measurement methods.
6. WANDT, EDWIN, and BROWN, GERALD W. *Essentials of Educational Evaluation.* New York: Henry Holt and Co., 1957. Chapter 1.
7. WRIGHTSTONE, J. WAYNE; JUSTMAN, JOSEPH; and ROBBINS, IRVING. *Evaluation in Modern Education.* New York: American Book Co., 1956. Part I: nature and scope of evaluation.

CHAPTER

2

Stating Goals

Four years ago Mr. Frank O'Brien, a fifth-grade teacher, experienced what he calls his *enlightenment about evaluation.* It was during his second year of teaching. When he sent out report cards, he included a note inviting any parents who wished to consult him about their children's progress. A Mrs. Kesling was one of the few to make an appointment to consult him after school. She was a middle-aged mother of five children. The youngest boy, Randy, was in fifth grade. In the first few minutes Mr. O'Brien learned that Mrs. Kesling knew a good deal about schools, having been trained as a teacher before her marriage and having subsequently been interested in schools as a parent.

The mother explained that her main reason for talking with the teacher was her concern over one of Randy's marks. Although he had received A's and B's in *study-reading,* in *spelling,* and in *writing and composition,* the boy had a D in *appreciation of literature.*

As she said, "I feel that Randy likes books very much and has a rather mature understanding of them for a boy his age. This grade of D in the subject called *appreciation of literature* amazed me. I felt that I had to know how he had earned such a mark. That's why I wished to ask how the children's appreciation of literature is judged."

Mr. O'Brien explained that "The mark is quite objective. I like to keep my personal opinion out of the grades as much as possible. Randy received the mark because of his very low test scores."

"I see. A test in appreciation?"

"That's right. It's quite a fair objective test. For one thing, the students are to match the names of authors with the characters in the stories read by the class this semester. Then they also identify passages from the stories, that is, they read a short paragraph on the test and tell which story it was from. They had several other types of items too."

"And was the whole mark based on that test?"

"Well, yes. Of course, it wasn't just one test. We had three of them during the semester."

"I see. Randy told me something about taking a test or two like that. He thought he hadn't done very well because he said the stories were ones he read a year or two ago in books from the library, so he didn't read the stories this year. Apparently he forgot some of the characters. Well, that takes a load off my mind."

"Then you understand about the mark?"

"Oh, yes. It's quite clear. You see, the reason I was confused was because he checks so many books out of the library and discusses them at home with the rest of us. As you probably know from having him in class, the books he reads are intended more for junior-high-age students. Then when he received this D we were very much concerned. But I see now that it was the three tests. That's all right."

Mr. O'Brien later said that he was surprised that Mrs. Kesling could be so easily relieved about the D and that she did not seem worried about making Randy study harder for such a test next time. The incident continued to bother the teacher because he could not reconcile the fact that some of the children who had got better scores on the matching test seldom if ever voluntarily read stories; and at least some of those who did check books out voluntarily probably would never discuss them with anybody, much less be able to talk about them with adults in a mature fashion. Yet Randy, who could do these things, had been given a D in appreciation of literature. Apparently something was amiss in the way Mr. O'Brien was judging children's progress in *appreciation.* As he thought about the ways he measured children's success in other classroom activities, he realized that he probably was misjudging some children very badly, despite his efforts to use "objective tests and keep personal opinion out of the marks."

This concern over ways of evaluating the children's work led him to talk with Mr. Harris, the Central School System assistant principal and curriculum director. The talks resulted in his enlightenment about evaluation, the essentials of which are explained below.

THE CORE OF THE PROBLEM: OBJECTIVES

Like Mr. O'Brien, many teachers are periodically embarrassed when they think about the ways they judge children's progress. They are distressed by realizing that the marks they give often are at variance with the actions or abilities demonstrated in a child's everyday life.

In an effort to improve his judgments of children it is natural for the conscientious instructor to begin tinkering with his tests or his report-card system or his methods of observing students, because it is this third step in the teaching process (evaluation) that appears at fault. Although the tinkering may correct a few mechanical aspects of evaluation, the basic improvement the teacher desires in his appraisal of pupils' growth often will not result from this approach. In many cases *the real fault lies in the way the objectives for the class* (or for the particular unit or lesson) *are stated.*

Discussing the way objectives are stated may appear at first glance to be much ado about nothing. However, there is evidence to support the observation that conscientious teachers who practice improved methods of defining their goals *can expect marked improvements in both their methods of teaching and the ways they measure children's progress* (*2,3,4,5,6,7,8*). The improved learning for children and the resulting increased personal satisfaction for teachers make a discussion of how objectives are stated an important step.

Focus of objectives

Objectives are commonly stated in a number of ways. They can be worded in terms of either the teacher or the student or the topic to be studied. That is, they can tell either what the *teacher aims to teach* or what the *student learns* or they can focus on the *topic or subject matter.*

Focus on Teacher	*Focus on Topic or Subject*
1. Teach appreciation of literature	1. Appreciation of literature
2. Teach reading	2. Reading
3. Teach fundamental communication skills	3. Communication skills

Focus on Student

1. Appreciates literature
2. Reads adequately
3. Communicates adequately

It is obvious that there is no fundamental conflict among these three methods. The distinction here is primarily one of focus: on the *teacher* or on the *topic* or on the *student*. There is nothing right or wrong with any of these ways of stating objectives. However, since numbers of educators have found that stating objectives in terms of students is more profitable, they prefer this approach.

Those educators who prefer the goals in terms of students use the following line of reasoning to support their practices: They begin with a definition of education as a *process of changing human behavior*. The teacher's job, then, is to help boys and girls change from non-readers into readers, from non-writers into writers, from children who fight and argue in a group into children who work effectively together, and so forth. The final goal of the school is to produce persons *whose behavior has been changed* so that they achieve a degree of success and happiness in our society. Following this reasoning, we find that the most profitable way for the educator to state his objectives is by describing the type of *behavior characteristic of the person who performs successfully*; that is, the person who performs successfully is the person who *has learned*. This is known as describing the objectives of the school in *terms of student behavior*. Because the student is the one who is being changed, the focus should be on his behavior, not on the teacher's nor in terms of the topic or subject matter.

In actual practice the importance of this distinction in focus can sometimes be observed in the behavior of different teachers. For instance, one instructor says, "Yes, we've successfully covered that objective. I taught it. I remember the exact day I went over division of fractions in class." This statement shows that the speaker thought of objectives in terms of teacher behavior or in terms of the subject matter. The teacher's job here was fulfilled, because he had met the objective: "To teach division of fractions" or "Division of fractions." However, as in the case of many lessons in school, the teacher can *teach* or *cover* a topic or skill, but this does not mean that the students *learned* or that their behavior has been changed.

On the other hand, the educator who uses student-focused objectives (in spirit as well as in word) tends to think in terms of "What did the students learn?" Or he thinks, "How did the students' behavior change as a result of this lesson?" Being student focused in his statement of goals, the teacher does not assume that the job is complete when he has "taught it" or "gone over it in class." Instead, he evaluates to see how well the students have learned. Only then can he make a statement about whether "we've successfully covered that objective." Since the students—not the teacher or the topic—are the ones the school proposes to educate, it appears more realistic to state objectives in terms of their changed behavior.

Mr. O'Brien granted that such a shift in focus would help him concentrate more on the students' needs and behavior. Consequently, he changed his objective from "teach appreciation of literature" to "student appreciates literature."

He asked, "Now, is that the right way to say it? It still doesn't seem to me that this objective is going to straighten out my problem." And he is right. He has corrected the *focus* of his goal, but he has not corrected the *specificity*.

Specificity of objectives

In addition to a difference in focus, objectives can differ in specificity. For instance, the three objectives indicated earlier were:

The student:

1. Appreciates literature.
2. Reads adequately.
3. Communicates adequately.

In this list number 3 is a more general objective than number 2. And 1 is more specific than either of the others. If we were constructing an outline of objectives, the more specific number 2 would be properly subsumed under 3, because reading is *one* of the communication skills. Objective 1 could then be subsumed under two categories below 2, for literature can be *appreciated* when it is either read or listened to. This section of our outline of objectives then could be:

The student:

1. Communicates adequately.
   a. Reads.
      (1) Understands newspapers.
      (2) Appreciates literature.
   b. Writes.

c. Listens.
   (1) Understands directions given in school.
   (2) Understands issues in debates on controversial topics.
   (3) Appreciates literature.
d. Speaks.

If we were teaching a particular reading or writing lesson we would wish to make these subtopics even more specific by breaking them down further into the skills or behaviors of which they are composed.

Thus it is seen that objectives can differ in how general or how specific they are. An understanding of this fact can help teachers improve their methods of teaching and evaluating.

Mr. O'Brien's objective, *student appreciates literature,* is too general to be an accurate guide in the classrom. The word *appreciate* is a favorite among the terms educators use in describing what they believe is worth while for children to learn. Students are to learn to appreciate art, music, literature, America, the culture of the Mayas, the contributions of the scientific method, modern transportation, and hundreds of other things. Although *appreciation* is inserted freely into lists of objectives, and teachers speak of giving "appreciation lessons," it is usually very difficult to discover what is really meant by such an objective. The meaning of the word is too general and vague. As a result, it is not only difficult for a teacher to determine how to help children reach the goal, but it is also difficult to determine whether or not the pupils ever reach it. The elusiveness of the term *appreciation of literature* led to the misunderstanding between Mrs. Kesling and Mr. O'Brien. She had observed certain of Randy's behavior (reading many advanced books and talking about them voluntarily with the family) and had interpreted this as evidencing an appreciation of literature. However, since Randy had not done well on the test about authors and their works, Mr. O'Brien had interpreted this behavior as evidencing a low degree of appreciation.

At this point it is well to indicate that teachers sometimes confuse their own introspections with the job of judging pupils' growth. For example, some teachers question the sense of making an issue of such a word as *appreciation* or of a term like *understanding of art*. They ask, "Why must we be more specific than that? I know when I appreciate literature or music. I know whether I understand art or understand the Italian Renaissance." This is quite possibly true. A person experiences within himself feelings and thoughts that convince him that he *appreciates* and *understands*. This is *self*-evaluation. However, self-evaluation is different from the teacher's job of judging students' appreciations or understandings. In appraising student progress, the teacher obviously cannot depend on introspection but must observe behavior. Consequently, it is profitable in stating objectives to specify behaviors or actions that give evidence of the extent of a pupil's appreciation or understanding.

Therefore, Mr. O'Brien retained *appreciates literature* as a general objective, but for teaching purposes he defined this in more specific terms. The curriculum director had explained to him how to state the objectives for teaching:

"Your goal is to change the children's behavior. And by *behavior* I don't mean the popular use of the term of having children refrain from being naughty. I use *behavior* in the psychologist's sense, meaning any action, whether physical or mental. Thinking is a kind of behavior, but since you can never see a person think, you as a teacher must depend on some other outward sign of behavior—some action like talking or building a boat—that shows some inner behavior like thinking apparently is taking place.

"If you state the kinds of behavior you expect from children by the end of your lesson—or by the end of the school year—you will find you have stated your teaching objectives. Just preface your list of objectives with a phrase like 'After being in my class the student . . .' or 'Following these learning experiences the student can . . .' Then make a list of the kinds of actual behavior that are desired of the child who has satisfactorily learned."

The teacher tried this technique with the literature objective. He attempted to make it specific by stating the actual, observable behaviors the student should show. As he tried to decide what kinds of actions he wanted from his students he could not help realizing that he had never before really thought out what he meant by appreciation of literature. After puzzling out his own beliefs he recognized that in his mind *appreciation of literature* actually involved two different groups of behaviors. It involved *understanding* the literature as well as *liking* the literature. Mr. O'Brien also realized that when he discussed appreciation of literature with other people, some of them really meant different things than he had in mind. For instance, some people used *appreciation* as a synonym for *understanding*, whereas others used *appreciation* to mean only *liking* or being drawn toward the literature. But even when he recognized that his definition of the term involved both understanding and liking he realized that he still had not defined it in behaviors that he could recognize in his students. Hence, he further analyzed each of these two categories into the following more specific actions.

In dealing with the matter of *liking* literature, he started his definition with the two behaviors Mrs. Kesling had mentioned informally. So the list began:

"After his learning experiences with literature, the pupil:

1. Voluntarily secures books to read.
2. Discusses with others what he has read."

The teacher then continued his list with other types of behavior he thought the student would show if he liked literature:

"3. Suggests that others read books he has enjoyed.
4. Voluntarily spends some free time reading."

After listing these evidences of liking books, Mr. O'Brien turned to his second category of *understanding* literature. He recognized that understanding can involve a great range of things, from the simple recognition of the plot sequence in *The Three Bears* to the complex analysis of character development and allusions to ideas from ancient times in *Hamlet*. Hence, he tried to state his understandings as a few basic types he considered suitable for the average fifth grader. The list included:

"The student who understands literature:

5. Relates the plot sequence in a story or play.
6. Describes the character traits of the main characters in the story.
7. Tells how one or two principal characters might be different at the end of the story than at the beginning, that is, tells how characters changed in the story and why.
8. Accurately locates the locale of the story on a map, if a definite geographical area is involved in the tale.
9. Tells which characters he liked best, and why. Tells which he liked least, and why."

As he finished his list the teacher wondered where his memorization of authors and their works should come in. Finally he decided that matching a list of authors and their works was really a forced type of *appreciation* or *enjoyment* and did not really fit with what he now recognized he meant by appreciation. Even though his former goal of memorizing authors' names had permitted him to use objective tests, the goal did not seem very worthy when he looked at the kinds of behavior changes he wanted the children to make.

Before discussing these objectives with the curriculum director, Mr. O'Brien added a tenth that he thought would cover any part of literature appreciation he might have omitted:

"10. Thoroughly enjoys stories and verse."

When the curriculum director read the goals he highly approved of the first nine. "They are real kinds of behavior. You can tell whether the students reach them. They are all clear except this last one. How do you tell whether a student *thoroughly enjoys stories and verse*?"

"If he enjoys stories and verse he likes to read them," Mr. O'Brien said.

"But how does he act?"

"Well, he spends time reading them and makes some effort to get hold of them. He probably talks about them to other people," Mr. O'Brien added.

"But *enjoys stories and verse* is not a kind of behavior you can observe. That statement is as vague as *likes* or *appreciates* literature. Notice that just now when you defined *enjoys stories and verse* you gave three kinds of behavior the study would show: spends time reading, makes some effort to get books, and talks about his reading. Aren't those the same as objectives 1, 2, and 4 in your list?"

Mr. O'Brien looked at his list. "You're right, of course. I didn't have to include the tenth one at all. Naturally, when I state specific objectives, I should list actual behaviors I can judge or observe some way."

"That's right. It's the key to this whole business of stating specific objectives in terms of student behavior. None of us has ever seen anybody *enjoy* literature or *like* books except by observing some behavior he shows, such as his suggesting the book to a friend or discussing it with someone."

"All right, but how is this going to help me teach and judge children's progress better?"

In answer to this question, Mr. Harris drew a chart containing three columns and titled them *objectives, methods,* and *evaluation.* He placed the teacher's behavioral objectives in the left column. Then he asked Mr. O'Brien to think of the best methods he could imagine to develop the desired behavior in the students. These methods, which would be the teaching techniques he would use in his class, were to be listed in the middle column. In the right column he was to list the ways he would find out how well the students' behavior had changed, that is, how well they had reached the objectives. By filling out this chart, Mr. O'Brien would be outlining in a concrete and convincing manner all the basic steps for his *appreciation of literature* program.

The next day, after completing the chart, Mr. O'Brien returned to discuss the methods and evaluation techniques he had listed. This was his chart:

OBJECTIVES	METHODS	EVALUATION TECHNIQUES
Following his learning experiences, the student shows he *likes* literature because he:	(In general all the methods listed would help students pursue the goals of liking literature.) *The teacher will:*	(Numbers in front of evaluation techniques correspond with numbers in front of objectives.) *The teacher will:*
1. Voluntarily secures books to read.	From time to time bring books to class. Give brief summaries of what stories are about. Read passages from books to class.	1. Have students keep lists of books read. Check with librarian or classroom library.
2. Discusses with others what he has read.	Give students opportunities to tell class about stories. Give them chances to draw pictures of scenes from books to show class.	2. Observe students in class. Talk with parents.
3. Suggests that others read books he has enjoyed.	Display book jackets on bulletin board. Give brief discussion of books displayed in class.	3. Observe students in class. Talk with parents. Have class book reports.
4. Voluntarily spends free time reading.	Provide time for entire class to go to library and browse and select books. Suggest particular books to individual students according to teacher's knowledge of their interests and abilities; do not force them, merely suggest.	4. Observe students in class. Talk with students and parents.
The student shows he *understands* literature because he: 5. Relates the plot sequence in a story or play. 6. Describes the character traits of the main characters in the story.	Read stories to (and with) class, and by use of leading questions show how to analyze plot, describe character traits, analyze character growth, locate story setting, give personal reaction to characters.	

OBJECTIVES	EVALUATION TECHNIQUES
7. Tells how one or two principal characters might be different at the end of the story than at the beginning. 8. Accurately locates the locale of the story on a map, if tale involves an exact location. 9. Tells which characters he liked best and least, and why.	(All the evaluation techniques help measure growth toward all goals.) Lead class discussions. Have students give book reports directed at objectives (oral and written reports). Give written tests.

Mr. O'Brien explained his chart:

"I put down the main methods I would use to reach those objectives. I would use all the methods under *likes* literature to reach goals 1 through 4 and all the methods under *understands* literature to reach goals 5 through 9. I mean that in this list there isn't one particular method for a particular goal. I think all the methods would help develop these kinds of behavior. I'd plan to use the methods throughout the year, since these are long-term goals and not just objectives for a particular unit. Across from each objective from 1 through 4 I listed the ways I think I could gather evidence about how well the children reached that goal. So the evaluation numbers correspond to specific objectives. That's why I have listed such things as the parent-teacher conference for more than one objective. Of course, I wouldn't have a separate conference for each objective. I just meant that objectives 2, 3, and 4 are kinds of behavior I could try to learn about in a conference with a child's parents. There is one more thing I might mention about the evaluation column. Some of the techniques listed there are more practical than others. For example, I probably would not be able to have a conference with each child's mother or father. Therefore, I would base my judgments more on the other devices, which are more practical for my class."

The curriculum director believed that the plan was sound and that the evaluation techniques suggested were logical ones for checking the objectives. When Mr. Harris commented upon the absence of a *matching test* among the evaluation techniques, the teacher pointed out that previously he had thought of evaluation mainly in terms of tests like the one requiring pupils to match authors with their works. However, in the present case he had begun by stating the objectives as the kinds of behavior he wished to result from his teaching. Consequently, he saw that evaluation means judging how closely a person's behavior approaches the objective. Sometimes tests are appropriate techniques for making this judgment, but many times other approaches are more appropriate or are best used in combination with tests.

Before leaving, Mr. O'Brien asked two final questions:

"Earlier today I was showing this scheme of mine to one of the sixth-grade teachers. She said it looked all right, but she thought I had too much in the objectives column. She said my objectives were really just 'likes and understands literature,' so those are the only things that should appear under objectives. She said these other more specific behaviors belonged over in the evaluation column, because those were the things I was looking for when I evaluated. What do you think?"

Mr. Harris said, "I prefer the way you have done it. These behaviors you have listed are ultimately your goals in terms of the ways you will see them reached by the children. Some teachers prefer to move these specifics into the evaluation column. This is all right too, if you like. What is important is that you actually do define them down into observable or measurable specifics, despite the column you assign them to. The scheme you have outlined in literature is a good one. It should work nicely."

Mr. O'Brien's second question was:

"Now that I've broken appreciation of literature down into two categories, liking and understanding, how do I lump them together again when I have to give a student a single mark on his report card? It's quite possible a bright student meets the understanding goals but doesn't like to spend much time reading on his own, so he would rank lower on the 'liking' objectives. Maybe he prefers playing ball in his spare time."

Mr. Harris admitted, "You're right. This means we'll have to look over the report card again for the middle grades. At least in the case of your class, it will need some revision so parents and students can better understand it. Let's talk it over next time the teachers of the intermediate grades meet."

EXAMPLES IN OTHER AREAS

The following chart presents a few examples of the relationship among objectives, methods, and evaluation in areas other than literature. Note that the types of evaluation devices used in each instance are determined by the particular behavior desired from the child as shown by the objective.

OBJECTIVE	METHOD	EVALUATION
After his experiences in this class the pupil:	The teacher:	
ART—*Grade 1*		
Draws with crayons or colored chalk, or paints with poster paints.	Provides crayons, paints and paper. Provides time for drawing, painting. Encourages child to draw as a reaction to his experiences in class and at home. Helps children plan murals and cooperate in drawing them as interpretations of their experiences in school, at home, and in the community.	Observation and anecdotal records. Samples of student work. Parent-teacher conference.
ARITHMETIC—*Grade 3*		
Adds, subtracts whole numbers accurately. Multiplies two-place numbers accurately.	Provides many opportunities for students to add, subtract, and multiply quantities in their daily lives. Has each child solve realistic problems in arithmetic book.	Personal observation and anecdotes. Informal oral tests and discussions. Written tests.
STUDY-READING—*Grade 6*		
Uses library card catalogue accurately. Finds topics in reference books.	Explains and demonstrates use of catalogue in library. Explains use of reference books. Sees that each student is assigned topics that necessitate use of card catalogue and reference books in relation to social studies and science experiences.	Observation of students' success in finding and reporting topics. Test on how to find material in library and in reference books.

The question is often asked, "But are these objectives, methods, and evaluation techniques placed on a chart like this supposed to be my actual lesson plans I would use each day?"

No, the type of chart suggested above is not a lesson plan. Instead, it is a technique for the teacher to use in doing over-all planning. The list of the teacher's objectives for the year would not necessarily be in chronological order with September objectives coming first and June objectives placed last. It is obvious that the second objective on the chart above (adds, subtracts, and multiplies) would be a goal toward which the third-grade teacher would strive throughout the year. (The other elementary-school teachers would also use this arithmetic objective, or at least portions of it.) The third-grade instructor tests the class and observes their accuracy in computing and in seeing what life situations demand adding, substracting, and multiplying. In this way the teacher judges which students are reaching the objectives most adequately throughout the year. Special help can be given to those who are not reaching the goals as fast as others. Therefore, the above chart is not a series of lesson plans or units. The details of methods and evaluation devices are not included. Rather, the chart is suggested as an aid for the teacher in stating:

Where we are going.

How we can best arrive there.

How we can find out how closely we have approached the goal.

During the school year the teacher spaces his units and lessons in such a way that by the end of the year the children will have moved closer to all of the goals; none of the objectives will have been forgotten or ignored. Because of their individual differences in abilities and in speed of maturation, some children will be expected to move closer to the goals than will others.

(See Chapter 15 for a year's plan of objectives, methods, and evaluation devices.)

LIMITATIONS IN EVALUATING

Teacher time for planning

Teachers like Mr. O'Brien who are newly introduced to the above approach to evaluation soon discover its limitations. One factor cited as a limitation is the lack of sufficient teacher time to do a thorough and immediate job of revising and charting all of the year's work in terms of student-behavior objectives. Indeed, since the task of sitting down to write all the specific objectives at one time for a grade may appear overwhelming, a natural reaction is to avoid doing any such revising at all, even though, as a seventh-grade teacher said, "I'm convinced that it would produce better teaching for students."

However, the task of writing *all* of the actual changes desired in students' behavior need not be done at once. Mr. O'Brien began by revising one area of his teaching: that of literature. As he worked through the semester he began to state goals in other areas more clearly, and in doing so he found that he no longer had difficulty deciding what evaluation techniques would be proper for his lessons and units.

The task of revising all the work in a particular grade in terms of specific behavioral outcomes probably could not be done easily in a year, because teachers have many other pressing tasks. Revising one area at a time will take the teacher gradually toward the goal and should result in better learning and better judgments of children's progress.

Time for evaluating

After outlining his objectives, methods, and evaluation devices and seeing how he could build lessons to meet his goals satisfactorily, Mr. O'Brien was disturbed by the fact that he now had listed many evaluation techniques for measuring student growth, but he realized that he would not have time to use all of these devices completely with his class. Mr. Harris provided the logical answer to his dilemma:

"Look at the possible ways you can evaluate the children. Then from these many possible ways, select the ones you think will give the best picture of the children's growth in the time you can dedicate to it. You never can do the task as thoroughly as you wish. You must be content to do what you can in the time you have."

Lack of opportunities to measure all behavior

In describing the way she altered her statements of objectives, Miss Colby, an eighth-grade teacher, indicated a difficulty she encountered in trying to measure the pupils' progress toward the goals. She said:

"One of the general goals for my students is to help them become democratic citizens. Following this newer approach to objectives, the students and I have broken down this general goal into specific behaviors. Here are a few of them:

"After their experiences in eighth grade the students:

1. Allow each person who wishes to present his point of view when a controversy arises.
2. Voluntarily suggest voting to settle controversial group issues.
3. Secure, or make an effort to secure, accurate information on

controversial issues about which they have an opportunity to help make decisions.

4. Vote in each election of all groups of which they are members.
5. Abide by majority decisions.

"I can see the value of stating these behavioral objectives, because it has changed my way of teaching. I formerly had a rather hazy goal of *producing democratic citizens*. It wasn't defined any more specifically than that. To meet such a goal I had the students read about our country's past, and my evaluation consisted mostly of objective tests, such as having them list the names of the presidents and answer questions about wars. But since we thought out the democratic behaviors the students are to reach, I now teach democracy differently. The children work on cooperative projects under my guidance in addition to their reading. Now they have training in acting democratically.

"Although we seem to be making good progress in learning, I face this one big problem: *How can I judge the specific behavior of the students when frequently I have little or no opportunity to observe or measure such behavior in their lives?* It's easy enough to judge directly a goal such as *speaks understandably*, because I hear the student talk in school. But how can I get a true picture of how well each pupil meets such a goal as: Votes in each election of all groups of which he is a member? I would have to follow him around on the ball field, at the Boy Scouts, and at home. It is true that in a conference with his parents I might learn something about such a goal (if his parents would bother to come for a conference). But I really can't see how a teacher can evaluate in school the actual behavior as stated by many of the goals."

Miss Colby's conclusion is obviously correct. Teachers do not have the opportunities or the time to measure directly all the desired changes in student behavior. A compromise is necessary. The following section outlines a solution that has been found satisfactory by numbers of teachers.

LEVELS OF BEHAVIOR, PLANNING, AND UNDERSTANDING

Judging direct behavior

Whenever feasible, the teacher judges children's behavior directly. For example, if the goal is *Adds fractions accurately*, he has the pupils add fractions. If the goal is *Allows each person to present his point of view when a controversy arises,* the teacher observes and records the pupils' actions in group work and in play. This is the best way to measure the students' progress, for it is the record of *actual behavioral change* desired in children's lives.

However, some goals do not lend themselves readily to direct measurement or observation by the teacher. The following would be an example in the area of science or health in a seventh-grade class:

"After experiences in seventh grade the student sterilizes water when its fitness for drinking is doubtful."

In the case of this objective, it is unlikely that the teacher will have adequate opportunities to *judge directly* how well pupils reach this goal. He probably will not see each pupil in a realistic situation of this type. Consequently, the teacher must compromise by measuring what the student would *plan to do* where the fitness for drinking was doubtful. Measuring the student's *plan* rather than his *actions* is obviously a compromise position, because people do not always behave as they say they plan to behave. (This is a limitation of public opinion polls before elections; at least a portion of the public votes differently from the way it reports verbally. In teachers colleges and schools of education it is not uncommon for a student teacher to perform in a manner different from that outlined on his written lesson plan. Men in stress situations such as war often do not act as they have planned.) Therefore, when the teacher measures what students *plan to do* rather than what they *actually do,* he knows that his evaluation of the behavioral goal may not always be accurate. When he appraises the plan he must *assume* (and hope) that the student later will act as he planned. Despite the exceptions cited above, this assumption is sound in a great many situations. Many times we do act as we have planned.

The planning level

Judging the pupil's direct actions is called evaluating on the *behavioral level.* The more indirect method of judging the pupil's plans is called evaluating on the *planning level.* The water-sterilizing objective that a teacher might have difficulty in judging in each student's life can be measured on the planning level through verbal or written test situations. A question could be asked directly: "How can polluted water be sterilized?" or "How would you purify unclean water to make it fit to drink?" This would test what the student would plan to do if faced by such a problem.

The teacher might also test on the planning level by constructing a problem simulating the real-life situation in which the desired behavior might appear. The following two examples would perhaps be more interesting for the pupils than the direct questions given above.

> *Example 1:* "The seventh graders went on a picnic to Kelsey Pond. They remembered to bring all the food, including a large bucket of weiners to roast, buns, potato chips, and two big pans of potato salad. However, they forgot to bring any soft drinks or water to drink. There was no faucet or well near by, and the school bus which had brought them would not return for three hours. During lunch they became quite thirsty. Harry started to scoop a drink of water out of the pond, but Carol stopped him by saying, 'I don't think that water is safe.'
>
> "Problem—What would you suggest they do? Give reasons for your answer."

In answering this the student would be expected to suggest that the seventh graders use the bucket or pans for boiling the water to make it safe for drinking.

> *Example 2:* "Water from snow melting in the mountains raised the level of the Missouri. As the river flowed across the plains it burst through its banks in many places. Although not many homes were damaged in the small town of Plattsville, several of the water mains were broken so that the water supply in homes was shut off. The people needed drinking water. What would you suggest they do?"

In answering this the student would be expected to suggest a means of obtaining safe water, such as securing flood water and boiling it to make it potable.

The above examples show that when the teacher finds it very inconvenient or impossible to judge directly a pupil's behavior, he can compromise by judging what the pupil would plan to do. Although this evaluating on the planning level is to some extent a retreat from the actual life situation, the teacher assumes that the pupil, at least in many cases, will act as he says he will.

The understanding level

It is true, however, that some objectives which most schools use as bases for their curricula cannot be judged adequately on either the behavioral level or the planning level. These objectives are commonly called *understandings*. Following are some typical objectives of this type from the area of social studies (*4:157*):

"The student:

1. Understands the need for government.
2. Understands the structure of government.
3. Understands how candidates are elected.
4. Understands how public opinion is formed.
5. Understands world interdependence."

Since *understanding*, like *appreciation*, is a rather abstract word, it is proper at this point to define the way it is used here. We can be guided toward a definition by asking, "How does a person behave to show that he understands?" Usually from the standpoint of the teacher who cannot observe the actual behavior of the student as a citizen in later years, the pupil who can *explain* or *tell* something accurately is given credit for *understanding*. The child who explains the living habits of the plains Indians is said to understand how plains Indians lived. Therefore, it appears fair in this instance to substitute *explain* or *tell accurately* wherever the term *understanding* appears in such objectives as the above. Defined in this manner, understandings are relatively easy to evaluate compared to actual behaviors of children, for understandings in this sense can all be measured by the traditional school tests, either oral or written.

Usually such goals as these understandings are based upon the assumption that the person who has achieved understandings (such as the five listed above) will use this knowledge at appropriate times in his life (such as when voting for members of Congress). It is assumed that he will use these understandings to *plan* his actions. Subsequently, he will *behave* according to his plans. In this way the teacher believes that understandings lead to adequate plans and thus to adequate behavior. This logic appears sound. As a result, many teachers base their programs almost completely on the assumption that this process is always true. However, there is considerable evidence to indicate that such factors as human emotions, conflicting human needs, poor evaluation techniques, and changing conditions in a person's life may cause a slip between an apparent *verbal understanding* and the *final behavior* that is supposed to result from that understanding.

For example, in the morning an entire class of eighth graders *understood* (that is, explained accurately on a test) the necessity for world interdependence, but in the afternoon not all of them were willing to sacrifice some of their spending money for needy children in Asia and Europe. The teacher had evaluated the students' understanding of the objective and they had passed the verbal test. However, only in the cases of some of the pupils did the tested understanding lead to what the teacher would call adequate behavior. Such instances as this (and others which can be seen when the citizen exceeds the speed limit or the boy on the way home from Sunday school steals pennies from a magazine rack) indicate that verbal understanding does not inevitably lead to consistent plans and adequate behavior.

For these reasons, evaluating on the understanding level is considered to be a less secure procedure for judging the changes in a person's life than evaluating on the planning or the behavioral levels. However, in cases where the teacher cannot readily judge either the actual behavior or the plans for behavior of students, he must evaluate how well the student understands the factors that could lead to desirable action.

Miss Colby's problem, which precipitated this discussion, was: How can I judge the specific behavior of the students when frequently I have little or no opportunity to observe or measure such behavior in their lives?

The answer is: Whenever feasible, choose an evaluation technique by which you can judge directly the *behavioral* goal. When this cannot be done readily, judge on the *planning* level. When neither of these levels can be used, evaluate the extent to which the pupil *understands* the information which can guide him to adequate actions.

PROBLEMS OF PREDICTING THE FUTURE

The foregoing discussion of levels of evaluating brings into focus an important issue that we have not yet faced directly. This is the problem of successfully stating *today* the exact behaviors that children will need to be able to carry out *tomorrow, next year,* and during the *next few decades.*

Throughout this chapter we have stressed the value of stating all goals in terms of the eventual behaviors people need to perform. We would have found this task much easier if we had lived in the Middle Ages. At that time life's pace was slower. Change came more gradually, so you could more surely predict this year the things a person would probably need to know and be able to do ten years hence. But today, with the rapid rate of change in our world, we find it very difficult to predict far ahead. We are continually amazed by scientific inventions, so that the wild fantasies of a short generation ago are reality today. Television and space travel are two cases in point. Social change is as amazing. Colonial nations over the world have recently gained independence. Weak nations have become powerful. Peoples that were allies a short time ago have turned enemies.

So the educator faces this conundrum: He knows that the more specifically he can state teaching goals in terms of the behaviors the learner will need to perform the more surely the school can teach the behavior and measure how well it has been acquired. On the other hand, the educator cannot know for sure what behaviors will be most needed in the future, so he cannot be as specific as he would like. Today's education must produce people readily adaptable to change.

The solution to this problem of stating specific behaviors yet providing also for unforeseen change seems to lie in the school's setting up two general kinds of goals. These may most simply be called *skills* and *knowledges*.

In the category of *skills* are placed those behaviors which we can predict, with considerable confidence, that people will need to solve life's problems in both the near future and the more distant future. Examples of these are skills in reading, writing, computing, working well with other people, approaching problems with scientific methods, using reference books to answer certain kinds of questions, keeping our bodies healthy, meeting our civic responsibilities, and such.

In the category of *knowledges* are placed: (1) those understandings and kinds of information that serve as bases for the skills outlined above, such as the knowledge underlying computational skill, and (2) those understandings and the information we think will help a person solve unforeseen problems that he will meet in life.

Let us inspect this second set of knowledges more closely, for it is this group that may cause the teacher puzzlement when he tries to state them as behaviors. We may take the area of science as an example. The school can make some relatively accurate predictions about specific behaviors based on scientific understandings that most modern Americans need today and will need in the future. For instance, we should learn not to put lighted matches or cigarettes near gasoline, kerosene, or oil. We should not plug in a radio while standing in water, as some people do when in the bathtub. If we want plants to grow, we should see that they get water. We should not unroll a length of undeveloped photographic film in the light. In case of atomic attack, we should hide in some covered-over place long enough to avoid radiation from fallout and contaminated air, water, and objects. But in addition to these behaviors, there are many others we will have to perform in the future that cannot be predicted specifically. To care for these others, the school tries to teach more general principles of science governing matter and energy and life processes so that the student who knows these principles can figure out for himself what behavior is best when he meets an unforeseen, unique situation for which he has not been specifically trained.

In the case of these kinds of knowledge goals, it is difficult or impossible to distinguish clearly among behavioral, planning, and understanding levels. This is because the goals themselves are understandings, not specific behaviors. Therefore, we frequently must evaluate these simply as understandings. Of course, you can, as has been done at several places in this book, state an understanding in terms of the behavior the teacher expects to see when he judges it. For instance, instead of saying "The student understands the ways germs are transmitted" you may say "The student *explains* the ways germs are transmitted." But in either case you are seeking to state a knowledge that will later be useful in a variety of situations, many of which cannot be predicted specifically ahead of time.

However, even though frequently we may find ourselves testing underlying understandings, it is still important whenever possible to push the evaluation as close as you can to behavioral or planning levels. In this way you not only measure the understanding itself as a verbalization, but you can judge whether the student can apply this knowledge to lifelike problems, even though you cannot predict all situations ahead of time. For example, to test for the objective "The student understands the way houseflies transmit germs," the teacher may well ask a question about the precautions that can be taken in the home to guard against the spread of germs by flies. Or he may describe an illness like anthrax in a family, and then ask for possible causes of the illness and methods that might have been used for prevention. Or students armed with a check list may inspect their homes or the school cafeteria to report on the adequacy of disease-prevention facilities there. In these ways an understanding is evaluated on a level that better measures how well it will probably transfer to solving life's problems.

FURTHER VALUES OF PREPLANNED EVALUATION

It is a common error to regard evaluation as something to do only at the *end* of a unit or semester. As a result, teachers often do not plan their techniques for judging children until the unit or semester is completed. This approach typically results in their compiling a final test to "cover the unit's facts" or in their resorting to a "rough estimate" of each child's progress in order to mark him. Waiting until the end to decide what evaluation techniques should be used may also result in guilt feelings for the conscientious teacher who realizes that he has not gathered the proper evidence to judge the children fairly. In addition, better evaluation methods throughout the semester enable the teacher to watch each child's progress and continually give him the proper help as he needs it.

A second-grade teacher explained, "I realized too late that I should have been keeping anecdotal records of the children's work throughout the term and I could have made rating scales and check lists to judge their growth better. But I had thought I would remember everything well enough. Now at the end of the term I have only a general idea of their development toward many of the goals. If I had better evidence I could be of more help to their parents and the third-grade teacher. The trouble is that I didn't look far enough ahead at the beginning."

This slipshod way of judging students' progress can be corrected when the teacher states the objectives in terms of the final behavior desired. The types of evaluation devices that will best measure the child's development then can be decided at the beginning, and the techniques can be used throughout the semester to gather adequate data. To make this decision about evaluation at the beginning rather than at the end does not entail additional work for the teacher, and it results in fairer evaluation and guidance of children's learning.

The question is sometimes asked, "But if the methods and evaluation techniques are decided upon at the beginning, doesn't that standardize or 'freeze' the semester's work? Doesn't that eliminate spontaneous activities and projects that might arise?"

No, the semester's work is not "frozen" by preplanning. The suggested chart is not a series of lesson plans. It is an over-all guide. The methods the teacher suggests in preplanning certainly will be supplemented by approaches that arise from the children's needs, their suggestions, and interests.

Many teachers do not plan their work alone. Instead, they enlist the class's aid in cooperatively planning the day or unit. In these cases the teacher guides the children to a statement of goals ("What do we want to learn?" or "What skills do we want to have after this unit?"). The class then plans ways of reaching these goals. And it is also proper that they decide at the beginning of the unit, "What will be good ways for us to find out how well we learned or how much we changed?" Therefore, whether the plan is mainly the teacher's or the students' it is valuable to decide at the beginning the principal steps to be taken with objectives, methods, and evaluation.

AN IMMEDIATE APPLICATION

This textbook has the same general function as a class in school, that is, a teaching function. Consequently, it has been constructed on the principles outlined in this chapter.

The general goal of the book is to help prospective teachers and in-service teachers judge students' progress effectively. When this general goal is stated in terms of *student* behavior (in this case the *student* is the prospective elementary or junior high school teacher), it becomes: "The teacher evaluates children's progress effectively." After using this book it is hoped that the elementary or junior high teacher's behavior will show that he evaluates effectively.

To what kinds of specific behavior does the term *effectively* refer? That is, how is this general goal made specific enough so that it is understandable and usable? The types of specific behavior which the writer believes are the marks of a person who evaluates children's school activities effectively have been stated, and the content of the book is based upon them. At the end of each chapter the goals that chapter was designed to achieve have been stated so that the reader may try to judge how effectively he has reached these behavioral objectives. *The sum of the behaviors listed at the ends of all chapters comprises the definition of what is meant here by the term "evaluates effectively."*

This book, then, has been designed as it is suggested that a curriculum or a course should be designed. The desired objectives have been stated in terms of "What behavior will be shown by a person who has reached these goals?" The body of the book becomes the method of arriving at the goals and as such is the writer's attempt to answer the question, "What methods will help us best to reach the objectives?" Suggestions are given at the end of each chapter about ways the effective elementary-school teacher himself or his instructor might use to evaluate, at least partially, "How well did we reach the goals?"

GOALS OF INITIAL CHAPTERS

Why have Chapters 1 and 2 been written? What are the behaviors expected to result from them?

Chapter 1. The intention of Chapter 1 was to introduce the reader to the general steps in the teaching process and to provide a setting in which to view the evaluation techniques described in subsequent chapters. In behavioral terms, the understandings that were the goals of Chapter 1 were:

The effective elementary or junior high teacher:

1. Explains the relationship among philosophy, objectives, methods, and evaluation in education.
2. Explains the relationship between the terms *testing movement* or *measurement movement* and the term *evaluation movement* as used in education during the past thirty-five years.

Chapter 2. The intention of Chapter 2 was to move from the understanding level of Chapter 1 to the actual behavior desired of the effective school teacher. Chapter 2 objectives have been included because the writer is convinced that diligent use of the suggested approach can markedly improve a teacher's methods and evaluation techniques.

The effective elementary or junior high school teacher:

1. Writes educational objectives in terms of student behavior.
2. Bases teaching methods upon the stated objectives.
3. Evaluates students' progress by judging how closely they approach the behaviors outlined in the objectives.
4. Whenever possible judges student behavior directly. When this is not feasible, judges on the planning or understanding levels.
5. Does not use one type of evaluation device exclusively but suits the evaluation device to the particular objective being measured.

The subsequent chapters of this book describe the use of a variety of evaluation techniques. It is hoped that this will aid the teacher in building a repertoire of devices from which to choose for the task of judging children's progress.

Suggested evaluation technique for this chapter (Planning Level)

1. Select or create a number of objectives for a particular elementary or junior high grade.

2. State objectives in terms of student behavior.
3. Outline methods which might enable children to reach each objective.
4. Indicate evaluation devices by which children's progress toward each goal might be measured.

(It is assumed that steps 1, 2, and 3 will be reached more effectively at this point than will 4, because additional knowledge of a variety of evaluation techniques is probably necessary for a more adequate treatment of 4.)

SUGGESTED READINGS

1. BLOOM, BENJAMIN S. (ed.). *Taxonomy of Educational Objectives.* New York: Longmans, Green and Co., 1956. A significant attempt to describe educational objectives in a way that can greatly improve communication among educators by offering a standard classification system.
2. FURST, EDWARD J. *Constructing Evaluation Instruments.* New York: Longmans, Green and Co., 1958. Chapters 2 and 3 treat: determining what to evaluate and defining behavior.
3. KINNEY, LUCIEN B. "Operational Plan in the Classroom," *School and Society,* 68 (September 4, 1948), 145-48. Planning with behavioral objectives.
4. SCHWARTZ, ALFRED, and TIEDEMAN, STUART C. *Evaluating Student Progress in the Secondary School.* New York: Longmans, Green and Co., 1957. Chapter 3: Identifying Educational Outcomes. Chapter 4: Determination of Classroom Objectives.
5. TRAVERS, ROBERT M. W. *How to Make Achievement Tests.* New York: The Odyssey Press, 1950. Pp. 6-29 illustrate using behavioral objectives in building tests.
6. WANDT, EDWIN, and BROWN, GERALD W. *Essentials of Educational Evaluation.* New York: Henry Holt and Co., 1957. Pp. 5-9 illustrate uses of behaviorial objectives in planning methods and evaluation.
7. WRIGHTSTONE, J. WAYNE; JUSTMAN, JOSEPH; and ROBBINS, IRVING. *Evaluation in Modern Education.* New York: American Book Co., 1956. Pp. 17-21 discuss defining objectives.
8. WRINKLE, WILLIAM L. *Improving Marking and Reporting Practices in Elementary and Secondary Schools.* New York: Rinehart and Co., 1947. Pp. 93-99 treat objectives in relation to marking and reporting.

PART II

Using Evaluation Instruments in the Classroom

THE MOST USEFUL EVALUATION TECHNIQUES AND DEVICES FOR ELEmentary and junior high teachers include: teacher-made objective tests and essay tests, standardized achievement tests, aptitude and intelligence scales, paper-pencil personality tests, projective techniques, casual observation and anecdotal records, sociometrics, participation charting, and rating scales and check lists for judging student skills and work products.

Part II explains each of these techniques and illustrates its use in elementary and junior high classrooms. In addition, one chapter is designed to assist the teacher who does not yet understand educational and psychological statistics that are often used in describing test results.

CHAPTER

3

Creating Class Tests

TO IMPROVE THEIR SKILLS in constructing and using classroom tests, the teachers in the Central School System held a series of six weekly in-service study sessions. An educational psychologist from a nearby university served as their leader.

The group spent most sessions analyzing and improving tests which the teachers themselves had used or intended to use in their own classrooms. But before they were ready to make wise judgments about their tests they needed a session for developing criteria for appraising them. In order to develop these criteria in a lifelike and interesting fashion, the group leader passed to each teacher a copy of two different tests which he suggested needed evaluating and possibly improving.

These two sample tests, covering conservation and English-usage goals, are reproduced below. As you read them, try to judge their worth. Later in the chapter you will be able to compare your judgments with the kinds of analyses that resulted from the Central School study sessions.

CONSERVATION TEST—FIFTH GRADE

True or False

1. Contour plowing refers to the practice followed in some areas of the country that tend toward erosion of plowing furrows up and down hills rather than curving the furrows around the hills.________

2. Planting the same crop year after year in the field sometimes uses up the plant food in the soil.______
3. Last year in our country more people died in accidents than in any previous year.______
4. It is important for citizens to prevent fires in forests and grasslands.______

Multiple Choice

6. One way to help farm land rebuild itself is to (*a*) plant the same crop every year, (*b*) spray it with DDT, (*c*) rotate crops and let it grow to grass every two or three years, (*d*) sell it to a better farmer.
7. You can put out a fire by covering it with a (1) bucket of sand, (2) kerosene, (3) gasoline, (4) feathers, (5) dry sticks.

Matching

______ 8.	erosion	A.	sources of good information about conservation
______ 9.	how to make water good for drinking	B.	wear away land by water
______ 10.	Department of Agriculture	C.	prevent water from flooding land
______ 11.	reforestation	D.	planting new trees on old land
______ 12.	dikes	E.	ground that has the plant food gone
______ 13.	depleted land	F.	boil it

This conservation test was intended to evaluate for the following objectives:

"After their study of conservation the pupils:

1. Explain the need and methods for the conservation of:
   - 1.1 soil.
   - 1.2 water.
   - 1.3 forests.
   - 1.4 grasslands.
   - 1.5 minerals.
2. Practice conservation wherever possible in their lives."

LANGUAGE QUIZ—SEVENTH GRADE

A. If you wish you may use your dictionary to do these:

1. Divide each of the following words into syllables and mark the accent:

dinosaur *silence* *oil* *lackadaisical* *carnivorous*

2. Write the meaning for each of these words:

tremendous *sissors* *menu* *syllable*

B. There are mistakes in the way some of the sentences below are written. When you find a mistake, draw an X through it. Then write the way you would correct the mistake.

1. Janes chair was too high?
2. Jack put his' hat on backward's.
3. Send the book to washington elementary school.
4. when are you going to play ball.
5. Carl asked "Why won't you go to the movie's. Youll like Roys ranch picture.

C. Fill in the blanks.

1. A ________________ tells you in what ________________ a word ________________ long ago.
2. One way to show ownership is to put ________________ at the end of the word.
3. ________________ is what a sentence should always begin with.

D. In five or six sentences tell some of the things you do when you go home from school. (Be sure to pay attention to capitals and punctuation.)

This language quiz was intended to evaluate for the following objectives:

"As a result of their learning, the students:

1. Use possessives accurately in their writing.
2. Use capital letters, periods, and question marks in appropriate places.
3. Use a dictionary to discover the meaning, syllabification, spelling, and pronunciation of new or difficult words."

In the Central School weekly study sessions the analyses of teacher-made tests centered on seven principles of test construction that concerned (1) the focus of test items on course objectives, (2) appropriateness of the type of item for the specific objective, (3) construction of items that are clear and specific, (4) construction of items that discriminate, (5) mechanical aspects of the test, (6) objectivity in scoring the test, and (7) opportunity for students to prepare adequately and to complete the test.

TEST VALIDITY

Principle 1: The test should evaluate only for the stated objectives. It should give most weight to the most important objectives. That is, most of the test items should emphasize the most important objectives unless other evaluation devices are also used to measure for them, such as sociometrics, rating scales, and anecdotal records. If other evaluation techniques are used, a test can properly be designed to evaluate for a limited number of objectives.

What is validity?

The term *validity* is used in the field of evaluation with a rather precise meaning, not synonymous with its general use in everyday conversation. In evaluation validity means that *an appraisal device really measures accurately for a stated objective.* In this chapter the term *test validity* refers to how accurately a teacher-made test measures for course objectives the teacher has specified.

At first sight this definition may appear so obvious that it may not seem worth discussing. But, since you can step into thousands of classrooms and find teachers unknowingly creating invalid tests, it must be true that the real meaning contained in this definition is not obvious at all and that it needs further explaining.

There are numerous reasons why a test can be invalid. For instance, a test may not measure accurately because the wording of the items gives away the correct answers even to pupils who do not know the material well. Later we will consider ways to avoid such errors. But first we will inspect the most basic of the causes of test invalidity: it is that the teacher has not been careful to include only items that focus specifically on clearly stated course objectives.

An easy way to check a test for this characteristic is to have the objectives listed, and inspect each item on the test to see that it measures for one or more of the goals. We can try this with the two sample tests at the beginning of the chapter.

Do the items match the objectives?

In the case of the conservation test we see that, although item 3 does indeed relate to conservation of human resources, it does not measure for one of the stated objectives. They all focus on natural resources.

3. Last year in our country more people died in accidents than in any previous year. __________

Hence item 3 is not a valid measure of any stated goal, so it should be eliminated. And item 10 (referring to the Department of Agriculture as a source of information about conservation) is a doubtful item in light of the objectives.

The other test items seem logically to fall under information related to conservation of the resources specified in the goals, so they meet this criterion of focus on objectives. (It should be obvious that this task of deciding would be easier if the objectives were stated in even greater specificity. But even at their present level of specificity, we can make rather accurate judgments.)

Turning to the language quiz, we note that item B-5 contains errors in the use of commas, quotation marks, and contractions, which are not part of the stated objectives. Therefore, these errors should be corrected by the teacher and should not be made part of the tested material.

B-5. Carl asked "Why won't you go to the movie's. Youll like Roys ranch picture.

Item C-1 seems to be aimed at the use of a dictionary, but not at the particular uses stated in objective 3. Thus it is not a valid item.

C-1. A ________ tells you in what ________ a word ________ long ago.

Objective 3: Use a dictionary to discover the meaning, syllabification, spelling, and pronunciation of new or difficult words.

The rest of the items in the language quiz seem to relate to specified goals.

Is there a proper balance between items and objectives?

The easiest way to see whether there is a proper number of items to measure for each objective is to inspect every test question and write its number beside the objective it is aimed at. In some cases we will find that a single question will focus on more than one objective, so we will write the item number beside each of these objectives.

After we have listed the item numbers beside each objective, we need to know which objectives the teacher considered most vital and thus necessitate the greatest number of test items. In the cases of the conservation and usage tests, the teachers considered all objectives of about equal importance, so we can expect each goal to receive about the same emphasis as the others.

When we check the conservation items against their objectives we see that there are no items really aimed at testing a student's knowledge of the need for conservation. Most questions touch upon methods only. More items seem to be directed at objective 1.1 than at the others. Objective 1.5 appears to have been given very little direct attention.

Finally, we note that there are no questions focused on objective 2 (practice conservation wherever possible in their lives). This brings up the issue of whether you can give a paper-pencil test to measure for this goal, or should some other evaluation device like a check list or rating scale be used. If the teacher has another way of judging pupil progress toward this objective, it may be best not to include it on the test. (This issue will be considered in more detail under principle 2.)

Inspecting the language quiz, we see that almost every objective has a few test items directed at it, with the exception of the goal concerning the use of a dictionary to discover correct spelling. Possibly this goal would be tested for indirectly by item D, but the way the item now reads it is doubtful because the child could restrict his short essay under D to words he already can spell.

Thus, through this analysis we have seen a simple method of estimating whether the items on a test are well balanced as compared to the objectives. This approach is suited to analyzing a test which has already been developed.

To construct a test which will be well balanced, the teacher obviously needs to use a variation of this same approach. That is, he first writes down specific goals. Then beside each goal he writes the number of items which he believes should be developed to give the objective its proper emphasis in the testing.

APPROPRIATENESS OF ITEMS

Principle 2: The kind of test item a teacher selects to evaluate for a specific goal should be as appropriate as possible to that goal. The kind of item should also be appropriate to the age level of the pupils taking the test.

Kinds of items

Most test items are some variety of the following types: multiple-choice, matching, completion, true-false, and essay. By inspecting each of these types briefly we may see more clearly their advantages and limitations and thus better understand what kinds of goals each is most appropriate for.

Multiple choice

A multiple-choice item is composed of two parts. The first is an incomplete statement or a question. The last part consists of several possible ways of completing the statement or answering the question. The student's task is to choose the correct or the best of these possibilities.

Multiple-choice questions are perhaps the most useful of the objective items. They can be used from first grade on up. At both elementary and junior high levels they are especially useful in testing for abilities to:

1. Recognize the *cause* of something:

______The balloon tied above the radiator became larger because:

a. The longer air was in the balloon, the thicker it got.
b. Air in the balloon expanded as it got warmer.
c. The rubber of the balloon got looser and stretched.
d. The air in the balloon got cooler than the room air.

______In the story of *Flame, the Deer,* the family had to move to town for the winter because:

a. The family liked the town better than the ranch.
b. The children wanted to be near their new friend, Jerry.
c. The forest fire had ruined the farm crops.
d. Father thought he could sell the white buffalo robe.

2. Recognize the *effect* of something:

______Imagine you have made an electromagnet by winding wire around a nail. What happens if you wind still more wire around the nail?

a. The magnet will get stronger.
b. The magnet will get weaker.
c. The magnet will need more batteries to make it work.
d. The nail will get very hot.
e. The nail will bend when the wire is hooked to batteries.

______If you multiply one fraction by another fraction, the answer will always be:

a. A whole number.
b. A smaller amount than either of the fractions.
c. A larger amount than either of the fractions.
d. A mixed number.

3. Recognize the *definition* of something:

______The person who is the head of our village government is called the:

a. Town Manager.
b. Chief of Police.
c. Mayor.
d. Village Clerk.
e. Councilman.

______A point of the mainland that sticks out into the ocean is called:

a. an island.
b. a bay.
c. an isthmus.
d. a peninsula.

4. Identify *errors:*

______What mistake did Jack make in this division problem?

```
      206
22) 4545
    44
     145
     122
      23
```

a. Did not subtract correctly.
b. Did not carry correctly when dividing.
c. Did not carry correctly when adding.
d. Did not carry correctly when multiplying.

______Draw a line under the picture that was not part of our story. (These directions are given orally by the teacher to a primary reading group.)

5. Recognize the *purpose* of something:

______The job of the state legislature is to:

a. Carry out the laws.
b. Punish people who break laws.
c. Collect taxes.
d. Make new laws.

______Why do you put water in the radiator of a car?

a. To keep the engine from getting too hot.
b. To keep the pistons from grinding inside the engine.
c. To keep the gasoline from exploding in the engine.
d. To keep the brakes from getting too hot.
e. To wash the inside of the engine.

Therefore, at the elementary and junior high levels the multiple-choice item can make its greatest contribution in testing a student's ability to *recognize* cause, effect, definitions, errors, and purposes. To a lesser degree it tests recognition of similarities, differences, and the order of arrangement of steps in a process.

Now it is proper to see when multiple-choice items are not appropriate:

First, they should not be used when the objective can be measured more directly. That is, if you wish to judge a child's skill in singing a song by sight, it is much safer to have him carry out the actual singing than to give a multiple-choice test over musical notation. In most instances multiple-choice items test on the understanding level, not the planning or the behavior level.

Second, multiple-choice questions measure *recognition* of facts, not *recall*. That is, all the student has to do is recognize which of the printed possibilities is correct. But with completion or essay questions, the student faces the more difficult task of recalling to mind the right answer. Hence, in the conservation test the items relating to farm land and to putting out fires are easier to answer as multiple-choice items than they would be if they were in essay form and asked merely what methods could be used to replenish depleted land or asked what methods could be used to extinguish different kinds of fires. If you wish to measure the student's ability to recall facts, to plan how he would attack a problem, or to organize his own ideas and present them, multiple-choice items will not serve you well.

Matching

Matching items typically consist of two columns. The terms or figures in one column are to be matched up with their most appropriate counterparts in the other. Since matching items usually test only for rote memory rather than for skills of analysis, they do not have as varied uses as multiple-choice items.

At elementary and junior high levels matching items find their greatest usefulness in measuring a pupil's ability to:

1. Recognize *terms and their definitions:*

———Draw a line from each word to its picture. (These direct' are given orally by the teacher to a primary reading clas

Directions: In front of each phrase in column I write the letter of the word in column II that matches the phrase.

Column I

______ 1. Part of the flower in which seeds are formed

______ 2. Container of "flower dust" that is blown or carried by bees to another flower

______ 3. The part of the flower whose color seems to attract bees and butterflies

______ 4. The stalk that supports the flower blossom

______ 5. Leaves just beneath the blossom

Column II

A. pollen sac
B. petal
C. stem
D. pistil
E. sepal
F. stamen
G. bud

2. Recognize *symbols and their names:*

Directions: In front of each item in column I, write the letter of the matching music symbol in column II.

I		II	
______1.	half note	A	♩
______2.	quarter note	B	𝄻
______3.	quarter rest	C	♪
______4.	whole note	D	𝅝
______5.	half rest	E	𝅗𝅥
______6.	whole rest	F	♭
______7.	eighth note	G	𝅘𝅥𝅯
______8.	sixteenth note	H	𝄾
		I	𝄽
		J	♯
		K	𝄼

In addition to matching terms with their definitions and symbols with their names, students can match causes with effects, problems with their solutions, and parts of mechanical devices with their names.

A major limitation of the matching item is that it cannot measure more complex understandings or students' abilities to organize their ideas and present them. But because it is rather easy to construct, teachers often turn to it when it is really inappropriate. For instance, before constructing the test teachers sometimes do not pay close attention to writing *specific objectives of learnings that are really significant for the child's life.* So they end up creating test items of men's names to be matched with the state they were from or with the name of an essay or book they wrote. Whereas, it would be more significant to measure pupil understanding of social and scientific movements of the times and their influence on our life today.

When we think back to the matching item on the conservation test we see that we can find fault with it on at least two major counts.

First, it has mixed several different kinds of things: definitions of terms relating to conservation, a government agency, and a method of making water potable. All the items within the matching list should be homogeneous, all of the same ilk. That is, they should all be definitions of terms or all sources of information or all conservation practices, but not mixed as they are now. Second, it is likely that the question about making water drinkable would be better as a short-answer or multiple-choice item, if indeed it belongs on this test at all. The same is true of the Department of Agriculture item. The other parts of the question relate to definitions and thus could appropriately be part of a matching item if it were more carefully constructed.

True-false or alternative-response items

A true-false or alternative-response item is one that presents a statement and then requires the pupil to judge it true or false. Sometimes the test requires the student to answer either *Agree* or *Disagree, Right* or *Wrong, Yes* or *No, Correct* or *Incorrect*. In any event, the student is to choose from two possible ways to answer.

At the elementary and junior high levels the true-false item has very limited usefulness. It tends to be a popular question type with some teachers because it seems easy to construct. (They simply copy sentences from the textbook.) It is easy to score. But there is little doubt that it has been used out of all relation to its value.

It is true that this type of item enables the teacher to cover much subject matter during one class period of testing. But too often what is really tested is the student's ability to memorize exact statements taken from the text rather than his application of facts to lifelike situations. To a great extent true-false items are limited to testing goals related to students' understanding the terms or central concepts in an area of study, such as geography or science. And very often these terms and concepts can be better measured by some other type of question.

One of the greatest disadvantages of alternative-response items is the likelihood of getting a question right just (1) by chance or (2) by faulty reasoning rather than by real knowledge. Or, on the other hand, a student may get the question wrong because (3) he knows more than the teacher expected him to. Let us inspect these three factors more closely.

1. Chance. If a pupil who takes a true-false test does not know any correct answers, and thus guesses at all of them, he can be expected to get half of them correct on the average. This is because his chances of securing a correct answer only by guess is ½ (that is, 1 over the number of alternatives). Hence, with alternative-response tests, the teacher cannot be at all sure that a student really knew the subject matter when he marked an answer correctly. It may have been blind guess.

2. Faulty reasoning. Consider the following statement:

T F 1. Washington was the American general and Lafayette the French general who commanded the troops which made the British surrender at Boston to end the Revolution.

A student who marks this false is credited with a correct answer. However, with such a complex item as this the teacher never knows what part of the answer the student considered false. Perhaps the pupil thought the French had nothing to do with the American Revolution but that Boston sounds like a logical place to surrender. Or perhaps he thought Lafayette was the French king and not a general when the surrender occurred at Boston. Thus, the item has not measured the student's knowledge accurately.

3. Student knows too much. Most statements in life, except statements of things like names and dates and places, are not simply true or false. They usually range someplace between, depending upon the conditions in the particular case. For example, here is a question relating to law processes from a junior high test.

TRUE FALSE 1. When one man kills another, the police try to arrest the killer and put him in jail to await trial.

The teacher considered this statement to be true. But one of the wiser students thought up numbers of exceptions, such as the war hero who kills many of the enemy and receives a medal rather than a jail term. So he marked it false because it was not an invariably true statement. He got it wrong because he considered more complex aspects of life than the teacher had expected him to.

Because of these disadvantages of the usual kind of true-false question, several variations have been developed to take the ambiguity out of such items. These newer forms usually require the student to add reasons for his answer or to correct the false portion of the statement.

In the *true-false-with-reasons* type the student is instructed to answer each item either true or false, and below the item he is to write why it is true or false. In this way the teacher knows whether good or poor reasoning or information led to the selection. (Some teachers have students write reasons only for the false items, assuming that the facts behind the true ones are obvious.) There are several methods for marking true-false-with-reasons items. Some instructors give credit for the true-false answers and then award additional credit if the reasons are correct. Such a practice may make the teacher appear to be a *good sport* in the eyes of the students, but from an evaluation standpoint this procedure is inconsistent. If a student marks any item false (which is the correct response) but gives the wrong reasons for the fallacy in the statement, it does not seem sensible to award him *any* credit for any part of his answer.

With true-false-with-reasons items, a statement sometimes can be correct if marked *either* true *or* false. This occurs when a question does not treat a simple case of fact but treats a situation for which evidence can be presented on both sides. One pupil may give excellent supporting reasons for marking it true. Another may give valid reasons for marking it false. The validity of the reasons they give becomes the basis for the teacher's marking these types of items, not the fact that the question was marked true or false. It is evident that such test questions are really short-answer or short-essay types, and the original statement merely stimulates the student to a response. Some teachers point out that this kind of question is more lifelike than the simple true-false variety. They say that in everyday discussion among friends or in committee meetings, one person may make a statement. Another person responds to this statement, not with a simple "I agree" or "I disagree" but adds his reasons for his agreement or disagreement. This is the true-false-with-reasons situation.

Here are three statements from an eighth-grade test which could be either true or false, depending upon how the reasoning was organized to support the student's conclusion.

1. The ending of the American Revolution caused widespread disruption in the colonies.
2. In westward expansion in the United States, the white men rightfully took over land where the Indians roamed.
3. The movies present a true picture of the cowboy's life.

A second variation of the true-false item also demands that a student find the actual fallacy in the statement in order to receive credit. In this form a blank is placed at the end of the statement. The procedure for marking this somewhat complicated type of question is indicated in the directions.

Directions: If an item is true, put a plus (+) in the blank at the left, and go on to the next item. If an item is false, put a zero (o) in the blank at the left and then *cross out the word or words that make the statement false.* After crossing out the false words, write in the blank at the right side the word or words that would make the item true. Here is a sample of how to do it.

__0__ 1. The planet nearest to the sun is ~~Venus.~~ __MERCURY__

Another form of this type uses the following directions:

Directions: Each of the statements that follow is either true or false. If the statement is *true,* draw a circle around the *T*. If the statement is *false,* draw a circle around the *F,* and then change the part of the statement that is *not* underlined to make the whole statement true. As you see, the first item is already done for you.

T (F) 1. Leprechaun is the name of a giant friend of Paul Bunyan.
a kind of Irish elf.

Completion, fill-in, or short-answer items

The three types of test items discussed so far (multiple-choice, matching, true-false) measure the student's ability to *recognize* a correct answer. With the exception of the modified true-false varieties, he does not have to *recall* a correct answer and write it down. But with completion or short-answer questions he faces the task of finding the correct answer in his own head, not on the test form.

A *completion* or *fill-in* item consists of a statement that is not quite complete. It is the pupil's task to insert the one or two words that have been left out.

1. Ice begins to melt when the temperature rises above ________ Fahrenheit.

If the item is stated as a question for which the pupil is to supply a response, it is called a *short-answer* question.

2. What are the names of the states whose borders touch Colorado?
____

In its simplest form, the completion item is best suited for testing the recall of facts. This is usually true also of the short-answer variety. But the short-answer type can become increasingly challenging and demand more complex answers. Then it becomes an essay item.

Essay items

Teachers sometimes ask, "Aren't multiple-choice and matching questions better than essay tests?" The answer to this depends on what objectives the questions are supposed to test for. As already indicated, for objectives like understanding factual matters, simpler causes and effects, definitions, and such, the multiple-choice variety will usually be most efficient. But if the teacher intends to measure a student's ability to organize his knowledge into a plan of action to solve a somewhat complex social or scientific problem, the essay variety is more appropriate. It is also better suited to testing the pupil's ability to analyze the advantages and disadvantages of a plan of action (such as the city's plan for a recreation program or the nation's plan for lowering tariffs).

The essay type is obviously not well suited to the lower grades of the elementary school, and its usefulness in the middle and upper grades is much less than at high school and college levels. Often in the elementary and junior high grades the teacher does not include an essay question as part of a major test. Instead, she poses the question or issue and explains its meaning clearly, then simply asks the students to write an answer to it during the coming class period. These papers or compositions are used to measure for the more complex critical or organizational abilities the teacher is interested in learning about, but they are not presented as being part of a formal test.

In this brief survey of common types of test items we have attempted to suggest situations for which each is well suited. This is intended to aid the teacher when he looks over his objectives to determine what kinds of items are most appropriate to the objectives and the students' ability level. Sometimes as he inspects the objectives the teacher will see that he can properly use a test composed entirely of one variety of item, such as completion. In other cases several kinds of items will be needed to suit the objectives best. And in attempting to find items that measure most directly for the goals, the teacher will sometimes come up with varieties or combinations not usually discussed in books on testing.

For example, in the language-usage quiz at the beginning of this chapter, the test-maker included a short-essay item at the end to secure a sample of how the children used punctuation and capitalization in their actual writing. The intention here was good, for the test-maker was not satisfied only with finding students' skills in recognizing errors in printed material (as tested by items under section B), but he was securing evidence on the behavioral level. However, there was one disadvantage to his essay question. He could not be sure that in five or six sentences each student would include all the punctuation (like possessives and question marks) the teacher was testing for. Students could avoid using some of these. Therefore, to ensure a good sample of the way every student handled these forms of punctuation, the teacher should change this essay to a dictation item. That is, he should have the students write down several sentences which he dictates to the class. In this way he can be sure the students have to use the punctuation they have been studying.

(In passing, it might be well to note that when administering a test it is best to give such dictation items as this at the beginning of the test, not at the end or in the middle. By having this at the beginning, all students complete it together and then turn to the written part of the test which each pupil completes at his own pace. If the teacher waited to give the dictation at the end, some students would have finished the test and moved on to other tasks, whereas the slower workers would still be struggling with earlier items which they could not complete because the teacher wanted to begin the dictation.)

In addition to using a dictation item to check for these punctuation objectives, the teacher also would be expected to judge regular written assignments, such as stories and friendly letters, to see how well pupils' knowledge of punctuation was actually serving them in everyday writing.

Application to life

Often it is well for the teacher to design items that give immediate application to a situation directly connected with the pupil's daily lives. Thus the items are not only appropriate to the objectives and age level of the pupils, but they are also appropriate to everyday life situations. Here are three examples of items teachers created with current, local applications.

Item 1

A sixth-grade teacher created the following problem to measure the students' progress in map reading and scale drawing. She copied a portion of a map of the local area as a basis for the item.

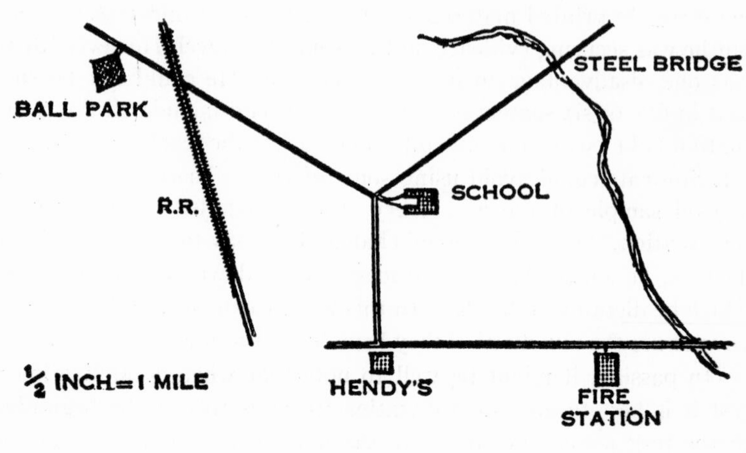

Fig. 2

Directions:

1. Draw a circle around the place where the scale is shown on this map.
2. With the help of your ruler, find out how far it is from school to Hendy's Drug Store. Write the answer here________.
3. How far is it from the ball park to the steel bridge? ________
4. If there were a fire at the ball park, how far would the fire engines have to travel to reach the park? ________
5. If the fire engines drove sixty miles an hour all the way to the ball park, how long would it take them to reach the fire? ________

Item 2

In a fifth grade the teacher examined pupils' knowledge of the symptoms of contagious diseases with items like the following:

This month pupils in our school began catching measles. Put an X beside each of the things that the doctor might expect to see in examining a person who is catching measles:

______ 1.	small blisters on face	______ 6.	red spots on face
______ 2.	running nose	______ 7.	stiff neck
______ 3.	much coughing	______ 8.	swelling of ankles
______ 4.	fever	______ 9.	red spots on body
______ 5.	watery eyes	______ 10.	sneezing

Item 3

Here is an eighth-grade item designed to test pupils' abilities to present numerical data in graph form.

In last week's election for city councilmen, the men running for office got the number of votes listed below. Draw a graph which shows the votes each man received.

Henderson	14,117	Tryon	2,119
McGeough	9,471	Silsby	572
Cavalli	5,042	Djivitz	54

ITEM CLARITY

Principle 3: Test items should be so constructed that the student understands the question asked or the problem to be solved. The type of answer desired should be understandable to the student who knows the material.

Some teachers through carelessness or mental clumsiness write items in a manner that makes it difficult for the student to understand what is expected of him or what the issue at hand really is. Other teachers seem to feel that part of the game of testing involves tricky wording or awkward item-construction to catch the student. But it must be remembered that the test should measure the individual's ability to meet class goals, not his ability to guess what is hidden behind the teacher's complex words or clumsy item-construction.

For example, true-false items should be stated as simply as possible, not like item 1 of the conservation test:

1. Contour plowing refers to the practice followed in some parts of the country that tend toward erosion of plowing furrows up and down hills rather than curving the furrows around the hills.

This would be a better item if stated:

1. Contour plowing means cutting furrows straight up and down a hill.

Double negatives are likewise confusing:

Poor item:

T F 2. It is not possible for the city council not to agree to a special election if the election board requests it.

Better item:

T F 2. The city council must agree to any special election requested by the election board.

With multiple choice items it is best to write the stem of an item so that it is the *first* part of the statement, and the choice will complete it. It is only confusing to make the choices the middle part of the item, such as:

Poor item:

3. The term—(1) reforestation, (2) erosion, (3) silt, (4) depletion—means wearing away land by wind or water.

Better item:

3. The wearing away of land by wind or water is called (1) reforestation, (2) erosion, (3) silt, (4) depletion.

The sly detail. Tricky true-false items, the truth or falsity of which depends upon a minute, inconspicuous detail slipped into the sentence, are usually not good evaluation questions.

T F 4. Old Faithful is a famous geyser in Yellowstone National Park that erupts every hour.

This is false, because the teacher required the students to know that Old Faithful does not always erupt each hour, but the interval is usually closer to 65 minutes. Some teachers are fond of such sly details that trip students up on historical facts, dates, names, and times which, as far as the real goals of the course are concerned, are unimportant.

Faulty completion questions

Generally completion items should be stated in such a way that one crucial or important word or term has been left out. One specific answer should be correct, and other answers a student might give would be incorrect. Sometimes it is all right to have two or three possible words that would be correct (usually synonyms), and the teacher gives credit for any one of them.

Completion items often exhibit the weakness shown in the questions under section C of the language quiz.

1. A __________ tells you in what __________ a word __________ long ago.
2. One way to show ownership is to put __________ at the end of the word.
3. __________ is what a sentence should always begin with.

Item 1 is known as a butchered sentence, since so much is left out that the sentence may well not make sense even to the pupil who has the correct information. Such an item tests the student's photographic memory of an author's or a teacher's phraseology rather than the true objectives of the course.

Item 1 is notable also for the variety of words which might be appropriate in the blanks. For example, the first blank could contain *dictionary, glossary, cyclopedia, library, person specializing in etymology*. The second blank could logically be filled with *country, nation, language, root form, place, dialect, area, district, language family, part of speech, spelling, manner, way,* or any number of other words. For an instructor to insist that only one or two of these answers are correct would be unjust, for all of them can be supported. And if a question allows such a variety of answers as does this one, it probably will be difficult for the instructor to explain why this item is really appropriate to the objectives being tested for.

Item 2 above has some of the same faults of allowing a variety of answers.

When constructing completion items it is well for the teacher to place the blank at the end or near the end of the sentence. This enables the pupil to read the first part of the sentence, and by the time he has reached the blank he understands what answer is to be inserted. If the blank appears at the beginning of the sentence, the pupil must read through the sentence, often looking back and forth at the words, and then go back to the beginning to see what the proper word will be. Thus, placing the blank at the end reduces the number of mechanical stumbling blocks in evaluation. Item 3 above has this fault. Its form would be better as:

3. A sentence should always begin with a __________ letter.

Although the form of item 3 is now improved, it still is not a very good item because of the use of *always*. Here the teacher has expected the student to write "capital" as the answer. But the more sophisticated student will think of the few exceptions (i.e., "*x* stands for an unknown quantity") and thus probably miss the item. So a completion item is not the most appropriate form in this case.

In completion items it is usually wise to make all the blanks the same length. If each blank is made the approximate length of the word it represents, then the size of the blank may tend to give away the word to the student who is not well prepared. On the other hand, if there is a marked discrepancy in the length of the blanks, the student who is fairly sure of the correct answer may be misled into believing the size of the blank represents the size of the word when it does not.

Stating essay questions

Here are some typical essay questions:

Discuss the place of the Supreme Court in the state government.

Write at least ten sentences about Eugene Field's writing.

Who was Benjamin Franklin?

These are generally poor kinds of questions because they give the student so little direction about what aspects of each of these broad subjects the teacher wishes discussed. Sometimes capable students receive poor marks on essay questions because the question is too general, and the student chooses to write on one aspect whereas the teacher has a different aspect in mind. For example, the student may have written about Benjamin Franklin as an inventor and a writer and publisher, but the teacher wanted information about Franklin as a political figure and statesman. Hence, it would have been better if the teacher had written the question as:

"Tell the important contributions Benjamin Franklin made as an official of the United States government."

It would be easier for the student to know what aspect of the Supreme Court the teacher wanted discussed if the question were more specific:

"Explain:

a. The duties of the State Supreme Court.
b. The number of judges in the State Supreme Court.
c. The way these judges are put in office.
d. The way a judge can be removed from office."

The Eugene Field question would be better if stated:

"Think of what you know about Eugene Field and his writing. Then:

a. Tell when he lived.

b. Tell where he lived.
c. Tell what kind of writing he is famous for.
d. Tell what kinds of people he wrote for."

As will be noted later, specifying essay and short-answer questions not only gives clearer guidance to the student but also enables the teacher to mark the papers more objectively.

In constructing essay questions the teacher should also be careful to limit the scope of the question to material that can be completed by most of the students within the class period allowed for it. Generally it is better to have all students write on the same essay question rather than give several questions and allow students to choose which they wish to write on. If the question is directed at an important objective of the course, the teacher needs a measure of each student's progress toward it. If the teacher allows a choice among several questions, he is not sure that the questions are all of the same importance or weight in assigning grades to the students.

DISCRIMINATION

Principle 4: Items should discriminate between the student who has met the objectives and the student who has not.

Portions of teacher-made tests often can be answered as well by students who have not met the objectives (or have not even been in the class or learned the material) as they can be answered by students who have reached the goals. Such items are poor because they do not discriminate between the adequate and the inadequate students. There are various causes for questions lacking this quality of discrimination. A few of these causes were outlined under principles 1 through 3. Others are discussed below.

Grammatical clue

Sometimes the grammar the teacher uses in the test gives away the answer. This allows the student who does not know the material to answer correctly. Item 7 in the conservation test contained such a clue.

7. You can put out a fire by covering it with a (1) bucket of sand, (2) kerosene, (3) gasoline, (4) feathers, (5) dry sticks.

Opportunities for guessing

Test questions are less discriminating when the student who has not reached the goals can secure a correct answer by guessing. A teacher can estimate the chances of guessing the correct answer in objective items by creating a fraction. The numerator is 1 (that is, the number of correct answers to that single item) and the denominator is the number of possible choices the student has for answering. Therefore, with the traditional true-false question, the chances of guessing correctly are ½ or 50 per cent of the time. A multiple-choice item with four choices provides an opportunity to guess correctly only ¼ of the time. Consequently, the larger the number of choices the less likely it is that the inadequate student can guess the answer correctly. Multiple choice items usually contain four or five choices. Matching items usually have a greater number, but more than eight or ten choices makes the item unwieldy.

Plausible choices. These statistics concerning the chances of guessing the answer are true only if all the choices in a multiple-choice or matching item are plausible answers. If any of the choices the student is offered is not a likely possibility in the eyes of the student who does not know the material well, then the item is a much less discriminating one, and the student has a better chance of guessing the correct answer. To determine whether a particular choice would be a logical deceiver for a given class, you need to know something about the maturity of the students. It is likely, however, that choice 3 in item 7 on page 69 would not be a plausible answer to most fifth graders.

Homogeneous items. Related to the problem of logical choices is the matter of homogeneous choices, a factor which is frequently overlooked by teachers when they construct multiple-choice and matching questions. Items 8-13 of the conservation test lack homogeneity. When the test-maker constructed this question he should have made all the terms in the left column the same kinds of things: *either* definitions related to conservation *or* conservation methods *or* agencies or bureaus, but not a mixture of all of these.

_______ 8. erosion	A. sources of good information about conservation
_______ 9. how to make water good for drinking	B. wear away land by water
_______ 10. Department of Agriculture	C. prevent water from flooding land
_______ 11. reforestation	D. planting new trees on old land
_______ 12. dikes	E. ground that has the plant food gone
_______ 13. depleted land	F. boil it

Obviously, a person who knows nothing about conservation could take the test and get several of the blanks correct merely by reasoning out the form of the statements.

Including extra choices. In matching items it is well to include more choices in the right column than there are questions in the left column. In this way the student who knows four of the five questions on the left cannot get the fifth correct simply by taking the only leftover answer from the right column.

Another technique for increasing the discrimination qualities of matching items is to give the following type of directions. Then, when the student has answered one question, he has not eliminated the one he chose as a possible answer to another question.

Directions: In the blank next to each item in column I, write the number of the best answer from column II. Some answers in column II *may be right more than once.* Some may *not* be right at all.

Column I	Column II
______Called Father of Our Country	1. Franklin D. Roosevelt
______Was President during War between the States	2. Benjamin Franklin
______Headed Roughriders in Spanish-American War	3. Thomas Jefferson
______Was General during American Revolution	4. George Washington
______Started United States post office department	5. Theodore Roosevelt
	6. Abraham Lincoln
	7. Alexander Hamilton

True-false clues. Several types of clues are often found in traditional true-false questions. These clues tend to enable a student to answer the question even when he does not know the desired facts.

True-false items that use the terms *possibly, probably, many, some, often, perhaps,* and other such vague, qualifying words are usually true. An item that is definite in quantity will discriminate better. True-false items that have statements of extremes, such as *never, always, none, all, nothing, entirely,* or *in every case* are most often false. An item that is definite but not to such extremes quantitively will usually discriminate better. Students who are "test-wise" are aware of such clues, and without knowing the proper information can secure correct answers merely from the form of the statement. Item 2 in the conservation test had this fault of the vague qualifying word.

2. Planting the same crop year after year in the field sometimes uses up the plant food in the soil. ________

If you do not know the answer to this, the best guess is TRUE, because almost everything in this world can occur *sometimes*. This item also suffers from other faults. It does not specify what crop is planted, what plant food the item writer has in mind, nor whether the crop was harvested or plowed under. All these details could affect the answer.

Obvious items

Questions whose answers are so simple for the grade-level that they are obvious to all the students do not discriminate between adequate and inadequate students. Everyone gets them right. Or in some cases the better student may think the obvious item is a trick question and may think up good, though perhaps subtle, reasons for answering it incorrectly. In the conservation test item 4 is probably too obvious for fifth graders.

4. It is important for citizens to prevent fires in forests and grasslands. ________

In some cases the teacher will legitimately include relatively easy items which all or most of the students will do correctly. However, when this policy is followed the intention is usually to give all the pupils a feeling of success in being able to answer questions over what they have studied. The teacher is not interested so much in discriminating among the students as in giving them a survey of the past work and a feeling of accomplishment. The decision about how difficult the items should be depends on the teacher's purpose in giving the test.

MECHANICAL ASPECTS

Principle 5: The test should be organized so that the student sees readily what he should do and how he should do it. The mechanical organization of the test should not be a stumbling block to accurate evaluation of the student.

Directions

Clear directions for marking each section of the test should be given. The students should not miss questions merely because the directions are not clear. The conservation test omitted any directions, so it failed to provide the student with adequate guidance. Although the language quiz did include directions, they were not always clear. For example, the instructions for sections A and B did not tell where answers were to be written.

Here are samples of directions for different types of items used with upper-grade children.

True-false. "In the space at the left of each statement mark whether the statement is true or false. Mark plus (+) for true. Mark zero (o) for false."

Multiple-choice. "In the blank beside each item, write the letter of the answer that finishes the item *best.*"

Matching. "In the blank at the left of each item in column I, place the letter of the *best* answer from column II."

Completion or fill-in. "Each of the following sentences is incomplete because a word has been left out. In the blank in each sentence write the word that *best* completes the sentence."

In the elementary school it is often true that the type of item appearing in a test is new to the children. In these cases, and especially in the lower grades where children do not read well, the teacher should take sufficient time to explain how each kind of item should be answered. A good way to do this is to have the entire class, with the teacher's guidance, work one or two sample problems before beginning the actual test items. The samples can be provided either on the blackboard or on the test paper. Here is an example of one type of multiple-choice test used with third graders who have been learning about the earth and stars. The teacher gives these directions orally:

"Here are some sentences about the earth, the moon, and the stars. There is a blank in each sentence where a word has been left out. From the words under each sentence, choose the one that should go in the blank. Write this word in the blank. Let's all try the sample one together."

Sample: Our earth is closest to ____________.

MARS THE MOON THE SUN JUPITER

"Now you do these by yourself."

1. The moon is made of ____________.

HOT GAS ICE WHITE MUD SILVER ROCK

2. The moon is shaped like a ______.

BALL PLATE CUP HALF-DOLLAR CAKE

To ensure that even the poorer readers can complete the item, the teacher reads each sentence with the class, and everybody completes his own answers.

This sample of a third-grade test is not suggested as *the* correct form. Rather, it is only one form among the many from which the teacher has to choose. The guiding principle should be: Will the children understand this adequately? The teacher may need to try two or three different approaches to discover which works best with his particular grade level.

Answer system

Besides making directions clear for taking the test, the teacher should try to make the system of answering as consistent and easy as possible for a student to understand.

In the conservation test the teacher was careless in numbering the choices in items 6 and 7. In 6 he used numbers, in 7 letters. Such inconsistency occurred when the teacher drew these two items from a file of cards on which he kept items, and on the cards he had sometimes used numbers, sometimes letters. This inconsistency, brought about by the teacher's carelessness, merely adds another possibility for a mechanical detail to prevent accurate measurement of the student's real accomplishment.

It is also helpful if the blanks for answering true-false, multiple-choice, and matching items are placed in a straight row down either the right or the left margin. By following this pattern the teacher can construct a correcting key which speeds up the task of marking papers, and students always know where their answers should go. In the middle or lower grades, however, it is easier for the children to take the test if they do not have to move one symbol, such as a code letter or code number, from one place to another. Consequently, item 2 below would be better than item 1 for middle-grade children.

Item 1

Directions: Find the best answer to each question. Write the letter of that answer in the blank beside the question.

1. In which national park will you find the cliff dwellers' homes? (A) Yosemite, (B) Zion, (C) ______

Mesa Verde, (D) Yellowstone, (E) Rocky Mountain.

Item 2

Directions: Look at the words under each question to find the right answer to the question. Draw a circle around this answer.

2. In which national park will you find the cliff dwellers' homes?

   (A) Yosemite
   (B) Zion
   (C) Mesa Verde
   (D) Yellowstone
   (E) Rocky Mountain

Another difference between the two sample items above is the placement of the possible choices. In the first the possible answers follow the question in the same paragraph. In the second the answers are listed. If sufficient paper is available, the second form is preferred because it presents the possible choices in a more distinct manner for the student. This is especially important when each choice contains several words or perhaps a sentence.

Typography

The teacher should be careful to check for typographical errors in mimeographed or dittoed tests. Such errors mislead the student, slow him down, and frustrate him when he is under the emotional pressure of the examination.

In the language-usage quiz the word *scissors* is spelled *sissors,* thus confusing the student who is not yet a good speller; because it is possible that with the more phonetic misspelling, he cannot even find the word in the dictionary.

The rush of the teacher's day often makes it difficult to take the time to proofread a mimeographed or dittoed examination. It is easier to say, "The stencil is probably right." In this way errors creep into tests and act as barriers to fair measurement of students' development.

OBJECTIVITY IN TEST SCORING

Principle 6: The test should be corrected as objectively as possible. Without sacrificing objectivity, the correcting process should be as speedy and simple as possible for the teacher or students doing the marking.

Teachers commonly find test correcting to be a tedious, irksome task. It not only takes time, but with such items as essay and short-answer questions doubt often enters the teacher's mind. He wonders whether he is doing justice in the way he is judging the students' answers. The following suggestions are designed to help teachers do a more efficient job of test scoring.

Objective versus subjective questions

True-false, multiple-choice, and matching items are usually called *objective* questions. Essay and short-answer items are usually referred to as *subjective* questions. Completion and fill-in items are sometimes placed in one of these categories, sometimes in the other.

Teachers frequently believe that when they use the objective types they are taking personal opinion out of the evaluation process, and when they use subjective types personal opinion is involved. But it should be clear that these terms *objective* and *subjective* refer only to the correcting or scoring process, not to the process of creating test questions. With true-false, multiple-choice, and matching varieties the correct answer has to be determined at the time each item is constructed. These answers then can be placed on an answer key and anyone, whether he understands the subject matter or not, can correct the test accurately. Thus, correcting is an objective, mechanical process not demanding personal judgments on the part of the scorer. But with essay questions the precise answer and the organization of the answer often have not been determined specifically ahead of time, so during the correcting process the scorer must exercise judgment about the adequacy of the answer. To a lesser degree this is true also with completion items because the teacher may have to decide whether one word is as acceptable as another for filling a blank in the sentence.

These facts about the process of correcting tests sometimes screen the fact that the *process of creating items is subjective* whether the questions are multiple-choice, completion, or essay. That is, the teacher's opinion determines what kinds of questions should be asked and also what kinds of answers, as in true-false items, will be acceptable. Consequently, when an instructor is selecting test questions he should not be misled into thinking that *objective* items do not entail the personal opinion of the teacher and therefore are to be preferred. As noted earlier, he should select the kind of question that will be most appropriate for the particular objective and the age level of his pupils.

Correcting essay and short-answer tests

If the teacher decides that an essay or short-answer item will best suit his purposes, he would be wise to follow a procedure such as this:

1. Write the question so that the student clearly understands what kind of answer is desired.

2. *Write down specifically the factors or ideas that should be included in an adequate answer to the question.* It is at this stage of the testing procedure that so many teachers fail. They neglect to outline beforehand the precise kind of answer they desire. Later, when a teacher comes to the task of correcting the students' answers, he is puzzled, irrational, inconsistent, and indecisive. Some teachers do not outline the answer ahead of time because they find the task rather difficult. This simply means that the question itself usually has been worded in such a general, ill-defined manner that the teacher himself does not know precisely what he expects. If he himself cannot do it readily, then how does he expect the students to answer it?

3. Determine what he intends to do about the nonsubject-matter aspects of the test, such as handwriting, neatness, spelling, and sentence structure. Some students have a fluid writing style and may be able to pour out a smooth paragraph that reads well but is actually devoid of facts and thus is a clever and often successful bluff. Other students who have the facts or reasoning well in hand may not express themselves well and as a consequence make a poorer literary showing. In either instance the writing style tends to influence strongly a teacher who does not realize that he is judging more on penmanship and spelling than on the content of the essay. The best way to separate these two factors, style and content, is first to outline the contents of a good answer as described under 2 above. Then the teacher may wish to give a different mark for the style of the essay. Or perhaps he wishes to ignore handwriting and spelling in this test. In either case, he should determine ahead of time how he intends to treat these factors so that they do not become mixed up in the scoring process.

4. Determine a number of points to be given for the inclusion of each idea or element listed under 2 above. If a predetermined numerical weighting is given to each element of the answer, the teacher may add up the points a student receives for his answers and arrive at a more objective mark. The following essay question for an eighth grade might be handled in this manner:

"Question: What are the three main divisions of our state government? Tell the main work or responsibility of each division."

The teacher outlines the main elements of an adequate answer:

"1. Legislative or lawmaking division. Makes laws for the state.

"2. Executive or administrative division. Does the work of carrying out the laws, such as building roads, collecting taxes, and taking care of state forests.

"3. Judicial. Decides which people are breaking laws. Decides if laws are constitutional."

The instructor decides to give one point each for naming the three divisions and two points for telling the function of each division. If the function is described but not specifically nor very well, only one point is awarded for this part. A total of nine points would be possible for the entire item. Therefore, it is seen that when the question is stated clearly and the teacher decides upon the main points to be included, an essay question can be judged rather objectively.

5. Correct question 1 on all students' papers first before going on to question 2, if several essay questions appear on the test. In doing so the teacher has to keep in mind only the elements of that one first question as he marks the papers. After marking the first question on every paper, he can follow the same procedure with question 2. This practice tends to increase the accuracy of grading and to reduce the inconsistencies that arise when a teacher marks all seven or all ten essay items on one student's paper before moving on to judge the next student's answers.

Before leaving this discussion of methods of scoring essays, we should recognize that in some cases it is difficult or impossible to state an exact number of points for particular elements of an answer. This is true because the question may be designed to test primarily a student's ability to organize material or construct a plan of attack on a problem. In such cases, the teacher, as he reads the essays, can decide "this answer is somewhat better than that one," but he finds it difficult to assign specific scores to the answers as he reads the papers. Many instructors solve this dilemma by placing the papers in five or six piles according to their comparative goodness. For a particular essay item the teacher may decide that the pupils' answers fall into six gradations of adequacy. After placing the papers in six piles, and perhaps rechecking a few by reading them again, he assigns a number to each group. These numbers might be from 1 (the poorest) to 6 (the best). However, some teachers believe that even the poorest papers in the class often have several correct ideas, and, therefore, to give these students a score of 1 on the question may cause them to feel that they have received almost no recognition for the ideas they did have. Consequently, these teachers prefer to award 10 to the top papers, 9 to the next, and so on. In this way the lowest of the six piles receives a score of 5, which is more encouraging to the student who knows a fair portion of the material even though he is comparatively poorer than the majority of his classmates. As a result, it is the individual teacher's responsibility, after placing the answers in piles according to their adequacy, to estimate what type of numerical weighting for the item should be used to make a fair judgment of the pupils' progress.

Scoring objective items

As with essay and short-answer tests, the specific answer desired for true-false, multiple-choice, matching, and completion items should be determined at the time each question is created. Then the

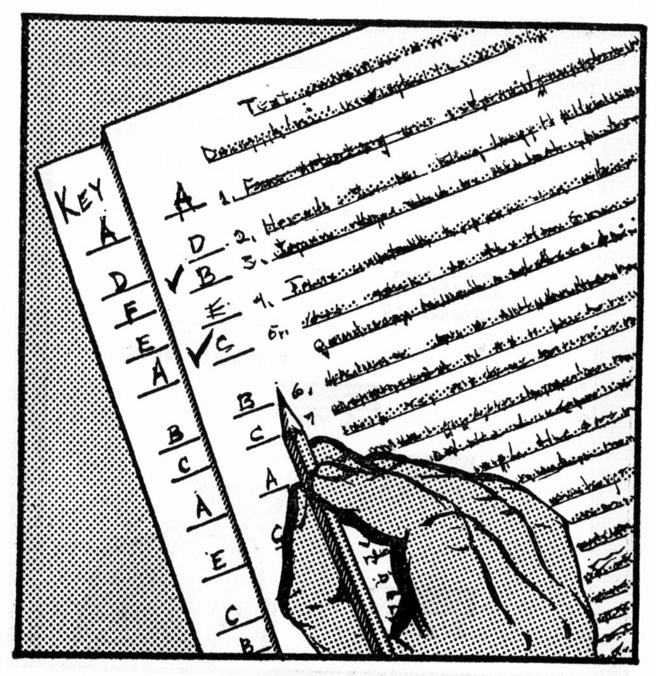

Fig. 3. Sample answer key

teacher's scoring task is reduced to the process of (1) marking each item and (2) determining a total score for the test.

Marking each item. A little attention to the physical arrangement of objective tests makes rapid, accurate marking possible. When objective items are on a mimeographed or dittoed sheet, it is easiest for the teacher to have all answer blanks down either the right or the left margin of the paper. In correcting the papers the teacher can place an answer key adjacent to the row of blanks and quickly check incorrect answers.

Usually in correcting completion tests the teacher can work efficiently simply by placing the answer sheet beside the student's test paper and compare answers on the two sheets. But if many completion-test papers are to be scored, the instructor may wish to place a sheet of typing paper on top of the test sheet. Through the typing paper he can see dimly where the completion blanks lie and can cut rectangular holes in the paper to expose what the child has written in each blank. Then just below each hole on the typing sheet he can

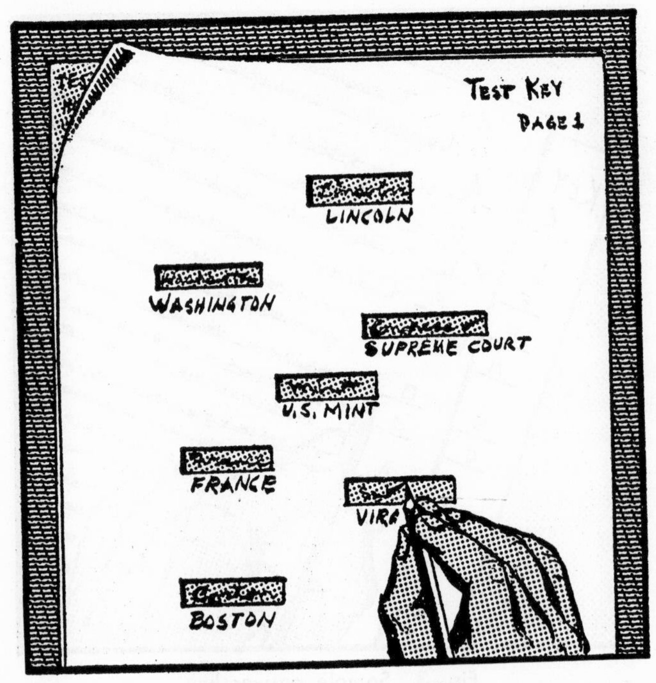

Fig. 4. Sample answer key

write the correct word or words for each blank. In this way the answer sheet can be placed on a child's test, and the slots expose his answers, which can be compared quickly with the correct answers written below each blank on the key. This speeds up the correcting process when a large number of tests are to be marked.

The correcting key with rectangular slots can also be used for correcting the type of multiple-choice item which requires the pupil to underline the proper word or phrase. Here is an example:

Directions: Draw a line under the word or words that best finish each sentence.

1. A kind of material that carries electricity very well is called:

(an insulator) (a conductor) (an automation)

2. If you must touch electric wires with a screw driver when fixing the wires, a safe kind of screw driver to use would be one with a steel shaft and a:

(steel handle) (copper handle) (plastic handle)

Determining a total score. To determine what the total test score should be, the teacher must decide how much each item is to be worth and whether or not to substract an amount for guessing on objective questions.

The first of these problems is solved simply by the teacher's determining how important one item is compared to the others. Thus, he may decide the multiple-choice items test more important objectives than the matching items, so he awards two points for each correct multiple-choice item and only one for each matching item. Or he awards one point each for an objective item and five each for the short-essay items.

The second problem concerns whether the teacher should try to punish the student for attempting to guess at answers which he is not sure of. Remember that the chance of getting a true-false item correct simply by guess is 1 out of 2, or ½. The chance of getting a five-choice multiple-choice item right simply by guess is 1 out of 5. Hence, with the assumption that a student will not be as apt to guess on true-false if he knows he might lose more than if he simply left the item blank, some teachers count one point off for each answer left blank but two off for each wrong answer. In effect, this is the same as subtracting the wrong answers from the right ones and not computing blank ones in compiling a total. (It should be obvious that the student who gets many answers wrong can end up in the hole with a minus score. This is often rather discouraging to him.)

If the teacher is to be consistent in reducing true-false answers in this manner he should also reduce multiple-choice and matching items by the appropriate fraction. That is, on four-choice multiple-choice items, the wrong ones should count against the student more than the ones he left out. The usual correction formula, which is based on the assumption that the person who does not know the answer simply makes a random guess, is:

$$\text{Score} = \text{RIGHTS} - \frac{\text{WRONGS}}{\text{N} - 1}$$

In this formula N refers to the number of possible choices in the answer. For instance, on a 50-item multiple-choice test in which each item had four possible choices a student got 40 questions right, 8 wrong, and he left 2 out. His final corrected score would be 37⅓.

$$40 - \frac{8}{4 - 1} \text{ or } 40 - \frac{8}{3} = 37\tfrac{1}{3}$$

Often teachers do not use this correction-for-guessing procedure because it is a bother and because the assumption on which it is based (that every wrong answer is a random guess) cannot be supported. That is, people who take tests often have most of the information necessary to answer an item correctly, but by slight misinterpretation they make the wrong choice. Or perhaps two of the possible multiple choices are fairly good answers, but one is judged by the teacher to be better than the other. In this case the student did not make a pure guess, but he knew a good deal about the item—more than he would have known for items he left out. Thus it seems hardly fair to reduce his score for guessing when he did not guess. The catch is, of course, that the teacher never knows which wrong answers were near-hits based on almost accurate knowledge and which were simply random guesses. Since either policy can be defended (correcting for guessing or not correcting for guessing), each teacher will have to accept the practice that is more compatible with his beliefs and the kinds of tests he gives.

OPPORTUNITY TO PREPARE FOR AND COMPLETE TEST

Principle 7: The student should have an opportunity to prepare adequately for the test. With certain exceptions (such as speed tests in intelligence scales or in typing or shorthand tests) *he should have time to complete the test.*

Material covered

Some teachers include material on a test that students did not know they were to learn. Usually this is not done with malice aforethought but through not paying close attention to testing for the real objectives of the class. Carelessness on the teacher's part may cause him to use a test from past years or to use a standardized achievement test for which the students have had no adequate opportunity to prepare. This is obviously an unfair practice if the teacher is trying to discover how much of what he has taught has been learned by the class.

Warning of a test

A common issue that teachers debate is the surprise, or *pop,* quiz. Some say, "A student should be prepared at any time to be tested. Thus, there should be no need for warning him ahead of time. Unannounced tests are the only proper type. They keep the students on their toes."

Others say, "Surprise tests are unfair. Students sometimes put different amounts of stress on different subjects or projects during a semester. For example, a boy may be helping make a stage scenery for the seventh-grade play. He may not keep up so well on his science reading, which he plans to stress after the play. To give a surprise science test is unfair, because he probably could have arranged his time if he had known a week before that the test was due. When a teacher gives surprise tests, the students may develop some fear of entering class each day, for they wonder, 'Is it going to be today?' I believe that for the purposes of mental hygiene it is only fair to let the children know when they are to be evaluated."

By weighing these factors against each other the individual teacher must decide for himself what method of forewarning, or lack of forewarning, is best for the pupils' continued growth. Some teachers use frequent short tests but warn pupils ahead of time so that the date and the material to be tested over are thoroughly understood by the class. In this way the pupils are constantly evaluated and constantly keep up with their work, but they are not afraid of a possible surprise quiz each day they enter class.

Time to complete test

Most tests that teachers create are intended to be *power* tests. That is, they are intended to measure how much a student knows, whether he can produce this knowledge immediately or whether he needs more time to answer the questions. Therefore, for situations like these the teacher should provide enough time for all, or almost all, of the pupils to answer all the items. (For practical reasons, teachers often cannot wait until the very slowest student has finished because this holds up the work of the rest of the class too much. But a rule of thumb can be adopted, such as stopping the test after 90 per cent of the class have finished, which is fair to the great majority.)

In some instances *speed* tests are desired, for the time it takes a pupil to complete a task is part of what the teacher is measuring. This is true in reading speed tests, in some kinds of arithmetic tests that stress speed of computation, and in typing tests. But with most teacher-constructed examinations in the elementary and junior high schools, speed should not be a factor. The teacher should design the length of the test to give most students ample time to answer all items.

USING TEACHER-MADE TESTS

Like other evaluation devices, teacher-made tests can be used in numerous ways. The more prominent functions of tests at elementary and junior high levels include: (1) diagnosing students' strengths and weaknesses, (2) motivating specific lessons, (3) providing evidence of progress to report to the student and his parents, (4) providing data for predicting probable future success, and (5) reflecting effectiveness of teaching techniques.

Diagnosing strengths and weaknesses

Oftentimes tests are regarded only as devices for judging pupils' achievement so that they can be marked at the end of a unit or a semester. However, when we consider that in school we are trying to help the child to grow continually we see that a more important way to use tests is for diagnosing his strengths and weaknesses. Continual evaluation, including testing, provides the teacher with information that can be used to help fit the program to each child's needs as the year progresses. To discover only at the end of the unit on Mexico that a fourth-grade girl has understood almost nothing of what she has read does not help the girl learn about Mexico. However, if this had been discovered earlier in the six-week unit, extra help in reading and simpler materials on Mexico might have been provided. To discover only at the end of the unit that a boy at the beginning had already known almost everything about Mexico that was covered in the textbook does not help the boy grow. However, if this had been discovered earlier, through written or oral questions, he could have been given supplementary reading or projects that would have challenged him and not allowed him only to coast along learning nothing new.

Consequently, tests are useful tools for diagnosing areas in which a pupil needs more help or more challenging materials.

Motivating students

Just as a test may be given at the beginning of a unit to provide the teacher with information about what the children already know, so a test at the beginning can motivate the class to want to learn the materials in the coming unit. The following items from a sixth-grade test given at the beginning of the study of "The Oceans" provided the class with some goals of the unit as well as promoted immediate interest.

1. What does a jellyfish look like? How does it live?
2. What is the biggest fish in the ocean? How could you catch one?
3. If you were out on a raft in the middle of the ocean, and you had no food, how would you be able to live?
4. What is plankton? How could we get some?
5. What food have you eaten in the past month that came from the ocean?

Providing evidence for reports to parents

In the middle and upper grades tests provide much of the evidence that the teacher uses in reporting a pupil's progress to the pupil and his parents. This is the most common use of tests in schools today, although the diagnostic use of tests for improving teaching should probably come to be the most prominent function of tests in elementary and junior high schools.

Providing data for predicting future progress

Usually intelligence and aptitude tests are used for predicting the probable success of a student in certain types of work. In a less formal way teachers use classroom tests for this same purpose. In general, the child who is doing well in arithmetic today, as revealed by tests, will also do well in the future in that area. This also tends to be true of other subject-matter areas. The prediction of the more immediate future is considerably more reliable than long-term prediction. However, from the standpoint of helping students select elective courses in junior high or high schools, records of students' success on classroom tests can be quite helpful.

Reflecting teachers' effectiveness

When most of the pupils in a class do rather well on a test, and only a few do poorly, the teacher usually can conclude that in general he has done an adequate job of teaching what the test covered. However, when most of the class does poorly on a test, it is time for the teacher to inspect himself more closely. Because the teacher is a human and emotional being who, like his students, is striving to feel adequate in his world, it seems only natural for him to blame the students for "no background" or "no brains" or "laziness" when they score universally low on a test. But if after this initial emotional reaction the instructor can analyze what might have been wrong with his objectives, methods, or test items, he will probably improve his teaching techniques and consequently reduce the number of such blows to his ego in the future.

OBJECTIVES OF THIS CHAPTER

The effective elementary or junior high school teacher:

1. Creates tests:
   a. Which evaluate for the true objectives of the class, giving most weight to the most important objectives.
   b. Whose items are as appropriate as possible to each objective and to the maturity level of the pupils.
   c. Whose items are clearly understood by pupils.
   d. Whose items discriminate between the student who has met the objectives and the student who has not.
   e. Whose mechanical organization is an aid, not a stumbling block, in the accurate evaluation of students.

f. Which can be scored efficiently and objectively.
g. For which pupils have had adequate opportunity to prepare.

2. Uses tests for:
   a. Diagnosing students' strengths and weaknesses.
   b. Motivating students.
   c. Providing evidence for reports to students and parents.
   d. Providing data for predicting future progress.
   e. Reflecting teachers' effectiveness.

Suggested evaluation techniques for this chapter

1. Inspect the objectives for which the *conservation test* and the *language-usage quiz* at the beginning of this chapter were to measure. Then create two new tests, or revisions of the present ones, which will measure more accurately for the objectives than do the original ones. Before creating test items it would be wise to make the objectives more specific than they are at the beginning of the chapter. If this is done, it will be easier to construct good test items.

2. Using the objectives listed at the end of this chapter, construct a number of test items which would measure (at least on the planning or understanding level) the extent to which a college or university student has achieved these objectives.

3. Write objectives for a unit or a series of lessons in an elementary-school class. Indicate for which of these objectives a teacher-made test would be an appropriate evaluation device. Construct test items to measure for these objectives.

4. *Improving a Test in Social Studies*

   Miss Angela has taught a sixth-grade unit on Canada's Maritime Provinces. Her principal objectives have been to have the students:
   a. Describe the geography of Newfoundland, Labrador, and Nova Scotia.
   b. Describe the life of the people of the Maritimes, including their homes, occupations, origins, customs, and recreation.
   c. Compare the lives of boys and girls in the Maritimes with those of our area.
   d. Estimate the probable future of the Maritimes.

   To evaluate how well the students had reached these objectives by the end of their study, Miss Angela gave the following test. You are to inspect it, and on a sheet of paper write your judgments of the test, item by item. If any items need improving, make the desired changes. If any need eliminating, discard them.

If any are worth while, indicate why.

Test on Canada's Maritime Provinces

Your Name ______________________ Date __________

1. Newfoundland is important to transoceanic travel because:
   a. ______________________
   b. ______________________
   c. ______________________
2. Newfoundland is the __________ of many transatlantic cables.
3. __________ laid the first transoceanic cable.
4. __________ invented the telegraph.
5. __________ is the capital of Newfoundland.
6. The major occupation in Newfoundland is __________.
7. The mineral __________ was discovered in the rocks used as __________ by the fishermen of __________ and is like to become an important __________ chiefly to __________, __________, and __________.
8. The words Nova Scotia mean __________ __________.
9. Labrador's future lies in her __________ wealth of __________ and __________.
10. The Maritime Provinces of Canada are __________, __________, and __________.

5. *Improving Arithmetic Test*

Miss Curtis had the following objectives for a portion of the arithmetic program in third grade: "As a result of their study the pupils:

a. Use two-column addition in real-life situations.
b. Use subtraction in real-life situations.
c. Use simple multiplication to solve lifelike problems."

To measure their progress toward these objectives, she gave the following test. Evaluate it as you did the test under exercise 4 above, using the same kind of criteria.

Name ______________________

1. Four boys wanted to put their money together to buy special tent stakes for the Scout patrol. The stakes cost 82 cents. Tom had 21 cents. Jim had 23 cents. Carl had 19 cents. Ralph had 25 cents.
   Did they have enough to buy the stakes? __________
   How much money did they have left over? __________
2. For a class Halloween party James was to bring enough paper sacks so that every pupil could make a mask. There were five rows of desks in the room. There were five students in each row. How many paper sacks did James need? __________

3. How many bookmarks, 5 inches long, can be cut from a yard of ribbon? How much ribbon will be left? ________
4. In his bank checkbook Bill had 30 blank checks. He has used 17 of them. How many blank ones does he have left? ________
5. At the circus that came to town last week Larry and Jane's father took them to see it and gave Larry 3 dimes and 2 pennies and he gave Jane a quarter, a nickel, and 2 pennies. Did each of them get the same amount? ________

6. *Improving Social-Studies Test Items*

The items below are from a seventh-grade test over a study of New York State transportation. The main goals of the study are: "(1) The student explains the development of transportation facilities in New York since colonial days, and (2) the student explains how modern living in New York is dependent on present-day modes of transportation." In light of what you know about tests, explain what is wrong with the following items:

1. (Multiple-choice) One of the outstanding developments of the past century was the invention of the radio by (*a*) Morse, (*b*) Edison, (*c*) Bell, (*d*) Marconi, (*e*) Fulton.
2. (Multiple-choice) Probably the lowest-cost type of transportation for bulky freight is a (*a*) semitrailer truck, (*b*) barge, (*c*) railroads, (*d*) air freight.
3. (Multiple-choice) The "Golden Spike" which completed the first transcontinental railroad was driven near Salt Lake by (*a*) Thomas Jefferson, (*b*) Andrew Carnegie, (*c*) U. S. Grant, (*d*) Leland Stanford, (*e*) Jefferson Davis.
4. (True-false) Among the large number of prominent waterways and ocean-connected routes that have figured importantly in the internal transportation history of the Empire State, the St. Lawrence River is notable because it has enabled ocean-going vessels to navigate hundreds of miles inland.

SUGGESTED READINGS

1. FURST, EDWARD J. *Constructing Evaluation Instruments.* New York: Longmans, Green and Co., 1958. Part II extensively treats construction of achievement tests.
2. GERBERICH, J. RAYMOND. *Specimen Objective Test Items.* New York: Longmans, Green and Co., 1956. Examples of 227 different kinds of objective test items for measuring many kinds of goals. An excellent source of sample items.
3. GREENE, HARRY A.; JORGENSEN, ALBERT N.; and GERBERICH, J. RAYMOND. *Measurement and Evaluation in the Elementary School.* New York: Longmans, Green and Co., 1953. Chapters 6 and 7.

4. Ross, C. C., and Stanley, J. C. *Measurement in Today's Schools* (Third Edition). New York: Prentice-Hall, Inc., 1954. Chapters on objective and essay test items.
5. Schwartz, Alfred, and Tiedeman, Stuart C. *Evaluating Student Progress in the Secondary School.* New York: Longmans, Green and Co., 1957. Chapters 6-8 give clear guidance to test construction suitable for elementary and secondary levels.
6. Thorndike, Robert L., and Hagen, Elizabeth. *Measurement and Evaluation in Psychology and Education.* New York: Wiley and Sons, 1955. Chapters 3 and 4.
7. Wandt, Edwin, and Brown, Gerald W. *Essentials of Educational Evaluation.* New York: Henry Holt and Co., 1957. Chapters 2-3.

CHAPTER

4

Using Standardized Tests

1. Achievement Tests

DURING THE CENTRAL SCHOOL faculty meeting the principal, Miss McKenzie, announced that:

"There seems to be a definite need for doing a better over-all job of measuring or testing our students in comparison with those in other schools. It's important to know about the ability of children transferring away from or into our school. And also we should have some better way to see how well our program compares with those in other schools. There's another thing that's important, too... that's telling to what extent certain of our pupils are capable of doing the work we ask of them. If we could measure their ability better, we would know what to expect of different children. Quite a few of you have brought these matters up before. I have talked it over with the superintendent, and he agrees that we should form a committee to recommend a procedure for doing this... that is, establishing some kind of testing program. I am going to ask the following people to serve with me on this committee: Miss Chavez, Mr. Harris, Mrs. Schultz, Mr. Endo, Miss Alder, and Mr. Carpenter."

In subsequent meetings of this committee, the members studied the best methods of solving the problems Miss McKenzie had proposed. They decided that the problems fell into two general categories: (1) comparing their students with those of other schools and (2) estimating within their own school the extent to which individual children were capable of doing various types of tasks and schoolwork.

Mr. Carpenter contended that "This whole business can be solved satisfactorily with a few standardized tests. They'll give us all the information we need, and it will be very little bother for us."

Miss Chavez said, "Perhaps standardized tests can help some, but you have to be careful not to put too much faith in them. Some schools do a lot of damage either by using them wrongly or by using ones that aren't constructed well. There are some pretty poor tests on the market along with the good ones."

The group agreed that before buying and using any standardized tests they would have to be sure they knew which tests were well constructed and what the tests could do adequately. Since the decisions to be made on the basis of the proposed program would affect the children's lives (such as placement of transfer students and guidance of children's classwork), the teachers wanted to be sure they used the right tests in the right manner.

In solving their problems, the committee members learned a great deal, which is summarized in the succeeding sections:

WHAT IS A STANDARDIZED TEST?

Broadly speaking, a standardized test is one which has been given to so many people that the test-makers have been able to determine fairly accurately how well a *typical* person of a particular age or grade-in-school will succeed in it. The standards are usually reported in terms of how well "average five-year-olds" or "average adults" or "other sixth-graders" answer the items. The items on well-constructed standardized tests have been analyzed statistically to eliminate poor items and to insure that only valid and discriminating ones are included. These tests require a standard method of administration, that is, they are to be administered to the students in exactly the same manner each time so that the results will be comparable. Standardized tests are usually constructed by experts and are printed and sold by test agencies, book publishers, or universities.

Like teacher-made tests, the standardized variety is intended to be a short-cut method for measuring a student's behavior. If a teacher wishes to judge how well a child reads, she cannot take time to question him thoroughly on everything he reads during a year. Instead, she gives him a test of selected reading material in hope that the way he reads this material will be an *accurate sample* of the way he reads all other material throughout the year, at home as well as at school. The teacher uses tests just as the geologist uses a drill sample when he searches the earth for oil or minerals. He samples a portion of the earth's layer, assuming that the sample is representative of the surrounding country. The teacher uses tests to sample areas of a student's knowledge, aptitudes, and behavior, assuming that the test is an accurate sample of this area of the student's personality.

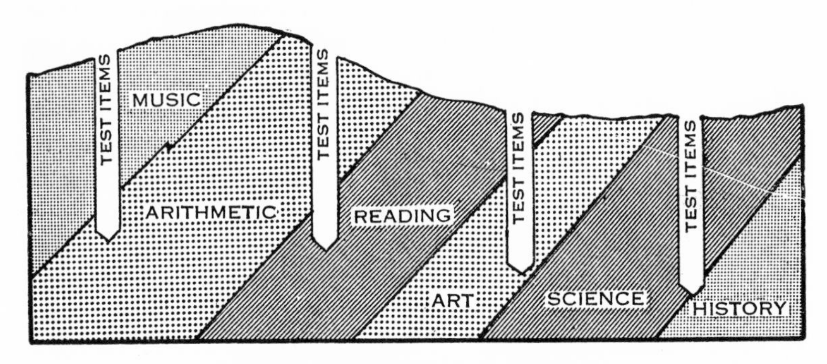

Fig. 5. Tests sample abilities

Obviously, inaccurate or misnamed tests, or tests administered improperly, give a distorted sample of a child's behavior. This distorted record may mislead the teacher and cause her to treat the child in a manner detrimental to his growth and mental health.

WHAT KINDS OF STANDARDIZED TESTS ARE AVAILABLE?

Usually the name of a test tells what it is intended to measure. However, a teacher should not necessarily take the test name at face value, for some tests do not do what the name indicates, and many others do not do their assigned tasks as accurately as the teacher might wish. In general, however, the test name is the best guide to the author's intentions.

The test name usually tells three things:

1. What area in a person's life is being sampled, such as, *reading* ability, *general academic* ability, *mechanical* ability, achievement in *science* or *arithmetic,* personal and social *adjustment,* and so on.
2. The person or organization that created or sells the test.
3. How the test is intended to be used, that is, whether it is intended to *predict* a student's future, to *diagnose* his present

strengths and weaknesses, or to measure his present *achievement.*

The first two categories above are usually self-explanatory, but teachers are sometimes confused by the words which indicate the third category, such as, *aptitude, prognostic, intelligence, ability, readiness, achievement,* or *diagnostic.* They ask, "What is the real difference between an ability and an achievement test? And what's the difference between an aptitude and an intelligence test?" Basically, these words (prognostic, aptitude, and so on) tell *how* the test-makers intended the test to be used, but the test might also be used in ways other than indicated by the name. The difference between a science achievement and a diagnostic science test is not so much in the content of the test as it is in *how* the teacher uses it. In fact, it is quite possible for a teacher to use one test, such as a reading test, for *all* of the above purposes.

For example, a second-grade teacher administers a standardized reading test to her class. She is using it as an *aptitude* (or it could be called *reading-intelligence, reading-ability,* or *reading-prognostic*) test if she uses the children's scores in trying to *predict their future success in reading.* She is using it as a *readiness* test if she is trying to estimate whether the children are ready for their next step in the reading process. She is using it as an *achievement* test if she is trying to evaluate or to mark how much the child has learned up to the present time (focusing on past growth without concern for predicting the future). The teacher is using the test in a *diagnostic* capacity if it enables her to analyze the child's strengths and weaknesses in reading at the present time (in terms of reading speed, understanding words, understanding sentences, understanding paragraphs, and so forth). Thus, the name of a test often tells *how* the authors intended the test to be used, but how the test is actually used in school depends upon the judgment of the teacher. If this judgment is based on an enlightened knowledge of proper test selection and test use, the children are more likely to be helped by standardized testing instead of being harmed, as is sometimes the case.

Standardized tests are commonly divided into three categories: (1) achievement, (2) aptitude or intelligence, and (3) personality. These categories are not mutually exclusive; they overlap considerably, for, as was seen above, one test might be used to do a number of jobs for a teacher. Despite the overlapping, these three divisions provide a convenient method of discussing how to choose and use standardized scales. The present chapter treats achievement tests. Chapter 5 discusses aptitude and intelligence scales, and Chapter 6 treats personality tests.

TYPES OF ACHIEVEMENT TESTS

An achievement test is designed to measure *how well a person has been trained in a particular skill or area of knowledge.* This type of test focuses primarily on *past attainment* in schoolwork rather than on prediction of future success, as an aptitude test does.

In the next section of this chapter we will present criteria by which a teacher can judge any standardized achievement test. We will not try to describe specific tests or recommend particular ones, for the number of available tests is large, and a test that would be most appropriate for one school would not be appropriate for another. (Descriptions of some of the most useful achievement tests are found in Appendix A.)

Some idea of the number of different achievement examinations in use with pupils of elementary-school ages has been offered by Greene (*5:734–51*) who lists 92 standardized tests in reading, 35 in arithmetic, 17 in languages, 12 in natural science, 11 in social science, 9 in health, and 3 in spelling. He also lists 63 batteries of achievement tests available for pupils at various elementary-school levels. (A *battery* is a series or collection of tests that cover more than one subject, such as reading, arithmetic, social science, and language. Some of the individual subject-matter tests described by Greene are also portions of the batteries he mentions.)

Although it is not feasible to describe all these tests, a better general understanding of their contents may result from a brief statement about a few typical varieties.

Reading tests

Both oral and silent reading tests have been produced for use with elementary-school children.

The oral test is usually composed of paragraphs of increasing difficulty which the child is to read to the teacher. Obviously it is not a group-testing situation. The teacher notes the mistakes made by the pupil and can compare his score with those of a standardization sample. This type of test has the advantage, especially with younger pupils, of informing the teacher of the amount of skipping, guessing, and miscalling of words a child is doing. It also helps the teacher diagnose the types of words or punctuation that are causing difficulty.

Silent reading tests are more common than oral ones. They enable the teacher to test large groups of pupils at one time. The most common varieties are termed *general* reading tests. They are usually composed of a series of sentences or paragraphs, each of which is followed by one or more questions the pupil is to answer about the passage. The reading material often becomes increasingly more difficult and the questions more involved. In some tests, however, the material is aimed at a particular level, such as third- or fourth-grade reading ability, and remains at that level throughout the test. Since general reading tests are usually timed, the pupil's score depends upon both speed and comprehension.

Many times teachers are not only interested in a child's general silent reading speed and comprehension, but they wish to know specifically the strong and weak factors in his reading. Is a pupil's lack of vocabulary causing reading difficulties? Or does he have trouble understanding sentence structure? Does he fail to draw logical conclusions or inferences from what he reads? In such cases the teacher wants a *diagnostic* reading scale. Some tests are divided into several sections, each of which yields a score intended to help the teacher decide which of the more specific factors that contribute to reading ability is causing a child trouble.

There are many specific types of reading tests, each designed to do a particular task. Some are effective; others are not. By applying the criteria suggested in the next section, the teacher can best determine the usefulness of a given standardized reading test for his class.

Arithmetic tests

Like reading tests, arithmetic tests can be of either a *general* or a *diagnostic* nature.

General arithmetic tests are often called problem-solving or arithmetical reasoning tests. They are composed of many practical uses of arithmetic in everyday life, business, architecture, and surveying. They yield scores that tell how accurately a person thinks about quantities and relationships in common situations.

The general arithmetic test, however, does not *diagnose* the strong and weak areas of a pupil's quantitative thinking. It does not reveal whether a pupil's difficulties may lie in (1) his ability to compute from rules and rote memory, (2) his abstract reasoning ability, or (3) his ability to handle geometric relationships. A student may be capable in one of these areas and not in another. Consequently, *diagnostic* arithmetic tests have been developed to yield scores that separate one of these factors from another. Other tests divide up arithmetic skills even further, so that they contain separate sections on addition, subtraction, multiplication, and division (of whole numbers, fractions, and decimals) as well as ones on symbols and rules, number concepts, and problem solving. Such diagnostic tests are especially useful to the teacher who wishes to survey his students' achievement in these areas with the view of providing aid for those having specific difficulties.

Many standardized diagnostic tests in all subject-matter fields have been properly criticized for having too few items in each section to be valid measures of a student's skill in the area. It is important to remember that a test is a sampling of a pupil's knowledge or skill, and an insufficient number of items in a test will provide an inadequate sample of this knowledge. The larger the number of items in the test, the greater the reliability will be. Therefore, it is important when inspecting a diagnostic test to see that each section contains a substantial number of items so that it will yield a fair and helpful judgment of the student's achievement.

Social studies tests

Nearly all of the standard tests in this area treat history, civics, or geography, which make up the principal high-school social studies. Most social studies tests for the elementary school are designed for the upper grades. Some state departments of education have produced geography tests to be used with students in the state. Other tests are produced by test bureaus.

Standardized tests in social studies commonly are composed of multiple-choice items testing facts and, in the case of geography, items that require location of places on maps.

Science tests

Standardized science examinations are usually designed for upper grades. They test for scientific facts and principles and also for conclusions that can logically be drawn from given data (that is, scientific method). Multiple-choice, completion, and true-false are the most common types of items.

Language tests

Capitalization, punctuation, sentence structure, grammar, spelling, and sometimes handwriting are included on language tests. A number of different types of items are usually included, such as a story with errors to be corrected by the student, sentences which the student is to judge as being in either correct or incorrect English, and sentences in which the student is to identify the grammatical form of an underlined word.

Achievement batteries

The most common type of achievement battery is composed of individual sections covering such areas as reading, arithmetic, language, social studies, health, and science. These areas are usually broken down into further divisions which make the tests more diagnostic in character.

For example, one popular battery includes the following tests: reading, vocabulary, literature, numbers, arithmetic fundamentals, arithmetic problems, spelling, language usage, English, history, geography, and science. For the primary children the battery also has tests on word pictures, word recognition, and word meaning.

Another battery consists of: reading comprehension (including following directions, sentence meaning, paragraph meaning), reading speed, spelling, arithmetic computation, number comparisons, problem analysis, arithmetic problems, language usage (words and sentences), punctuation and capitalization, expressing ideas, literature (sections on motives and moods and on miscellaneous facts), geographical ideas and comparisons, miscellaneous geographical facts, lessons of history, historical facts, and health.

As these listings indicate, the more comprehensive batteries have been designed to evaluate pupil achievement in almost the entire school program.

However, two cautions are necessary when a teacher or administrator contemplates using an achievement battery.

First, each test in the battery should itself be long enough to yield an adequate sample of the students' achievement in that area. It may be a temptation for test constructors to reduce the number of items on each section of the battery so that the whole series of tests does not take up too much school time. However, the shorter the test, the poorer the sample of achievement it will be likely to yield.

The second caution relates to the objectives of the particular class compared with the objectives of the test-makers. When they constructed the examination, the experts had their own idea of what material in social studies, science, and arithmetic children should learn in a given grade. The school, however, may have been working toward different, and equally good, objectives in these areas. It would be improper to try to measure children's progress toward goals different from those for which the test battery was designed. Unless the school is working for the same specific goals in each area that the test was designed to measure, the test will not evaluate properly the students' achievement.

HOW TO SELECT STANDARDIZED ACHIEVEMENT TESTS

Teachers use achievement tests more than any other type of standardized scale. As indicated earlier, there are a great many such tests published in all of the common subject-matter areas. Because of the abundance of achievement tests and because they vary in quality, the teacher needs pertinent criteria by which to judge them. The following criteria help insure accurate choice of tests: test name, publisher, reliability, validity, norms, time, administering and scoring, and price.

Name

As previously indicated, the name of the test is usually a good guide to how the test-makers intended their scale to be used. However, in some cases the name misleads, rather than helps, because the test does not measure accurately what its title states. To purchase a test on the basis of its name alone can lead to the use of an unreliable or invalid measuring scale.

Publisher

As a teacher reads about tests and inspects copies of the better standardized varieties, he comes to recognize the companies that are noted for publishing only well-constructed tests. The larger test bureaus, prominent textbook publishers, and universities tend to be most dependable.

Reliability

An important requirement of a test is that it *yield consistent results*. This trait of consistency in a test is termed *reliability*.

When we analyze what test consistency really involves we see that the term *reliability* can have more than one meaning, depending upon the circumstances. It is important to recognize this fact when you select standardized tests, so that you will know what reliability data to look for and how to interpret it.

Our discussion may well begin with an example of seventh graders who took a social-science-facts test. The scores of six students, typical of the class range, were:

Student	*Score*
Ralph	97
Sally	84
Ted	78
Verne	62
Wallace	57
Evelyn	41

From these results the teacher concluded that Ralph was markedly superior to the others. Below him the students ranged down in well-defined steps to Evelyn, who was obviously very poor in social-science facts. However, these results did not agree in all cases with the teacher's impression of the students' work. So, having corrected the papers during lunch period, the teacher that same afternoon gave the same test again. The results on this second administration are shown here, compared with the morning scores.

Student	*Morning*	*Afternoon*
Ralph	97	63
Sally	84	72
Ted	78	49
Verne	62	87
Wallace	57	63
Evelyn	41	67

The teacher was quite disturbed by these results which he had obtained by his *test-and-immediately-retest* technique. Something was obviously wrong. We would assume that in a typical seventh-grade class some of the students knew social-science facts better than others did. The test had been given in an attempt to secure an accurate sample of these students' knowledge. The test results, therefore, should reflect *consistently* on every testing which students were best informed, which were moderately well informed, and which were poorly informed in social science. But the results of the test are puzzling. Which time did the test give the correct sample of the students' behavior, morning or afternoon? If the teacher is thinking of grading the students' progress on the basis of the test, which score should he choose, the first or the second?

If the teacher selected the first score and gave letter grades to rate the pupils' success, Ralph would probably have received an A and Evelyn would probably have been given a very low mark. But if the second results were used, Evelyn would have been marked slightly higher than Ralph. The other students' scores were equally confusing. Which time did the test secure an accurate sample of the students' progress? Or perhaps neither the morning nor the afternoon scores represented an accurate picture of their relative command of social-science facts. The teacher has no way of knowing. This test yielded *inconsistent* results from one time to the next.

And what caused the inconsistency? As we look at the testing situation, we judge that something was wrong with the testing procedure or the items themselves, causing the students to answer erratically from one time to the next. We reject the probability that some students learned a great deal and others forgot a great deal of social-science facts during the lunch hour, which could have been another reason for inconsistent scores.

Upon inspecting the test the teacher observed that indeed the items included numbers of rather ambiguous true-false and matching questions. In addition, many of the items concerned facts never touched upon in the students' schoolwork. When questioned, the students admitted that ambiguity led them to guess in many cases. Students apparently changed their guesses between morning and afternoon.

Retest after an interval. If the teacher had waited longer to do the second testing—perhaps a few weeks or even months—there would have been a mixture of two factors to cause the unreliability: (1) shortcomings of the test procedure and the items themselves, as well as (2) changes in amount of student knowledge, motivation, and alertness over the period of time. Thus we see that when an interval comes between testing and retesting we are not sure how much each of these two factors has contributed to any resulting inconsistency between the two sets of scores.

So far in this discussion we have inspected two ways of judging test reliability: (1) test and immediately retest with the same examination, and (2) test, wait for an interval of time, then retest with the same examination. But there are other ways of judging reliability. The most popular of the other methods involve developing two parallel forms of a test and comparing one half of the test with its other half. Let us inspect these methods to see how they differ from the test-retest procedures.

Alternate or parallel forms. To use this method of describing the reliability of a test the test-makers compose two or more forms of the test. The questions on one form are *similar* to those on the other because both forms are designed to sample the same area of the student's behavior or knowledge. Although the questions on the two forms are similar, they are *not identical.*

If you administer Form II immediately after Form I, you have two possible causes of inconsistency in the results: (1) poor test items or erratic test procedure and/or (2) the fact that Form I may sample something other than does Form II, so the forms are not really parallel.

Use of second form after an interval. If you wait a period of days or weeks or months between administering Form I and Form II, you have added another possible cause of inconsistency. That is, the individuals themselves may have changed, some learning more than others during the interval or some gaining in motivation.

Split-half reliability. Another way of measuring the reliability of a test is termed the *split-half* method or the *odd-even-halves* method. In this case the students take only one test one time. Then the test-maker compares their scores on the first half of the test with their scores on the second half to see if the test is *internally consistent.* That is, with the split-half method you discover whether the first half of the test measures the same things as the second half. A variation of this method involves comparing the students' scores on the odd-numbered items with their scores on the even-numbered items.

Thus we have seen several kinds of test consistency, or reliability, and several ways to judge them:

1. The test-immediate-retest method reflects the consistency of the testing procedure and something about item clarity.

2. The test-interval-retest method not only estimates the consistency of the testing procedure and item clarity but also shows how consistently the test results stand up over a period of time.
3. The split-half method gives an estimate of the internal consistency of the test.
4. The parallel-form method yields an estimate of the consistency of test procedure and the clarity of items of each form as well as indicating how closely the two forms parallel each other in measuring the same things.
5. When time elapses between administering Form I and its parallel Form II, we have a most complete measure of reliability, because as we compare the students' success on the two forms we are estimating (*a*) consistency of test procedure and clarity of items themselves, (*b*) comparability of the two forms, and (*c*) the amount the students vary individually over a period of time.

Now that we have inspected these five approaches, our problem is to decide which of these is preferable and how to find out the reliability of a published test. But first let us recall the example of the social-science-facts test. By simply looking over the six students' scores we could see that the test results between morning and afternoon were very inconsistent. However, if we were computing the reliability of a test in order to standardize and publish it, we would want the scores of many more than six students. We must be sure these six were not just peculiar cases that were not typical of ordinary seventh graders. By securing the scores of several hundred or several thousand students on such a test we can judge its reliability with much more confidence. However, this brings up a problem, because a test-maker or a teacher could not make a very accurate judgment of reliability by looking at the paired scores of two or three thousand students. This many scores would be merely a jumble of numbers, probably more confusing than helpful. Therefore, test-makers take advantage of the *correlation coefficient,* which is a *single statistical number* that tells accurately the degree of reliability of a test given to hundreds or thousands of people. (See Appendix B for an explanation of correlation.)

When a teacher wishes to judge the consistency of a particular test, he should look in the test manual for a correlation coefficient describing the reliability. This *reliability coefficient* will be reported in some such form as:

Doe Arithmetic-Reasoning Scale	"Test-retest $r = .93$"
Smith Science-Achievement Test	"Form I and Form II correlation $= .87$"
Western Reading Examination	"Split-half (odd-even) $r = .91$"

In the first of these three examples the students' scores on the first testing were correlated with their scores on the second testing. The correlation of .93 indicates a high degree of consistency from the test to the retest. We would be able to interpret this correlation more completely if we knew how much time elapsed between test and retest. For instance, if the retesting was done immediately, we would judge that the testing procedure and item clarity were consistent. But if a substantial time interval separated the first testing and the retest, we would know an additional important fact about the test: that its results are consistent over a period of time and that even after the interval the students who did well the first time also did well on the retest. This kind of information tells something about the ability of the first testing to predict a student's score on a later testing.

In the Smith Science-Achievement example, the students' scores on Form I were correlated with their scores on Form II. The relatively high relationship (.87) shows that the two forms indeed are quite parallel and sample almost exactly the same knowledges or skills.

The report on the Western Reading Examination indicates a high degree of internal consistency among items within the examination, but it tells nothing about the consistency of the testing procedure nor the consistency of scores over an interval of time.

Of these various kinds of reliability estimates, the alternate or parallel-form method is usually considered the most desirable, especially if some time has elapsed between the administration of Form I and Form II. This is the most desirable situation because if you receive a high correlation you know that the test not only (1) is consistent in the measuring procedure and apparently in item clarity, but (2) the two forms measure the same things, and (3) the results are consistent over a period of time so that you can predict a student's future score more accurately. The main problem with the parallel-form method lies in the difficulty of producing two nonidentical tests that will give nearly identical results (that is, that will yield high reliability). The classroom teacher usually appreciates a test which has more than one form, especially if he is to use the test more than once during the year (such as at the beginning and the end of the semester). The alternate forms eliminate the chance of the child's remembering answers from one testing to the next, as he may do with the test-retest method.

If a test does not contain two or more forms, reliability is usually estimated by the split-half or test-retest method or both.

After teachers realize that the reliability of a test is important, they ask, "How high should the correlation coefficient be in order to make the test reliable enough to use with confidence in my class?"

There are many highly reliable achievement tests on the market today. A teacher usually should not be satisfied with a test whose reliability coefficient is lower than .85, and preferably it should be above .90. Considerable confidence can be placed in a reliability above .90. The lower the reliability coefficient drops, the more inconsistent the test is, and with an inconsistent test the teacher does not know whether to believe the children's scores or not. Therefore, the inconsistent test is inaccurate and very likely will do more harm than good as a means of judging a child.

Not all test manuals report reliability coefficients. In these cases a teacher may use the *Education Index* to see if any journal articles have been written about the test in question. The sources of test information described in Appendix A will provide additional data about the test along with comments from relatively unbiased experts in the field of testing. If no reliability figures can be found for the test, it probably was not standardized properly and therefore is of questionable value to the school.

Validity

Although in everyday life many people use the terms *reliable* and *valid* interchangeably, for judging tests the two terms have specific and different meanings. As already indicated, the *reliability* of an achievement test means its consistency. On the other hand, the validity of an achievement test means *the degree to which it accurately tests for the objectives of the class.*

The distinction between reliability and validity can be demonstrated by a science survey test administered to a sixth grade. As this standardized test had a reported reliability coefficient of .92

(alternate-forms), it could be regarded as a highly reliable test; it secured consistent measurements. But in order to judge whether it was valid for this particular sixth grade, the teacher had to *inspect the items on the test and judge to what extent these items would measure for the science objectives in this sixth grade.* The sixth-grade teacher had two general objectives in science. They were: "As a result of the science experiences the student:

1. Is better acquainted with his physical environment.
2. Uses scientific methods for solving problems."

These broad over-all objectives were broken down into more specific objectives which outlined the particular areas of the physical environment studied during the semester. The main areas were: *the work of electricity, how plants grow, why weather changes, and how animals are adapted to the places they live in.*

A few of the specific behavioral goals for the "scientific-method" objectives were:

"After these science experiences the student:

1. Selects from a mass of data the portions pertinent to solving a defined problem.
2. Reserves judgment on an issue until he has secured data pertinent to it.
3. Revises conclusions to make them compatible with newer pertinent data."

The standardized science test consisted of questions on the following topics: levers, simple machines, properties of water, stars and planets, fire, formation of the earth, electricity, animal life, and plant life.

By comparing the objectives of the class with the test items, the teacher decided that the test had very limited value for judging the science achievement of the students in this sixth-grade class. The test had no items that measured how well the students used scientific methods for solving problems, and only three of the areas on the test were among those covered by the class objectives. For purposes of grading the students, this test was not very valid, even though it had proved to be reliable. The examination probably would be more valid as a pretest for the teacher to give at the first of the semester to survey what the students already knew in the areas covered by the test. Used in this latter way, the test would help the teacher learn something of the students' backgrounds (a valid use of this particular test) but it would not be useful for grading their achievement during the semester (an invalid use of the test in this class).

From this example it is seen that when the question is asked, "Is this test valid?" the proper reply is: "Valid for what? First you must tell me your goals or the area in life you are trying to measure before we can decide whether the test adequately samples that area or that behavior."

Norms

A test becomes *standardized* by being administered to a relatively large group of people whose scores are recorded and analyzed. This group upon which the test is standardized is usually termed the *normative group,* or it is sometimes called the *standardization group* or the *sample* or *sampling* group.

The records of the group's successes on the test are called the *norms.* The following examples are typical of kinds of norms which might be reported for two reading-achievement tests.

When selecting a standardized test the teacher or administrator is interested in the normative group in order to answer the question: How much faith can I place in the norms or the average-grade-scores reported for this test? There are two main factors to consider in answering this question.

First, the teacher wants to know if the children upon whom the test was standardized are like the children in his room, socially and

Test I—*Bi-State Reading Examination*

Normative Group or Sample—1,100 Children in New York City and Jersey City schools. Grade range from 3 through 7.

Norms by Grade	*Month Test Given*	*Average Test Score for Grade (Combined Speed and Comprehension)*
3	October	39
3½	March	43
4	October	46
4½	March	51
5	October	56
5½	March	64
6	October	70
6½	March	83
7	October	94

Test II—*Doe Reading Speed and Comprehension Test*

Normative Group—4,550 children in urban and rural communities in California, Colorado, Illinois, and New Jersey. Grades 4 through 8. The sampling group was distributed in the following manner:

State	*Urban* (Pop. 10,000 or more)	*Rural* (Pop. less than 10,000)	*Total*
California	839	420	1250
Colorado	480	220	700
Illinois	720	300	1020
New Jersey	937	643	1580
	2976	1583	4550

(No significant difference was found between the scores of the urban and rural nor among the states.)

Norms by Grade	*Average Score*		*Number in Sample at Each Grade Level*
	Speed	*Comprehension*	
4	48	27	820
4-6	53	30	
5	58	34	1048
5-6	66	40	
6	74	46	927
6-6	84	54	
7	94	62	895
7-6	107	71	
8	116	80	860
8-6	127	87	

educationally. If a reading test was standardized on children in London schools, the teacher should probably question its results when he administers it to his sixth grade in Walla Walla, Washington. It would be better not to use the British test at all but to select a scale such as the Doe Test described above. The Walla Walla children are more likely to be comparable to the Doe normative group (rural and urban California, Colorado, Illinois, and New Jersey). Thus, the teacher observes where the test was standardized and tries to estimate how nearly his students are like those in the normative group. The more alike they are, the more faith he can place in the average-scores-by-grades as applied to his students.

Second, the teacher wants to know how many children were in the standardization group. Generally, the larger the number of persons in the normative group the more faith one can place in the norms as being an accurate sample of children at each grade- or age-level.

If a sixth-grade teacher had the choice of using one or the other of the two tests above (the Bi-State or Doe), he probably would place more confidence in the norms of the Doe examination; that is, if other factors such as reliability and validity were equal. The sampling for the Doe Test is broader geographically, and the number at each grade-level is specified. In addition, the Doe norms are given for speed and comprehension individually. This should help a teacher who wishes to know which children have average comprehension but slow speed, which read rapidly and comprehend well, and so forth.

It is through an inspection of such data as the above on the normative groups of different tests that a teacher or a principal tries to make an accurate estimate of which test yields norms that can be applied to his students with most confidence.

Time

Tests vary greatly in length. Children can complete some types of standardized examinations in fifteen minutes, whereas other tests (usually a battery or series of several long tests) may demand a large portion of a week's school time. Therefore, when selecting a test for a particular class, the teacher will wish to know the average time needed for the test, so that demands on the children's time may be compatible with their attention span and the school program.

Administering and scoring

When judging a test, a teacher will do well to note how it is administered and scored.

The directions for administering should be clear so that a teacher with little or no special training in testing can administer it accurately to a class. The directions should answer all questions that students might ask about how to take the test. Otherwise the teacher has to use his "best judgment" in answering students' questions about procedure, and without clear, printed directions the teacher may give advice which was not given to the original standardization group.

Any such departures from the methods used with the normative group reduce the validity of the norms. A teacher who administers a test in a manner different from that used in the original standardization (such as allowing more or less time than that recommended for its completion) cannot rightfully use the published norms in interpreting the scores.

Like the administering, the scoring should be simple and objective. Complicated methods of scoring which demand that the tester make personal judgments reduce the validity of the norms because some scorers may be more lenient than others or they may interpret the marking techniques differently. Tests that are objective and can be scored easily appeal to teachers, for such scales take little time to mark. However, there is a danger in placing too much emphasis on the "quick-scoring" features of a test when selecting achievement examinations. This fact was brought to a test expert's attention recently when an elementary-school supervisor said:

"Yes, we are beginning a thoroughgoing achievement-testing program. These are the tests we are using. What do you think of them?"

When the expert asked why the school had purchased this particular test series, the supervisor said:

"Well, the salesman said they were very good . . . very widely used. And they are quick-scoring. See the scoring keys here? They are very easy to use. Our teachers like them. The price is good, too. They don't cost as much as some of the others."

The expert glanced through the test manual which described the battery of examinations. There were no statistical data on reliability or validity. There were average scores listed for each grade, but there were no data on the size of the normative sample or on the kinds or location of children who composed the standardization group. A salesman's pleasant manner plus the appeal of quick-scoring and relatively low cost had sold more than a thousand tests to the school with promise of future sales. In this case the supervisor had placed the stress on the less significant criteria for test selection. The validity of a test for use with a particular group of children is much more important than the quick-scoring features. Perhaps this test series was as good as any other. However, because data had not been published about the most vital features of the series, there was no way of knowing its worth. It is poor educational practice to judge and to alter children's lives on the basis of poor or questionable measuring instruments when more valid instruments are available.

Price

The cost of a test should be a minor consideration. Officials in charge of finances in some schools do not necessarily agree with this point of view, primarily because they do not understand the differences among tests nor the effect of using poor tests in guiding children's education. A teacher or supervisor may have to take a strong stand and to indicate that, as in the case cited above, making price the most important consideration in test selection may result in damage to children rather than assistance.

When, then, should price be considered? If two tests appear to be of about equal reliability and validity and are about equally adequate in sampling and in methods of administering and scoring, then the lower-priced test is the one to select. (It is well to note that a higher-priced test is not necessarily the better test.)

SOURCES OF ACHIEVEMENT TESTS

It is helpful for a teacher to read a discussion of types of achievement examinations. Still, the best way for him to become acquainted with the content and types of items is to inspect some of the actual standardized tests. For this reason a list of test sources and publishers has been provided in Appendix A. Upon request, publishers will furnish catalogues of tests and, in some cases, will send sample achievement tests for your inspection.

USING ACHIEVEMENT TEST RESULTS

Teachers and school administrators sometimes are guilty of misusing standardized achievement tests.

A teacher may misuse a standardized test for any of several reasons, such as (1) having poorly defined objectives for children to reach, (2) being ignorant of what a particular test validly measures, (3) lacking ability or training in using methods other than standardized tests for evaluating student progress, or (4) "taking the easy way out" when seeking evidence upon which to base a child's semester grade. All of these misuses are interrelated.

An administrator may misuse standardized achievement tests by (5) having blind faith in the tests' ability to judge children's progress adequately and (6) judging (and subsequently promoting or dismissing) a teacher on the basis of her students' scores on standardized tests.

Teachers' objectives

Some teachers do not think out the objectives of their classes clearly. That is, they do not decide exactly what types of behavior changes they are trying to bring about in their students. When questioned about the purposes of their classwork, they may say, "I just teach straight material" or "We pretty much follow the textbooks" or "It's regular fourth-grade work" or they may give some other vague answer. In some cases teachers answer this query by citing a list of objectives from the state syllabus or the city course of study, but observation of their classes indicates that these cited objectives are really only vaguely related to the classwork. When a teacher does not really know what outcomes he wants from his students, he cannot evaluate the outcomes. Some teachers, realizing they need some measure of the students' progress, give standardized tests and thus believe they have obtained an accurate, objective evaluation of what the children have learned. This might be termed *testing by default* rather than *testing through intention.*

Ignorance of a test's validity

Frequently students leave a class remarking, "What a test! Some of those questions were about things we had never taken up in class. It's that way every time she gives one of those printed exams." Such accusations are often true.

Some teachers have considerable respect for any standardized test, probably because it is formally printed and sold commercially. They, quite logically, judge the test by its name. If the test is called a *Language and English Usage Examination,* they are prone to believe it is an accurate measure of "language usage." Whereas, upon closer inspection of the test they would discover that it demanded considerable mastery of parts of speech and therefore is not an accurate measure of the "language usage" of their own students who have *not* been taught grammar formally but have been taught acceptable language usage by having their common errors corrected.

An examination titled *Arithmetic Problem-Solving Test* sounds, on the surface, universally valid for elementary-school children in the upper grades. However, unless the teacher knows specifically the areas covered and the types of items in such tests, he cannot know whether the test is a valid measure for his students.

Lack of training in other evaluation techniques

Some instructors depend too heavily upon both standardized and teacher-made tests for judging children's progress. These educators do not intend to misuse tests. Instead, they do it because they lack ability or training in the use of other evaluation techniques. Perhaps much of a child's growth in school could best be judged by anecdotal records, sociometrics, rating scales, participation charts, student reports, and other devices. However, a teacher who does not understand these techniques, or believes he needs a specific test score to describe a student's growth, may depend too heavily on the objective test. The usual result is a distorted judgment of pupils, for only the "standardized-testable" part of their school experience will be adequately measured.

The "easy way out"

For many—perhaps most—teachers the unhappiest moments of their careers come when they must make out report cards. Increasingly, teachers are able to make grading a less painful task by developing effective reporting systems (see Chapter 14) and by utilizing varied evaluation devices throughout the semester. However, there are other teachers who do not systematically evaluate children's development throughout the year. When the end of the semester arrives and grades are due, they have a problem to face. Some solve the problem by giving grades on the basis of personal, and oftentimes rather casual, impressions derived during the year. But if this technique is used the teacher may find himself burdened by doubts and guilt feelings which arise from a realization that certain children are being misjudged. In addition, the teacher who grades only on impressions has no concrete evidence to show the child, the parents, or the principal if the mark should be contested and an explanation requested.

However, there is another alternative for the teacher who has not evaluated systematically throughout the year. He can give a final test and base the semester marks on the test scores. Some teachers use standardized tests instead of ones they construct because printed tests have been developed by experts and appear to be more official and valid. How could a teacher feel that he had misjudged a child when the score the child earned on the standardized test was the basis for the mark? It is in this way that a teacher may "take the easy way out" when grading time arrives. But only in the rare case when he is sure the test really measures all the objectives of his course can he defend such a practice.

Administrators' faith in tests

School administrators, too, may cause the misuse of standardized tests by having blind faith in the printed examinations' ability to measure children's development accurately. Without considering carefully enough the specific objectives of each class, they may insist that all instructors use a certain test series and base the children's marks chiefly upon "this good objective evidence." An educationally sounder attitude for a principal or supervisor to take in aiding a teacher would be:

"Use these tests only insofar as they can measure the changes you desire in the children. You will need to use other methods in addition to judge children fairly. Don't depend too much on these tests just because they yield a definite numerical score which is convenient to use for marking."

Marking the teacher

An insightful junior-high principal recently observed that "Nobody is better able to evaluate a teacher's effectiveness than the students. They spend long hours under his tutelage, and some of them become apt judges of human behavior."

True as this may be, it is not the students but the school administrators who have the responsibility for evaluating a teacher's effectiveness, and the administrators must do this job without benefit of the students' opportunities to observe a teacher's normal classroom activities day after day. Even when the principal visits the sixth grade three times a year, the lessons he witnesses may not be typical samples of the teacher's and students' behavior. Consequently, administrators seek more secure methods of appraising a teacher. Some have solved this problem to their own satisfaction by *rating a teacher according to how well his students succeed on standardized achievement tests.* If an administrator believes these tests are true measures of student development, then he may conclude that the students of the best teacher will earn the highest examination scores. The poorest teacher will be revealed by the low average of his class's scores.

There are at least two obvious fallacies underlying such reasoning. The first fallacy exists because children's individual differences show up on tests. For example, in a school with three sixth grade classes, Miss Lindholm has a number of students who are slow learners. These students' academic limitations are reflected on the standard test given to all sixth graders. Consequently, the low scores adversely affect the administrator's rating of Miss Lindholm's teaching ability. If these same slow learners had been in another room their low scores would not have affected Miss Lindholm adversely; rather, they would have caused another teacher's record to show up poorly.

The second fallacy is the belief that tests adequately measure progress toward *all* the worth-while educational goals. Mr. Stanton has set up the goal of "working effectively in a group" as an important aim for his class. Since it is doubtful if any objective test can measure how well he helped his students reach this goal, this facet of his teaching cannot be judged from the students' scores on a social science or reading test.

There is evidence from a number of states that this practice of administrators grading teachers on the basis of pupils' standardized test scores is being supplanted by fairer appraisal techniques. Yet the practice is not uncommon today.

Proper uses

The above discussion of the use of test results has stressed negatives; that is, it has stressed misuses to be avoided. What, then, are proper uses of standardized achievement tests?

This was the question which the committee appointed earlier in this chapter by the principal, Miss McKenzie, set out to answer. The committee's answer is contained in the following statement which they prepared for the Central School faculty after studying the selection and use of standardized achievement examinations. Mr. Harris, as a committee member, said:

"This is only a preliminary report. We will need several more weeks before we can make full recommendations. Up to the present we have concentrated on investigating standardized *achievement* tests. Our next step will be to make a concentrated study of *intelligence* and aptitude tests. We feel that until we have completed the second portion of our study we cannot recommend a full testing program, because achievement and aptitude or intelligence tests seem to be closely related. Today's report consists of policies concerning achievement testing which we strongly endorse.

"First, we wish to give our recommendations concerning two basic skills: *reading* and *arithmetic computation*. After inspecting reading and arithmetic tests, we decided that the basic objectives of these tests coincided with our reading and arithmetic computation objectives. Consequently, we believe that it might be appropriate to use standardized tests in these two areas. There are some very good reading and arithmetic tests which have carefully established norms based on children much like those in our school. We think it might be well to test all our children perhaps at the third-grade level, at the sixth, and at the eighth. In this way we would know something about how our students read and compute in comparison with children in similar communities. We believe that such a testing program at these three levels would also aid us in placing transfer students, since we get quite a number of them now that our community is expanding. By knowing how our own students score in reading and arithmetic, we can test entering students and assign them to appropriate classes.

"The committee has stressed the word *might* when discussing the appropriateness of using standardized arithmetic and reading tests at three intervals in the elementary program. We say *might* because we do not think such a testing program essential. We believe that efficient teachers in our school already have effective ways to measure children's reading and arithmetic achievement throughout the year. However, we believe that well-constructed standardized tests in these areas could provide additional aid in diagnosing particular difficulties of individual children in reading and arithmetic, especially in the upper grades where we have not spent as much time on reading as such.

"We wish to emphasize that if such a program is initiated, the tests should be used for diagnosis, not for grading the children on report cards. To give children grades based only on their scores on these standardized tests would be contrary to the policy which we as a faculty have agreed upon in recent years; namely, that in marking a child we will consider not only his standing in relation to other children, but also his progress in relation to his own abilities and his needs.

"Second, we wish to give our recommendations concerning standardized tests in areas other than reading and arithmetic. During our deliberations we inspected batteries of achievement tests in such areas as elementary science, social studies, and literature. It has been the practice in numbers of schools to give many such standardized achievement tests periodically to determine how the children are progressing. In these schools it is common to base children's grades on their standardized test scores. Also the teacher's success, either in his own eyes or the eyes of a supervisor, is often measured by the children's scores. On the surface this may appear to be good educational practice and good evaluation. However, on closer inspection it is seen that this practice is defensible *only if the questions and topics on the standardized test coincide exactly with the goals of the class.* In the cases of reading and arithmetic computation we decided that our goals in these two skill subjects did coincide with the test-maker's. Almost any school would have the same objectives in these two basic skills. However, the objectives and the grade placement of material in such areas as science, social studies, and literature vary greatly from school to school. We believe that with the aid of leaders from our school system and the state education department, we faculty members are the best judges of what the objectives will be for our elementary science, social studies, and literature programs. By inspecting the items on standardized tests in these areas, we saw that the test-makers' judgments concerning the proper objectives and the subject matter at various grade-levels were somewhat different from our own. Consequently, it would seem foolish for us to use standardized tests in these areas when they are not designed to measure our specific goals.

"Through our reading and our discussion with teachers in other systems we have learned that in some schools which made wide use of standardized tests in many subject areas the tests have become the dictators of the curriculum. Too often the goal of the class becomes *pass the test.* The teacher's objectives, therefore, become merely the test questions. Any new methods and objectives, such as increasing group work to develop cooperation and problem-solving techniques among the children, must be secondary to passing the tests. We do not want our school to make that mistake. We want tests and other evaluation devices to be our servants in helping judge children. We do not want to be ruled by standardized tests.

"As a result, in regard to such areas as science, social studies, and literature we wish to make the following recommendation: Only when a test's specific objectives, as revealed by an inspection of the test items, coincide with the teacher's objectives is that test a valid measure to use.

"The committee has provided a number of sample tests in these areas for you to inspect in light of the goals of your particular classes. However, as a result of our studying these examinations, we are afraid that they will not be useful in very many instances. Other evaluation techniques, such as teacher-made tests, direct observation of the children, and rating scales are most likely more valid methods of measuring the pupils' progress toward our particular goals."

OBJECTIVES OF THIS CHAPTER

The effective elementary-school teacher:

1. Selects standardized achievement tests that have established reliability, validity, and norms appropriate for use with his pupils.
2. Administers standardized tests in the method established by the test-makers as being correct for the particular examination.

Suggested evaluation techniques for this chapter

1. a. For one elementary-school level (primary, intermediate, or upper), write several behavioral objectives in reading or arithmetic.
   b. By inspection of sample achievement tests in reading or arithmetic decide which test (if any) would be best to use in evaluating for the stated objectives. Did you have any objectives in the list which could not be measured adequately by a standardized test?
2. By inspecting the items on a standardized achievement test in any subject matter or area, determine what general objectives the test-maker apparently had in mind when he constructed the device.
3. With one or several persons functioning as subjects, administer a standardized test exactly in the manner recommended by the test-maker.

SUGGESTED READINGS

1. Gerberich, J. Raymond. *Specimen Objective Test Items.* New York: Longmans, Green and Co., 1956. Examples of 227 different kinds of items from standardized tests, many of them achievement tests.

2. GREENE, HARRY A.; JORGENSEN, ALBERT N.; and GERBERICH, J. RAYMOND. *Measurement and Evaluation in the Elementary School.* New York: Longmans, Green and Co., 1953. Several chapters describe and, in some cases, evaluate standardized achievement tests and batteries appropriate to elementary and junior high grades.
3. LINDQUIST, E. F. *Educational Measurement.* Washington, D.C.: American Council on Education, 1951. A sophisticated book on test construction and standardization.
4. THORNDIKE, ROBERT L., and HAGEN, ELIZABETH. *Measurement and Evaluation in Psychology and Education.* New York: Wiley and Sons, 1955. Chapter 11 compares values and characteristics of teacher-made and standardized achievement tests.

CHAPTER

5

Using Standardized Tests

2. Aptitude and Intelligence Tests

AT THE TEST-SELECTION COMMITTEE's next meeting Mrs. Shultz said to the principal, "There's one reason I think we ought to use good intelligence tests throughout the grades, and that's to see if we can group the children in our grades according to their IQ's."

"You mean ability grouping?" asked the principal, Miss McKenzie. "Such as having the four classes of first graders homogeneously grouped so that the children with the highest IQ's are in one room, next highest in another, and so forth?"

"Yes. I know that some people disagree with that idea because they say it makes snobs out of the ones in the highest group. I can see some social reasons for having them pretty well mixed the way we do now, but I still think homogeneous grouping according to a good IQ test is best. It really simplifies the teacher's problem to have children of the same ability in one room."

"We used to do that, you know," said Miss McKenzie, "and then we changed back to the present plan about ten years ago. This ability grouping is a bit confusing, because there are some good reasons for grouping and some good reasons for not grouping. But I think you are right in bringing up the issue at this time. That will be a good topic for the committee to investigate further."

Mr. Endo asked Mrs. Shultz, "Would you recommend grouping according to a general intelligence test? What about the children's art and music activities? What about their physical education and social affairs? What happens when they build a miniature town or they plant a garden as Miss Chavez' class did in connection with social studies units this year? If you group according to the usual general intelligence test you are going to find that when you do any of these activities your class will be heterogeneous, not homogeneous."

"What makes you say so? If we use a good test they will," said Mrs. Shultz.

"No, I'm pretty sure that's not true," Mr. Endo insisted. "What people commonly call *intelligence tests* don't measure abilities in art, music, and mechanical and physical activities."

"But if the student has high intelligence he's bound to be smart in almost everything. That's rather obvious," Mrs. Shultz said.

"I don't care how obvious it seems. It just isn't true."

The principal interrupted to point out that such an argument over an important issue was futile unless specific data were presented to settle it. The committee agreed that by dividing the responsibilities for reading the educational and psychological literature on the topic they would be able to settle this issue as well as others which related to aptitude and intelligence testing in their school. Their research led to the following information.

THE GROWTH OF INTELLIGENCE TESTS

The first practical intelligence test was developed to solve a school problem. In 1904 the Minister of Public Instruction of France appointed a commission of scientists, physicians, and educators to study the problem of improving instruction for feebleminded in the public schools. Alfred Binet, a psychologist who had for some years been trying to measure the "higher mental processes," was a member of the commission. He found that by asking children to do a number of simple tasks he could get a sample of the types of "higher mental processes" that apparently accounted for success in school. For this scale he selected tasks or items which (1) average children usually had equal opportunities to encounter and learn in their environment, that is, they were not unique or unusual tasks that only a few children had opportunities to meet, and which (2) older and more capable children did more successfully than younger and less capable children. By first trying out many kinds of tasks and then including in the scale only the ones which effectively discriminated between the more capable and the less capable children at a given age, Binet constructed the first intelligence test.

Samples of some items from the original Binet scale are given below. These activities were expected of normal persons at the listed ages.

Age 3	Points to nose, eyes, mouth.
	Repeats two digits.
	Gives family name.
Age 5	Counts four coins.
	Repeats a sentence of ten syllables.
Age 7	Shows right hand and left ear.
	Names four colors (red, green, blue, and yellow).
Age 9	Defines familiar word in terms superior to use, i.e., shows how it is related to other ideas.
	Recognizes value of nine pieces of money.
	Gives the names of the months in order.
Age 12	Uses three given words in one sentence.
	Gives sixty words in three minutes.
Adult	Gives three differences between a president and a king.

Binet, with the help of a collaborator named Simon, first organized his scale in a practical sense in 1905 and published a revision in 1908. This was the beginning of the intelligence-test and aptitude-test movement which has flourished for half a century.

For convenience of discussion, the kinds of intelligence tests in use today can be placed in five categories: (1) Binet, and its revisions, (2) individual performance, (3) group verbal, (4) group nonverbal and non-language, and (5) combination group test.

Revisions of the Binet scale

Shortly after Binet's early success with measuring the intelligence of French children, psychologists in other countries adapted the Binet scale for use with people of their own cultures. Several revisions were made in the United States, the most satisfactory being the Stanford University Revision which was first published by Lewis Terman in 1916. This was the most widely used individual test in psychological clinics for twenty years.

In 1937, after ten years of careful item-selection and standardization, a new Stanford revision of the Binet scale was issued. This test, the 1937 Stanford-Binet, was generally recognized by psychologists and educators as the best general intelligence scale available during the period 1937-1959 for children from about age 2 through 16. Two comparable forms (labeled L and M) were published so that a child who had already been tested with one form might be retested on the parallel form without fear of his remembering specific items from one testing to the next.

In 1960 the latest revision of the Stanford-Binet was issued. It is not actually a new scale. Rather, it incorporates in a *single form* the best subtests from the L and M forms of the 1937 scale. The new version is called the L-M Form. It retains the characteristic features of the 1937 version, but is composed of tests that were checked against a school and preschool population of about 5,000 children tested during the 1950's. Obsolete test material was eliminated. Items that were outdated were modernized, such as new pictures of a ship, a plane, and a telephone were substituted for old ones.

Whereas the earlier forms stopped at age 16, recent findings indicate that mental growth as measured by the Stanford-Binet continues beyond 16. Thus the IQ tables of the 1960 version includes ages 17 and 18.

Like all Binet revisions, the 1960 Stanford-Binet is an individual test. That is, one trained tester administers the items to one child at a time. It is not the kind of test a teacher can administer properly without special training. The scale consists of six items at each year level, except below age 5 where there are six items at each half-year level. These items are tasks, similar to those of the original Binet test, which the average child of a particular chronological age can do successfully but which an average child of a younger age cannot do. At the younger age levels the items tend to be more of the performance type, such as stringing beads in a pattern. At the older levels they tend to be of the verbal type, such as defining words. The new scale has alternative tests for all age levels, which helps make up for the lack of two separate parallel forms in the 1960 version. (Because the bulk of the items of the 1937 scale held up rather well in the retesting done during the preparation of the 1960 revision, it is reasonable to expect psychologists to continue to use the 1937 L and M forms when parallel forms are needed.)

Mental age. If seven-year-old Helen Quinn can pass all the items *below* her age and *at* her age-level but can pass none beyond her age, she is said to have a *mental age* (abbreviated MA) of 7.

That is, she has the typical ability of a seven-year-old, according to the test.

If a seven-year-old passes some tests at a level higher than year 7, he is given *two months' credit for each of these additional tasks,* and his mental age is scored higher. For example, in addition to succeeding on all at his own level, seven-year-old Ted Jensen passed four of the six items at the eight-year level (failed the other two at that level) and passed one at the nine-year level. In all, he succeeded on five items above the average for his chronological age. If he is given two-months' credit for each of these five extra tasks, he has a mental age of 7 years 10 months.

Intelligence quotient. The term *intelligence quotient* (IQ) is used to show the *relationship between a person's chronological age and his mental age* as shown by a test. The formula for computing IQ is $\frac{\text{MA}}{\text{CA}} \times 100 = \text{IQ}$. Therefore, to find a child's IQ it is necessary to divide the mental age by the chronological age, and multiply by 100. A few samples will show how this is done.

Seven-year-old Helen Quinn, mentioned above, passed all of the tests at her age-level but none beyond her age. Since her mental age and her chronological age are both 7, her IQ is 100: $\left(\frac{7}{7} \times 100 = 100\right)$. Theoretically, a child who is operating at *exactly* average for his age will be found to have an IQ of 100. However, in the practical sense, persons within the IQ range of 90 to 110 are all regarded as operating in an average manner for their age and for the qualities measured by the test.

Ted Jensen's IQ can also be computed from the data given above. He is exactly 7 years old. His mental age, as given by the test, is 7 years 10 months. Since in the case of his MA we are not working only with years but must consider months also, it is customary to change his CA and MA to months before completing the computation: $\left(\frac{94}{84} \times 100 = 112\right)$. Ted's IQ is 112. He is slightly above average.

A type of seven-year-old who will have difficulty with the usual academic schoolwork, such as reading and arithmetic, is Carol McLaughlin. Her mental age according to the test is 5 years 3 months. Chronologically, she is 7 years 1 month old. When these ages are

changed into months, her IQ is computed as 74: $\left(\frac{63}{85} \times 100 = 74\right)$.
Assuming that the test was administered accurately and that Carol tried to do as well as she could, the prediction for her success in the usual schoolwork is rather poor. She would be regarded as having "borderline" ability, that is, on the borderline between normality and feeble-mindedness. In school, children of ability comparable to Carol's ordinarily cannot keep up with the usual work and are frequently termed *slow learners*. Special classes are often provided for them.

Figure 6 shows the percentage of the nation's population at various IQ levels. Terms above the divisions in the figure are those commonly applied to the various IQ ranges.

Wechsler-Bellevue scale and WISC

It was seen that the type of scale which Binet created has been developed into the most useful *single scale* for sampling how well a school-age child probably can succeed in the usual kinds of academic work. The Stanford-Binet, being standardized on children and youth, is not a very effective measure for adults. David Wechsler, a psychologist at New York's Bellevue Hospital, developed an individual test of adult abilities. This scale, called the Wechsler-Bellevue Intelligence Scale, includes both *verbal* (such as similarities between words and memory for digits) and *performance* (such as making patterns with colored blocks) items. This test was originally standardized on 1,081 individuals in the New York City area. Wechsler tested people of all age divisions from adolescence to old age. The Wechsler-Bellevue scale is generally regarded as being the most effective individual measure of adult "general intelligence" in the United States.

In recent years simpler contents were added to the Wechsler-Bellevue so that it could be used with children between the ages of 5 and 15. In this downward extension the test is called the Wechsler Intelligence Scale for Children, commonly abbreviated as WISC. The form of the test is basically the same as the adult version (though at the youngest ages some tests change a bit in form). It includes subtests over verbal *material,* such as general comprehension and recognizing similarities, as well as *performance* subtests, such as picture arrangement and block design items.

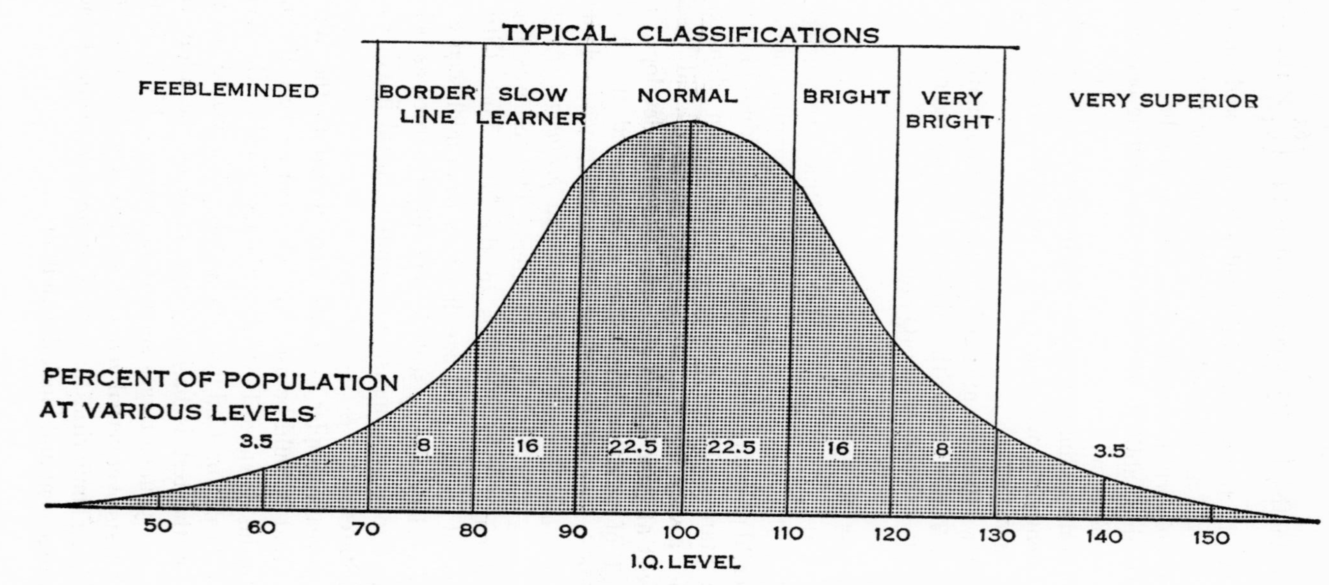

Fig. 6. Distribution of measured intelligence in population

Unlike the Stanford-Binet, the WISC does not involve a series of tasks at each age level that become increasingly more difficult at each higher age, so the child tries each level until he gets high enough to fail all tasks at one age level. Instead, the tester gives the child a chance at every subtest. Each subtest yields a separate score which is converted into a standard score for that task. (See Appendix C for

Fig. 7. Sequin Form Board

The form board is presented to the child in the manner shown. He is to see how rapidly he can place the forms in their proper spaces. (Manufactured by C. H. Stoelting Company.)

an explanation of standard scores.) The subtest standard scores are combined to produce total scores which convert to three different varieties of IQ's on tables of norms. You can find an IQ for the verbal subtests alone, another IQ for performance items, and a total IQ for all subtests combined. The Wechsler scoring system does not yield a mental age, so IQ's cannot be computed as with the Stanford-Binet but must be read from conversion tables.

The question arises, "Which individual intelligence test is better for use with children, WISC or Stanford-Binet?"

The answer depends somewhat on what kind of decisions you wish to make on the basis of the testing. For instance, the Stanford-Binet has a more definitely established value in predicting academic success. On the other hand, because the WISC yields both performance and verbal scores, it may prove useful in understanding the pupil whose verbal ability measures substantially lower or higher than his performance ability. Although the Stanford-Binet is usually more time-consuming and perhaps more difficult to administer, it seems preferred by many school psychologists because of its longer history of usefulness, its apparent greater reliability, and its suitability for children even as young as 2 or 3 years of age. The WISC, though designed for children as young as 5, is most suitable between ages 7 and 15.

Fig. 8. Feature Profile Test

Wooden cutouts are presented to the pupil in the pattern shown at left. When he has placed all of the forms in their correct places, the completed profile results. (Manufactured by C. H. Stoelting Company.)

Individual performance tests

A test of the Binet variety is effective with children who can speak and understand the language the tester uses. However, it does not provide an accurate measure of the abilities of some handicapped children, such as those who are deaf, mute, or are accustomed only to a foreign language. To test these children psychologists devel-

Fig. 9. Healy Pictorial Completion Test 1

A large picture of children playing is presented to the subject. As the test begins, the picture is incomplete, because it contains ten empty squares. From a selection of many blocks picturing objects, the subject is to select the ten blocks that complete the large picture in the manner shown here. (Manufactured by C. H. Stoelting Company.)

oped scales which can be administered by pantomime and which, for answering, require some *action* on the part of the subject rather than a verbal answer. Typical performance items are:

1. *Form boards.* Holes of various shapes are cut into a board. The test consists of fitting properly-shaped blocks into the holes.
2. *Picture-completion boards.* The child is shown a picture from which a small square is omitted. From a selection of small blocks with portions of pictures on them, the child is to choose the correct block to complete the larger picture.

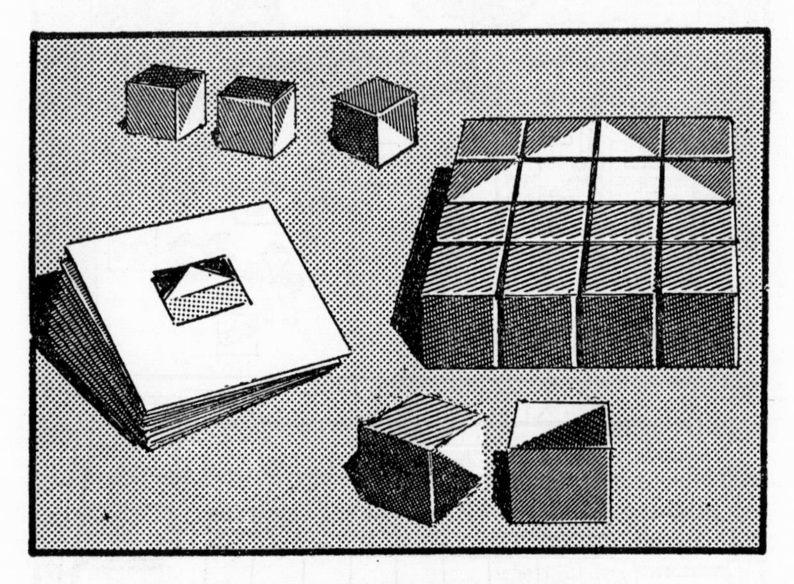

Fig. 10. Kohs Block Design Test

The subject is presented with varicolored cubes with which he is to reproduce colored designs shown to him on the examiner's cards. (Manufactured by C. H. Stoelting Company.)

3. *Cube test.* Four cubes are tapped by the tester in a given pattern which is to be repeated by the child.
4. *Mazes.* A printed pattern of lines on a sheet of paper form a maze. The child is to draw a line from the beginning to the end of the maze without crossing a printed line or going into a "dead end" of the maze. He is usually timed to determine

how fast he can complete the route. There is a series of standardized mazes, graded from easy to difficult.

Arthur Point Scale of Performance. Probably the most popular individual performance test which clinicians use with children ages 3 to 15 is the Arthur Point Scale of Performance. It consists of a number of different tasks such as those described above. There are two comparable forms of this scale. Each form contains different items; if a psychologist tests a child with one form and then wishes to retest the child, he can use the other form without feeling that the child might remember answers from the first testing, as might

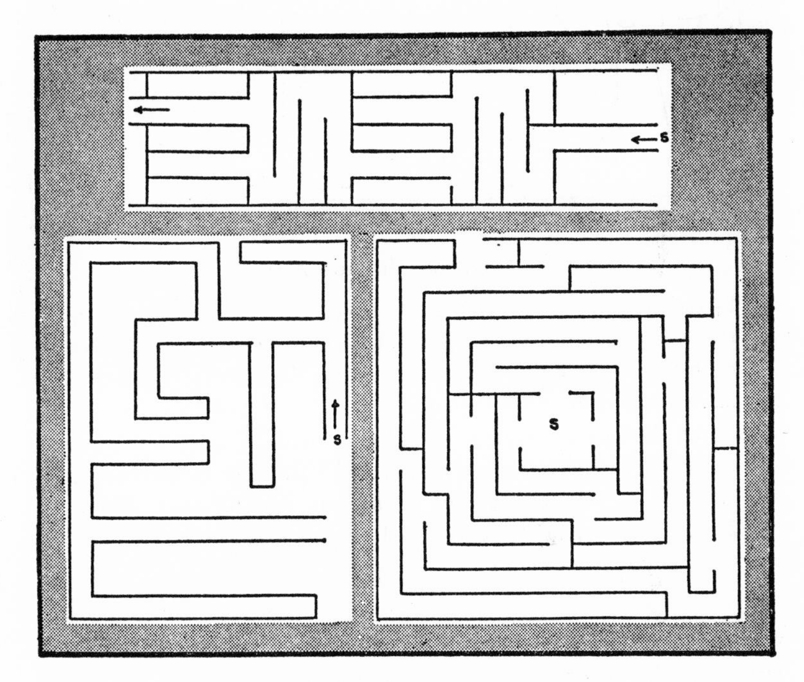

Fig. 11. Porteus Mazes

A series of mazes, from simple to difficult, require the subject to draw a line from the starting point (S) to the open end of each maze as rapidly as possible. In doing so he must not cross any printed lines. In the figure above the top maze is designed for age 6, the one on the left for age 8, and the one on the right for adults.

be true if only one form were available. As with the Stanford-Binet, special training is necessary for the proper administration of these performance tests.

Goodenough Draw-A-Man Test. Another kind of performance test is based on the fact that children's ability to draw a realistic picture of a man increases as they grow older. The Draw-A-Man intelligence test, developed by Florence Goodenough in the 1920's,

Fig. 12. Goodenough Draw-A-Man Test

By drawing the picture at the left, a boy, age 7 years 2 months, received a mental age of 5 years 3 months and an IQ of 73. The center drawing by a boy, age 5 years 10 months, yielded a mental age of 6 years 9 months and an IQ of 116. The drawing at the right by a boy, age 10 years 1 month, yielded a mental age of 10 years 9 months and an IQ of 107. (From Goodenough, Florence L., *Measurement of Intelligence by Drawings,* World Book Company, 1926. Reproduced by permission of World Book Company.)

was standardized for children between the ages of 3½ and 13½. However, the accuracy of the scale appears to diminish in the upper age ranges, possibly because of special training or special ability some children display in art. Unlike the Binet and its variations and other performance scales, this test is easily administered and takes only a brief time. The child is simply asked to draw a picture of a man. The scoring, however, is more complicated. For a test score, the child receives a certain number of points depending upon the elements he has included in his drawing. A table is used to convert the point score to a mental age, and an IQ can then be computed. Soon a new edition of the Goodenough scale is to be published to bring up to date the scoring and standards that were originally established in the 1920's.

Easel Age Scale. Another measure based on art work that is of particular interest to teachers in the preschool and primary grades is the Easel Age Scale, published in 1955. It was developed over a period of ten years by Dr. Beatrice Lantz of the Division of Research and Guidance of the Los Angeles County Schools.

The scale is not a formal test. Rather, it is a set of standards for judging the characteristics of tempera paintings created by children.

To develop the scale Dr. Lantz collected and photographed 3,000 easel paintings made by children ages 4 to 9 in the Los Angeles area. She analyzed the paintings to identify characteristics that might distinguish the more mature from the less mature child. As a result a painting is scored on four characteristics: (1) forms portrayed, (2) amount of detail, (3) the meaning of the objects for an adult, and (4) the relation of the objects to one another. These subscores are summed to yield an *easel score,* which in turn is converted to an *easel age* by means of a table.

The test manual indicates that all paintings should not be scored, because certain types are expressions of a child's emotions rather than indicative of his mental and physical maturity. These exceptional paintings are scored "Q" (meaning questionable for purposes of estimating maturity or ability) and are set aside for study of the possible emotional problems involved.

In the early part of the manual the author says the purpose of the scale is to "help provide information valuable to the understanding of the adjustment, the maturity level, the learning readiness, and the interests of the young child." [1]

At present this broad claim for the scale should be viewed with some reservation until more secure evidence is provided concerning its validity for fulfilling each of these roles. The best current guide to its usefulness as a method of estimating mental maturity is furnished in the form of correlations with three mental measurements used in the standardization study: (1) Goodenough scale, (2) Pintner-Cunningham Test of General Ability, and (3) California Test of Mental Maturity. Correlations of the Easel Age Scale with these

[1] Beatrice Lantz, *Easel Age Scale* (Los Angeles: California Test Bureau, 1955), p. 1.

measures range around .75 and higher for the primary grades, thus suggesting the scale may prove quite helpful in estimating a child's mental maturity. It awaits more testing out in the classroom and clinic. As the author suggests, "The Easel Age Scale is offered as a beginning framework, and it is hoped this framework will stimulate further research." [2]

Group verbal tests

Because individual scales take considerable time and demand the services of trained testers, psychologists after 1910 attempted to develop group tests. These attempts were climaxed in 1917 with the development of the first well-standardized verbal group examination, the Army Alpha test. This scale was used to measure "general intelligence" among the men being inducted into the United States Army during World War I. To some extent this test, along with others created about the same time, was the ancestor of the dozens of group tests available today. These are commonly termed *paper-pencil tests,* for the subject is given a test booklet containing questions which are answered by marking the booklet. A great many of these group scales have been designed particularly for judging the abilities of school children.

The kinds of items included on different group verbal tests vary considerably. Test authors have not always agreed upon the types of items that can best sample a person's abilities. The following items are samples of the kinds elementary and junior high school teachers may see on tests that may be used with their classes.

Vocabulary and word relationships. Items relating to the definition of words and relationships among words make up a very large proportion of the problems on verbal group tests. These verbal problems take many forms. Among them are:

1. *Word Meaning* (Circle the correct answers.)

INGENIOUS means the same as (a) ingrown (b) clever (c) jolly (d) handsome (e) endless

2. *Word Opposites*

COMPLEX is the opposite of (a) duplex (b) insist (c) complicated (d) compliment (e) simple

3. *Verbal Analogies*

[2] *Ibid.,* p. 10.

FLOOR is to HOUSE as DECK is to (a) sailor (b) home (c) cards (d) ship (e) funnel

4. *Classification* (Circle the word that does not belong with the others.)

cat lion leopard horse tiger

5. *Mixed Sentences* (Words in sentence are mixed up. Decide whether what the sentence says is true or false.)

to gone some school never have people

6. *Logical Selections* (Underline the two words which tell what the thing in capital letters *always* has.)

A CAR always has (a) frame (b) driver (c) weight (d) gasoline (e) windshield

Arithmetic and number relationships. Many tests include arithmetic problem-solving items. A small number of scales utilize other items involving numbers, such as codes to solve or number series to complete.

1. *Arithmetic Reasoning*

If candy canes are 3 for 10 cents, how many can be bought for 60 cents?

2. *Number Series.* Try to find how the numbers in the row are made up. Then in the spaces write the next two numbers.

6 3 8 4 10 5 12 6 ____ ____

Group non-verbal and non-language tests

Because the verbal group tests demand reading ability, they cannot be used effectively with persons who do not read well or do not understand the language. Thus, *non-language* and *non-verbal* group tests have been developed. Like the verbal group tests, the non-language and non-verbal scales are paper-pencil tests.

Non-language tests are composed entirely of pictures and figures. As directions are given by pantomime and by samples demonstrated by the tester, the child does not have to understand either spoken or written English. These tests are administered the same way to persons speaking different languages. Obviously they are best suited for testing groups of foreign and hard-of-hearing children.

The content of *non-verbal* tests also is entirely pictorial, so that subjects do not need to read or write. However, in these tests the directions are given in English. Consequently, they can be used only with persons who understand spoken English. Group tests for children in the primary grades are commonly of the non-verbal type. The administrator gives spoken directions as the children take the test. Reading-readiness tests given in the kindergarten or first grade to help determine whether children are capable of beginning reading are also pictorial in nature.

The following examples illustrate some of the kinds of items that compose various group non-verbal and non-language tests. Not all of these types of items would appear on a single test. Some test-makers prefer certain types of items. Others prefer different ones.

Following directions. The three items illustrated here indicate how simple directions that children are told to follow may increase gradually in complexity. First the child is asked to draw a circle or ring around the duck. Then he is asked to draw a line from A to B in the center figure. His next task is to draw a line from A to B to C in the figure at the right. This section of the test would then continue with additionally complex directions to follow.

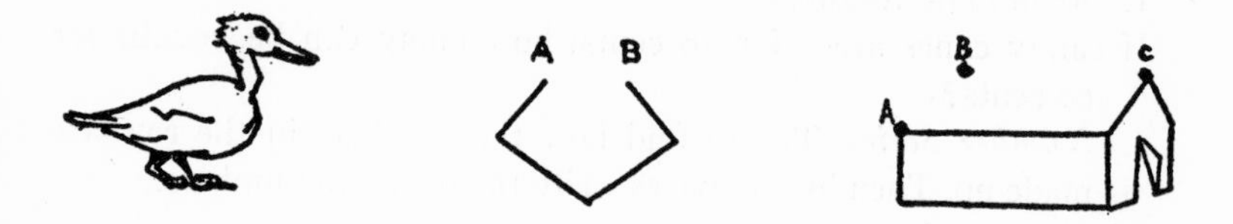

Completing designs. The pupil is presented with pairs of designs. If one line is added to the second design in each pair, the two designs will be identical. The pupil is asked to "Put in the mark that is left out of the second picture."

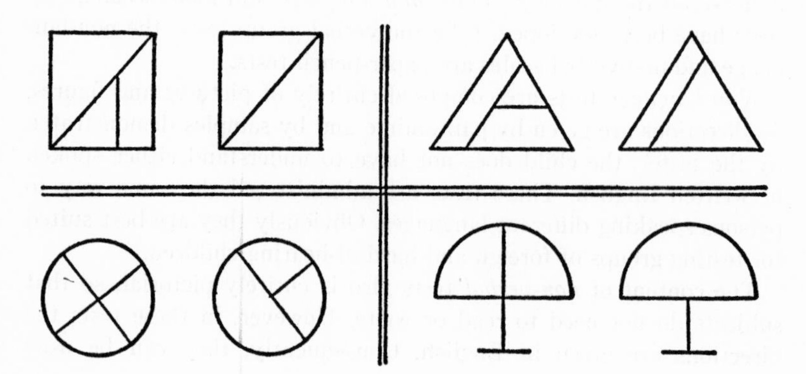

Copying designs. The student is directed to "Copy each of the designs in the space underneath." In addition to being used on nonverbal group tests, this kind of item also appears on individual tests of the Binet type.

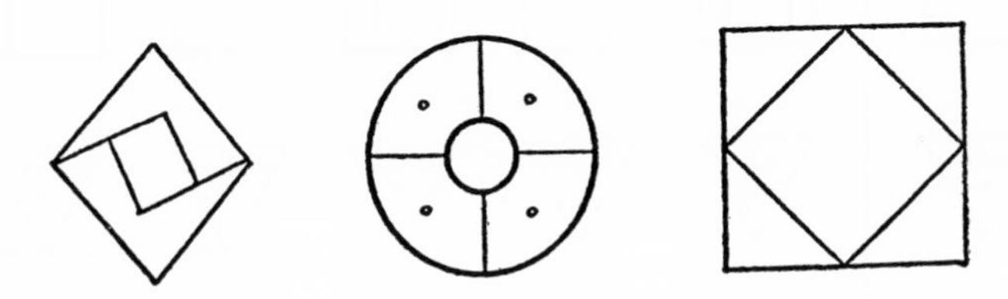

Comparing pictures. Picture-comparison items are very common on group tests. The pictures may be lifelike or abstract designs. Items range from very simple ones to very complex ones.

Among the simplest kind of picture-comparison is the paired-picture type. The child is directed to put an S in the space at the left if the two pictures are the same and to put a D in the space if they are different.

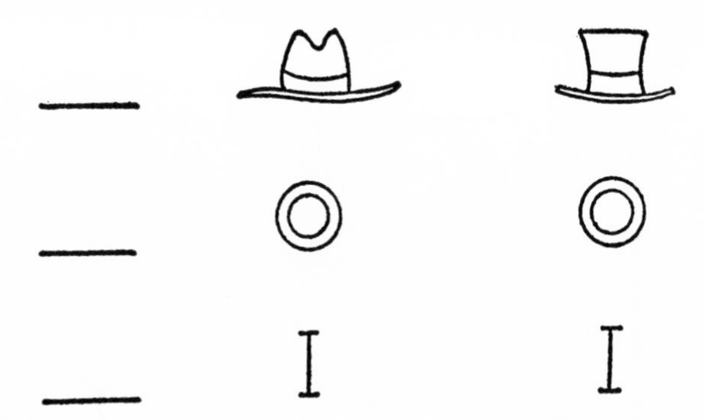

A more difficult type requires the pupil to circle the picture that is like the one at the left of the black line.

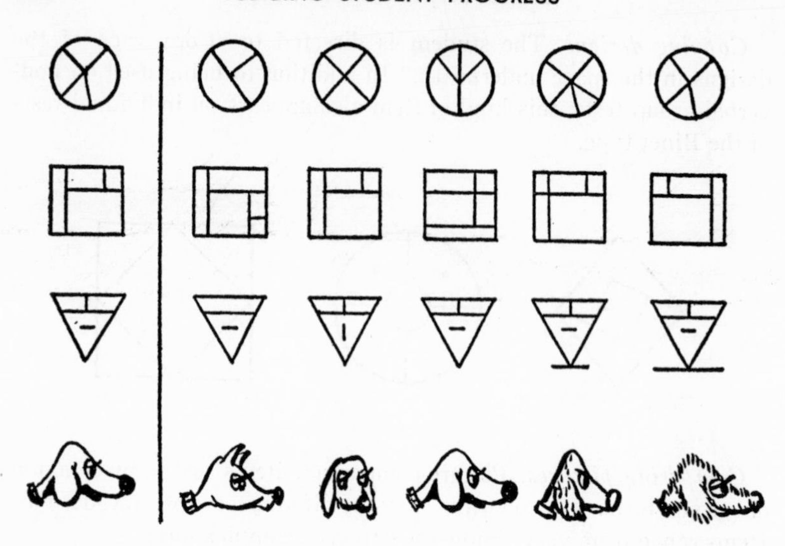

A still more complex item demands an ability to identify like objects in different positions. The directions given to the pupil are: "In each row find the drawing that is a different view of the first drawing, and draw a circle around its number."

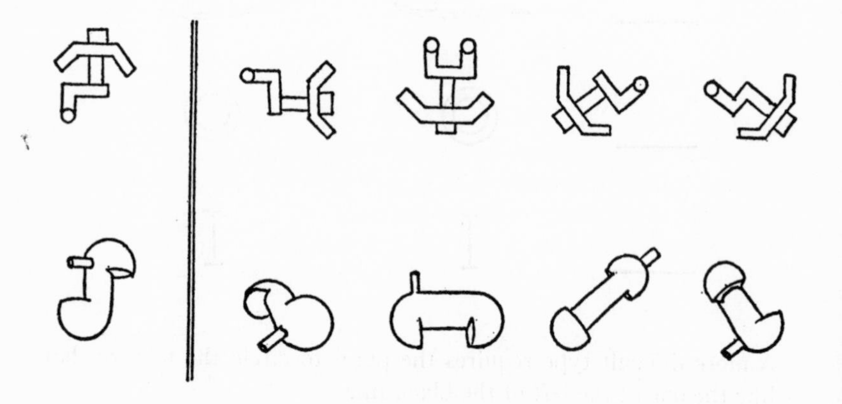

Drawing missing parts. Instructions to the pupil are: "Mark on each picture the part that is left out."

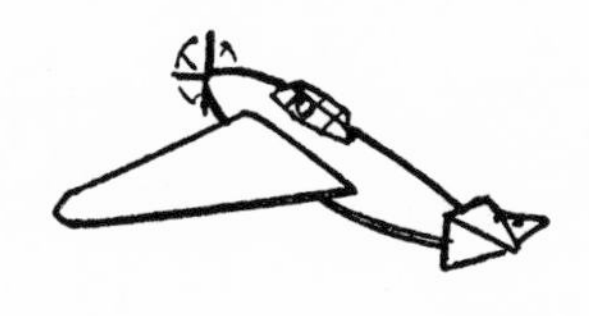

Identifying characteristics of objects. Each line on the test consists of pictures of five objects. For each line the pupil is asked a question that relates to qualities of the pictured objects. In the first row of the example below the pupil is directed to "Draw a line through the one that can go fastest." In the second row he is directed to "Draw a line through the one that is alive."

Ending stories. Each line on the test consists of pictures of four objects. For each line the tester reads a brief story that has an incomplete ending. The child is to complete it in a logical fashion by circling the object that would end the story.

The story for the first row of the example below is: "George came into the house after school. He said to his mother, 'I'm very hungry. May I have something to eat?' His mother said, 'Yes, take this____________________.' "

The story for the second row of the example is: "Some boys and girls were playing a ball game. John threw the ball up, but it did not come down again. It was stuck up in some branches. To get their ball back, John had to ask his father to climb up into the ______________."

Story-ending items can progress from these very simple forms to ones of some complexity.

Identifying symbol-digit combinations. The purpose of the test is to determine how rapidly and accurately pupils can compare pictorial symbols and the numbers under them and subsequently write the proper numbers under identical pictures. The first row of pictures in the test serves as the key that defines what digit should go under a particular picture. The rest of the test is composed of a number of rows of pictures in random order; however, in these test rows the picture symbols do not have their proper digits below them. The student is to write the proper number under each picture, such as a 1 under every picture of a hammer, a 2 under every chair, etc. In our example we have only the definition row or key row and one test row. In the actual examination there would be several test rows with symbols mixed in random order. Since the student is timed while taking the test, he cannot spend long studying the symbols.

1	2	3	4	5

Counting cubes. The pupil is presented with pictures of piles of cubes. Below each figure he is to write the number of cubes pictured.

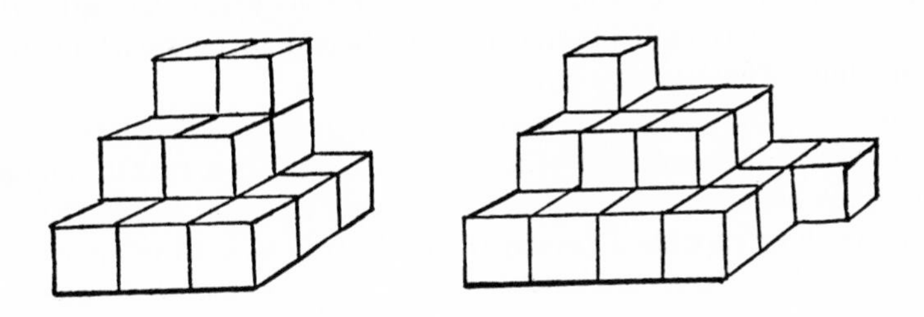

Identifying symbolic analogies. The subject is to find in each line the numbered figure that has the same relationship to figure C as is seen between figures A and B. In his mind the subject says, "A is to B as C is to________."

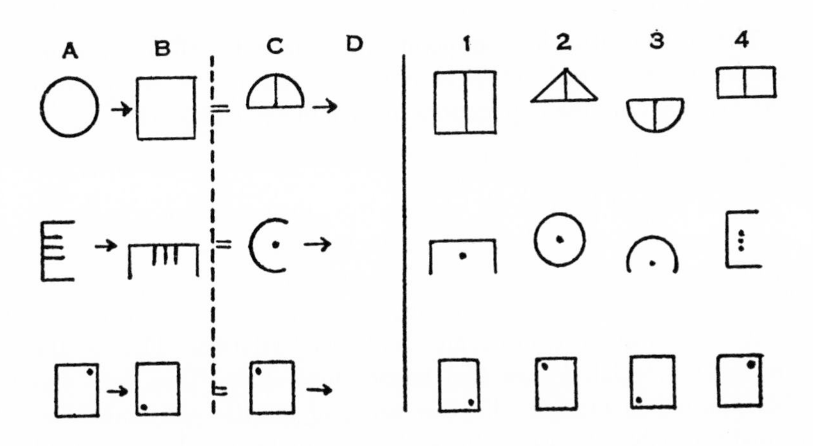

Combination group tests

Many group tests cannot be classified as either strictly verbal or strictly non-verbal, for they include sections of each type. For example, one popular test is divided into three sections: vocabulary, arithmetic, and cube counting. Another includes arithmetic reasoning, similarities among figures, judging spacial relations, syllogisms, and vocabulary. These would be called combination group tests.

THE MEANING OF INTELLIGENCE TESTS

In the Central School test-committee meeting Mrs. Schultz had expressed her view of what *intelligence* means when she said, "But if a student has high intelligence he's bound to be smart in most everything. That's pretty obvious."

Her view that there is a *single human quality* called intelligence that greatly influences all of a person's actions is a rather common one. This belief that *intelligence* is a single common factor that determines how capable a person is in all areas of his life appears to some people to be so obvious that they feel it is foolish to question its validity. However, in recent years numbers of psychologists have expressed increasing belief in the idea that a person may have different degrees of *intelligence* depending upon the area of life or the particular skills that are being considered. That is, they believe that intelligence is not one single factor in life, but a person may be more apt or intelligent in one area of behavior than he is in other areas (*12:11–20*).

These two contrasting viewpoints are commonly called (1) a *single-factor* or *general intelligence* theory and (2) a *group-factor* theory. What are the implications of each of these beliefs?

Single-factor theory

If the general intelligence view is true, then a person who shows great capabilities for learning in verbal areas (such as defining words and reading well) can also be expected to show great capabilities in handling numbers, writing, typing, filing index cards, as well as in music, art, mechanics, and social relations. That is, the *intelligence* which makes him adept along verbal lines will also be expected to pervade all other areas of his life and make him equally capable of success there. A chart of his capabilities would look something like Figure 13a. And logically, if a single-factor theory is completely true, by testing a person in one area we can predict his abilities in other areas. Hence, by sampling how well he defines words, we can predict how adept he is at learning to handle numbers, to spell, to paint a picture, to repair a television set, or to decipher a military code. If this theory is true, testing a person will result in a single score which adequately describes his potentialities.

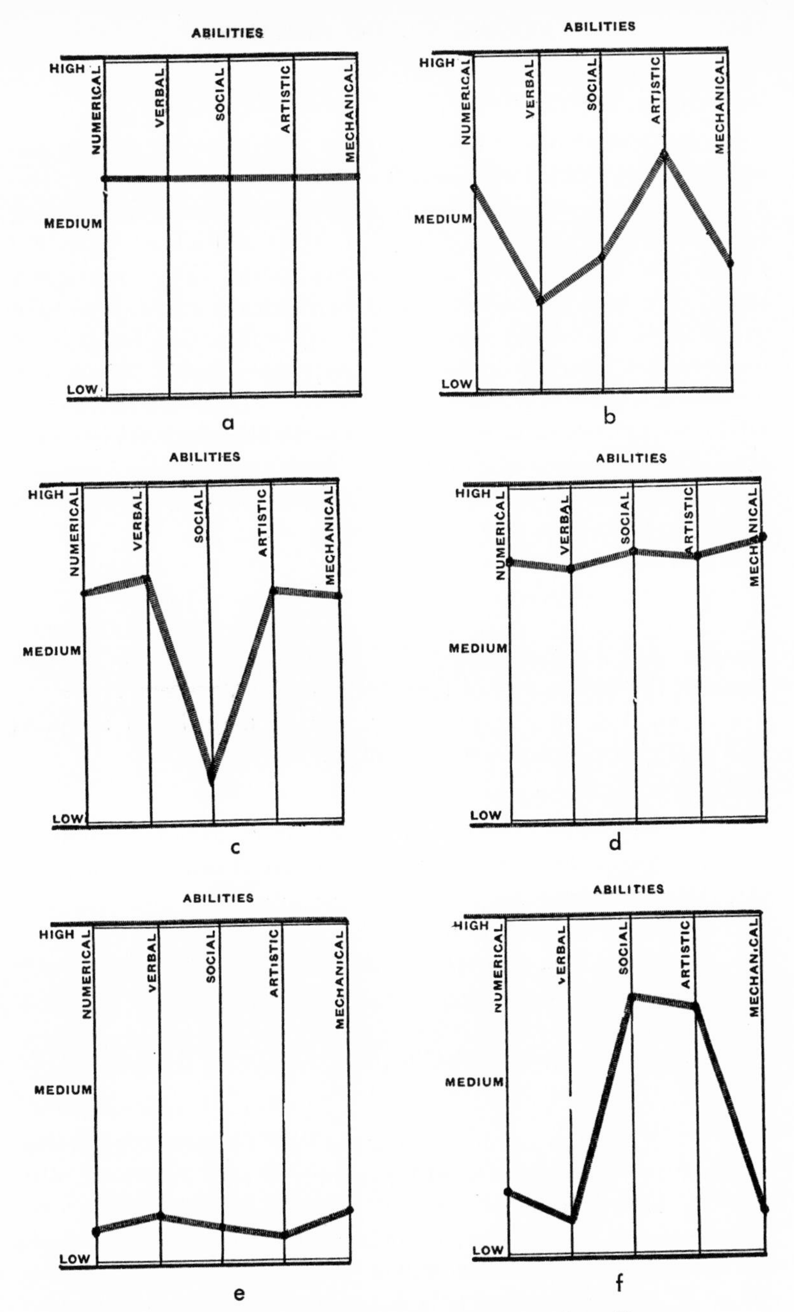

Fig. 13. Single- and group-factor theories of intelligence

Group-factor theory

On the other hand, if a group-factor theory is true, the person will not necessarily be expected to show similar ability in verbal, numerical, musical, social, and mechanical areas. He might be variable on all of these (Fig. 13b), or he could be high on many and low on one (Fig. 13c). He might be high on all (Fig. 13d) or low on all (Fig. 13e) or low on several and high on a few (Fig. 13f). Any number of combinations might be possible. And logically, if the theory is true that abilities are somewhat divided into groups, by testing a person in one area we cannot expect to predict accurately his abilities in other areas. For prediction purposes, we need a test for *each group* of abilities. We could not describe a person's potentialities by a single test score, but would need as many scores as there are factors or groups of abilities.

In recent years psychologists have used statistical procedures in attempts to identify the kinds of groups that abilities would be organized in if a group-factor theory of intelligence is true. Thurstone's analysis of intelligence into what he termed *primary mental abilities* is one of the best-known of these statistical studies. The seven factors or abilities he identified (*10:192–193*) after broad sampling with group paper-pencil tests are abilities to:

1. Deal with spacial relations.
2. Perceive details which are imbedded in irrelevant material (such as perhaps finding a word in a page of print).
3. Handle numbers.
4. Deal with verbal relations.
5. Deal with isolated words (such as building many small words out of a large word).
6. Memorize.
7. Reason inductively (that is, drawing a general principle that governs several tasks or activities).

As this list indicates, the areas treated by Thurstone are limited to ones commonly measured with paper-pencil tests. There are other areas of human behavior, such as personal relations, music, art, and mechanics, which have not been included in such an analysis, but according to correlation studies, these areas may well be composed of different factors or abilities. Consequently, the problem faced now by psychologists who subscribe to this theory is to identify more securely what groups of abilities exist and to determine the interrelationships among them as well as ways of measuring them.

A point of view

This discussion of theories of intelligence, treating a view of general intelligence and a view of group factors, has been much simplified. However, it does present in general the issue we face when we talk about intelligence and when we try to test for it in school.

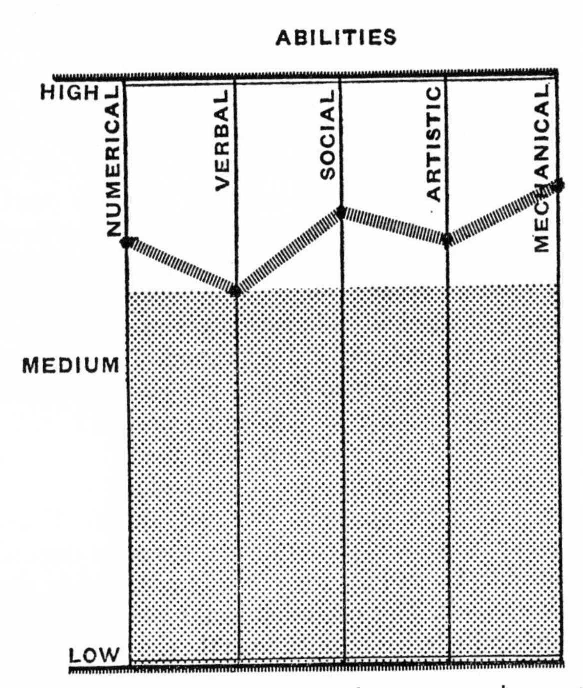

Fig. 14. Combined general and group factors to produce aptitudes

Which of these views should a teacher accept? Actually, there is no positive proof one way or the other at the present time. Possibly the truth, as some psychologists believe, lies somewhere between the two views. That is, there may be some general factor influencing all of a person's behavior at the same time that more distinct aptitudes make him more capable in one area of life than in another (Fig. 14). At least, from the practical standpoint it might be well for the teacher to accept this compromise view because the results of present-day intelligence and aptitude tests seem to support the idea that there may be some common factor in human abilities, but that a person is very likely to be more capable in one area than he is in another.

Up to this point in the chapter the words *intelligence* and *aptitude* have been used without being specifically defined. This is because a person's use of these words and his understanding of them depend somewhat upon his beliefs concerning general intelligence and group abilities. When Mrs. Shultz used the term *intelligence test,* she believed that each person has a general, all-pervading capacity in his life. She believed that some people have a general ability to do everything well; for others it is an ability to reach an average level; still others are capable only of doing consistently poorly in all areas of life. *Intelligence* for her meant the level of a person's capabilities all rolled into one IQ score. In contrast, Mr. Endo meant something more specialized when he spoke of *intelligence.* His idea was that the scales commonly called general *intelligence* tests measure aptness for academic schoolwork but do not measure very well capabilities in such areas as music, art, mechanics, social relations, and physical education. Therefore, the word *intelligence,* as Mr. Endo used it, was not all-inclusive but might better be termed *intelligence for academic schoolwork.*

Some psychologists and educators have used the term *aptitude* to specify capabilities only in more specialized areas, such as music aptitude or mechanical aptitude. However, the word aptitude is also used today by some experts to mean the same thing that Mr. Endo meant when he used the word *intelligence;* that is, they speak of *academic aptitude.* This confusion in the use of these terms, intelligence and aptitude, has resulted from the changing ideas in recent years about the nature of intelligence. As far as is known today, it is probably true that the term *intelligence* (as indicated by measurements of existing general intelligence tests) means primarily an *aptness for academic schoolwork and discerning the relationships among words and symbols.* Consequently, it appears to be more accurate to speak of *academic intelligence* rather than intelligence in general. Or some teachers may prefer to follow the lead of a number of psychologists who reject the term *intelligence* because of its "too-broad popular connotation" and prefer instead to use the word *aptitude* when speaking of any human capabilities. When they speak, they attach an adjective to the term to indicate more specifically which capabilities they mean, such as *art* aptitude, *clerical* aptitude, or *music* aptitude. In reading or talking about intelligence, it is well for the teacher to determine in which of these ways the writer or speaker uses the term.

What practical use does this discussion of general and group factors have for elementary-school teachers? And is it really important? Yes, it is very important. This discussion should cause teachers to be wary of using a child's IQ as established by one test to estimate his ability in other areas not closely related to the kinds of material on that test. It should cause teachers *to seek actual evidence telling what aptitudes in life a test measures before they choose a test for use in school or before they use test scores in directing children's lives.*

How does a teacher find proper evidence of the area of life a test samples? Some people accept the word of a test salesman or a catalogue from a test publisher as sufficient evidence that "it does an accurate job of measuring children's abilities." The publisher may be correct in such statements; however, since he has the biased view of a person trying to sell tests, more secure statistical evidence than merely a verbal opinion is desirable.

Other instructors may accept the view of another teacher who has used the test "and it seemed to be pretty good." However, the best evidence is found in correlation coefficients which describe how closely the test relates to some area in life. The way the correlation coefficient tells what a test really measures and whether the name of the test is accurate is indicated by the following coefficients which Burt found when he correlated children's scores on a Binet test with grades earned in specific subject-matter areas:

Correlation between	
Intelligence and composition	.63
Intelligence and reading	.56
Intelligence and arithmetic (problems)	.55
Intelligence and spelling	.52
Intelligence and writing	.21
Intelligence and handwork	.18
Intelligence and drawing	.15

"These correlations show that the Binet tests do not measure aptitude for all scholastic lines equally well. The tests correspond quite closely to the children's ability in the linguistic and abstract subjects—composition, reading, spelling, arithmetic. Children with high IQ's in these subjects are generally superior to those of lower IQ's in these subjects, but they are not markedly superior in writing, handwork, and drawing, that is, in mechanical and motor abilities. Although the correlations between the intelligence tests and the latter functions are positive, they are so low as to be practically negligible." [3]

As shown above, tests of the Binet variety are relatively good indicators of how well a child will succeed in the academic subjects. But these tests do not predict art ability or mechanical ability well. If a test is named accurately and is a good measuring device, it will correlate highly with the function in life which its name indicates.

Kinds of test validity

The establishment of the kinds of abilities in life that an *aptitude* test samples adequately is termed test *validity*. In foregoing chapters we defined the validity of a classroom or standardized *achievement* test as *the degree to which it accurately tests for the objectives of the class*. Thus, since we have now used the term *test validity* in more than one way, it is appropriate to inspect various things validity can mean in the field of evaluation.

In establishing the validity of a test we can turn to either rational or empirical sources of evidence, depending upon how we wish to use the results of the test.

Content validity

When a teacher wishes to determine how effectively a test measures the achievement of his students, he turns to rational evidence. That is, he estimates the content validity by inspecting the test items and matching them with the course objectives or content.

However, in the case of tests intended to estimate aptitudes, it is most helpful to use empirical or statistical sources. The following terms have been used to describe three varieties of validity established by determining statistically the relation of the test to some

[3] Arthur L. Gates, Arthur T. Jersild, T. R. McConnell, and Robert C. Challman, *Educational Psychology* (New York: Macmillan Co., 1950), p. 253. Quoted by permission of the publisher.

other measure: (1) concurrent validity, (2) congruent validity, and (3) predictive validity.

Concurrent validity

As its name implies, this refers to evidence of validity secured by comparing the test results with some *other measure taken at the same time.*

For example, let us imagine we have created a paper-pencil test to measure frustration level, that is, to measure how much frustration a child can tolerate before he "blows up" emotionally or shows some other symptom of marked disturbance. To determine whether our test does what we hope, we also secure teachers' ratings of children's frustration tolerance as observed in class or on the playground. Then we use statistical procedures (we find a correlation coefficient as described in Appendix C) to learn how children's test scores compare with teacher ratings. In this instance the teacher rating is the *criterion* measure we use to determine how validly the test measures current frustration tolerance. If the relation between test and criterion is quite high, we then assume that in judging a new group of children we need not get teachers' ratings of frustration tolerance but can use the handier medium of the test to judge this aspect of a child's emotional make-up.

Other examples of concurrent validity include (1) correlating a paper-pencil Fair Play Scale with students' rankings of each other on sportsmanship, (2) correlating a paper-pencil test on Use of Tools with ratings by the teacher of a pupil's actual handling of tools in the industrial arts shop, (3) correlating student scores on a Written English Usage Test with the number and kinds of errors made on class written assignments.

In each of these cases we hope for a very high correlation between the test and the criterion. If this high relationship obtains, we can thereafter confidently use the test alone as the measure of the characteristic rather than having to depend on more difficult, time-consuming methods such as ratings, observations, or counts of errors.

Congruent validity

This term refers to securing evidence of validity by comparing the test with a *similar measure or test* of the same characteristic.

For instance, let us say we create a new test of "general intelligence" for children. We wish to establish its validity in predicting school success. So we measure a sample of pupils with both our new scale and the Stanford-Binet. We compute the correlation between the two. If the correlation is very high, we can rather confidently say our test does predict school aptitude, because it measures about the same thing as the Stanford-Binet, whose ability to predict school success is already established.

This kind of evidence was seen in our earlier discussion of the Easel Age Scale. The author of that measure tried to determine the usefulness of the scale for estimating mental maturity by correlating it with three other measures: the Goodenough test, the Pintner-Cunningham, and the California Test of Mental Maturity.

It should be evident that the success of this procedure rests on how well these other tests themselves correlate with something in life. That is, from the standpoint of validating the Easel Age Scale it means nothing to find a high correlation between the scale and the Pintner-Cunningham test unless we also have good evidence concerning what the Pintner-Cunningham itself really measures.

Because it is costly and time-consuming to validate a new test by comparing it with other kinds of evidence in life, test-makers like to follow the more convenient procedure of correlating the new test with an already established one. When teachers read validity reports about a test they should always be careful to search out also the validity of the criterion measure (like the Pintner-Cunningham above) before accepting a high correlation as meaning the new test is a valid measuring instrument.

Predictive validity

When you seek the predictive validity of a test you try to learn how well it *foretells a student's later success* in school, in a vocation, or in some facet of living like social adjustment. Therefore, to establish the predictive validity of a test you must administer it and then wait till some time in the future when you will use a different type of measure (called a *criterion* measure) to compare the test scores with.

This is the type of validity involved when the intelligence-test scores of six-year-olds are later correlated with school marks in junior high. Other examples of predictive validity include (1) correlating music-aptitude test scores at the beginning of the sixth grade with ratings of musical performance at the end of the year, (2) correlating reading-readiness test scores at the end of kindergarten with reading performance at the end of first grade, or (3) comparing scores on the Arthur Point Scale at first-grade level with marks in arithmetic and reading at the fifth-grade level.

Summary of validity

Thus it is seen that if you are interested in the content validity of an achievement test you inspect test items to see how well they sample the content of classwork. But if you are interested in concurrent, congruent, or predictive validity you look to statistical studies to see what other measures the test correlates with.

Where should a teacher or school administrator look to find statistical evidence of the validity of a test?

Probably the first place to look is in the examiner's *manual* that accompanies the test. Manuals for the most carefully constructed tests report what the test was validated against in life (such as school marks or ratings of efficiency in doing the task) as well as what types of people were in the standardization group, what forms of the test are available, and what the reliability is. When using test manuals as sources of validity data, it must be recognized that test publishers and authors have an understandable bias in favor of the test. They are unlikely to be very critical of the test or of the way validity has been attempted. Hence it is well to look also to other sources of information.

The *Education Index* and *Psychological Abstracts* can guide you to journal articles and research on tests.

The one most helpful reference is the series of Mental Measurements Yearbooks edited by Buros. These volumes summarize research on specific tests and offer the opinions of experts who have no vested interest in the tests.

The following references at the end of the chapter also contain descriptions and, in some cases, evaluations of tests appropriate for elementary and junior high pupils: 2, 3, 7, 9, 10, 11, 14.

If little or no definite information about the validity of the test can be found in these sources, the test is of doubtful value.

Some tests that are published have been constructed primarily by the "armchair" technique. That is, an educator or psychologist, sitting in his armchair, creates items which seem to him to be good ones for testing musical aptitude or "general intelligence" or science aptitude. Without going through the tedious and costly process of standardizing and validating the scale on a fairly large number of people, the test creator has it published because he has personal confidence in the scale's worth. This test will lack *proven* validity and proper standardization. If such tests were used in situations that had little or no social consequence—such as merely using them as games for amusement at a party and then forgetting them—the fact that their validity is not proven would be unimportant. However, since the scores of such tests are used in schools to "tinker with children's lives," a teacher or administrator should select only the most carefully constructed scales.

HOW TO SELECT APTITUDE AND INTELLIGENCE TESTS

The criteria listed in Chapter 4 for choosing an achievement test are also the criteria to use in choosing an aptitude or intelligence scale. These include: test name, publisher and publishing date, reliability coefficient, validity coefficient,[4] norms and sample, methods of administering and scoring, the time the test demands, and the cost.

As a result of the foregoing discussion, the reader should be able to decide which among several tests would probably be the most effective in measuring a child's aptitudes. The following problem situation provides an opportunity to attempt such test selecting.

The school in which you teach is beginning a group testing program to be used with all children. You are asked to help select an academic aptitude test to be given by the teacher to every fifth grader each year. The supervisor for intermediate grades asks your opinion about four particular tests. After some research you have secured the data below about each test.

The Problem:

1. Rank the four tests according to which is best for this job, which is second best, and so on.
2. For each test, list the *reasons* you had for giving it the particular rank that you assigned to it.

[4] NOTE: With aptitude tests a correlation coefficient which describes the test's reliability is usually called the *reliability coefficient*. The correlation coefficient which describes how well the test compares with some ability in life is called the *validity coefficient*.

The data on tests

Kentworthy-Jones Intelligence Scale

Constructed by George Kentworthy and Stanley Jones. Published 1942 by York-Ohio Test Bureau. Age range from five to fourteen. Test is administered to one subject at a time by a trained tester. Reliability of Form I versus Form II = r. + .93. Norms established on 1300 children age 4 through 15 in Nebraska, Illinois, and Iowa. Correlation with school grades + .54. Testing outfit costs $4.00 but can be used with hundreds of children before needing replacement. Test record blanks for individual children are 5¢ each. Items include both verbal and performance types; verbal items increase with age.

Mid-Atlantic School-Aptitude Test

Author: M. L. Lenwig. Published 1954 by Mid-Atlantic House. Test-retest reliability = + .64. Manual states that "the test is valid for predicting school success as judged by teachers and experts." Paper-pencil test. It is easily administered by tester who reads directions to the subjects. Quick-scoring feature enables tester to score one test a minute. Accompanying statistical table easily converts scores to IQ's. Price: 10¢ each in lots of 100 or more; 12¢ each in lots of 50 to 100; 15¢ each in amounts under 50.

Steen Mental Aptitude Scale

Author: Melba R. Steen, Ph.D. Published by Wynote State Teachers College. Copyright 1934. Steen scale is intended to be used with school-age children (5 through 12). Three forms are available according to age level (Form A for children 5-7, Form B for children 8-12, Form C for children 13-17). Split-half reliability of forms: A is + .81; B is + .91; and C is + .87. Test is paper-pencil variety with both performance and verbal items; there are more verbal items on Form C than B, and more on Form B than A. Norms established on 1700 children in rural and urban areas of Michigan. Correlation with teacher's ratings of children's ability is + .31 for Form A; + .67 for Form B; and + .53 for Form C. Correlations with school grades are about the same as with teachers' ratings. Price: 18¢ each. Booklets cannot be used more than once since answers are recorded on them.

Tri-State Intelligence Test

Authors: J. B. Marsh and T. S. Clarkson. Publisher: Tri-State College. Copyright 1946. Paper-pencil test administered by tester who reads the directions to the subjects (directions appear on front of each test booklet). Two forms (I and II) correlated with each other + .92. Test standardized for children between ages 6 and 14. Both verbal and performance items are included. In a study of 1018 school-age children from city, town, and farm areas of Ohio and Pennsylvania, the test correlated with 1937 Stanford-Binet + .89. Price: 17¢ each in lots of more than 100, 20¢ each in lots of less than 100. (Manual and six scoring keys $1.00 extra.)

An efficient way to evaluate the four tests in the list is to consider first the *most important* and *crucial* criteria for test selection and decide if all of the examinations meet them adequately. Any test which does not meet the crucial criteria can be rejected, and the remaining ones can be inspected in terms of the next most important requirements. The above test data might be inspected in the following manner:

Age range

The test which is finally selected is to be used with fifth graders. A typical group of such children will range in age from 9 to 12 years; however, they will have a greater span of mental ages. All four of the tests being considered appear adequate for the age ranges of fifth graders.

Group test

It is understood that the test is to be administered to the students by their teachers. Usually teachers do not have the special training needed for administering individual tests properly. And even the few with such training often do not have time to test all children individually. Consequently, the academic aptitude test we are seeking is a group examination. Inspecting the four examinations, we see that three meet this requirement. The Kentworthy-Jones Intelligence Scale, however, is an individual test and would be improper for this particular situation even though it has several important desirable features, such as its reliability and validity.

Next in order of importance are *reliability, validity,* and the *standardization* sample.

Reliability

If a test is not reliable (that is, not highly consistent) the scores it yields are to be suspected. An inspection of the reliability coefficients reported for the three remaining scales shows that the Tri-State Test is highest (two forms .92), the Steen Scale next (split-half ranging from .81 to .91), and the Mid-Atlantic is lowest (split-half .64). There is no specific coefficient that is listed as a minimum for acceptable reliability, but, as indicated in Chapter 4, many test experts are not satisfied with reliability coefficients below about .85. Reliability above .90 is common among standardized tests. In light of this we can regard the reliability of the Mid-Atlantic Test as being unacceptable. This test can be eliminated from further consideration. The two remaining ones in our list have high enough reliability to warrant comparison according to other requirements for good tests.

Validity

Because we are trying to measure fifth-graders' aptitudes for academic types of schoolwork, we are interested in how well each test discriminates between the child who will succeed in academic work and the one who will not. Thus, we wish to know what the test has been *validated against in life.* This *thing* in life that is used to indicate what a test validly measures is called the *criterion.* The Steen Scale has two criteria: school grades and teachers' rating of children's ability. Obviously, these two criteria are closely related. The validity coefficients reported for forms A, B, and C are .31, .67, and .53, respectively. *Unlike reliability coefficients, validity coefficients can be lower than .80 and .90 and still be useful in estimating children's aptitude for schoolwork.* A validity coefficient of .67 between test scores and school grades indicates that the test, along with other data about the child, would be rather helpful to the educator in predicting the pupils' academic success. A coefficient of .31, though helpful, would be of much less value in estimating school success.

The criterion for the Tri-State Test was neither school grades nor teacher ratings. It was the 1937 Stanford-Binet. This is an example of attempting to establish the validity of a test indirectly. Instead of correlating the test directly with a criterion in life, such as school grades, the Tri-State authors correlated their test with an existing scale whose validity already had been securely established. The 1937 Stanford-Binet correlates quite highly with school success. The Tri-State authors used this rather popular indirect method of validation in order to avoid the costly and tedious process of other types of direct validation. Since the Tri-State correlated highly with Stanford-Binet scores (.89), it is fairly safe to assume that the Tri-State Test measures about the same characteristics as the Stanford-Binet. Therefore, such indirect validation is acceptable if the two tests correlate highly and if the *criterion test*—Stanford-Binet in this case—*has secure direct validation.*

In comparing the validity of the Steen and Tri-State examinations for the assigned task, we could conclude that both the Tri-State and Form B of the Steen would be helpful in estimating pupils' school aptitude. The Tri-State Test, although validated indirectly, would probably be better.

In discussing validity, it is interesting to note that the Mid-Atlantic Test, which was rejected because of poor reliability, has no statistical statement concerning validity. Instead, it boasts only the unsupported generalization that "the test is valid for predicting school success as judged by teachers and experts." Even if the test had been reliable, such flimsy evidence concerning validity would warrant rejection of this test.

Sampling

The norms for both the Steen and Tri-State scales were established on relatively good-sized samples in both rural and urban areas. (It is true, however, that norms for many group tests are established on much larger samples than these.) In selecting a test the teacher or administrator would have to estimate the extent to which the children on whom the test was standardized resemble the children in the local school. Generally we assume that the children in most areas of the United States have similar enough backgrounds to enable norms established in one state to be used in other states. Although this assumption is probably sound in the majority of cases, it may not be proper in the cases of children with language difficulties (foreign tongue spoken at home) or those raised in the lower social classes. There is some evidence that the usual intelligence and aptitude tests discriminate against these two types of children (5, 6).

Considering that our fifth graders are typical American school children, we judge that the Steen and Tri-State scales are about equal in adequacy of the sample upon which the norms were based.

Test forms

Each of these two tests has more than one form. However, the purpose of the additional forms differs in the case of each scale.

The Tri-State has two equivalent forms which can be used interchangeably. If in order to make a more accurate evaluation of a child's aptitude a teacher wished to administer a second academic aptitude test some time after the first was given, the alternate form of the Tri-State could be used without the danger of the child's second score being influenced by his memory of items on the first test. In contrast, the Steen Scale does not have equivalent forms. The three forms of this scale are designed for three different age ranges. In testing a child a brief time after he took the first Steen test, the teacher would have to use the same test form over again.

It might appear at first glance to be advantageous to have the three separate forms of the Steen Scale for different age groups. In practice, however, this can be a disadvantage. One form of the test may not measure adequately the abilities of all the fifth graders. The Steen form the teacher would use with fifth graders would be Form B intended for children ages eight through twelve. It would be necessary to inspect the tables of norms to determine whether Form B would have enough *top* (that is, enough difficult items) to test adequately a ten-year-old with a mental age of fourteen (IQ 140) or fifteen (IQ 150). Consequently, when separate forms of a test are available for different age-levels, it is necessary for the teacher to inspect the norms carefully to be sure the test has enough range to measure accurately the higher and lower students as well as those of average ability.

In regard to test forms, the Tri-State appears to be more adequate than the Steen Scale for use with fifth-grade pupils.

Authors

Because nothing is known personally about the ability of the authors of these two tests, knowing their names in this case is of no help in distinguishing which is the better test.

Publishers

The better-established test bureaus and publishing firms and the university and college presses are fairly consistent in issuing well-constructed tests. Which test publishers are most reliable becomes evident after experience using tests or after inspecting the names of the publishers of tests that are rated highly in such books as Buros' *Mental Measurements Yearbook*.

Without further data about the publishers of the Steen and Tri-State tests, it is assumed that they are reliable because most college test bureaus have proved to be so in the past.

Copyright date

After tests have been judged adequate on such crucial criteria as norms, reliability, and validity, the copyright date should be considered. The more recent test is usually the preferred one, for it probably was constructed on the basis of newer and improved methods of test development. The Tri-State was published in 1946, the Steen in 1934.

Price

The cost of the two tests is approximately the same, so price is of no consideration in choosing between them.

Conclusion

The above type of analysis would probably lead to the selection of the Tri-State Intelligence Test for evaluating academic aptitude among the fifth graders. The Steen Scale would be second choice. The Mid-Atlantic Test with its questionable norms and validity and its unreliability would be a poor scale upon which to base judgments of children's aptitudes. If an individual test rather than a group test were desired, the Kentworthy-Jones Scale probably would be good. However, for the present requirements it would be inappropriate.

RECOMMENDED TESTING PROGRAM

The Central-Union School test-selection committee, as the result of their work, made the following report to the faculty:

"Through our study we have learned that there are available today well-constructed group tests which can help teachers estimate a child's ability to succeed at certain tasks. Most of these tests are much better for judging aptitude in academic schoolwork, such as reading and arithmetic, than work in such areas as art, music, physical activities, and social skills. Apparently at the present time there are few if any group tests that measure aptitudes in these latter areas very adequately.

"We believe that our students could profit by taking well-constructed academic intelligence tests (that is, tests which measure aptitude for academic schoolwork) at three levels: grades one, four, and eight. Scores from such tests at these three levels, along with other data about the pupils, should aid us in judging how well each child is succeeding in academic schoolwork according to his ability and in estimating what his probable future success may be.

"We have specified 'well-constructed' tests. By this we mean tests with established reliability and norms appropriate to our students. The tests should not be accepted as valid measures of academic aptitude unless actual statistical data have been gathered to show how well they measure what the test name indicates.

"When teachers administer these tests to their classes, they should do so in the exact manner described in the test manual. Otherwise the scores will not be valid.

"The group tests will be given to all children. However, as you realize, group tests are not as accurate measures of children's aptitudes as are individual tests administered by a trained examiner. Consequently, for those children who score low or whose scores are at great variance with the quality of their schoolwork, an individual test will be provided to determine more clearly their probable abilities. Teachers will not administer the individual tests because special training is necessary for the proper use of such scales. Sometimes emotional conflicts in a child's life, which are not readily recognized as such by a teacher, will cause his intelligence-test score to be at variance with his schoolwork and his real ability. A psychologist through individual tests often is able to discover such emotional conflicts in a child's life, whereas the teacher has neither the time nor the special training to do so.

"The question of homogeneous grouping of our students according to their ability has been brought before the committee. A number of years ago Central-Elementary had ability grouping based upon a general intelligence test together with school grades. The system was abolished because the administration felt some worthy social goals were being neglected by having the children separated in this manner. We have reinspected the issue and realize that there is much evidence on each side of the question of homogeneous groups. For the present our committee recommends that only the very slow learners be grouped together to secure special help. The average and rapid learners, we believe, should be mixed together in classes as is now the policy; and within each of these classes we teachers will attempt to provide, as we do now, additional interesting work to challenge the fast learners while the average students are proceeding at their own pace. Aptitude tests and school grades, considered with teacher and parent observations of the children's maturity, are suggested as the basis for this type of grouping."

OBJECTIVES OF THIS CHAPTER

The effective elementary-school teacher:

1. Selects intelligence or aptitude tests that have established reliability and validity and are most appropriate for use with the individuals to be tested.
2. Accurately computes and explains intelligence quotients.
3. Explains the difference between a single-factor theory of intelligence or aptitude and a group-factor theory.
   Explains the bearing of these concepts on the treatment of children in school.
4. Administers group tests in the manner established by the test-makers as being correct for the particular test.

Suggested evaluation techniques for this chapter

1. Compute the IQ of a boy 8-years-3-months-old whose mental age on a test is 7 years 2 months.
   Find the mental age of a girl whose IQ is 127 and CA is 15 years 3 months.
2. By the use of manuals for academic aptitude tests or such a book as Buros' *Mental Measurements Yearbook* (or both), select a test which you believe would accurately measure the schoolwork aptitudes of a large group of third-grade children. Do the same for eighth graders.
3. You teach a class of 32 sixth graders. There are three openings in a special music class, and you are to select the three children from your room who probably will gain the most and will do well in the music group. How will you make your selection? What bearing will the children's scores on an academic aptitude test given earlier in the year have on your decision?

SUGGESTED READINGS

1. American Psychological Association Committee on Test Standards. "Technical Recommendations for Psychological Tests and Diagnostic Techniques: Preliminary Proposal," *American Psychologist* 7 (August, 1952), 461-75.
2. ANASTASI, ANNE. *Psychological Testing.* New York: Macmillan Co., 1954. Good source of principles of psychological testing, individual and group intelligence tests, aptitude tests, and personality measures.
3. BLAIR, GLENN MYERS. *Diagnostic and Remedial Teaching.* New York: Macmillan Co., 1956. Describes tests and ways of using them in diagnostic work at elementary and secondary levels.
4. BUROS, O. K. Four yearbooks containing expert analyses of many tests. If a test is not reviewed in one of the volumes, it is usually covered in another.
   (a) *The 1938 Mental Measurements Yearbook.* New Brunswick, N.J.: Rutgers University Press, 1938.
   (b) *The 1940 Mental Measurements Yearbook.* Highland Park, N.J.: The Mental Measurements Yearbook, 1941.
   (c) *The Third Mental Measurements Yearbook.* New Brunswick, N.J.: Rutgers University Press, 1949.
   (d) *The Fourth Mental Measurements Yearbook.* Highland Park, N.J.: Gryphon Press, 1953.
5. COOK, JOHN MUNSON, and ARTHUR, GRACE. "Intelligence Ratings for 97 Mexican Children in St. Paul, Minn.," *Exceptional Children* (October, 1951), pp. 14-15. Illustrates use of Arthur Scale with children not skilled in the English language.
6. DAVIS, ALLISON. *Social-Class Influences upon Learning.* Cambridge, Mass.: Harvard University Press, 1951. Criticisms of intelligence tests as being aimed at upper and middle classes.
7. FREEMAN, FRANK S. *Theory and Practice of Psychological Testing.* New York: Henry Holt and Co., 1950.
8. GOODENOUGH, FLORENCE L. *Mental Testing.* New York: Rinehart and Co., 1949.
9. GREENE, EDWARD B. *Measurements of Human Behavior.* New York: Odyssey Press, 1952.
10. GREENE, HARRY A.; JORGENSEN, ALBERT N.; and GERBERICH, J. RAYMOND. *Measurement and Evaluation in the Elementary School.* New York: Longmans, Green and Co., 1953.
11. HILDRETH, GERTRUDE. *Learning the Three R's.* Minneapolis: Educational Publishers, 1947. Discussion of tests for elementary schools.
12. National Society for the Study of Education. *Intelligence: Its*

Nature and Nurture. Thirty-ninth Yearbook, Part I. Bloomington, Ill.: Public School Publishing Co., 1940. Varied views of intelligence and a survey of research.

13. TERMAN, L. M., and MERRILL, M. A. *Measuring Intelligence*. Boston: Houghton Mifflin Co., 1937. Explanation of creation and use of 1937 Stanford-Binet. The 1960 manual for the new Stanford-Binet brings the 1937 book up to date.
14. THORNDIKE, ROBERT L., and HAGEN, ELIZABETH. *Measurement and Evaluation in Psychology and Education*. New York: Wiley and Sons, 1955. Clear discussions of ways to select tests; includes analyses of tests useful at elementary and junior high levels.
15. WECHSLER, DAVID. *The Measurement of Adult Intelligence*. Baltimore: Williams and Wilkins Co., 1944. The basis of the Wechsler-Bellevue is explained.

CHAPTER

6

Using Standardized Tests

3. Personality Tests

THE PRINCIPAL opened the next meeting of the test-selection committee by saying, "We have investigated achievement and aptitude tests, so I believe our task is about over. However, there is one more area which Mr. Endo felt we probably should consider. Would you tell us about it?"

Mr. Endo explained, "This has to do with children's personalities and their adjustment in a broad sense. It's not really a subject-matter goal like reading or geography, but I'm sure we all consider it important because it is related to the actual kind of children we are trying to turn out: well-adjusted ones. If we were to state it in terms of a goal we want the children to reach, we might put it something like this: We want each child to be able to satisfy his personal needs and also to meet his responsibilities in our society without having to escape reality, to attack other people, to act babyish, or to rationalize unduly. I'm sure we would agree on this as an over-all goal. Now this is the reason for bringing the subject up here. As all of us probably know, there are some kinds of personality tests published which are supposed to help a teacher learn about the mental hygiene of the pupils, such as what disturbs them or how they feel inside. These tests are supposed to show things about a person that he usually doesn't tell people or you usually can't find out in other ways. Actually, I don't know much about these personality tests or whether we should be using them in our school. I know some schools use them, so I think it is something we should look into at this time when we are making suggestions for improving our testing program."

Miss Adler, a kindergarten teacher, said, "I think you're right. And there is one thing I would like to add. Some of these tests can't be given to my kindergarten children because they are written. But I understand that you can tell a lot about a child's personality from the kinds of paintings he makes, and I would like to know more about that. How good are children's paintings as tests of their personalities?"

"I don't know," said Mr. Endo. "The tests I was thinking about particularly were paper-pencil ones which the youngsters fill out. They would obviously be for the upper grades. But I agree that we ought to try to find out about paintings and drawings, too."

Miss Chavez asked, "What about the inkblot tests? They are supposed to reveal personality. I don't know how much training it takes to give them, but perhaps a teacher could learn with some instruction."

Mr. Carpenter said, "Aren't we perhaps taking some of these things a little too seriously? Children's painting and inkblots don't seem to be very logical things to base an educational program on. Aren't they mostly psychological research tools?"

That is what the committee decided to find out. They decided that by inviting the county school psychologist to meet with them the following week and by reading journal articles recommended by the psychologist they could make a valid decision about the place of personality tests in the elementary school. Their discussion and reading led to the following understandings.

PERSONALITY MEASUREMENT

Although there is no real agreement among psychologists on what *personality* means, for purposes of discussion here it may be regarded as meaning the *total observable behavior and the "inner life"* of an individual. Such a definition covers the whole existence of a person, and to make an adequate measurement of *personality* in this sense would necessitate the use of all the measuring devices discussed in this book plus many others. Even then the picture of the human personality would be far from complete, for man's knowledge of himself and of methods of evaluating himself are today far from adequate. Although every evaluation device (such as personal observation, sociogram, aptitude test, interview) contributes something toward this total picture of a person, there exists *no one device* which is capable of measuring *personality* completely.

What, then, are the so-called *personality tests* which have been developed? Generally, they might be regarded as being the psychologists' attempts to do one, or both, of two things: (1) to judge a *particular facet* of the total personality, such as vocational interests or "honesty" or "social adjustment," and (2) to seek out the inner life or the *inner-springs-of-action* which make one person view life differently and act differently from another person.

There are many types of tests relegated to this all-encompassing category of personality measures. However, only two of these general types seem to be of importance to elementary-school teachers. These are: (1) the personality or adjustment inventories, and (2) the projective techniques.

PERSONALITY OR ADJUSTMENT INVENTORIES

Numerous adjustment inventories are published for both children and adults. Although they appear under a variety of titles (such as personality inventory, adjustment inventory, adjustment survey, test of personality factors, test of personality adjustment), their forms and functions are similar. They are primarily of the paper-pencil variety and thus are commonly called *paper-pencil personality tests*. Typically, an inventory consists of a list of questions which the child answers by circling a *Yes* or *No* response. A question-mark or a "don't-know" category is sometimes provided for use when the subject is undecided about the answer he wishes to give. However, the child is urged to try to answer either *Yes* or *No*. Here are a few typical questions:

1. Do you feel that people do not like you? YES NO ?
2. Does your bed get wet at night? YES NO ?
3. Do you often have bad dreams? YES NO ?
4. Do you like to talk with strangers? YES NO ?
5. Do you get nervous when you speak in front of the class at school? YES NO ?

Other inventories take a more indirect approach in seeking answers about a child's personal life and thoughts. An example of this indirect type of inventory would be:

1. Mike is a good sport. He never cheats at games.
   Am I just like Mike? YES NO
   Would I want to be like Mike? YES NO

In the elementary school these printed personality tests have been developed for use with children in the intermediate and upper grades (about fourth grade and up), for they demand the ability to read fairly well. They are administered to a group, or sometimes to an individual, in a standard manner described in the test manual. The manual, in addition, tells how to score the test, and standards are usually given to indicate what type of response pattern (such as a high number of *Yes* responses) is indicative of "poor" or "good" or "average" adjustment in the opinion of the test author.

These paper-pencil tests have several advantages. The scoring and administering follow a standard procedure. The tests are usable with large groups of children who can read and write. They do not demand a highly trained tester to administer them.

However, there are a number of important limitations to present-day paper-pencil adjustment inventories. In most cases they demand a definite "Yes-No" or "Like-Dislike" answer; they do not allow for qualifying statements concerning an item. For example, when Carl Conn reads the question "Do you feel that people do not like you?" he may answer *Yes* because he knows of three people who do not like him, although he feels generally well liked. If Carl could qualify his statement and explain it, he would indicate that three do not like him. Such a *Yes* answer in Carl's case has a different significance from the *Yes* for Franklin Brown, who is generally disliked and knows it. The inventory does not reveal the differences between the two boys. Some test authors have tried to avoid this definite *Yes-No* difficulty by providing a scale of 8 or 10 degrees, so that the child can make a check mark to indicate whether he means "completely *Yes*" (checked on the far left) or "sometimes *Yes* and sometimes *No*" (checked in the middle). The following item is an example of this type:

Do you have dreams that frighten you?

YES ____ ____ ____ ____ ____ ____ ____ *NO*

In general, however, these tests provide no opportunity for a child to explain his own particular situation.

A second disadvantage of the paper-pencil inventory is that a relatively astute child who is acquainted with what his society considers "good" and "bad" or "nasty" and "nice" can see through the questions and discern what type of answer will probably make him appear well adjusted. Consequently, a child who does not wish to divulge his feelings and thoughts can accurately fake some of the answers to appear better adjusted according to the norms, although actually he is quite disturbed. It probably does not take a great amount of insight for a sixth or seventh grader to know which answer to the following questions indicates the more desirable kind of person. If he wishes to do so, he should be able to avoid revealing his disturbance by his answers.

1. Do you often have headaches? YES NO
2. Do you often feel that people are talking about you? YES NO
3. Is it hard for you to go to sleep at night? YES NO
4. Do you think you worry too much? YES NO

A third limitation of the paper-pencil inventory lies in the possibility that the test may fail to uncover the problem of even the conscientious child who does not try to fake it. This may occur if none of the questions on the test happens to touch upon the child's specific area of disturbance. The paper-pencil test is limited in its scope to the particular questions the test-maker included. It is true, however, that children who are very maladjusted are commonly disturbed in the several areas of their life, not just one. Since at least some of these areas are covered in the typical inventory, the child would be likely to be discovered.

Validity

When judging the worth of such tests, the elementary-school teacher is primarily interested in having answers to two questions: How have these tests been validated? How well have they differentiated between well-adjusted and poorly-adjusted people?

Validity for inventories has been sought principally through the careful selection of items; therefore, it would appear logical that a child who answered the bulk of 200 questions, like those above, in a negative manner, would be a disturbed child. Although this logic makes sense, the actual statistical validation of inventories has much to be desired. As Stephens has written, empirical validity "... has been a difficult problem since it is hard to get a good criterion of adjustment against which the questionnaires can be checked. At present we had better regard the question as unsettled. The various questionnaires most probably measure some aspect of adjustment, but it is unlikely that they measure precisely the same thing that the psychiatrist has in mind when he announces that a given person is poorly adjusted."[1]

USES OF ADJUSTMENT INVENTORIES

What, then, are the valid uses of such inventories? There are probably two main ones. The first is as a group-screening device. The second is as a psychological *springboard* for a personal interview.

Many children who take such tests answer them as truthfully as they can. They do not try to fool the teacher or psychologist. A few of these children will make scores which, according to the test norms, are indicative of considerable maladjustment. The rest of the students will score within a "normal" range. It is very possible that the children with the "disturbed" scores actually are disturbed. Therefore, the test has been helpful in screening these apparently maladjusted children from the group so that they can be studied more carefully and can secure special attention. However, it is also likely that there are others in the group who received "normal" scores but are actually disturbed children. Their normal scores could be accounted for by their conscious or unconscious faking or by the fact that the questions were limited to areas in which they were not obviously disturbed. As a result, the teacher or administrator should recognize that although the paper-pencil inventory may be a quick method for screening out a few children who are disturbed and need special attention, it is unlikely the test will indicate nearly all of the disturbed ones. Consequently, the personality inventory has a limited use as a group-screening device to select disturbed children for special attention.

A second valid use of a personality test in the elementary school is as a springboard for personal interviews with children. By talking over the questions privately with a child, the school guidance worker may establish a friendly relationship with the child and be able to ask, "Is there any particular reason you answered *Yes* to this question: 'Do you feel your parents are sometimes unfair?'" Such an interview, in a non-critical and a very friendly atmosphere, may serve as an entree for the child to unburden himself of something which has disturbed him and which he would like to have discussed before but never had been able to find the proper occasion

[1] J. M. Stephens, *Educational Psychology* (New York: Henry Holt and Co., 1951), p. 536. Quoted by permission of the publisher.

nor to summon the courage to do so. In this case the inventory has aided in helping a child.

Do these two functions, to screen a group and to initiate an interview, warrant the widespread use of such inventories in elementary schools? A sixth-grade teacher, after studying such tests, gave what she termed a "practical opinion" which is shared by numbers of other teachers.

"These tests would be impractical in my room. Through my own observation in the first five weeks of school I have found a number of children who need special help from me. And two of them really need some outside help . . . from a psychologist or guidance clinic. As it is now, I can't find enough of my own time or get enough outside help to aid adequately the obviously disturbed children in my room. It would seem useless for me to give such personality tests to discover any more disturbed ones when we can't properly take care of the ones we have found already. Besides, I am not so sure that I as a teacher am capable of using such tests properly. I haven't had enough training to know what a score really means in a child's life."

The present writer would agree basically with this teacher's opinion. Most teachers do not have a problem finding the children who need help. Rather, they face the problem of finding methods by which to help the children who obviously need aid. The overaggressive girl, the painfully shy and reticent boy, the girl who cries unconsolably at the least rebuff can be discovered without a paper-pencil test. Since the teacher has other evaluation techniques available, and because special psychological help and extra teacher-time are still rare in many schools, the test as a screening device is not practical in most classrooms. In addition, unless such tests are administered and interpreted by a well-trained guidance worker or psychologist, they may do more harm than good for children. For example, one teacher of an upper grade administered a test, corrected it, and then wrote the norms on the board, indicating that "scores below this point on these different scales show poorly adjusted people." This handling of the test scores resulted in a great deal of unwarranted worry on the part of students whose scores even approached the supposed "maladjusted" point. If these students were not maladjusted before entering the class, the teacher's actions were surely giving them cause to become disturbed by the time they left.

In regard to initiating interviews, the typical teacher who has established good rapport with the children will have many topics to discuss with each one and should not have to depend on an item from a personality test to initiate a personal talk. Consequently, in its present state of development, the paper-pencil personality test, with its questionable validity and limited uses, probably has little, if any, place in the elementary or junior high program.

PROJECTIVE TECHNIQUES

The principle underlying projective methods of personality evaluation may be understood by the following informal experiment with a number of older students. The drawing below was shown to them.

Fig. 15. Experimental projective design

Each was asked to write what it looked like to him. These were a few of the responses:

Student 1. A bird with his head under his wing.
Student 2. Looks like an eye. I don't know what the other black business is.
Student 3. A farm. Black dots in the back look like corn stalks tied together. Lines look like planted rows of beans or any

crop. Looks like a barn with three fence posts in front. Clouds are in back.

Student 4. Looks like the sun getting up in the morning. Kind of looks like a mess.

Student 5. Looking from airplane and see fields.

Student 6. Tombstones in a military cemetery.

Student 7. Looks like a city with a lot of roads coming into it. The big line is a building. Can't figure out what the middle thing is.

Student 8. I think of landscaping, pretty grass, purple mountains.

Student 9. Sun coming up on areas of farm land.

Student 10. Airplane view of fields.

Here was a variety of responses to the drawing. Some students' interpretations were more alike than others. After the students responded, some asked, "But what is it really?" They wanted to know the *correct* answer. It was *really* lines of ink on paper, nothing more. However, each student had given an interpretation of what it looked like to him. Even though each recognized it was obviously produced by ink on paper, the drawing "meant" something else to him. Where did this *meaning* come from? Where does the *meaning* come from when a person says, "That cloud looks like a ship"? Obviously the *meaning was projected from the students' personalities.* The drawing merely reminded each one of some meaning. There was no meaning in the ink on the paper. The drawing had served as the type of evaluation device called a *projective technique* or *projective method*, for it stimulated each student to reveal his individual method of interpreting part of his environment. (In this discussion the term *projection* is used in an inclusive sense rather than the more limited meaning applied to it by some psychologists and psychiatrists.)

In recent years psychologists have tried out many types of stimuli in an attempt to discover ones that reveal significant clues to a person's *inner life* or the *core of personality*. Projective techniques are based upon the theory that the way a person interprets an inkblot or the way he finishes an incomplete sentence may be a good sample of his way of interpreting the world and his relationship to it. Advocates of projective testing claim a number of advantages. White (*11*) writes that these projective methods are better able to uncover three types of material not reached by other measures: (1) the things which a person himself realizes, but because of embarrassment or reluctance will not reveal; (2) material which is "repressed," that is, present but not consciously recognized by the subject; and (3) facts which the individual does not notice, about which he is not equipped to make comparisons with others, such as his personal defense mechanisms.

Included among the many types of projective techniques being used by psychologists are the Rorschach inkblot tests, picture association methods, handwriting, speech, dramatic play, sentence and story completion tests, word association tests, expressive movements, and art productions. (The picture on page 170, which is not part of an actual test but is merely an example of the operation of projection, could be considered one kind of picture-association method.) A brief description of a few of the more popular techniques will acquaint the teacher with their use in relation to the elementary school and junior high grades.

Rorschach

Best-known of the projective techniques is the Rorschach Test, which consists of ten standard inkblots first organized as a measuring device by a Swiss psychiatrist, Hermann Rorschach. Although Rorschach had introduced his inkblot technique in Europe shortly before 1920, the test did not come into widespread use in America until after 1935. The test is usually administered individually, although a group test with the blots flashed on a screen has been used to some extent. The Rorschach demands a well-trained tester to administer it, for the tester must write down a record of everything the subject says as he looks at the cards and describes what each inkblot looks like to him. Even more training is needed for interpreting the Rorschach record, and the actual personality meaning of particular responses to the cards is not well established.

The trained clinical worker uses the Rorschach not as a sole indicator of personality factors but as one source of clues that should be interpreted in relation to personal interviews, observations of the children, aptitude tests, teacher observations, and records of home background and behavior. The teacher will not be administering the Rorschach. Thus he does not need a thorough knowledge of it. Instead, he needs to know only the general purpose and nature of the test so as to have some understanding of a psychological report that might be made upon a child in his room who has had special psychological testing and, perhaps, treatment.

Fig. 16. Inkblot test

This inkblot is similar to those in the Rorschach Test. The subject is asked what the inkblot looks like or what it resembles. He may look at it from any position.

The following is an example of such a record of an eighth-grade girl who was referred to the school psychologist by the teacher who wrote:

"Jeanie's problem lies in her social adjustment and relationship with other children. She is inclined to be loud and self-assertive and extremely belligerent when crossed. She becomes enraged over small incidents in games and over fancied or very slight incidents in class and gives way to violent outbursts of temper."

The psychologist studied Jeanie by interviewing her, administering several tests (found Stanford-Binet IQ to be 147), and by securing records of her school behavior and home background. Among the tests was the Rorschach, which the psychologist said helped reveal, along with other data, "... a hostility toward the world and others about her. For example, on her first response she sees a cat with eyes giving forth 'a wicked glow. (There is) vicious hate in its eyes.' Her record is full of aggressive objects, animals, and people: she sees hatchets hanging on a mantelpiece, a man-eating barracuda 'after something,' a bat of the type 'which pulls your hair out,' etc. Individuals with so much inner aggression see the world as a hostile place and frequently feel that others are attempting to injure them. This, coupled with her feelings of being rejected by others, may account for Jeanie's attempts to strike back in any way she can, both verbally and physically."

The above excerpt is typical of the type of reference to a Rorschach record that appears in special case studies of individual children who are having difficulties in school.

Although clinicians have achieved some insights and gratifying results with this projective device, the structure of human personality is so complex that it is extremely difficult to validate the test adequately. However, in clinics and universities throughout the world today many studies are being conducted to determine the meaning of various responses to Hermann Rorschach's ten inkblots.

Thematic Apperception Test

Probably the second most widely used projective device is the Thematic Apperception Test. It consists of a series of drawings, many showing people carrying on some type of activity, the nature of which is usually not very clear. The subject is asked to tell, or sometimes to write, a story of what he thinks is happening in each picture. By seeking a pattern of responses or of attitudes that run through the subject's stories about the pictures, the psychologist tries to determine the primary concerns, frustrations, and motives in the person's life. As its name suggests, the test aims to reveal the theme that runs through a personality.

Like the Rorschach, this is a specialized instrument. Teachers would not be administering it to their classes or to individuals in the class, for much training is required for its safe use.

However, in relation to the language arts program of upper-grade classes it is not uncommon for teachers to present the children with some type of picture as a stimulus for a piece of creative writing. That is, the teacher can place three different pictures on the bulletin board: perhaps one of a boy fishing, one of a girl looking at the advertisements in front of a theater, and one of a car pulling a house-trailer over a hill. The students are to choose one of the pictures and write a story that the picture might be telling. The main purpose here would be to stimulate creative writing and to give practice in writing. But a secondary outcome may well be the

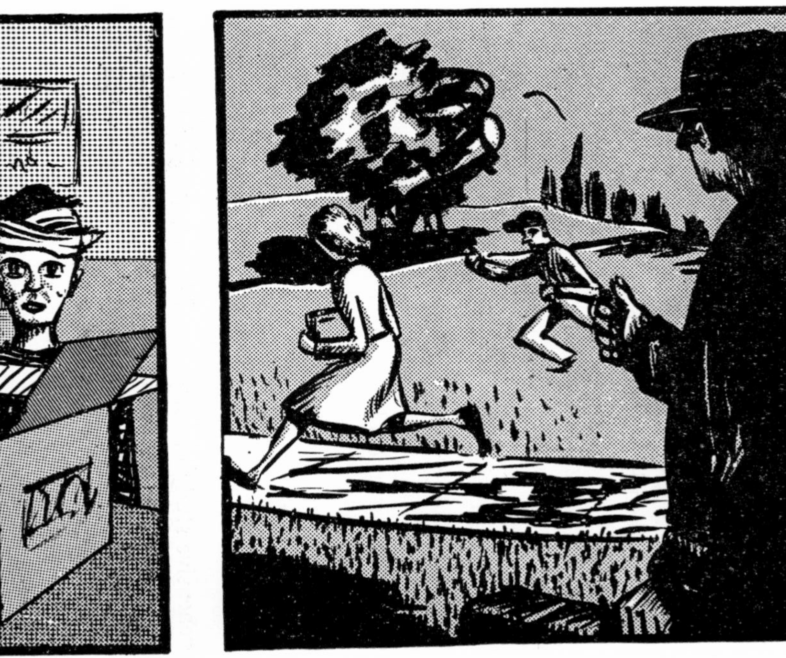

Fig. 17. Picture-association device

These pictures are similar to those in such picture-association tests as the Thematic Apperception Test, Symonds' Picture Story Test for adolescents, and the Children's Apperception Test. The subject is to tell or write a story of what is happening in each picture.

possible clues that the creative interpretations of the pictures give about the needs and concerns of the student who wrote the story. The teacher must be very cautious in trying to interpret such students' stories, for one sample story in the hands of even a trained clinician is very shaky grounds for interpretation of personality structure. However, taken in relation to many other types of information the teacher gathers about the student, the story about the picture can offer additional clues to understanding the individual child and to adjusting the school program to fulfill his needs.

Play

Children's play is another projective device. The fact that dramatic play often reveals the way a child interprets life or the way he feels about happenings in his life is obvious to the primary-grade teacher. Children, especially those in the primary grades, often cannot or will not talk about their frustrations or concerns, but when playing house and acting the parts of mother or father they may reveal significant aspects of their personalities or their preoccupations.

In a comprehensive study of early-school-age children eight functions of dramatic play were identified. Children were found to use play (1) to imitate adults, (2) to play out real life roles in an intense way, (3) to reflect relationships and experiences, (4) to express pressing needs, (5) to release unacceptable impulses, (6) to reverse roles usually taken, (7) to mirror growth, and (8) to work out problems and to experiment with solutions (*5:27–28*). Obviously some of these functions overlap. A given play episode may involve one or more of them.

This list of eight important functions, established on the basis of a great many observations of children's free dramatic play, indicates that play is a valuable tool for revealing personality factors. The list also suggests that adequate interpretation of a particular play episode in a child's life is not a simple matter.

Examples of four of these uses of play may make the distinctions among them clearer.

Imitation of adults. Two girls and one boy were playing the roles of Mother, Daughter (called Sister by Mother), and Father.

MOTHER: "Sister, you stop making so much noise. Daddy's trying to rest. He's worked hard all day and doesn't want you fooling around all the time. I'm going to cook supper."

DAUGHTER: "I want to go out and play, Mama."

MOTHER: "No, you've been a naughty girl all day. You'll have to stay in. Go right to your room, and don't make noise either or I'll be in there fast."

This type of incident also reflects relationships and experiences. This is especially true when such incidents show strong emotion involved.

Expression of pressing needs. In this case the apparent need is for an early type of affection and mother-child relationship.

In the doll corner Albert sat on the floor feeding a wetting doll with a small baby bottle. He looked to see if the doll had wet. He said, "She's wetting. That's something." He paddled the doll a moment on the rear, then laid it across his knees and looked at the amount of water still in the bottle. He sucked the nipple, took the bottle out and looked at it. Then he sucked the nipple again, slowly lay back on the floor and closed his eyes, sucking all the while. When an adult walked nearby, Albert opened his eyes.

ADULT: "Don't you want to get up from the floor?"

Albert removed the nipple, said, "I'm too little" and dropped the bottle. He put his thumb in his mouth and lay sucking it.

Release of unacceptable impulses. Direct expression of such impulses as aggression toward other children or adults is usually forbidden. Frequently, it comes out in a more indirect form during play.

Sandra spoke to the rag doll in her hands: "Did you bite your little friend? No, no. Now I'll have to bite you." Sandra bit the doll's arm tentatively, then harder. She rapidly bit various parts of the doll, paused to say, "There. Will you be good? Oh, you won't?" She bit the doll again.

Working out of problems and experimenting with solutions. In the play yard Ricky, Tod, Janice, and Lenny gathered around a large wooden packing box that stood bottom-up near a sand pile.

RICKY: "This will be our train."

TOD: "We get on top?"

RICKY: "No, get in it."

JANICE: "We can't."

RICKY: "Turn it over."

All tugged at the box, but, since they were on different sides, one was pulling against another.

RICKY: "Get on this side. Lenny, over here."

All pushed on one side of the box and turned it over.

JANICE: "Get the shovels. We'll put coal in the engine." She ran to the nearby sand pile, picked up one of two shovels. Ricky picked up the other.

LENNY: "Where's one for me?"

RICKY: "Use that." He pointed to a toy bucket. Lenny filled the bucket with sand to carry to the train. Ricky and Janice carried shovels full of sand to the box. Tod watched a moment, then used a small cardboard box from the sand pile to carry sand.

As these examples indicate, play is a most useful evaluation tool in the kindergarten and primary grades where time and equipment are provided in the school program for free dramatic play. One play incident may not be of great significance in telling of a child's view of life. But a series of incidents should give important indica-

Fig. 18. Miniature life toys

Psychologists who work with children often present a child with miniature life toys that may represent the home environment. As the child plays with the toys, the clinician may receive hints about the sources of the individual's emotional difficulties.

tions of some of the child's inner life that might not be revealed in direct conversation with an adult such as the teacher. The eight functions of play listed above are recommended as useful guides to the teacher who seeks the meaning of episodes in which children are observed.

In addition to observing dramatic play, psychologists use miniature-life toys in play sessions with young children. With toys that the child could identify as models of his home furnishings and the members of his family or neighborhood, he often is able to play out the fears and conflicts he feels. Frequently, the child cannot, or will not, tell his feelings about his schoolmates, his family, and his other companions. But the miniature-life toys allow him to achieve a psychological distance from himself so that he can play out problem situations and disturbed feelings without fearing that he is revealing his own life. When playing out unacceptable emotions or when expressing needs, he can feel safe by saying, "The doll did that. Of course, I wouldn't do such a thing."

In the clinic the miniature-life toy sessions not only bring to light important information about his frustrations and ideas of life but they also frequently result in a reduction of the child's disturbance. Consequently, play can function not only as an evaluation technique but also as therapy. As with other projective methods, the significance of much play is still incompletely understood. More research is needed.

Child art

Children's paintings and drawings have received much attention in the past decade as probable reflectors of personality. There are many magazine articles, numerous books, and an increasing number of summer-school courses in colleges directed at the interpretation of children's paintings. Despite the numbers of studies in which attempts have been made to determine the correlation between types of child art and personality functions, the real meaning of child art is not at all commonly agreed upon among psychologists. The greatest limitation in the use of drawing and painting for diagnostic purposes has been summed up by White (*11*) who writes that although there is "... no lack of ingenuity and stimulating ideas, the crying need is for validation."

The interpretation of children's drawings is a very complex process. Factors that must be considered include organization and content of the picture, color (varieties and amounts), types of lines, continuity of the whole, variety of forms, perspective, number of pictures in a sequence, contents of each picture in the sequence, size of paper, format of paper, placement of forms in the space, preference of media (such as poster paint, chalk, or crayon), and age of the child. Investigators have tried to determine what a particular element, such as use of vertical lines or placement of forms in one corner, means in children's lives. However, for the person who is seeking specific answers, the results have been very disappointing. The conclusions from one investigation conflict with the conclusions from another. Some experts claim that overpainting a picture reveals a need for the child to hide his feelings. Others say each overpainting is merely another episode in a story the child is telling in paints. Some believe tans and browns reveal depressive feelings; others heartily disagree.

This does not mean that a child's paintings may not help reflect personality factors. Rather, it suggests that red and blue circles probably mean something different in John's life from what they mean in Max's or Marie's lives. Hartley, Frank, and Goldenson have summed up the current state of affairs:

"The situation that really obtains seems to be the reverse of what teachers and clinicians are seeking. It would appear that one needs to know the child in order to understand his paintings. And conversely the paintings do not, in and of themselves, illuminate the child." [2]

Does this mean that artwork is not to be used by teachers, even partially, for assessing the needs and concerns of the child? No, artwork can help the teacher, for it often precipitates a discussion by the child. What the child says as he paints or as he shows his picture to the teacher may provide clues to his personal problems or his interpretation of life. But the way he does this will be peculiar to his own life and should not be generalized to the way other children would paint. An example of this is seen in the way a nursery-school girl painted during an experiment which involved her being frustrated by an adult prior to the painting session.

The child steps to the easel. She takes the brush from the black paint and starts at the right of the paper, making long vertical strokes that

[2] Ruth E. Hartley, Lawrence K. Frank, and Robert M. Goldenson, *Understanding Children's Play* (New York: Columbia University Press, 1952), p. 248.

overlap and cover the right quarter of the sheet. The brush goes off the bottom of the paper with each stroke.

CHILD: "This is an airplane. Look at its wings. Another wing." She still makes black verticals as she talks, punctuating her talk with the strokes.

CHILD: "People might get dead. *Bad* people might get dead. People might get dead. People might get dead. People might get dead in that plane. People might get dead in that plane. Hey, can I make a bomb? I want to make a bomb."

ADULT: "Whatever you like."

CHILD: "I want to make a potty." She paints a purple spot with crisscross lines in the center of the paper. She scrubs the paper hard. "People might get sick in that plane. People will come and shoot them. Now I am going to make a book. I am going to make a new Christmas light and a Christmas tree."

It would not be very helpful for the teacher to see only the final picture painted by this girl. However, the picture is valuable when we observe the process of painting it and hear the child's comments. Other sources of information about the girl tended to substantiate the hints from the painting session that the girl, though apparently calm and not outwardly disturbed when frustrated by adults, was actually disturbed and expressed it indirectly, as in painting. Other children in the identical frustrating situation would paint in their own individualistic ways and the meaning of the situation for them would apparently be different. Each would handle the situation in his unique manner (*9*).

Therefore, at the present time the *process* of painting and the *comments* made by children as they work or as they display the painting provide the most secure and valid sources of information about the meaning of art products in each child's life.

Other creative work

Children's free expression and creative work in other areas, such as the writing of stories or the development of spontaneous plays, is considered projective material. A child's concerns in life, his ideals, and his fears sometimes can be found in his creative writing in school. As with other kinds of evaluation, several such productions from a pupil will provide a better sample of his behavior than will only one story he writes. As dramatic play is more valuable to the primary teacher, so creative writing is more applicable to the middle and upper grades. Numerous topics serve as interesting stimuli for pupils' written work and also frequently provide information about the pupils as personalities. Common topics include: *My Life* or *My Autobiography, If I Had a Thousand Dollars, The Person I Most Admire, The Movie I Liked Most, What I Want To Be, A Fear I'd Like To Overcome,* and *A Daydream.* Stories children write on subjects of their own choosing are also valuable. The interpretation of this literary material in relation to the child's personality is not a simple matter. For instance, an eighth-grade boy has written an unconventional cowboy story in which the bad man first killed the hero, then married the pretty girl and ended up living happily with his stolen gold on the prosperous ranch he had secured through blackmail. Interpreting this in terms of the boy's personality, who is to say whether the eighth grader is *rebelling against authority* or is *trying to be individualistic to gain the teacher's attention* or is *cynically commenting on life's injustices?* Caution and much additional data are necessary before the significance of this one short story in relation to the boy's personality structure can be determined.

A variation of the short story, poem, or composition as projective material is the unfinished story. In this case the tester begins the story (one with considerable suspense), and the subject is asked to complete it.

Another variation of a written projective method is the sentence-completion test. There are commercially-produced tests of this type which consist of the first words of incomplete sentences that the child is to finish. Typical unfinished sentences are:

1. I am afraid that__________________________.
2. I like________________________________.
3. My mother____________________________.
4. Why do_______________________________.

A further type of projective material used occasionally with elementary-school children is the Three Wishes. In this case the clinician or teacher asks the child what he would wish for if by magic he could have any three wishes he wanted. His answers may provide additional insights into his interests, his worries, and his needs.

Summary

The foregoing discussion of projective techniques has merely touched the surface of a fascinating and rapidly growing area of personality assessment. The techniques discussed here have been the ones of most use and interest to teachers. For those further interested in this area, items 1, 2, 4, and 5 in the bibliography are recommended.

USES OF PROJECTIVE MATERIALS

In order to demonstrate that they understand the proper use of projective techniques with elementary and junior high children, teachers should be able to answer these questions: (1) How adequate are projective methods as personality measures? (2) To what extent should the teacher use projective materials with children, and what part of projective testing should be done only by trained clinicians?

Adequacy of projective techniques

Although projective methods have been found to be fruitful approaches to the appraisal of personalities of school children, the standardization and validation of the methods leave much to be desired. With more secure validation, projective techniques promise to yield more useful and accurate information than other personality measures. Unlike paper-pencil tests, answers to projective tests are difficult to fake, for the most acceptable or "correct" response is not obvious. In addition, they are not limited only to areas (such as social adjustment or family adjustment) which the test-maker thought important; instead, the projective material serves merely as a stimulus to set off non-restricted reactions of the pupil, rather than as a series of definite questions to be answered *Yes* or *No*.

Of the projective techniques available, "...none has yet established itself as a completely satisfactory instrument that may be safely used as a single accurate, objective diagnostic tool. They may be regarded as unique and valuable additions to the tools of the clinician working with school-age children (*a*) if interpretive results are regarded as *hypotheses* and *clues* to things which the subject is unable or unwilling to discuss concerning his own 'private world,' (*b*) if these results are obtained by a careful, trained examiner, and (*c*) if the techniques are used only with full awareness of their limitations and in conjunction with the findings of other measuring devices and case material." (*10*)

Teacher's and clinician's roles

Because the proper use of projective techniques depends upon special training and a knowledge of research in the field, the general use of these materials for personality diagnosis should rest upon the shoulders of the school psychologist who deals with children whose behavior deviates markedly from the average. A teacher recently remarked, "This Rorschach business is rather interesting. I was reading about it in a magazine. I'm going to get a book about it at the library and learn how to do it." Although the teacher's desire for personal and professional improvement is laudable, the expectation that he would be an adequate Rorschach tester after a few weeks of home study, or one year's study, is unrealistic and possibly dangerous. If the highly trained clinician has great difficulty deciding whether he has diagnosed a disturbed child's difficulties accurately, surely the teacher should be even more cautious in using the specialist's tools, which are yet in an early stage of development.

Tools like the Rorschach and Thematic Apperception Test should be left to the specialist. However, it is well for the teacher to be acquainted with the terms *projective technique* or *Rorschach* or *TAT* so as to know what they mean when they appear in the psychological report about a school child who has been tested by a specialist.

Then, should the elementary or junior high teacher ignore any possible personality clues in the children's short stories? Should the teacher never give any kind of sentence-completion test or never ask the children to write what they would ask for if they had three wishes? These are controversial questions. However, the present writer's opinion is that the classroom teacher surely should not ignore clues from any phase of a child's behavior (be it his action on the playground, his work on committees, or his short stories) which help the teacher understand him and fit classwork to his needs. The writer believes that the teacher should (1) make cautious use of hints and clues about meanings in a child's life that are revealed in projective materials, (2) limit his use to techniques that are normally associated with the school program (essays, stories, spontaneous puppet plays, dramatic play, art activities) and not attempt to use highly specialized techniques, (3) use projective materials only with full awareness of their limitations and in conjunction with the findings of other measuring devices and case material.

Two examples of educators using artwork as a reflector of something about a child's life will illustrate the difference between what the writer regards as proper use and improper use of projective material by a teacher.

Miss French teaches kindergarten in San Francisco. When children draw or paint, she admires their efforts and hangs up their pictures as a display around the room. Frequently she asks, "Do you want to tell me anything about it?"

One day a small, blond boy, George Baker, pointed to his painting and told her, "That's a house, and that's a boy looking out the window. He'd like to go out and play, but he can't. He has to stay in, but he'd like to go out."

Fig. 19. George's drawing

Being curious about this picture's significance, Miss French made inquiries about George's home and arranged a conference with Mrs. Baker. During the interview she learned that Mrs. Baker worked most of the time, and Mr. Baker attended college. When Mr. Baker was not in school, he was earning money by doing mimeograph work in his basement. The family lived on a busy street. Consequently, George was not allowed to play outside without some supervision, and he could not be supervised when his mother worked and his father operated the mimeograph machine. By knowing these facts, Miss French better understood the pressures operating in George's life and could understand something of his feelings about having to stay in after school. She could understand why such feelings might result in such a picture as he had drawn. Miss French said that this information helped her provide more outdoor activities at school for George to make up for his restricted play life at home. The conference also made the Bakers more aware of their son's concern, and they said they would try to arrange more outside play for him and a chance to make more friends in his neighborhood. Therefore, through cautious interpretation of George's painting and his story about it, Miss French contributed toward a happier life for the boy.

Miss Doe was recently hired as the art supervisor of a large elementary school. She stressed the belief that children should have opportunities for free expression in art, a philosophy most of the teachers agreed with. In addition, Miss Doe continually sought evidences of children's inner life in specific elements of their paintings (such as color or line); this was a practice about which most of the teachers wondered. The art supervisor invited the assistant principal to one of the second-grade classrooms one Friday afternoon shortly before the children were to go home. She did this to demonstrate how the paintings, when interpreted properly, revealed the core of a child's frustrations and motives. Several paintings were attached to the bulletin board. Miss Doe nodded at one, which she indicated had been painted by Carlo, and she pointed out the way the confused lines were indicative of the confusion in this particular second-grade boy's life. He was from a broken home in which there had been much violent argument before the parents' separation. In school he was often sullen and quick to anger. Miss Doe pointed out that these characteristics of the boy's personality (confusion from the broken home, resentment of parents, sullen attitude and underlying anger) were evident in his painting, which consisted of crisscrossed reds and blacks.

By this time the second-grade children in the room had put their coats on and were leaving for home. Several children began to unpin their paintings from the bulletin board. Janice, a girl in braids, unpinned the red and black painting. When Miss Doe stopped her,

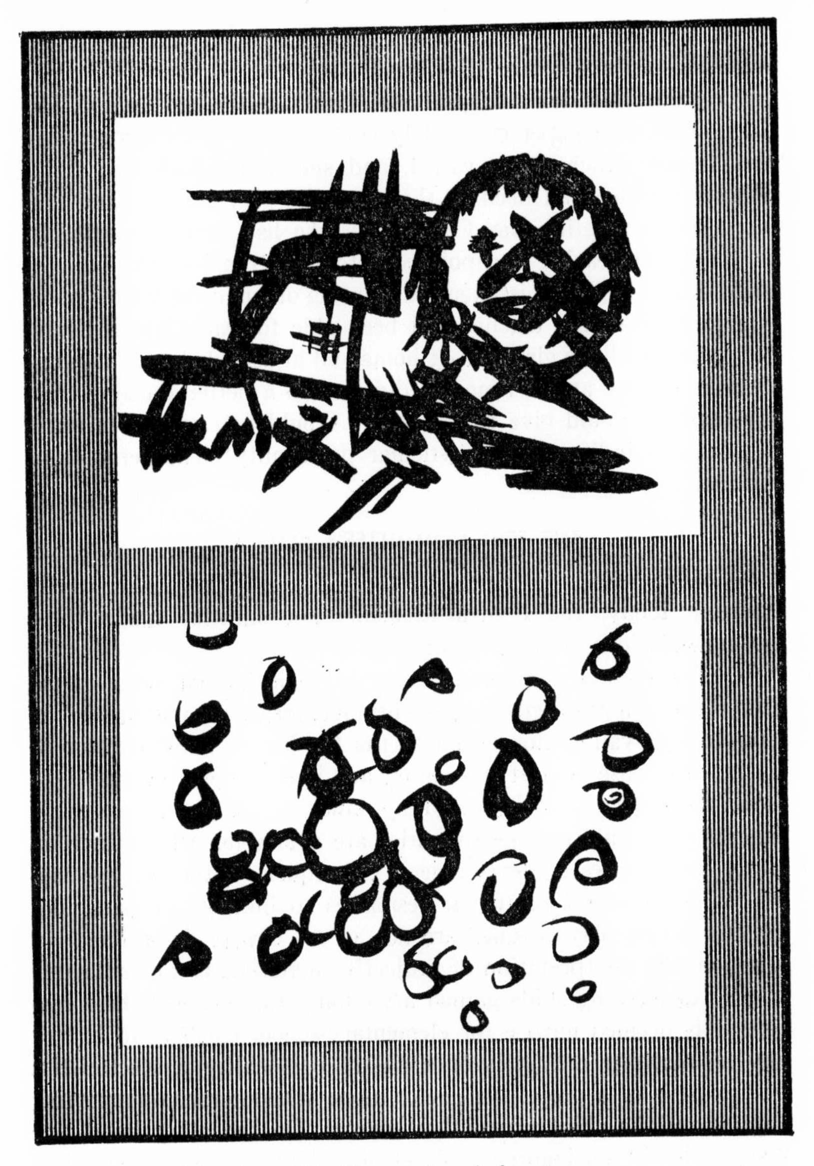

Fig. 20. The confused drawings
The art supervisor took the top picture to be Carlo's. But the top one was by Janice, and the bottom one by Carlo.

Janice said it was her painting and the teacher had said they could take their pictures home. Miss Doe insisted the picture was Carlo's. Janice said, "No, it's mine. That's Carlo's . . . the next one." The girl pointed to a paper completely covered with green circles. The second-grade teacher was called, and she said Janice was right. When Miss Doe had been in the room the previous day and had asked which painting was Carlo's (for she had been interested in his case), the teacher had pointed across the room to the bulletin board. Miss Doe had mistaken the painting of Janice at the distance. Janice, from all the teacher had been able to learn, was a happy and successful little girl both at home and at school. Janice's unpinning the picture at the time she did seemed a better warning than any textbook could give that teachers should be cautious in using paintings as indicators of particular personality characteristics of children.

THE TEST COMMITTEE'S REPORT

Following a brief description of several kinds of personality tests available today, the Central-Elementary committee made these recommendations to the faculty:

"1. *Paper-pencil personality tests.* In their present stage of development, paper-pencil adjustment inventories do not appear to offer enough valid information to the teacher or administrator to warrant their use in most elementary and junior high schools.

"2. *Projective techniques.* Many kinds of projective materials for studying children's personalities are available. All are in relatively early stages of development. Consequently, the real psychological meanings of particular responses to inkblots or particular actions during play sessions are not as yet clearly determined. In addition, the interpretation of projective materials is a complicated process demanding skills gained after long training. For these reasons it is deemed unwise for elementary-school teachers to hazard any far-reaching estimates of a child's personality characteristics on the basis of a projective device alone without much supporting data about the child from other sources. On the other hand, the teacher should not ignore any facet of a child's activities, including such things as his drawings, paintings, and play patterns. Careful observation of the child's actions in the projective situations should lend additional evidence to build a more complete and rounded portrait of every individual in a classroom."

OBJECTIVES OF THIS CHAPTER

The effective elementary or junior high teacher:

1. States advantages and disadvantages of paper-pencil personality inventories and of projective techniques.
2. Uses paper-pencil inventories only for class screening or initiating an interview, if he uses them at all.
3. Does not attempt to use highly specialized projective devices.
4. Uses data from normal classroom projective situations (such as children's stories or dramatic play) with considerable caution and only in conjunction with supporting evidence from other sources.

Suggested evaluation techniques for this chapter

1. For an age-level of your choice, construct a ten-sentence test of the sentence-completion variety. Design the test to elicit student responses directed at one or two areas of their lives. The area might be parent-child relationships, peer relationships, school success, feelings of confidence about tasks attempted, physical and mental health, or attitudes toward authority. Have a fellow teacher or university classmate of yours inspect your test and offer opinions about how well he thinks: (*a*) pupils will complete the sentences without feeling unduly threatened psychologically, (*b*) the questions will elicit responses pertinent to the areas of life you are interested in investigating, (*c*) pupils of this age will understand the meaning of the sentences. After adding any revisions to the test in light of your companion's evaluation, try out the test with a group of children.
2. Select an area of life in which you would like to investigate student reactions or feelings, such as home relations, boy-girl relations, peer relations, or feelings toward rules and authorities. Search through discarded popular magazines to find five pictures that might elicit pupil reactions concerning the areas you are interested in. Cut out and mount the pictures. Then try them out with a group of children, using a standard form of instructions that you write, such as: "Write a short story telling what is going on in the picture. Tell what the people are saying or thinking. You may want to tell what happened just before the scene in the picture."

   If you are working with an individual child, you may wish to have him tell the story orally rather than write it.

   Try to determine what cautious, safe conclusions (if any)

can be drawn about the children's attitudes from the stories they constructed.

3. Write three incomplete stories designed to elicit pupil reactions that reflect feelings or attitudes about some area of their personal life, such as child-adult relations, feelings toward freedom and control by parents, or a self-concept. Try these out with several children to determine whether the stories do indeed stimulate pupils to give responses that might be useful in understanding the area under investigation.

SUGGESTED READINGS

1. ANDERSON, HAROLD H., and ANDERSON, GLADYS L. *An Introduction to Projective Techniques.* New York: Prentice-Hall, Inc., 1951. Experts explain the theory and use of specific, more advanced devices.
2. BELL, J. E. *Projective Techniques.* New York: Longmans, Green and Co., 1948. Survey of techniques and early research on them.
3. BUROS, O. K. Four yearbooks containing excellent evaluations of many kinds of tests.
   (a) *The 1938 Mental Measurements Yearbook.* New Brunswick, N.J.: Rutgers University Press, 1938.
   (b) *The 1940 Mental Measurements Yearbook.* Highland Park, N.J.: The Mental Measurements Yearbook, 1941.
   (c) *The Third Mental Measurements Yearbook.* New Brunswick, N.J.: Rutgers University Press, 1949.
   (d) *The Fourth Mental Measurements Yearbook.* Highland Park, N.J.: Gryphon Press, 1953.
4. GREENE, EDWARD B. *Measurements of Human Behavior.* New York: Odyssey Press, 1952. Clear discussions of various techniques.
5. HARTLEY, RUTH E.; FRANK, LAWRENCE K.; and GOLDENSON, ROBERT M. *Understanding Children's Play.* New York: Columbia University Press, 1952. Interesting, detailed study of the use of popular projective techniques with nursery-school and kindergarten age children.
6. MALLER, J. B. "Personality Tests," in J. McV. Hunt, ed., *Personality and the Behavior Disorders,* Vol. I. New York: Ronald Press, 1944.
7. ROTHMAN, ESTHER, and BERKOWITZ, PEARL. "The Language Arts Program as Personality Projection," *Understanding the Child,* National Association for Mental Health, Vol. XXII, No. 1 (January, 1953).
8. STEPHENS, J. M. *Educational Psychology.* New York: Henry Holt and Co., 1951.

9. THOMAS R. MURRAY. "Effects of Frustration on Children's Painting," unpublished doctoral dissertation. Stanford University, 1950.
10. THOMAS, SHIRLEY M. "Selected Projective Techniques for the Study of Personality of School Children," unpublished doctoral dissertation. Stanford University, 1949.
11. WHITE, R. W. "Interpretation of Imaginative Productions," in J. McV. Hunt, ed., *Personality and the Behavior Disorders,* Vol. I. New York: Ronald Press, 1944.

CHAPTER

7

Using Statistics

ONE MORNING just before school began, Mr. Harris, the assistant principal, stepped into the room of Miss Jane Solski, one of the three fourth-grade teachers.

"Say Jane, I'd like you to take charge of giving those arithmetic achievement tests to the fourth grade. You give Miss Cohen and Mrs. Jensen enough for their classes, and be sure they understand the directions for administering the tests properly. And I'd also appreciate it if in a couple of days you would give me a brief summary of how the three classes compared. I'm collecting information to see how the three groups stand according to their apparent ability."

Miss Solski gave the other fourth-grade teachers the tests to administer and asked them to give her the students' scores as soon as the tests were corrected. She told them, "I don't need the individual children's names, just a list of the scores so that we can compare the groupings. Later we can look over the individual scores for guidance of particular children."

In each class 50 pupils took the test. The highest possible score was 85. Following are the lists of scores from the three classes:

Class I (Miss Solski): 67, 61, 64, 58, 61, 68, 65, 65, 63, 71, 57, 74, 72, 60, 65, 66, 69, 66, 66, 62, 72, 66, 66, 65, 62, 63, 69, 66, 62, 64, 66, 64, 71, 62, 64, 66, 67, 62, 69, 67, 64, 66, 65, 68, 63, 66, 65, 67, 64, 64.

Class II (Miss Cohen): 67, 73, 68, 71, 70, 72, 66, 71, 69, 70, 75, 69, 68, 71, 68, 64, 71, 67, 74, 69, 69, 72, 65, 71, 70, 71, 73, 66, 67,

67, 71, 74, 58, 71, 68, 71, 67, 73, 70, 69, 70, 68, 73, 71, 71, 70, 68, 69, 70, 69.

Class III (Mrs. Jensen): 67, 71, 72, 58, 63, 62, 66, 73, 67, 66, 61, 63, 64, 59, 69, 74, 71, 59, 65, 66, 68, 70, 73, 60, 66, 63, 75, 58, 67, 61, 61, 62, 66, 68, 71, 72, 60, 67, 66, 59, 61, 73, 68, 61, 70, 63, 74, 72, 71, 71.

The easiest thing for Miss Solski to do would be to hand these lists of scores to Mr. Harris, but such a report would not fulfill his request for a "brief summary of how well the three classes compare." In this form the scores are a jumble of numbers which make little or no sense. However, there are several simple ways the fourth-grade teacher could organize the scores so that they would show immediately how the classes compare. *This is the function of statistics: to organize a mass of data into some understandable form.*

Class I (Miss Solski)		Class II (Miss Cohen)		Class III (Mrs. Jensen)	
Score	*Students*	*Score*	*Students*	*Score*	*Students*
75		75	/	75	/
74	/	74	//	74	//
73		73	////	73	///
72	//	72	//	72	///
71	//	71	𝍸 𝍸 /	71	𝍸
70		70	𝍸 //	70	//
69	///	69	𝍸 //	69	/
68	//	68	𝍸 /	68	///
67	////	67	𝍸	67	////
66	𝍸 𝍸	66	//	66	𝍸 /
65	𝍸 /	65	/	65	/
64	𝍸 //	64	/	64	/
63	///	63		63	////
62	𝍸	62		62	//
61	//	61		61	𝍸
60	/	60		60	//
59		59		59	///
58	/	58	/	58	//
57	/	57		57	

Fig. 21. Tally sheet

TALLY SHEET OR GRAPH

One method of arranging the scores would be to make an ordered list of them, and beside each number place a tally mark for each student who achieved that score. In this way Miss Solski would be able to develop a tally sheet. Note that she would not list all possible scores from 0 to 85 but only the range of scores from the highest to the lowest that any of the children achieved; in this case it is from 57 to 75.

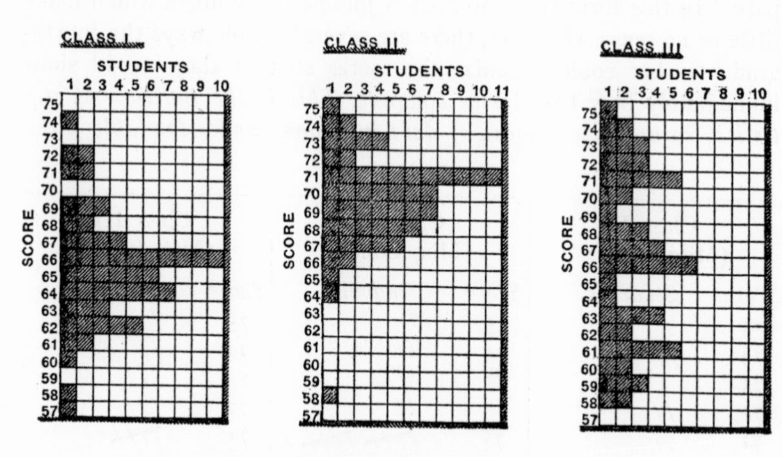

Fig. 22. Bar graph

The same data shown on the tally sheet could be recorded instead on a bar graph (sometimes called a *histogram*) on which the number of students attaining a particular score would be indicated by the length of the bar (Fig. 22). Or the data might be reported as a profile (often called a *frequency polygon*) as seen in Figure 23.

The tally sheet or graph helps answer the assistant principal's question. Brief inspection of one of the graphs indicates that Class II was generally superior to I and III. It also shows that the students' scores within Class I and within Class II were bunched together more than those of Class III, where the students were strung out over a wide range.

Although the tally sheet or graph would help Mr. Harris, he might well remark, "I can see that Class II was best, but I can't quite make out which was second best, I or III." Therefore, the tally sheet gives a general comparison among classes, but a more specific report of

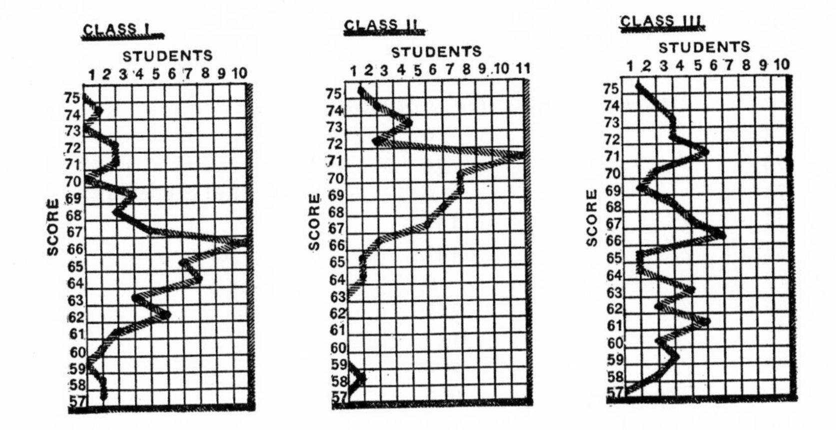

Fig. 23. Frequency polygon

their achievement is desired. Which was second best? And which did the poorest?

COMPUTING AVERAGES

There are two good ways Miss Solski can determine the average attainment of each class more accurately than by looking at the graph.

Mean

One way would be to find the *average score,* which is called the *mean.* The mean (sometimes referred to as the *arithmetic mean* or *arithmetic average*) is computed simply by adding up all of the scores and dividing that total by the number of students who took the test. The process for doing this with Class I is shown in Figure 24.

As Figure 24 indicates, each score is multiplied by the number of students who attained that score. This product is placed in a column at the right, and the column is added. The sum at the bottom is divided by the number of tally marks, that is, by the total number of students who took the test. The resulting answer is the *average score* or the *mean* for the class.

The formula for computing the mean is:

$$\frac{\text{Total of all scores}}{\text{Number of students}} = \text{Mean}$$

CLASS I ARITHMETIC TEST SCORES

Score	*Students*	*Score Times Students*
75		0
74	/	74
73		0
72	//	144
71	//	142
70		0
69	///	207
68	//	136
67	////	268
66	~~////~~ ~~////~~	660
65	~~////~~ /	390
64	~~////~~ //	448
63	///	189
62	~~////~~	310
61	//	122
60	/	60
59		0
58	/	58
57	/	57
	Total	3,265

Number of Students = 50

```
       65.3
50)3265.0
   300
    265
    250
     150
     150
```

Mean = 65.3

Fig. 24. Computing mean from raw scores

By computing the means for the three classes and by comparing them, Miss Solski clears up any doubt about which class averaged second best and which was last. Class III with a mean of 66.3 is slightly better than Class I with a mean of 65.3. Obviously, Class II with a mean of 69.5 is considerably better than the other two.

Median

There is a different kind of average that would also answer the principal's question about which class was second best and which was poorest. This kind of average is called the *median* and is sometimes used instead of the mean because it is easier to compute for scores that have already been listed on a tally sheet or graph. The median is the *half-way student*, or, more precisely, it is the point on the scale of measurement above which are exactly half of the cases and below which are the other half.

In the simplest form, the median or half-way student can be found by counting the tally marks. In the cases of these fourth-grade classes in which 50 students took the test, the half-way point would be between student 25 and student 26 in each class. Since there would be no student at this half-way point, the point half-way between them would be called the median. If there had been 51 children in each class, child 26 would be the half-way student, and his score on the test would be called the median. When there is an even number of children, the half-way point comes between two children's scores.

Looking at the tally sheet, we see that within each of the three classes student 25 and student 26 both achieved the same score. Thus, the median in Class III is 66 compared to the median of 65 for Class I. The Class II median is 70. Like the mean, the median in this case would answer the assistant principal's question about which class came out second and which was last. It should be noted that the mean and median for a distribution will be the same or almost the same *unless* one end of the distribution of scores tends to be strung out farther from the center than does the other end.

In some cases a more accurate determination of the median, carried out to tenths or hundredths, is desired. For example, if there had been a Class IV to take the test in addition to the other three, the half-way point for Class IV might have been at score 66, the same as Class III. Then Mr. Harris might have asked, "Are classes III and IV, each with a 66, exactly the same on the average, or is one just very slightly better than the other as far as medians are concerned?" In this situation, where several students have the same score at the center of the class, the teacher can use the method described in Appendix B, Part II, to answer Mr. Harris' question. In general, however, such a problem does not arise in the elementary school. If two classes have the same median, as in this example, any such very slight difference is of no practical importance to the teacher or administrator. For practical purposes the medians of classes III and IV are the same.

Computing different medians

It is important at this point to indicate a characteristic of most test scores and measurements which is sometimes ignored but which can be important when computing medians and also percentiles, as we shall see later. When we make a measurement, we decide what unit will be most practical for us to use. For example, in measuring the length of a ship we decide the most practical unit will be feet, and we report the length as 121 feet. In making such a report we realize that, as with almost all other measurements, the length is not precisely 121 feet from the standpoint of extremely precise measurement. Actually our ship is very slightly longer. However, since the length is closer to 121 feet than it is to 122, we report it as 121. We see, therefore, that when we use the term *121 feet* we mean any measurement closer to 121 feet than to either 120 or 122 feet. Our term *121 feet* actually represents an interval ranging from 120.5 to 121.5. The number we commonly use and report, 121, is the middle of this interval. Likewise, the term *122 feet* would represent measurements in the interval from 121.5 to 122.5. And 122 is the midpoint of that interval.

Like these measurements, test scores in education and psychology are also regarded as being not specific and definite points but being a range around a point or score. Therefore, we reason that the student who receives a score of 45 is really scoring within an interval whose lower limit is 44.5 and whose upper limit is 45.5. Of two students who receive total test scores of 45, one may really be slightly better than 45 but closer to the 45 than to 46. The other student may not actually be quite as good as 45, but he is closer to it than to 44. Consequently, in our testing system, which uses only whole units, these two students have received scores within the same interval.

One value of thinking of a score, such as 45, as really representing an interval from 44.5 to 45.5 is seen when the median falls between two scores or intervals. Here is such an instance of dart-game scores at a class party.

Scores	10	11	12	13	14	15	16	17	18	19	20
Number of Students Receiving These Scores	1	4	4	3	7	8	2	3	4	1	1

In the situation above, 38 students tried tossing darts at the target. Beginning at the bottom of the distribution, we count 19 students and find that the median will be between scores 14 and 15. Thus, it will be 14.5 since this is the point of division between intervals 14 and 15.

In another situation there may be no students within the interval or at the score where the median would fall. When this happens, the median is the midpoint of that blank interval. The median falls at this middle score, 14, even though no one has received the score.

Scores	9	10	11	12	13	14	15	16	17	18
Students	3		5	3	1		3	3	4	2

Sometimes it happens that two or more blank intervals occur where the median should fall. In such instances, the median becomes the midpoint of these blank intervals. In the following example the median would be 13.5 or the midpoint of scores 13 and 14.

Scores	8	9	10	11	12	13	14	15	16	17	18
Students	1	1	3	5	3			6	5		2

The average to report

The question now arises, "If there are two kinds of averages, the mean and the median, which should I choose to report?"

If this were a book on statistics for research workers, it would be worth while to discuss subtle distinctions between these two kinds of averages. However, it is sufficient for elementary-school teachers to realize that the *median* is usually easier to compute, especially when a fairly large number of scores is involved. The *mean,* on the other hand, is more commonly understood as "the average," and it has certain advantages if more complex statistics are to be computed. The teacher may choose the one he prefers, but he always should identify which one it is he is reporting.

SPREAD OF SCORES

If the fourth-grade teacher chose to report only an average (either mean or median) without including the tally sheet in the report, it is obvious that she would be misleading the assistant principal about how well the classes had succeeded. Receiving the report that Class I had a mean of 65.3, Class II a mean of 69.5, and Class III a mean of 66.3, Mr. Harris would logically conclude that classes I and III were almost alike, whereas Class II was somewhat superior. However, inspection of the graphs shows that *reporting only an average for a class does not tell an accurate story.* Despite their similar means, classes I and III are markedly different. In Class I the scores tend to bunch together around the average, whereas in Class III they are strung out gradually over a wider range.

Such a fact about the ranging of scores would be important to the administrators in a school where it was deemed desirable to group children in classes according to their success in schoolwork.

The administrators would want all of the children whose abilities were similar to be placed in one class. This fact of the range of scores would be equally important in a school where the administrators *did not* want children homogeneously grouped into lower and higher ability sections. In the case of either school's policy, information about the spread of talent within classes would be important. Consequently, it would be a mistake to report only the averages of the classes without some measure of whether the scores were bunched or spread out. In Class III there are obviously quite a number of children at each of the levels (low, middle, and high) on the arithmetic test. But a mean or a median alone does not tell this fact.

If Mr. Harris saw the tally sheet, he would see the obvious difference between classes I and III. However, it would not be necessary to provide the sheet to tell this story, since there are ways of describing accurately and briefly whether the scores are grouped tightly together around the center or are strung out.

Why not the range?

When they wish to show the extent to which scores are dispersed, some teachers use the rather obvious though inaccurate method of reporting the *distance from the lowest to the highest score in each class*. This statistic is called the *total range*. The fact that the range does not tell a true story of the spread of scores of the *majority of the class* is demonstrated by the fourth-grade groups. In these classes the range is the same in each case, 18 points inclusive. But such a report to the administrator would mislead him to believe the classes were the same as far as the bunching of scores is concerned. The reason the total range is misleading is that it is determined by the *extreme top and bottom scores only;* whereas, what Mr. Harris really wanted to know was how much the bulk of the class or the majority of the scores bunched together. The range, although easy to compute, should *not* be used in Miss Solski's report.

Although the range should not be used, there are other kinds of statistics that will tell an accurate story about the extent to which scores are dispersed. Two kinds of *measures of dispersion* or *measures of score-spread* are useful for teachers to know. The first, *distance between percentiles,* is closely related to the median, for it is computed in about the same manner, that is, by counting tally marks. This distance between percentiles is simple to compute and to understand and therefore is a handy tool for the elementary-school teacher to be able to use. It will be explained in the following pages. The second type of measure of dispersion, called the *standard deviation,* is seldom computed by elementary-school teachers but is commonly used in research on school problems. A knowledge of the standard deviation is less essential in the teacher's daily work but is very helpful for understanding educational articles and standardized-test manuals. The standard deviation and its relation to the normal-distribution curve are explained in Appendix B, Part III.

Percentiles

In order to understand how the distance between percentiles can be used to describe how much the scores of a class are bunched, it is first necessary to understand what percentile means. The term *percentile* (sometimes called *centile*) is used to indicate a *point below which a certain percentage of the class's scores fall.* From this definition we see that the median, which is the point below which one-half of the cases fall, can also be called the 50th percentile.

Percentiles have various uses in an elementary-school classroom. For instance, the teacher can use the percentile to describe where a particular student ranked in relation to his classmates. As an example we may use Helen Stimson who had a score of 60 on the arithmetic test in Miss Solski's class. (See Fig. 21.) The teacher wishes to tell what percentage of the class scored below Helen. Only two other students had lower scores than she did. To find the percentage of scores below Helen, the teacher divides 2 (the number of scores below Helen's) by 50 (the total number of students in the class). The resulting per cent is 4. Thus, it can be said that Helen scored above the 4th percentile. That is, she scored above the point below which 4 per cent of the class fell. The formula for discovering the percentile at which a student scored would be this:

$$\frac{\text{The number of students below this individual}}{\text{Total number of students}} = \text{Percentile}$$

Distance between percentiles

Another use for percentiles, and the one of immediate interest to Miss Solski, is to describe *how much the scores of one class bunch together compared with the scores of another class.* It was seen above that the teacher should not use the total range to describe how much the scores of the bulk of the class spread out or bunch together, because a unique student at the top or bottom extreme of the class can distort the general class picture. However, if the teacher can move farther up the scale from the bottom and then move a short distance down from the top of the class, he can be more sure of describing how the bulk of the class spread out, not just the extremes. Using percentiles is one way of solving this problem.

For example, the teacher could use the popular technique of reporting the range of scores of the middle half of the class. This eliminates deviates at the top and bottom extremes. It is probable that Miss Solski would use this technique because it is easy to compute.

The range of the middle half of the class is called the *interquartile range*. It is found by counting (counting students, not score points) one-fourth of the way up from the bottom and marking that score, then counting one fourth of the way down from the top student and marking that score. Obviously, by doing this we are marking the point where the 25th percentile falls (a quarter of the way up from the bottom) and where the 75th percentile falls (a quarter of the way down from the top). The middle half of the class is found between these two scores. In the case of the fourth-grade classes, Miss Solski would count 12½ students (that is, ¼ or 25 per cent of the 50 students in each class) up from the bottom and 12½ students down from the top. This would give her the following scores:

	Class I	*Class II*	*Class III*
¼ way down from top (75th percentile)	67	71	71
¼ way up from bottom (25th percentile)	63	68	62
Interquartile range	4 points	3 points	9 points

Thus, Miss Solski is able to show that Class II had the greatest bunching together of scores, for the middle half of the class scored within 3 points of each other. Class I had a slightly greater spread of scores with the middle half of the class getting marks within 4 points of each other. On the other hand, in Class III the students had such varied success with the test that the middle half of the group was strung out over a range of 9 points. Now it can be seen that Miss Solski could summarize accurately how the bulk of the classes' scores were dispersed by reporting the distance between the 25th and 75th percentiles for each group. Or, if she preferred, she could use the distance between the 20th and 80th percentiles or the distance between the 15th and 85th percentiles as a method of describing how much the bulk of the classes' scores spread out. The administrator, reading her report, would know that the larger the number of the distance between percentiles, the more the scores spread out (as in Class III with a 9). The smaller the number, the more the scores bunched together, as in Class II with 3 points between the 25th and 75th percentiles.

By following the above reasoning, Miss Solski would not have to include her original tally sheet with the summary, but she could give the assistant principal the following accurate, brief report. (Note: It is especially helpful for a teacher to eliminate the tally sheet when she has to report scores for a fairly large number of tests or classes. The tally sheets can be both unwieldy and confusing if there are many of them or if a very large number of students has been tested.)

To: Mr. Harris
From: Miss Solski
Regarding: Arithmetic Achievement Tests Administered to Three Fourth-grades.

	Class I (Miss Solski)	*Class II* (Miss Cohen)	*Class III* (Mrs. Jensen)
Number of Students	50	50	50
Median	65	70	66
Distance from 25th to 75th percentile	4 points	3 points	9 points

These few numbers tell how the classes compared in general. If Mr. Harris is acquainted with simple classroom statistics, he will be able to read the story from this summary. However, if Miss Solski is not sure that the assistant principal or some other teacher will interpret the figures correctly, she might include a short interpretation with the report, such as:

"As shown by the averages (medians), Class II in general scored considerably higher than classes I and III. The majority of Class II students had very similar success on the test (the middle half of the class made scores within 3 points of each other). In Class I the scores also tended to bunch around the class center. However, in Class III the students' success was quite varied, as evidenced by the middle half of the students scoring over a range of 9 points, more than twice that of either of the other two classes."

A special case of percentiles. Occasionally a percentile, such as the 25th, falls between two scores rather than directly within an interval as in the above cases. When this happens, the problem is handled in the same way outlined for a median that falls between two scores. That is, the midpoint between the two scores becomes the percentile.

SUMMARY

It is seen by the discussion in the foregoing sections that two types of statistics are commonly used to describe how well a class has succeeded on a test.

The first type is a measure of how the class as an *average* succeeded, that is, where the center of the class tended to be. The median, which is the half-way student, and the mean, which is the average score, are two types of averages.

The second type of statistic needed to describe a class's success is a measure of the extent to which the scores *bunched* around the center or *spread out* from the center. The distance between percentiles was suggested as a simple method of describing this dispersion of scores.

INTERPRETING SIMPLE STATISTICS

The example of the fourth-grade classes indicates how a teacher can take a mass of raw scores and by using graphs or statistics can in a simple manner tell what these scores mean. However, unlike the above situation, the teacher is often not the one who reports the statistics but is the one who must interpret them. When a person interprets statistics, he merely begins with the final product described above (for example, the report to Mr. Harris) and mentally works backwards. That is, he interprets the numbers presented by trying to reconstruct in his mind the steps that led up to them. The following example shows how this is done.

Mr. Kelly teaches health practices to two eighth-grade classes. He wished to know whether a textbook method or a project method of teaching the classes would be better for his students. Consequently, he decided to combine lectures with assigned textbook readings as the method of instruction in Class I. In Class II he planned to cover the same facts of diet, sanitation, and control of disease by carrying out demonstrations in class and by assigning students to work in groups to complete experiments and projects under his guidance. Before beginning this unit of teaching he constructed a 50-item test covering his objectives for the six-week health unit. On the first day of the unit he gave the test to both classes to determine how much the students already knew about the topics (pretesting). Then, after the six-week period he gave another equivalent form of the same test to each class (final testing). Our present task is to use the following statistics which Mr. Kelly gathered to answer these questions:

1. Were the two classes relatively the same at the beginning?
2. Did the classes improve as a result of the unit?
3. Were the two classes relatively the same at the end of the unit?
4. What effect did teaching the health unit have on the bunching or spreading out of scores?
5. Judging by the results of these 50-item tests (which admittedly constitute a somewhat limited type of evaluation), which teaching method did Mr. Kelly apparently use more successfully?

HEALTH TESTS

	Class I		*Class II*	
	Pretest	*Final Test*	*Pretest*	*Final Test*
Number	37	37	35	35
Median	10	32	11	40
75th %ile	14	38	15	46
25th %ile	6	25	6	30
	—	—	—	—
Distance between %iles	8	13	9	16

To interpret these statistics and answer the questions, you may be able to picture in your mind what the distribution of scores for each of these four testings must have been to yield such results. Or, if at first it is difficult to imagine what the distributions would look like, you can easily draw a portion of the apparent distributions on a piece of paper; this simplifies the process of interpreting. For example, the health-test results might be plotted in this manner. Numbers 0 through 50 (or perhaps it may be done quicker by 5's) are written up the left margin of a sheet of paper. Across the top the four test titles are indicated. Next, an **X** is placed where the median for each testing is found. Then a line drawn across at the 25th and one at the 75th percentiles will show how the middle half of the classes' scores bunched together or spread out. Such a procedure would result in a chart like Figure 25.

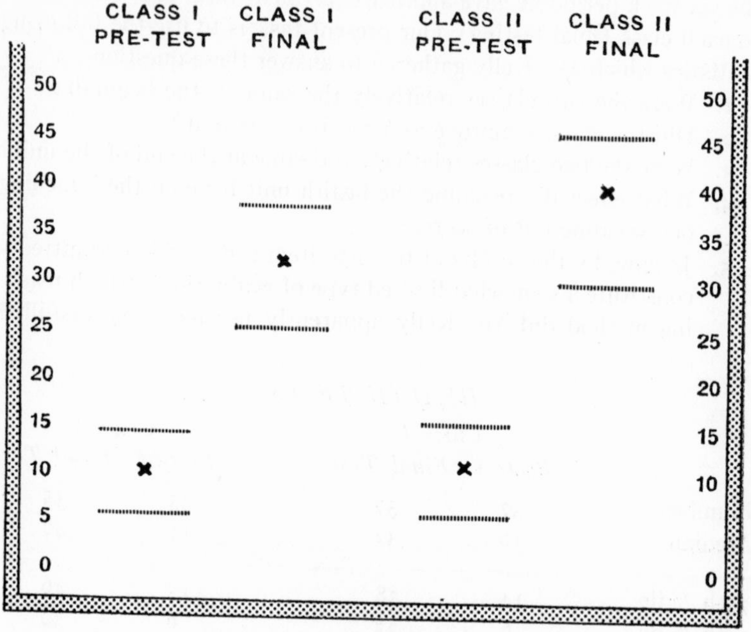

Fig. 25. Interpretation of test results

The process of interpreting statistics is done most rapidly when the reader can do the plotting in his imagination without actually needing to sketch out the data on paper. However, when in doubt it is best to do the simple type of plotting described here.

When the results are sketched out in this manner, the answers to the questions are readily seen.

1. Yes, the two classes were relatively the same on the pretest. Their averages were almost alike, and their scores were bunched together to about the same extent.
2. Yes, both classes improved as a result of the health unit.
3. Class II, taught by the project method, improved more than Class I, taught by lecture and text readings.
4. In regard to the spreading-out of scores, in Class I the middle group of students were bunched together more closely on the pretest than on the final. This same pattern of change

from pretest to final was true in Class II; however, in Class II the scores on the final were even more spread out than in Class I. From these data we conclude that on the *pretest* the students within a class were more like each other (that is, more homogeneous) in regard to health information than they were at the end of the unit. Apparently, some students learned a great deal during the six weeks and therefore their scores shot up markedly on the final. Other students learned, but not so much; as a result their scores did not show such a marked improvement, which would cause the observed stringing-out of the scores on the final.

OTHER USES OF PERCENTILES

Two uses of percentiles have been described so far: (1) to indicate what percentage of his classmates a student scored above, and (2) to indicate how the scores of a class spread out or bunched by showing the distance between two percentiles.

Percentiles are also quite useful in comparing a child's scores on several tests of different lengths. For instance, a sixth grader, Sam Stelt, took four tests which the teacher had constructed and administered during the semester. The tests had the following numbers of total points possible:

Test A = 90 Test B = 40 Test C = 54 Test D = 20

Sam's scores on the tests were:

Test A = 73 Test B = 30 Test C = 39 Test D = 19

A parent, an administrator, or another teacher, seeing only the raw scores Sam received, would very likely conclude that the boy did best on Test A, for he received the highest number of points on it. The raw scores might also lead to the conclusion that Sam did about as well on B as he did on C and that he did quite poorly on D. Such conclusions would be very inaccurate. These raw scores are not at all comparable because: (1) there were different total points possible on each and (2) it is possible that the items on one test were easier than those on another; the raw scores on an easy test are not comparable to those on a difficult one even when the total points possible on each are the same.

However, Sam's scores can become meaningful and can be compared if they are changed into percentiles. To do this, the sixth grade teacher looked at tally sheets for the four tests in order to locate in each case where Sam ranked in comparison to his classmates. The teacher found that he was twenty-fourth up from the bottom of his class of 35 students on Test A, twenty-seventh from the bottom on Test B, nineteenth on Test C, and thirty-fourth on Test D. Using the formula for computing a student's percentile rank (that is, divide the number of people below a student's rank by the total number in class), the teacher determined the following percentiles for Sam.

Test A = 66th percentile   Test C = 51st percentile
Test B = 74th percentile   Test D = 94th percentile

Now it is seen how Sam actually compared with the rest of the class. He was above average (50th percentile) on all tests. He succeeded best on Test D, next best on Test B.

Some teachers and guidance workers like to use a graphic method of recording test scores that have been converted into percentiles. The percentiles usually are listed up the margin and a vertical line is used to represent each test. The child's percentile scores then can be marked at the proper place on each line. Such a form as that shown in Figure 26 can be mimeographed to indicate the number of tests to be included. Then it is a simple matter for the teacher to write the student's name and the date of the test, and to place an **X** on the vertical lines at the proper percentiles. When all the tests are recorded on a pupil's record sheet, it is common practice to connect the **X**'s to form a *test profile,* that is, to form a picture of the child's success on the tests.

(Note on making the test profile sheet: As shown in Figure 26, when centiles are listed up the margin to form a chart it is customary to bunch the numbers together at the center and spread them out at the ends, because this describes more accurately the relationships among students in the center and at the extremes of a distribution. There is more difference between the students at the 5th and 10th centiles than there is between the students at the 45th and 50th centiles.)

REPORTING TESTS TO PARENTS

Occasionally, a teacher or administrator finds it appropriate to discuss a child's success on aptitude or achievement tests with his parents. Because the raw scores on a test have little if any meaning to a parent, the test results are probably best reported as percentiles. In most cases the teacher can make the pupil's achievement clear by such an explanation as: "Jim did better than 60 per cent of his classmates. Forty per cent did better than he."

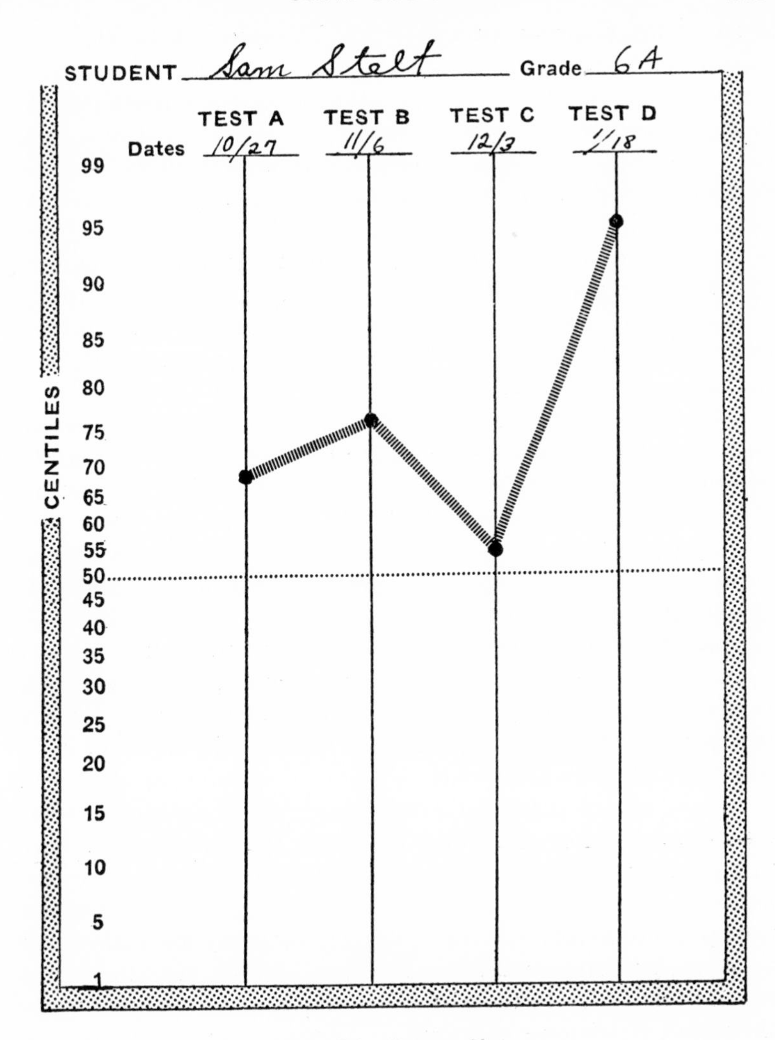

Fig. 26. Test profile

Sometimes, however, parents confuse *percentiles* with the absolute type of per cent scores which traditionally have been used by many teachers for marking children. For example, some teachers give 50 questions on a test and then grade each child on the *number of questions* he completes correctly. Consequently, a child with 45 correct answers out of 50 questions receives a mark of 90 per cent. Typically, some arbitrary score such as 65 or 70 or sometimes 75 is set as the minimum passing grade. This *per cent of questions right* is obviously quite a different statistic from the percentile which is the *per cent of students below a particular pupil's mark.* However, because many parents were graded on a per-cent-of-questions basis when they were in school, they are apt to be confused if the teacher indicates their daughter "scored at the 55th percentile." They believe the girl is a failure because her percentile is below what the parents believe to be the traditional minimum of 70, whereas in reality she is slightly above average. To obviate any such confusion it is recommended that the phrasing "Larry scored higher than 35 per cent of his classmates" be substituted for "Larry scored at the 35th percentile."

If the teacher believes that this suggested phrasing still is confused with the per-cent-of-questions concept by parents, it may be well to change the term from a percentile to a rough fraction, such as, "Larry was higher than a third of his classmates but lower than two-thirds of them." Another alternative is to indicate Larry's standing on a chart of percentiles or to show which tally represents his score on a tally sheet or graph.

A question that continually vexes teachers when this topic is discussed is: "Should I report achievement and aptitude test scores to parents? Won't they often misinterpret these scores, or won't they perhaps put undue pressure on a child to do better when he really is doing his best?" The question is certainly an important one, especially in light of the findings in recent years concerning the mental hygiene of children in school. One mother may learn that her son is below the average on an academic intelligence test, and as a result she may assail the boy for a presumed laziness or may publicly despair of "his ever becoming anything, and after we've tried to do so much for him, too." In this case the family would probably be better off not knowing the test results, because the parent is misusing them and is showing clearly that she misunderstands the implications of a below-average score on this single academic intelligence test.

On the other hand, parents have a right to know the extent of their children's progress. When results of tests and other evaluation devices are presented accurately and cautiously by the teacher, parents often profit from this knowledge and use it properly to develop realistic expectations for their children.

This discussion of handling and reporting test scores has been intended as an aid to the teacher or administrator of a school that has a policy of comparing a child with his classmates. Such a policy, though the most common one, is not universal. In schools that compare a child only with his past achievements, not with his classmates, the use of percentiles would be limited or absent. For a discussion of the different philosophies underlying such policies toward marking, see Chapter 13.

STATISTICS AND SCHOOL MARKS

Teachers often look to statistics for what they term a *scientific* or a *psychologically correct* way of grading students. They may have heard about percentiles or the normal curve (See Appendix B for discussion of the normal curve), and they hope that statistics can remove personal opinion from marking. However, this is a vain hope. All that statistics can do, as indicated earlier, is to organize a mass of data into an understandable form. After the data are organized, the teacher must make a personal decision about how the students are to be marked. Statistics do not tell us *scientifically* or *correctly* the way we should assign letter grades (such as A, B, C, D, and F) or number grades (such as 70, 80, 90, and 100) if we use such grading systems. When students' test scores are plotted on a tally sheet, the teacher must make a personal decision about which students pass and which fail. Statistics cannot determine this. Only the teacher's philosophy of education can do so.

Some teachers have been misled into believing that statistical procedures eliminate subjectivity. This misconception has resulted from the fact that many schools (usually high schools and universities) assign given percents of letter grades throughout the institution. For example, some schools follow the practice of assigning the middle 50 per cent of the class grades of C on the theory that these students are *average*. Within the upper quarter of the class, 20 per cent receive B and 5 per cent A. Within the bottom quarter of the class, 20 per cent receive D and 5 per cent F. Other schools, also operating on the theory that their students are "normally distributed," use different percentages of letter grades. For example, another common practice is to assign the top 15 per cent A, the next 35 per cent B (which takes us to the median), the next 35 per cent C, and the bottom 15 per cent D and F (depending upon how far below the bulk of the students those in the lowest 15 per cent fall).

Thus, it is seen that statistics can tell who ranked in the upper 15 per cent or 25 per cent of the class on a test, a series of tests, or on the semester's work. However, the decision as to what (if any) letter or number grade these students receive, or whether they should pass or fail, is a personal judgment of the teacher or the administration of a school. School marks, in the last analysis, are assigned on the basis of the philosophy of the educator. They are subjective.

OBJECTIVES OF THIS CHAPTER

The effective elementary or junior high teacher:

1. Reports test results to administrators, other teachers, and parents in a form they can clearly understand.
2. Accurately computes means, medians, and percentiles.
3. Constructs tally sheets or graphs to show test results.
4. Accurately interprets means, medians, percentiles, tally sheets, and graphs.

Suggested evaluation techniques for this chapter

1. You have taught a sixth-grade unit on local geography and history. Class activities included interviews with some of the older local residents, a bus trip around the county, a visit to the historical society's museum, reading old newspapers and history books, reading old and new maps of the area, and constructing maps of the route followed on the bus trip. Before teaching the unit you gave a pretest of 100 items covering facts about local geography and history and about map-reading and map-making. Eight weeks later, as part of your final evaluation of the unit, you administered this same test. Following are the scores received by the students on the pretesting and final testing.

PRETESTING: 27, 30, 55, 37, 25, 34, 60, 47, 22, 22, 29, 33, 18, 27, 33, 44, 22, 17, 18, 27, 32, 38, 47, 37, 22, 32, 27, 32, 22, 20, 35, 21.

FINAL TESTING: 78, 79, 86, 90, 82, 82, 74, 88, 92, 72, 57, 78, 83, 85, 90, 65, 75, 93, 94, 93, 78, 46, 85, 55, 82, 92, 90, 82, 85, 84, 85, 82.

A. From these data construct tally sheets to show how the pupils succeeded on the pretesting and the final testing.

B. For each of these two groups of scores compute the mean, median, range, and distance-between-percentiles (75 and 25). For each testing tell which two of these statistics it would be important to report if you wished to indicate the class's progress without having to include the tally sheet or a graph. Why did you select these two particular kinds of statistics?

C. Write a brief interpretation of these statistics (the two you reported under B) for a person who does not have an adequate understanding of them but who wants to know how the class succeeded before and after the unit.

2. The following statistics have been reported to describe the success on an arithmetic-fundamentals test of the students entering eighth grade for a three-year period. After inspecting the statistics, write a brief interpretation of how the groups compared. Your interpretation should be worded in such a way as to be understandable to a person with no knowledge of statistics.

First-Year Group	*Second-Year Group*	*Third-Year Group*
Number = 103	Number = 94	Number = 113
80th centile = 74	80th centile = 87	80th centile = 94
50th centile = 63	50th centile = 62	50th centile = 62
20th centile = 52	20th centile = 43	20th centile = 34

3. Janet Clarkson, a fifth grader, received the following raw scores on five tests this semester:
   I. Problems Using Fractions and Whole Numbers = 15
   II. Addition of Fractions = 61
   III. Reading Comprehension Test A = 53
   IV. Reading Comprehension Test B = 58
   V. Test on Science Unit about Earth and Sky = 27

In this fifth grade of 36 pupils, Janet attained the following rank on each test:
   I. Fifth student from the top of the class.
   II. Eighth student from the top.
   III. Sixteenth student from the top.
   IV. Eighteenth student from the top.
   V. Eleventh student from the top.

Using the information above, convert each of the raw scores into a percentile. Then plot these percentiles on a chart and draw a profile of Janet's success on the five tests compared with the success of her classmates.

SUGGESTED READINGS

1. TATE, MERLE W. *Statistics in Education.* New York: Macmillan Co., 1955. A more complete treatment of statistics.
2. THORNDIKE, ROBERT L., and HAGEN, ELIZABETH. *Measurement and Evaluation in Psychology and Education.* New York: Wiley and Sons, 1955. Chapter 5 contains a direct, simple discussion of elementary statistical concepts developed around clear illustrations.

CHAPTER

8

Observing Students

DURING HER FIRST YEAR of teaching in second grade Miss Claire Latimer learned that a teacher who depends primarily upon her unwritten memory of children's actions is likely to be an inaccurate judge of children's progress. Two incidents brought this bluntly to her attention.

The first occurred when the P.T.A. held open house for parents. On this occasion parents visited the rooms and had opportunities to chat individually with the teacher for a while. As she talked with parents, Miss Latimer increasingly had the feeling that she was telling most of them about the same thing:

"Yes, Jimmy is getting along satisfactorily in his work. He's making regular progress in reading and generally gets along all right with the other children. I think he likes to draw and seems to like music. He's coming along in arithmetic, too. His speech is also improving."

Miss Latimer depended upon her memory for most of the material. Occasionally, she related some specific incident in a child's life to illustrate the way he was succeeding, but the tale she had to tell most of the parents was much the same: "progressing at his own speed" or "might be stronger in this area." She realized that most of the specific incidents she had noticed in class that illumined the uniqueness of each child had slipped from memory, even though at the time she had thought she would remember them without writing them down.

The second incident that showed she needed better material about her children occurred when Mr. Harris, the assistant principal, asked Miss Latimer and a first-grade teacher, Mrs. MacDonald, to discuss with him the cases of two boys who had unexcused absences from school. One was from Miss Latimer's second grade and the other from Mrs. MacDonald's first grade. Each boy had been absent October 17 and November 10 in addition to three consecutive days of the current week. Mr. Harris said that the mothers of the two boys, who lived in the same neighborhood, were to talk with him that afternoon. Before speaking with the parents, he wished to have more information about the two boys "... so that we can see what is behind this and help them."

When asked about the boy in her grade, Miss Latimer said:

"Harold's rather inattentive. And, of course, missing school once in a while doesn't help any. But he's done fairly well. He's in my group of average readers, and he's about average in arithmetic. Sometimes he acts up or gets into a quarrel with some of the others, but he hasn't been too bad in class."

Mr. Harris wanted to know if she could think of any more specific incidents that might lead to a better understanding of Harold. She said that she had nothing specific other than: "He just gives the general impression of being pretty average in his work, but sometimes inattentive and quarrelsome."

When Mrs. MacDonald was asked about the first grader who had been missing school the same days as Harold, she said:

"I've been watching Gary. I wouldn't want to hazard much of a conclusion about him as yet. But I do have some anecdotal records in his folder, and I think they give some insight into Gary's actions and perhaps his motives."

She opened a manila folder titled *Gary French* and read the following incidents:

Wednesday, September 17—Today began morning circle time. (That's the time every morning when each child has an opportunity to stand before the group and tell about anything interesting that has happened to him recently.) Gary was one of three children who said they had nothing to tell group. Gary is next-to-largest boy in class.

Thursday, September 18—Circle time about animals. Gary stood beside where I sat in front of children seated on floor. He was one of last children to talk. He looked at floor as he said in fairly loud voice: "I got a dog. That big. I rassel him on the floor."

Carlos: "Doesn't he bite you?"

Gary: "Naw. I can put my hand in his mouth. Won't bite me, but he'll bite other people."

Tuesday, September 30—11:30—Gary asked for more books about trains to look at. He said he would be glad when he could read the words.

Monday, October 6—Noon, after lunch—Sue Link ran into room followed by Dora and Jane.

Sue: "Mrs. MacDonald, Gary's fighting a second grader on the playground, and the playground teacher stopped them."

I asked: "Fighting a second grader?"

Sue: "Two second-grade boys were fighting over a swing. One was Gary's friend, that Harold. Gary went and hit that other boy, and Harold got the swing, and the other boy cried, and the teacher came."

Friday, October 10—Class discussed fathers' jobs. Gary said father was engineer on a "streamliner train." According to my records, Gary's father was a farmer killed in threshing accident four years ago, and mother moved with Gary to town to live with her sister. Both mother and sister are department-store clerks.

Thursday, October 16—End of noon hour. Sue Link ran into room early, said Gary was fighting on sidewalk across from school. Said he and second grader named Harold were fighting another boy.

Sue: "A boy was chasing Harold and Gary knocked the boy down."

I told Sue it was not necessary to report such things to me, that the playground teacher would take care of it. Sue has been reporting other children's behavior to me about once a week.

October 16—2:00—Class walking trip to vacant lots a block from school to collect plants and animals. Gary brought back toad, four kinds of weeds or flowers, found pictures of two of them in flower book when we returned.

Gary: "Look, Miss MacDonald, I found it better than anybody."

Tuesday, October 27—Afternoon—Gary fell asleep with head on desk while class listened to records. He woke up when class left for gym.

Wednesday, November 5—A.M.—After I read class story of boy whose father was sea captain who took the boy to see all kinds of interesting animals around the world, Gary asked: "Can you get a daddy like that if you really want?"

PAUL: "You said your daddy's a engineer."

Gary snapped at him, said: "Well, he is. Shut up." Later Gary scuffled with Paul in coatroom as group dressed to go home.

Tuesday, November 11—Gary absent yesterday. This morning said he lost excuse his mother gave him. During circle time Alice told about space-ship program she saw on television. Gary asked to talk next, looked at group, and said: "We was down at the station where the trains are. We saw the streamliners, and we saw a man with a little car pulling suitcases on it. He gave us a ride. And we got close to the engine, too."

PAUL: "When?"

GARY: "Yesterday."

SUE: "You said you were sick yesterday."

Gary looked at me, chewed his fingernail. After pause said: "Not yesterday. Sunday I saw the trains. I was sick yesterday." He sat down, looked at floor rest of circle time.

Wednesday, November 19—Gary 20 minutes late. Said he helped Mr. Roberts (gym teacher) find school soccer balls older boys threw into vacant-lot weeds when playing before school. Mr. Roberts later supported this story.

Monday, December 1—During music hour Gary said again and again, "Let's sing the puffer-billy." He has asked for this song about trains every day since we learned it last week. As usual, class agreed and we sang it.

Wednesday, December 10—Circle time. Discussion of Christmas desires. Gary wants space ship, jet plane, electric train, pistol, and "whistle just like Mr. Roberts'."

Thursday, December 18—P.M. music time. Gary said he learned Christmas song on record at home. I asked him if he would like to sing it. He said yes, faced group, sang first verse of "Jolly Santa Claus." Class applauded. Gary walked to seat looking at floor, grinning.

Tuesday, January 6—Circle time. Gary's New Year's resolutions included: "Be good and do what I'm told, come home when I'm called, and learn to read better."

After reading these incidents, Mrs. MacDonald gave a brief summary of Gary's standing in schoolwork:

"He's one of the best readers in class, above average in handwriting and counting, and he follows directions as well as most of his classmates. That's all I have on Gary so far. Of course, he was absent Monday, Tuesday, and today this week. Did they find where he's been?"

Mr. Harris said, "Well, apparently at the railroad yards or airport. He and Harold were picked up by the police about two hours ago, around 10:30, as they hiked out by the airport. The officers thought they might be lost. The mothers will be in this afternoon. I think your information gives us something to work on. I'll see you later, and we'll decide what plan to use in working with the boys."

As the two teachers left the office, Miss Latimer said that the record Mrs. MacDonald had kept on Gary astounded her. "Just listening to it made me feel that I knew more about him than many of my own children. I was ashamed not to be able to say anything more definite about Harold, although several things did come to mind as you read that record. Frankly, I'd appreciate your showing me exactly how you find time to do it."

This was the beginning of Miss Latimer's steps toward effective observation of her children. She had already taken the first step: she was convinced that noting and recording important incidents helped reveal the unique individual that each child is. In taking the further steps in doing this efficiently, she learned much more about the techniques of observation. The following sections explain her new findings.

KINDS OF OBSERVATION

Casual observation

There are numerous ways to observe children. Probably the easiest type of evaluation is *casual observation* of the way children act. Over a period of time this commonly leads the observer to a *general impression* of the child's behavior. However, for several reasons this *impression* may be a wrong one.

First, many of the classroom incidents, which the teacher thought he would easily remember, slip away as time passes. Also, in his casual observation the teacher may have noted only incidents that were *not* typical of the child's usual behavior. And because such observation is only casual and is not directed, many significant incidents may be missed.

Thus, unorganized observation, such as Miss Latimer carried on in second grade, helps a teacher judge children, but it is often unsatisfactory if a fair evaluation is to be made.

Anecdotal records

To record incidents that might otherwise fade from memory, many teachers jot down their observations on slips of paper and keep these in the child's folder, as Mrs. MacDonald did. Or they dedicate a page in a notebook to each child's activities. Such reports are termed *anecdotal records*. They are brief reports of happenings that seem significant in telling about a person's adjustment or his interpretation of his world. Or they tell about his main concerns in life or his progress toward goals that are not easily evaluated by other techniques.

At first glance the writing of useful anecdotal records appears to be simple. This is not so. There are certain standards which records should fulfill to be most useful and most truthful. In their book, *Helping Teachers Understand Children,* members of an American Council on Education committee report their experiences in aiding groups of teachers to improve in writing reports of child behavior. The committee observed that "... teachers have not been trained to evaluate behavior scientifically, on the basis of adequate information about particular girls and boys interpreted through valid principles of human development." (*1:6*)

Thus, it is necessary for a teacher to practice more scientific methods of recording children's actions. In order to do this he should try to *record only what actually happens*. He should try to keep his interpretation and decisions out of the report. The children should speak for themselves, in direct quotations if possible. Their actions should be noted accurately. Any interpretation or evaluation can well wait until numbers of anecdotes have been gathered, at which time the teacher has a better over-all picture of a student's behavior. On the third-grade level, here is an example of the difference between an *opinion-loaded* anecdote and an anecdote that is a straightforward statement of what occurred.

Observation 1. "Tony did a naughty thing today. He said bad words, swore at some other children on the playground. Then he thought it was funny, and he was quite surly when I reprimanded him about it."

Observation 2. "Tony and Fred and Jane threw sand at each other near the swings after lunch. When Jane and Fred stuck their tongues out, Tony shouted, 'Damn you damn sneaks.' Fred and Jane ran across the yard calling, 'Oh, that's naughty.' Tony shouted after them, 'Ha, ha, run away.' I called Tony to my room. He looked out the window as he stood at my desk. I said, 'You know, we don't want children using such words as that.' Tony said, 'They threw sand in my hair. Served them right to be called damn.' "

The second observation is a recording of what happened. If the teacher at the end of the term, or perhaps the principal who might see Tony's folder, wants to conclude, "Tony did a naughty thing... said bad words... thought it was funny... was surly," then that is his privilege. But any such personal interpretation should be based upon well-recorded anecdotes of what actually happened. It should not be part of the anecdotal record. Someone else might well interpret the incident differently, and the behavior should be described accurately to allow such interpretations.

Observation 1 above is colored with opinion and actually does not tell much. In its present form it is a better device for evaluating the teacher's attitude toward Tony than it is a record of an incident in the boy's life.

Some teachers use a modified plan of recording incidents. They let the incidents tell themselves, let the children talk for themselves, and try to make the report an accurate record of behavior. However, at the end of the record they jot down a few words of tentative interpretation or their own reaction to the situation, being careful to separate interpretation from the actual incident. In general, it is probably better to leave any interpretation until several incidents have been recorded.

Need for training. The fact that teachers usually do not write the most useful records without training was demonstrated in the A.C.E. committee's analysis of the entries written by teachers in their study groups. They found four main types:

"1. Anecdotes that evaluate or judge the behavior of the child as good or bad, desirable, or undesirable, acceptable or unacceptable ... *evaluative statements.*" (*1:32*)

Sample *evaluative statement:*

"Julius talked loud and much during poetry; wanted to do and say just what he wanted and *didn't consider the right working out of things.* Had to ask him to sit by me. Showed a *bad attitude* about it." (*1:33*)

"2. Anecdotes that account for or explain the child's behavior, usually on the basis of a single fact or thesis ... *interpretive statements.*" (*1:32*)

Sample of interpretive statement purporting to tell *why* the person acted as he did:

"For the last week Sammy has been a perfect Wiggle Tail. He is *growing so fast he cannot be settled.* ... Of course the *inward change* that is taking place causes the restlessness." (*1:33*)

"3. Anecdotes that describe certain behavior in general terms, as happening frequently, or as characterizing the child ... *generalized descriptive statements.*" (*1:32*)

Sample generalized description:

"Sammy is *awfully restless* these days. He is *whispering most of the time* he is not kept busy. In the circle, *during various discussions,* even though he is interested, *his arms are moving or he is punching the one sitting next to him.* He *smiles when I speak to him.*" (*1:33*)

"4. Anecdotes that tell exactly what the child did or said, that describe concretely the situation in which the action or comment occurred, and that tell clearly what other persons also did or said ... *specific or concrete descriptive statements.*" (*1:32*)

Mrs. MacDonald's anecdotes about Gary are primarily examples of specific descriptions. Observation 2, telling of Tony's playground experience, is also this type.

Mixed descriptions, which include elements of more than one of the four above types, are very common among teachers' records. In the experiment reported in *Helping Teachers Understand Children,* the teachers cooperating in the study over a period of two years "... gradually learned to include more and more specific description in their anecdotes and to refrain from immediate evaluation and interpretation. This, of course, is what we desired. But teachers are human, and even two years of practice did not serve to train them to limit their anecdotes entirely to specific description. We tried to get the teachers to withhold their evaluations and interpretations until they had accumulated anecdotes for at least two or three months so that their appraisals would be based on more extensive and objective evidence, but many of them continued to write anecdotes that were mixtures of all four types of statement.

"We must, however, admit that an examination of the anecdotes actually written showed certain advantages in not limiting them entirely to specific description. Some of the generalized descriptions gave excellent pictures of children in action. Again, some of the interpretations made on the spur of the moment captured the moods of interacting children in a fashion that would have been well-nigh impossible by straightforward description. Finally, some of the departures from description obviously indicated natural attempts on the part of teachers to apply new knowledge or insight or to express new points of view. We even suspect that the very writing of some interpretive and evaluative anecdotes had a part in crystallizing concepts or clarifying attitudes and so contributed to the development of understanding. All this is by way of saying that, while specific description is generally to be sought and applauded in anecdote writing, leaders should not insist on it too rigidly, because individual teachers will want and need the chance to try out and clarify their emerging concepts and attitudes in relation to the specific situations and children they are describing." [1]

In general, then, the teacher's goal is more specific description. However, on occasion other types of statements may appropriately enter the anecdote (or better, follow it) if they serve a special purpose. But they should not enter merely because the teacher does not know any better or because he is careless.

When to write the anecdote. The time to write the observation is a problem that concerns teachers who are newly introduced to the technique. The record will be more accurate if the anecdote can be written while it is happening, for the exact conversation and actions are reported as they happen. However, it is often inconvenient for the teacher to write an observation during a social-studies discussion or while walking along the corridor. Also, it is unwise to write anecdotes about older children when they can see the teacher doing it. Consequently, the teacher in the primary grades can more often write the observation as it happens. If a first grader asks the teacher, "What are you writing?" the teacher can truthfully satisfy the child's curiosity by answering, "I'm writing my lesson." With

[1] American Council on Education, Commission on Teacher Education, *Helping Teachers Understand Children* (Washington, D. C.: The Council, 1945), pp. 34-35. Quoted by permission of The Council.

older children this obviously will not work; therefore, the observation must be remembered and written as soon as possible after the incident.

Time-sampling

Another observational technique is time-sampling. Although it is more applicable to research, the method is occasionally useful to teachers.

Time-sampling consists of recording carefully a child's actions for a definite period at a particular time of day. Thus, a fifth-grade teacher might write everything a pupil does for a five-minute period or for a ten-minute period during a free-reading or study session. This gives evidence of the pupil's work or play habits, attention span, and pattern of movements. A different pupil might be chosen another day and watched for the same time. Or, a teacher who desires evidence about the varying patterns of behavior of an individual or of a class at different periods of the day would find time-sampling useful.

As a tool for research in child psychology, this technique "... is characterized by careful selection and definition of the behavior to be observed, by standardization of the observer's methods, by careful limitation of the length of the period of observation, and by the multiplication of observations to be certain that the behavior of the child has been sampled in an adequate fashion for such variables as situation, time of day, and other factors that may influence behavior.... Results that give a reliable basis for experimentation and prediction have been procured...."[2]

USES OF ANECDOTAL RECORDS

One of the main concerns of teachers is voiced in this common query:

"Children are very active. They do many things during a school day. Which incidents are important? Which should I record?"

The answer depends upon the use that is to be made of the records. Generally, there are two ways in which anecdotes are most useful:

1. As evidences of a student's progress toward school goals.
2. As clues to the particular motives, problems, and patterns of

[2] Willard C. Olson, *Child Development* (Boston: L. C. Heath and Co., 1949), p. 7. Quoted by permission of the publisher.

behavior that make each child unique and different from every other one.

Evidence of student progress

It is convenient when a teacher can evaluate students' development by such techniques as paper-pencil tests, situation tests, check lists, and rating scales, because these devices usually yield data that are easily scored or summarized. However, teachers continually see evidences of student progress which cannot be discovered by such means as tests.

For example, in her third grade Miss Andover wrote this anecdote about a boy who usually retreated from activities in which he would be involved with others or be noticed by them:

"Franklin said he didn't want an actor's part in the puppet show. When a stage crew was being selected, he and Lanny volunteered. During most of lunch period and for an hour after school, Franklin installed lights, nailed the stage together, and hooked up the curtain. He worked alone at noon, but Lanny helped him after school. They conversed freely with each other, appeared to work well together."

This incident provides evidence of Franklin's progress toward two of Miss Andover's goals for third graders:

"The student:

1. Willingly completes his share of group work.
2. Speaks before a group with apparent ease and confidence."

In the case of the first goal, the anecdote suggests Franklin is making substantial progress. Apparently he is not meeting the second goal very adequately at this point. It would be unwise for a teacher to draw a conclusion, other than a very tentative one, about the general extent of a student's progress toward a goal on the basis of a single anecdote such as this. However, over the period of a year, numbers of anecdotes provide a more substantial basis for drawing conclusions.

As is true with any evaluation device, anecdotes that apply to a particular goal (such as to 1 or to 2 above) are valuable if recorded at different times throughout the year. They show how a student's behavior changes or remains the same during the year. They help the teacher decide what methods of teaching work best with different children by indicating whether the present methods are producing desirable changes in the student's behavior.

The case of Franklin demonstrated this. Miss Andover had not experienced much success in getting Franklin to participate in group activities early in the year. She had praised him, urged him, and encouraged him to talk with her about his interests. These approaches had no apparent effect, but the puppet-show incident gave a first indication of progress. This was a possible clue to a method that would be successful in helping him toward the group-work goal. She later used his help in another puppet show and also in construction of a table display of "Houses of the World." Class members remarked about his good work. Anecdotes recorded at these times helped substantiate her growing belief that Franklin's manual skill was a good means of carrying him into group-work gradually and of breaking down his shyness. By keeping records appropriate to this group-work goal, she had at the end of the year a series of incidents that outlined clearly the boy's progress in relation to the methods she used with him. Consequently, the appraisal technique helped evaluate both the student's growth and the teacher's methods.

Anecdotal records are appropriate for judging certain kinds of behavior changes at any grade level. Below are examples of three other incidents which provided important data that could not have been obtained through such devices as tests.

Seventh grade. "Carol clearly explained three percentage problems at the board. None of the other class members had done them correctly. This is the first time she has done this."

(Goal: Student gives directions and explains process so others readily understand.)

Kindergarten. "George wiped his nose on his sleeve. I asked him if he had a handkerchief or tissue. He said yes, showed me a handkerchief, walked to a clay table, wiped nose on sleeve before picking up clay."

(Goal: Child uses clean handkerchief.)

Eighth grade. "Ralph brought a folder of pictures pertaining to our westward expansion unit. He had cut them from old magazines stored in his basement. Upon my suggestion he made a bulletin-board display of them."

(Goal: "Through personal initiative, student contributes pertinent ideas and materials to class.")

Clues to child's unique personality

Effective teachers realize that each child differs to some degree from every other one in his motives, his patterns of behavior, his feelings of confidence in tackling problems, his worries, his reaction to criticism and praise, and so forth. The teacher may best help children achieve happiness and be effective in their lives if he understands their individual personalities better, because only by knowing their unique motives and reactions can he estimate the best ways of helping each child learn and grow. For example, one student may feel crushed by negative criticism and will stop trying, but he will progress markedly when he is praised for his attempts. A second student may accept praise as his just due and will not work unless he is challenged or prodded by negative criticism. Another may learn best when combinations of praise and criticism are used.

Along with some projective techniques, the anecdotal record is probably the teacher's most fruitful single device for revealing the desires, concerns, and patterns of behavior of each child. This discovery process is what the psychologist means when he says teachers should try to *understand* every pupil.

Earlier in this chapter Mrs. MacDonald kept anecdotal records that helped her understand First Grader Gary French, in addition to giving her evidence of his growth toward educational goals. She did this by recording significant events. The new teacher frequently asks, "But how do I know what events are significant ones?"

There is no rule that gives a pat answer. The answer comes from experience in observing children and from keeping in mind the purpose: *understanding the child.* In the study referred to earlier (*1:37*), teachers beginning to record behavior at first noted most readily the classroom incidents that were of prime importance *to them as teachers.* For instance, they commonly reported children's success in school tasks (which is, as indicated earlier, one useful purpose for anecdotes). Or else they reported incidents in which the student helped or disturbed the *teacher* and her control, records of the *teacher's* emotional reaction to the child, or observations about *family status.*

After observing and recording incidents over an extended period, the teachers increasingly redirected their attention to recording happenings that were of more importance *to the child;* his concerns, motives, and the events that elated or disturbed *him.*

An emphasis on the *child* was seen in Mrs. MacDonald's records of Gary's actions. Some of the incidents Mrs. MacDonald noted about Gary were of no significance to her personally. They were not just Gary's good and bad deeds which affected her classroom. Instead, she selected incidents because they seemed to be *significant clues to Gary's problems* and his way of handling the world. She was guided by thoughts of: "What is the world like to Gary? What are his desires? What are his worries?"

As Mrs. MacDonald collected anecdotes about Gary, a picture of some of his probable concerns began to form. Consequently, when Mr. Harris needed information about the boy, the anecdotes which the teacher had believed significant gave clues to his motives and problems. Mr. Harris added these clues to other information which he gained during interviews with Gary and his second-grade companion, Harold, as well as with their mothers. As was hinted in Mrs. MacDonald's observations, Gary was apparently concerned about not having a father. His mother saw evidences of this ("He used to follow the man next door when he worked in the yard, but the man got tired of Gary's questions."), and it disturbed her, but she said she did not know what to do about it. Mr. Harris suggested that they talk with members of the local Big Brother movement, which was composed of men who befriended boys without fathers and became pals or big brothers to them. Mrs. French welcomed the suggestion, which subsequently was carried out. A thirty-year-old insurance man became Gary's big brother. On occasional weekends and late afternoons they went on picnics, played ball, built toy boats to sail, saw the circus, or visited the railroad yards and airport. As would be realistically expected, there was no major change in the boy's personality, but during circle time he increasingly talked about what his Big Brother Tom and he had done the day before. And Gary did keep his bargain to attend school regularly.

After being caught "playing hookey," Gary's second-grade friend, Harold, also began attending school regularly. From what the two boys and their mothers had said, it was evident that Gary, although younger, was the leader of the two. When Gary realized that he could trust Mr. Harris, the boy admitted that it had been his idea to "...go see the diesels when we were 'sposed to go to school."

Mrs. MacDonald's observations tended to support the idea that Gary was the leader and that Harold depended upon him, for the younger boy had helped in Harold's battles.

Harold's subsequent regular attendance probably was strongly influenced by the fact that Gary no longer missed school. A supporting factor may have been Harold's father, whom his mother later reported "... said some pretty direct things to the boy."

From the example of Gary and Harold, it is seen that brief records of specific behavior that is significant in revealing each child's pattern of life help the teacher and the school to fulfill the child's needs better. In this case Mrs. MacDonald's notes were of particular use to the school in understanding one boy's problems and helping solve them. In any school there will be more and less spectacular instances of the use of anecdotes.

Usually a teacher must keep observations about children for a period of time before really becoming convinced of their worth. Few instructors have the sudden awakening that the second-grade teacher, Miss Latimer, experienced when she compared her vague and generalized observations of Harold with Mrs. MacDonald's specific notes on Gary.

AMOUNT OF RECORDING

Teachers object when educational theorists recommend additional tasks which use up the teacher's valuable class time. As one fourth-grade teacher put it:

"I have thirty-one children. They're full of vigor and ideas. I have to be on my toes most of the time to keep interesting activities going on in class and to help them learn. I don't have time to write down every little thing each of the thirty-one does. Let's be realistic about teaching. Aren't anecdotal records just idealism run a little wild?"

The realistic answer is: *Do as much as you can.* Do as much as you think is valuable. Naturally, a teacher does not have time to make a record of each event, nor even one event per day per child. Mrs. MacDonald's records about Gary were made on an average of less than one each week. For some children there will be more significant incidents that are worth noting. For others there will be fewer. The teacher must make the decision. But one semester of collecting brief reports of significant-appearing happenings in the class should convince an instructor that the picture of each child's personality at the end of the semester can be seen in a truer light than if no reports were available. A teacher readily forgets many of the events in the lives of thirty-one fourth graders. Anecdotal records help him remember.

In numbers of schools a principal or supervisor becomes firmly convinced that anecdotal records are valuable. This conviction often leads to the speech or note to the faculty which reads:

"In order to provide better information about the children in our classes, we are beginning a school-wide program of keeping anecdotal records. It appears that three anecdotes about each child each week should be a minimum if we are really getting to know our children. Since these records will be valuable to the guidance director's office as well as to the individual teacher, a carbon copy should be made of each anecdote. The teacher is to retain the copy, and the original record is to be used in the pupil's folder in the main office. Each teacher is requested to place the week's anecdotes in a manila folder and leave the folder with the secretary in the main office before leaving school each Friday."

Despite the use of such words as *requested,* teachers know anecdotes are now *required.* They will comply with the order and will leave three anecdotes about each child with the secretary every week. Some will diligently collect the observations during the week. But, as has been observed in such situations, the bulk of the records probably will be written during lunch period or after school Thursday. And the remarks will be quite general, many of them almost identical, such as, "Florence is doing better work. She tried harder today but was somewhat restless in the afternoon."

Anecdotes written under these conditions, with teachers resenting the task, probably will be of little value in helping children. It is doubtful that many useful observations are produced by executive order. The best records will be produced by teachers who really want to know their children better, want to judge them on a more secure basis, and believe that jotting down incidents will help them do these tasks. An in-service program similar to the one described in *Helping Teachers Understand Children* is an effective way to convince instructors that anecdotes are worth the work.

OBJECTIVES OF THIS CHAPTER

The effective elementary-school teacher:

1. Writes anecdotal records that:

a. Tell specific behavior and minimize personal opinion.
b. Give evidence of students' progress toward school goals that are not so well judged by other evaluation devices.
c. Give clues to the particular motives, problems, and patterns of behavior that make each child different from every other one.

2. Records time-sample observations when data are desired about the rate and pattern of children's classroom behavior.

Suggested evaluation techniques for this chapter

1. Write observations of the actions of students in a class you teach or attend. Analyze your observations to determine whether they are evaluative, interpretive, generalized, specific, or a combination of these. Would your observations be best used as evidence of student progress toward school goals, as clues to the individual's personality, or as both of these?
2. Make a five-minute time-sample observation of two students. On the basis of these records can you draw any tentative conclusions about their patterns of behavior? If so, what would these conclusions be? What cautions should be used in interpreting time samples such as these?
3. The following anecdote was written by a third-grade teacher. By crossing out any words or phrases you believe would be best omitted, improve the usefulness of the record. "Henry Joaldie, the rather mean little boy with red hair and freckles, yesterday threw a handful of Jimmy Kling's marbles into the aquarium. Like his older sister, this Joaldie boy is a born trouble-maker. After throwing the marbles he ran across the room to the bulletin board and pulled out three thumbtacks, which he put on Jimmy's seat. Jimmy shouted, 'You dumb beak, you!' and swept the tacks off onto the floor. Henry laughed and ran to the front of the room, where I grabbed him by the arm. The little sneak squirmed out of my grasp and ran out the door. Jimmy, who is really very sweet and comes from a good family, tried to fish out the marbles. As he did this, the aquarium began to tip. Luckily, Helen Jensen grabbed it and straightened it up, but some water and two fish had spilled onto the floor. By this time Henry had sneaked in the back door again. Spanking is actually the only thing that will do him any good, because I've reasoned with him time and again only to have him do something like this. He scooped up the two fish and dangled them in front of Helen's face. When she turned her head away, he threw them at her. It's all right to talk about 'interesting the child' and using 'mental

hygiene' but some children, like this Joaldie boy, need a bit of good old-fashioned discipline once in a while."

4. Evaluate the following anecdote, written by an eighth-grade teacher, using the same procedure used for item 3 above. "Something happened this noon that made me feel sorry for Carol again. The pupils were all supposed to go to the gym the latter part of the lunch hour for recreational folk dancing that they have been learning in gym classes. When I came back to my room after lunch to do some work, Carol was in her seat in the back of the room, where she sits because she is the tallest girl in the class. When I asked her why she wasn't dancing in the gym, she said she wanted to work on her arithmetic. I knew this was not the real reason, because she is so tall and is afraid no boy would want to dance with her. And I imagine she is a bit clumsy as a dancer."

5. Below you find portions of several anecdotal records. You are to inspect them and judge whether they are *evaluative* statements, *interpretive* statements, *straight descriptive* statements, *unduly generalized,* or *desirably specific*. Use these code letters: I—Interpretive, E—Evaluative, D—Descriptive, UG—generalized, DS—specific. If a passage is more than one of these types, use more than one code letter.

   ______(1) Tommy is continually on the move. When he is not working he is wiggling or walking about the room to sharpen a pencil or find a sheet of paper.

   ______(2) Because she couldn't be the captain of the volleyball team again today, Laverne sulked all afternoon.

   ______(3) At juice time Frank spilled his crackers and juice on the table. When he began to cry, Susan put her arm around him and said, "It's all right, Frankie. I'll help clean it up. And you can have some of my juice and crackers."

   ______(4) Chris was unusually nasty today about the arithmetic tests I handed back. Usually he takes his mark in the proper spirit, but he certainly didn't today.

   ______(5) During music period the class marched, hopped, or skipped around the room according to the rhythm I played. Because Linda wouldn't move fast enough, Jack pushed her. This made her angry, so she hit him across the nose. He hit her back, and as usual she began to cry.

______(6) Len brought his Siamese cat to school today. During conference time he stood the cat on the table in front of the class and told how Siamese cats are different from others. He spoke clearly and answered all questions asked of him.

SUGGESTED READINGS

1. American Council on Education, Commission on Teacher Education. *Helping Teachers Understand Children.* Washington, D.C.: The Council, 1945. A most specific study of teachers studying children and keeping records about them.
2. Bieker, Helen. "Using Anecdotal Records to Know the Child," in *Fostering Mental Health in Our Schools.* Association for Supervision and Curriculum Development. 1950 Yearbook. Washington, D.C.: National Education Association, 1950. Brief, specific examples of uses for anecdotes.
3. Thorndike, Robert L., and Hagen, Elizabeth. *Measurement and Evaluation in Psychology and Education.* New York: Wiley and Sons, 1955. Examples of observational methods and ways to improve them: pp. 312-32.

CHAPTER

9

Evaluating Social Relationships

Miss Kenmore teaches sixth grade. What some teachers call the *social studies* part of their program, Miss Kenmore calls the *social living* part. She uses this term because it seems to describe best the goals she is trying to reach. She includes units built around such topics as "Modern Transportation" and "Life in China," which typically are called social studies. But she also includes more. She not only strives to have the children learn about the social aspects of the world around them, but she wants the children also to change in their own lives to become more secure and happier. Thus, she has definite personal *social-living* goals. She has stated them in terms of student behavior that she believes should be developed. By stating the objectives as definite pupil behavior, she knows she can better evaluate whether the children reach them.

Miss Kenmore believes that children have a need to be accepted and liked by others. She believes that, in general, the boy who is rejected or ignored by his peers is not as happy as he would be if he were welcomed by them. She believes that the girl who has friends to work and play with, to share secrets with, is happier than the one who is not accepted by others. Miss Kenmore believes that in a complicated American society, where people do not typically live isolated from others but are rather dependent on them, a child will be more efficient and happier if he can work well with other people and be accepted by them.

Because of these beliefs, Miss Kenmore has included the following objective as one of her most important social-living goals.

"The student is accepted by other children; that is, others choose him for group work, others encourage him or allow him to play with them, others frequently talk with him in a friendly way."

After stating the goal clearly she must find ways of determining which children are reaching it and which are falling short. Only by evaluating will she know who needs her special help and who does not.

Probably the easiest type of evaluation would be casual observation of the way the children get along with each other in class. This might be supplemented by anecdotal records to make the observations more permanent. However, Miss Kenmore is not satisfied with these alone, for they do not tell the whole story. They tell what *she* observes and tell *her opinion* of how socially acceptable the children are. She wants a better evaluation of progress toward the goal. One good way to secure a more complete picture of social adjustment is to use sociometrics.

SOCIOMETRICS

Sociometrics is the charting or measuring of social relationships by showing children's opinions of each other. In this way the teacher supplements what he observes and thinks about the students with what they think about each other. This is additional evidence of social acceptability.

In the classroom and on the playground children's opinions of each other can be observed informally when they choose teams or elect class officers. The teacher can see which children are most popular because they are often chosen. He can see which are least acceptable for various activities because they are seldom chosen or are chosen last. However, such informal observations usually do not yield as complete evidence as a teacher-planned study of child selections. Better-controlled handling of the students' choices is possible when the teacher asks each child to choose according to such statements as:

"My best *friends* are . . ." or "I would like best to *work* with these children . . ." or "I would like best to *play* with these children . . ." or "I would like best to have these children *sit near* me . . ."

Studies of sociometrics indicate that the wording of the statement or of the problems posed by it affects somewhat which children are selected. For example, some differences in choices might be expected if the statement were "The people I want on my side in football" instead of "The people I would like to work with on a committee making school carnival posters." The teacher must decide for himself what type of statement will provide the data he wishes about the children's opinions of each other.

It is generally agreed among sociometric experts that if the statement used implies that some action will result from the choices, this action should be carried out. The teacher should not fool the children just so that they will commit themselves on choices and provide him with material for a sociogram. For instance, if the pupils are asked to write the names of three people they would like to work with on carnival posters, he should actually have poster committees formed as much as possible on the basis of choices. Children may readily lose faith in the teacher who says after the choices are handed in, "Of course, that was just for fun. We really aren't going to have committees."

Some instructors wish to give children free rein in selecting as many classmates as they wish. This has the advantage of showing which children desire or choose many others and which voluntarily limit their selections to only one or two. However, when many choices are made, the teacher may have difficulty charting the choices later on a sociogram. Other instructors limit the choices by including the desired number in the statement, such as "I would like best to have these *three* children work at my table during art period." When the number of choices is limited, the teacher must realize that the children are not writing down the names of *all* the children they welcome or accept, but they are writing down only the ones they prefer most.

The practice of asking children to list only the persons they *want* or *prefer* has been criticized by some experts who point out that if a child is not selected by anyone, the teacher cannot say he was *rejected.* They say that some of those not selected will be rejected but others will be merely *overlooked.* To make a distinction between active rejections and those who are overlooked, some teachers ask for "those children I would *not* want to work with" in addition to "those I want to work with." A number of teachers, however, do not like the practice of asking children to cite those "I would *not* want" because they feel this makes the children seek pupils' names to list as ones they do not like. It may also make the insecure child acutely aware of the possibility that his classmates may be writing down his name under the "not want" statement. Thus, the teachers who do not approve of this technique of distinguishing between overlooked and rejected children believe the method is contrary to good mental hygiene in their classes and prefer to have the technique used only for research purposes. The decision of whether to include a "not want" statement is up to the teacher's judgment.

Simple tally graph

When the children hand in the slips of paper with their choices, the data do not make much sense until the teacher organizes them. There are several good ways to do this. Probably the simplest

Column I—Children's choices		*Column II—Tally Graph*	
Student	*Those He Chose*	*Student*	*Times Chosen*
1. Alfred	Ted, Chuck	Alfred	o
2. Alice	Joyce, Janet	Alice	///
3. Betty R.	Helen, Sally	Betty R.	/
4. Betty T.	Sally, Betty R.	Betty T.	o
5. Billy	Bob, Tim	Billy	///
6. Bob	Tim, Billy	Bob	~~////~~///
7. Carl	Billy, John	Carl	o
8. Chuck	Bob, Jim	Chuck	//
9. Edna	Alice, Janet	Edna	/
10. Fran	Alice, Jill	Fran	o
11. Frank	John, Ted	Frank	/
12. George	Tim, Bob	George	o
13. Gerald	Bob, Jill	Gerald	o
14. Helen	Jill, Sally	Helen	///
15. Janet	Edna, Joyce	Janet	///
16. Jill	Joyce, Helen	Jill	////
17. Jim	Mike, Chuck	Jim	/
18. John	Bob, Ted	John	///
19. Joyce	Alice, Jill	Joyce	///
20. Mary	Helen, Sally	Mary	o
21. Mike	Bob, Tim	Mike	/
22. Sally	Jill, Bob	Sally	////
23. Ted	Frank, John	Ted	///
24. Tim	Bob, Billy	Tim	////

Fig. 27. Tally graph

method is to list every child's name on a sheet of paper and put a tally mark for each time he was chosen. This shows how popular each child was or how acceptable the others regarded him for a given activity.

In her sixth grade Miss Kenmore asked each student to list the names of "the two people I would like to sit near." Column I shows the choices as they appeared on the slips of paper. Column II shows a tally sheet for the times each student was chosen.

The tally sheet is simple to make. It tells Miss Kenmore the children's desires as far as the class seating plan is concerned. Those with many choices are called *stars* by teachers who use sociometrics. Those with a single choice are sometimes termed *neglectees;* however, in this sixth grade where only two choices were allowed each child, the term neglectee might be questioned. If a third choice had been allowed, perhaps some of the apparent neglectees would no longer be in this category. The tally sheet also shows which children were not chosen at all. These children are commonly referred to as *isolates*. Those who choose each other are called *mutual* choices. The tallies, therefore, can help Miss Kenmore evaluate the social acceptance of her students in the class seating situation.

Sociograms

The tally graph, however, does not show the patterning of friendships or choices. If Miss Kenmore is to help the children who are isolates or neglectees become more acceptable, it is important for her to know how their selections relate to selections of the rest of the group. Was Frank chosen by someone he selected, indicating they have a mutual friendship, or was he chosen by someone he does not want to sit near? Are there any tight little social cliques in the room or do all choices center around one or two children? These questions, not answered by a tally sheet, are answered by a sociogram. With a *sociogram* (that is, a map of social relationships in the class) the instructor can see at a glance who the stars and isolates are and how the children relate themselves to each other.

There are several variations of sociograms. One of the most common consists of circles, each containing a child's name or his code number, with arrows indicating which classmates a student chose. Sometimes one geometric figure (circle or square) is used for boys and another (triangle or diamond) for girls.

Miss Kenmore charted the selections of her students (Fig. 28),

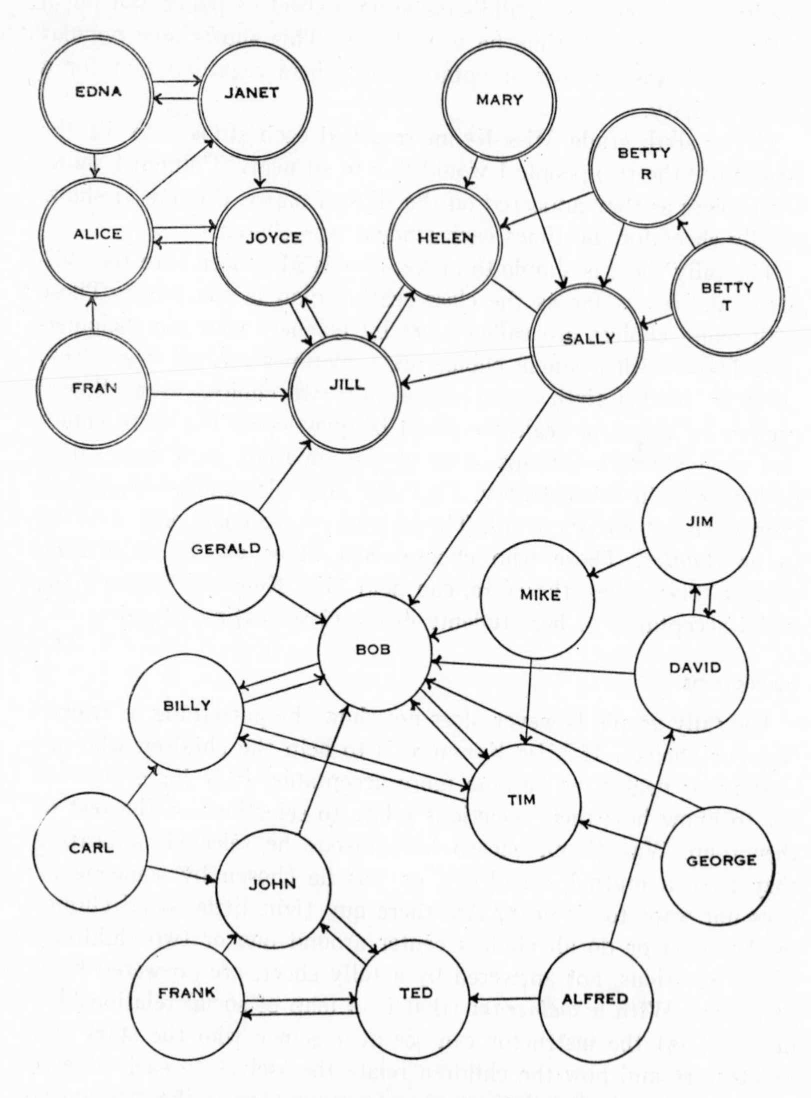

Fig. 28. Sociogram of sixth grade
Children chose "The two people I would like to sit near."

using circles for boys, double circles for girls. It is seen that the sociogram tells everything the tally graph does plus much more. Thus, creating a tally sheet *in addition* to this social-relationship map probably would be a waste of time.

Some teachers are interested not only in how many times a child is chosen and who chooses him, but also whether he is a first choice of his classmates, a second, or a third choice. To discover this, they phrase the leading statement somewhat in this manner: "I would like these three students as my best friends. My first choice is ____________________. My second choice is____________________. My third choice is____________________." Then, when the sociogram is plotted, a number *1* is placed on each arrow-line indicating a first choice, a *2* is placed on each line showing a second choice, and a *3* is used to indicate a third choice. Or, instead of numbers, colored lines are sometimes used to indicate first, second, and third choices. It is assumed that a child with first choices is more socially desired than one with an equal number of third choices.

Target Chart. A slight variation in sociograms is the target chart. It differs from the type illustrated in Figure 28 in that the *stars* are all placed in the bull's-eye of a target. The children who have fewer choices are placed in circles farther from the center. The *isolates* who have not been selected are found in the outermost circle. The choices of the eleven girls in Miss Kenmore's class have been charted on a target to demonstrate the technique. As shown in Figure 29, the use of code numbers rather than names permits the choices to be recorded in a smaller area. The advantage of the target is that it enables the viewer to see at a glance the relative number of times the children were selected.

The type of sociogram a teacher chooses to create for his class depends upon what kind of information he desires and how complicated the choices of the children are. If each child makes four or five choices and the class is large, the target chart may well be too clumsy to handle, for the maze of lines becomes difficult to keep orderly.

A note on construction. Learning to construct a meaningful sociogram takes a bit of practice. The neophyte will probably find more success if he begins the first sociogram on a relatively large sheet of scratch paper, with the intention of transferring it to a final sheet after the initial plotting has been experimented with. It is often helpful to place the stars on the chart first, then to organize

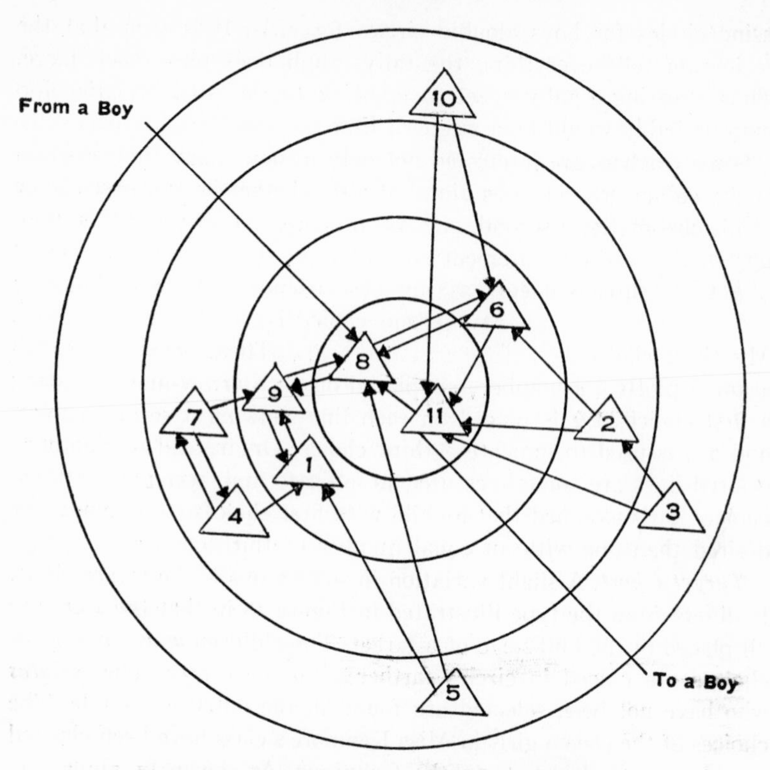

Fig. 29. Target chart of sixth-grade girls
Code numbers on the chart refer to the following girls:
1—Alice, 2—Betty R., 3—Betty T., 4—Edna, 5—Fran, 6—Helen, 7—Janet, 8—Jill, 9—Joyce, 10—Mary, 11—Sally.

the less popular students around them. The first attempt may result in what appears to be a maze of extended, twisting lines. However, by inspecting this trial chart, the teacher usually sees where some children may be regrouped so as to shorten lines and make the final sociogram more comprehensible.

USING SOCIOGRAM DATA

If the sociogram is really to result in help for the children and is not to be merely a fascinating pastime, the teacher must know how to interpret it accurately. Few other evaluation techniques show more clearly that one measuring device alone is insufficient for judging children's progress. The sociogram cannot be used alone. It tells *what* relationships exist among children. It *does not tell why* the choices occurred nor whether the choices a pupil received necessarily indicate good or poor social adjustment on his part. The sociogram gives hints. The teacher must look to personal observations, interviews with the child, anecdotal records, and records of home background to discover answers to these questions of adjustment.

The fact that a sociogram alone is insufficient is shown in Miss Kenmore's sixth grade. In this class four of the boys were isolates on the sociogram. If the sociometric data were used alone, we would assume that the boys were quite alike in social inadequacy and that the teacher would have to use the same method to get them into class activities to be better accepted. However, Miss Kenmore did not jump to such a conclusion. Instead, she took the hints offered by the sociograms and used them as a starting point for examining the children individually by other methods to see if each was really failing to meet social-acceptance goals. From anecdotal records, casual observation, and data about home background, the teacher made the following estimates of the meaning of the sociogram in these four cases.

Gerald . . . not chosen. He's new in our room. Just moved to town last week. He seems likable, but he's just beginning to get acquainted. I think he'll be all right when the others get to know him better. I'll wait and see.

Carl . . . not chosen. Carl is the smallest and youngest boy in class. I've never seen him playing with the sixth graders during lunch period or recess. Instead, he plays with the fifth graders who were his classmates until he was put ahead a year ago. Mrs. O'Brien (fifth-grade teacher) says Carl is one of the two leaders of the Blue-Aces, a gang composed mostly of boys in her room. Apparently, Carl is well accepted by his former classmates, and his social relationships remain at that level. Maybe it was a mistake to accelerate him last year, although he's doing very good work in my class. Despite the sociogram results, I think Carl is reaching the social-acceptance goal quite well. Perhaps I should have him work on more small committees with the sixth graders. However, I'm not going to worry too much about him. He's just not as mature as the others.

Alfred . . . not chosen. I could have predicted this. Alfred's record of behavior all through school has been poor. When he doesn't get his own way, he causes all kinds of difficulties. I've heard some of the children call him *Whiney*. I'm afraid that about describes him. I have talked with his mother twice and have discussed it with Mrs. O'Brien (fifth-grade teacher) who met Alfred's mother several times last year. I am convinced that he always has his own way there; he seldom is asked or required to compromise his own wishes for the good of others. Thus, he doesn't know how to handle compromises in school, and his classmates reject him. He is often the butt of teasing. I'm sorry for him, because he tries to get into group efforts, such as playing ball or painting a mural, but he usually ends up antagonizing the other children. He is definitely not succeeding in being accepted socially, and I believe it bothers him. I don't know what to do, since there appears to be little hope of helping his mother see there is anything wrong with the way he has been treated at home. She blames the school and the other children for Alfred's social rejection. The best I can do is to seat him near Ted, because he chose Ted, and Ted is more tolerant and less likely to be antagonized by Alfred than are some of the others.

George . . . not chosen. He's so shy and silent, I almost forget he's in class. However, from time to time I notice something he does that makes me realize that I should pay more attention to him. I have a number of anecdotes in his folder; they all lead me to believe that he wishes to have friends and be more accepted by the others, but he apparently feels too insecure to step forward and enter wholeheartedly into the group. He does his work steadily and causes no trouble. I'm quite sure he's not fulfilling his need for being welcomed by the others. I'm going to have to help him with some skill or hobby so that he can feel confident about showing it to the class. That might give him more confidence, and they would notice him more. In the meantime, I'll put him near Bob. For a sixth grader, Bob has a lot of social insight. I can talk with him more as I would with an adult, so I'll ask him to encourage George. It takes something like this sociogram to remind me to pay attention to George's needs. He's so shy and silent.

There are two notable aspects of Miss Kenmore's use of the sociogram. First, she did not interpret the sociometric data blindly, ignoring the other factors (gained from personal observation and talking with others) that gave insight into *why* the child has such a relationship in the class and *how* he apparently should be treated by the teacher. Second, Miss Kenmore did not work miracles as a result of the information she secured about the children. Instead, she used the information, along with her understanding of child development, to treat each child in such a way as to help him grow up more effectively, as far as she could predict. Teachers are not expected to work psychological magic. They are expected to use data to help see children's needs, their weaknesses and strengths, and to help them develop more effectively.

So far we have inspected sociograms as partial measures of a child's social acceptability within a class. Underlying this discussion has been the assumption that "social acceptability" is a desirable goal for children. In general, parents and educators would probably agree with this assumption that it is good for a child to be *accepted,* or, in a more active form, to be *welcomed* by his associates. However, the modern school aims not only to see that the child gets along well with others but that within himself he develops self-respect and confidence and a realistic acceptance of his own strengths and limitations. Consequently, we must not accept a high number of choices on a sociogram as necessarily representing good personal adjustment for every child. The *quality* of a child's relations with others must be inspected through observation and interviews. Jersild has presented a view of this qualitative factor which it is well for teachers to consider:

"We have fairly good methods for measuring behavior which we call social participation. We have usually assumed that the youngster who shows a high score in participation is in good shape. But if we could look at social participation from the viewpoint of the subjective world of the child, we would observe that seemingly similar scores may have vastly different meanings. One child, for example, is always on the alert to be with the group, to be accepted, and to lead. He comes up with ideas that others incorporate. He is resourceful as a group member. He seems to be well adjusted. Actually his sociability may be a sign of ill-health. He may be expressing a compulsion to live up to a self picture of being very popular. He needs to bolster his confidence in himself by means of continual evidence of being accepted by others. When seen from the point of view of his own lack of confidence in his worth as a person, his apparently good adjustment may be a symptom of maladjustment.

"On the other hand, a youngster may earn a high social participation score because he is spontaneous and wholehearted in his participation in group activities. He does not participate because of a chronic need to bolster himself.

"There may be a third person who has a low social participation score. His low score does not necessarily mean poor adjustment, for he is neither driven to seek the society of others nor driven to avoid it. He can enter into genuine relationships with other persons and enjoy them, but his style of life is not such that he needs continually to be in the thick of group activities." [1]

The observations made by Jersild about social participation also apply to social acceptance as reflected in sociograms. The quality in addition to the quantity of acceptance and the social participation that leads to acceptance must also be inspected.

Are sociograms practical?

This is a common question asked by those who say, "Doesn't a good teacher, who has observed the students closely over a period of time already know what the children's social relations are? Why bother to make a sociogram?"

It is true that after having a class for some time the observant instructor does know in general the degree of social acceptance of children in the group. A sociogram in these cases merely substantiates and refines the teacher's observations about the popularity of children and about the cliques or friendship groups formed in the class. However, teachers who use sociograms have found that even though they can predict the majority of class choices, they typically are mistaken in the cases of several children. These teachers, therefore, continue to use sociometrics because such methods refine and substantiate their observations and indicate possible mistaken judgments of a few children. For these reasons, and for others to be outlined later, they feel the work of a sociogram from time to time is worth while.

The following example shows how a first-grade teacher was aided in refining her observations of her children. Mrs. Botkin used the rest period several days to administer a sociometric test. During rest time, each child was called individually to the teacher's desk to "play a choosing game." Each was asked whom he would choose

[1] Arthur T. Jersild, *In Search of Self* (New York: Teachers College, Columbia University, 1952), pp. 112-13. Quoted by permission of the publisher.

as a partner to go on a walk. She gave them two choices. This sociogram was administered in March after the teacher had been with the 28 children for more than six months. Before asking the sociometric questions she had tried to predict from her casual observations how each child would be rated by his classmates. In general she made accurate predictions, but she was surprisingly wrong in the cases of two boys, Kenneth Jones and Charles Fronzi.

The teacher had assumed that Kenneth would be selected as one of the more popular. She wrote, "He has a creamy complexion, brown eyes, and wavy brown hair. He is in the advanced reading group and has the ability to do above-average work in school. In the early part of first grade he played a good deal with dolls; he always had many 'girl friends' around him and he kissed them a good deal."

On the sociogram Kenneth was selected only once, and that was by a boy. Observation following the sociogram showed that he probably was not welcomed by the others because he commonly disregarded other children's welfare and would not compromise his own desires. He always wanted his own way. This gave the teacher new insight into an area in which she could try to help Kenneth but had previously overlooked.

The second surprise produced by the sociogram was in the case of Charles. Mrs. Botkin's summary of observations pictures Charles as "... a quiet child. He is always clean and well dressed. Charles is very conscientious in all schoolwork. Charles' mother has spoken to me frequently about him. She says that the other children do not like him, that he is very unpopular. She does not allow him to play with other children at home, because she feels that they live in a very undesirable location, and 'I don't like him playing with the trash that live around us.'"

The teacher's report continues: "Charles seems to have great feelings of inadequacy; he does not have the confidence in himself that his ability warrants. He had a good deal of difficulty making the sociometric choices. When I asked the question, whom he would like to be with on the walk, he looked bewildered and repeated, 'to be with on the walk?' He looked around the class for quite a while and then said, 'That's pretty hard.' He chose Diane, a quiet girl of above-average ability in school. For his second choice he said, 'That's pretty hard, too.' He looked around the class and then stood for a long time. He looked at me again and said, 'Pretty hard.'

Finally he said, 'I know I couldn't have Meredith. Someone else would want her.' I told him he could choose anyone he wanted. Then he finally said, 'Meredith.'"

Because of her observations and the information from Charles's mother, Mrs. Botkin expected Charles to be overlooked by his classmates. On the sociogram Charles was selected eight times, the second largest number of choices received by a child.

The teacher recorded the following anecdote later: "I talked to Charles's mother after the sociogram results were tallied and tried to explain that Charles was apparently accepted by the others. She expressed great surprise at the results. I tried to encourage her to invite some of the children over to his house to play. She said she didn't want him playing with girls. Were there any 'nice, polite little boys' in our room? Charles had been chosen six times by boys, twice by girls." The mother took the names of the boys with the idea of following Mrs. Botkin's suggestion.

In this typical situation it is seen that the sociogram helped evaluate children's progress toward the goal of social acceptance and to refine the teacher's previous observations.

Repeating sociograms

By repeating the same sociometric question at a later date, a teacher is sometimes aided in seeing the changes that occur among children's choices.

This is shown in the case of a fourth-grade teacher who used a sociogram (whom I want as tablemates in the classroom) to determine patterns of social acceptance in the group. In this classroom, which had tables seating four students instead of the usual desks, the teacher allowed three choices per student. The sociogram revealed that one girl, Clarice, was isolated by her classmates. The teacher's observations indicated that Clarice was often rude to the others and that she dressed in a manner described as "careless and old-fashioned, not like her age-mates. Her hair is seldom brushed."

Thus the sociogram gave evidence of the pupils' lack of regard for Clarice, and the teacher's personal observations provided hints about why the girl was not selected as a tablemate. The teacher tried to help Clarice in two ways: by giving her special aid in working in a group and by asking her mother to visit class.

Clarice's mother worked in a laundry almost every day, so that she could not come until after school one day. Most of the first interview was spent by the teacher listening to the mother's complaints about Clarice ("She's lazy."), about two younger brothers, and about the difficulty of "getting the housework done after working all day." Gradually the teacher broached the subject of the way Clarice dressed compared with her classmates. The teacher said she thought Clarice's appearance affected her behavior in school and her acceptance by others. The mother at first partially resisted any suggestions and defended the girl's appearance by saying, "A person just doesn't have time to keep after her, and that girl can't keep her clothes nice when you do get her any." On the other hand, the mother was also concerned about helping her daughter become happier and more acceptable to her classmates, and she said she would see what could be done. In this case the teacher realized that money was not the important factor, because the father's job provided money enough to support the family without the mother's having to work.

In the following weeks the teacher noted that Clarice's appearance improved considerably, with "occasional days when her hair was uncombed and her clothes spotted and very wrinkled." A second sociometric test given when the seating arrangement was to be changed three months later, and supported by anecdotal records, revealed some progress in Clarice's becoming chosen and more acceptable to the group.

In this case, as in most realistic situations, the girl's personality was not rebuilt and no social-acceptance miracles were performed. However, the sociogram, supported by observations and parent interviews, did aid the teacher in diagnosing which children probably could use help toward attaining the friendship goal. The second sociogram helped evaluate how successful the teacher's methods were in aiding Clarice.

OTHER USES OF SOCIOGRAMS

The foregoing discussion has stressed the use of sociograms for analyzing the ways in which a student's classmates view him socially. The focus has been on the individual child and the extent to which he is chosen by others. There are at least three other important ways in which sociometric data aid the modern teacher. They are (1) to show the *patterns of groups* within the class, (2) to reveal the *kinds of choices* individual children make, and (3) to help establish a psychologically sound *basis for grouping children* for classwork.

Group patterns

The elementary school, more than any other social institution in America, is instrumental in bringing together a cross-section of the population for intimate contact over relatively long periods of time. It is true that some schools are in "good" neighborhoods, others are "across the tracks" or "down in the slums." Consequently, these classrooms do not reflect a real cross-section of American children. Despite the natural segregation of such schools because of the segregated nature of their neighborhoods, the elementary classroom remains the closest approach to congregating children of varied social classes, races, national backgrounds, and religions.

In a sense, the classroom is a miniature of the range of attitudes of the community, for the students bring with them their parents' varieties of attitudes toward other social classes, races, and religions. Sociograms are often effective devices for discovering how these attitudes operate within a classroom. Therefore, when analyzing a sociogram a teacher not only should pay attention to the number of times each individual was chosen but also should look for group *cleavages*. (*Cleavage* here means absence of choices between pupils as a result of their considering themselves as belonging to divergent groups. This group factor may be economic status, national background, religion, academic ability, race, or some special factor.) If cleavages and cliques do exist on the sociogram, the teacher should ask himself, "Have attitudes toward minorities or special groups caused these social patterns in my class, or has some other factor, such as my committee assignments or the seating plan, caused them?" By listening to students' comments and by observing their behavior, the teacher can answer this question.

Let us say the teacher does discover cleavages and decides that they are a result of community attitudes brought by the pupils into the classroom. What, if anything, should be done about it? A glance at the tensions among races, nations, and other social groups today indicates that one of the prime jobs of education is to reduce cleavages among peoples. The elementary classroom, as a miniature society, can be a valuable training ground for social understanding so that children will be better able than was their parents' generation to adjust to different social groups. The teacher, by using sociograms and observation for hints about cleavages, has the opportunity to manipulate the classroom society so that students who would not normally work closely with each other will come to know intimately, and consequently to understand, individuals of different social backgrounds. Research with sociometrics (2, 3) has shown that appropriate interaction among divergent groups within the classroom can provide significant intergroup understanding and cooperation. It seems to substantiate the saying, "When you know the man, you'll like him."

In the more formal type of classroom where the only action and only discussion is between teacher and student (commonly termed *coaction* because the children are expected to respond only to the teacher), information derived from a sociogram about group cleavage is usually of little use to the teacher. Such information does not help the teacher alter the classroom program to allow individuals of unlike religions or races to interact, because in the class that operates only on a coaction basis the students do not interact with each other. However, the more democratic type of classroom that is becoming more prevalent allows not only teacher-student discussion but also encourages *student-student interaction* during part of the class period. In such classes students work on committees together; they help each other in reading or arithmetic or geography. It is in situations like these that the teacher can manipulate choices for group work so that children of a minority will be spread among the committees, not concentrated only in their own clique or rejected by the others.

Throughout the above discussion we have assumed that the teacher desires the children's classroom experiences to carry them toward a goal that is an integral part of democracy:

"The student judges and treats other people on the basis of their individual characteristics, not on the basis of their membership in a particular group, such as a race, religion, or social class."

Let us grant that intermixing groups within the class can often be effective in reducing cleavage. The question now arises, "If you ask children for their choices of committee members and they do not choose classmates of a minority group, how can you honestly place minority members on their committees without violating the children's choices?"

This question can best be answered by the individual teacher who studies and understands the children in his room. The best answer for one classroom may not be the best for another. There are, however, some suggestions about grouping that have resulted from the experience of those who have worked most with sociometrics (*2, 3*). They recommend, first, that when a teacher administers a sociometric test, the action indicated in the test (such as reseating the class or forming science committees) should actually be carried out as soon as possible. Second, "...provide for each child the best possible arrangement from *his* point of view, but since the same consideration must be shown to all of his classmates, there will have to be some compromise." (*3:45*) By following these two rules of thumb, the teacher shows his respect for the students' choices. When the teacher inspects the sociogram with the intention of dividing the class into science committees, and he finds cleavages he wishes to combat, he may decide that the "best possible arrangement" can result sociologically if minority-and majority-group members are intermixed, even though they were not high on each other's list of choices. To do this the teacher may have to organize the committees by giving some students their third or fourth choices rather than their first or second.

One way this can be done is illustrated by an eighth grade in a California school where the teacher discovered cleavages through sociograms and subsequently divided up the class for committee work. The class was composed of 43 students, of which 23 were boys and 20 were girls. From grades four through seven the students had had very few opportunities for interaction during class. The eighth-grade teacher was gradually initiating them into group work. She had introduced it by saying:

"You all know the people you like to work with most. So we are going to use a new way to set up committees to work out the booklet about our community which we decided last week to make. There will be four or five people on each committee. On the first line write your name. On the second line write a number 1. On this line with the 1 you are to write the name of your first choice for a person to be on the same science committee with you. Number the next line 2 and write the name of your second choice. Use the next line for your third choice and the following one for your fourth, as I have indicated here on the blackboard. And remember, choose the people you want to be with on a community-booklet committee. They may be the same people you like to be with on art or science or party committees, or they may be different people.

It doesn't matter. You may not all get your first choices, but everybody will be on a committee with one or more of the people he has chosen."

The resulting sociogram revealed few boy-girl selections, a fairly common situation in numbers of classrooms. This does not necessarily mean that boys and girls do not want to be on the same committees in eighth grade; it often indicates an embarrassment about indicating their liking for one of the opposite sex when they are in this early adolescent period. To reduce this type of cleavage, and to indicate that there was no stigma attached to cross-sex choices, the teacher took advantage of as many boy-girl selections as possible in creating the committees.

A casual observer entering the eighth-grade room would note that four of the forty-three students were American children of oriental parentage (three boys, one girl). The observer might expect rejection or neglect of these pupils on the basis of race. However, this did not prove to be true. In fact, the boy who was selected most often (13 times) was Frank Iwamoto. Each of the other three was chosen several times. Thus the teacher was not concerned in this eighth grade with using the groups to promote acceptance of a racial minority.

As shown by a segment of the eighth-grade sociogram (Fig. 30), there was another type of cleavage that caused the teacher concern. A tight clique of four boys (George, Jack, Don, and Louis) showed up on the social-relations map. What the four had in common socially was the place they lived. All were from broken families and now lived in a home for boys which was run by a religious organization. This had created a tight bond among them. In addition, it apparently had caused the bulk of their classmates to consider them different and undesirable.

By inspecting the segment of the sociogram (Fig. 30) we see the choice the teacher had to make in composing the social-studies committees. She could have given the four boys their first or second choices and kept them together. But she decided that for their own good they should be placed in personal contact with other members of the class with whom they had little or no contact outside of class. Consequently, she placed George and Jack on a committee with Bill, Frank (the popular boy mentioned earlier), and Larry. (It will be noted that Larry was an isolate as far as the committee-choices were concerned. The teacher was glad to be able to give him three of his selections.) The two other boys in the clique, Louis and Don, were placed on a committee with Sam and with Jane and Helen. Jane and Helen were well-liked girls who had mutual first choices. As shown in the sociogram, Sam and Louis had both chosen Jane.

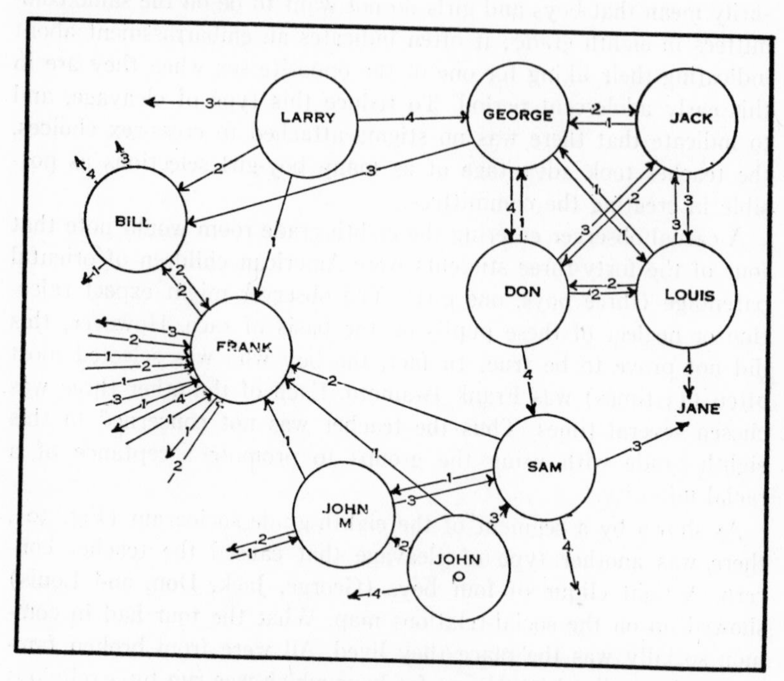

Fig. 30. Cleavage in an eighth grade

In this eighth grade, therefore, the teacher tried to organize the committees to establish the best possible arrangement for all. She not only focussed on the individual needs of children but on cleavages which she believed should be reduced if a happier society was to result in the classroom.

Reasons for students' choices

Just as adults select companions and join groups to fulfill their own needs, so children choose classmates that fulfill needs in their lives. The modern teacher continually seeks to learn his students' needs, desires, and concerns. He knows that fulfilling these needs is the school's major task. He realizes that the needs, and the strength of them, differ somewhat from one child to another. To find them, the teacher must study each child.

In this area of understanding pupils' motives and drives sociometry can make a unique contribution. It reveals the ways pupils themselves are attempting to satisfy their own needs. We do not assume that children are aware, except perhaps partially, that their needs govern their choices of companions and workmates. However, what children say about their choices can give hints to the teacher or psychologist about motives and concerns.

As indicated earlier, the sociogram tells only *what* choices are made, not *why*. To discover the *why* the teacher must observe the pupils' actions and must talk with them. Consequently, in using sociometry to discover more about individual children's motives and problems the teacher can use a *sociometric interview* or can ask children to *list their reasons* for their choices.

A sociometric interview is a discussion with a pupil based upon his answers to a sociometric test. The student should not feel that the interview is a probing into his personal life. Instead, it must be handled with tact, and the teacher must present himself as a friendly guide, not a critic. A less direct question, such as, "Was there a particular reason you can think of for your choosing Alice?" is probably preferred to a more blunt "Why did you choose Alice?" (See Chapter 15 for a fuller treatment of interview techniques.)

Before interviews about sociogram data are held, the teacher should inform the class of what to expect. He might say when administering the sociogram question, "The better you and I become acquainted, the more I can help make the class worth-while and interesting for you. If I understand your ideas and feelings, I can help arrange our class groups and class seating plan so that they will suit you. It will help me understand if you and I talk together about your choices for committee members or seat partners. So from time to time between classes and during our work I will chat with you individually. This way you can explain your ideas and feelings to me."

The informal interviews that result can be used to inform the teacher of child needs and can improve teacher-pupil rapport. Students in the upper grades often give direct and helpful reasons for their choices. Here are three examples from one seventh grade:

1. "I chose her because she's always nice and is the favorite of all the girls. We tell each other our troubles."

2. "He doesn't have to have his own way all the time. I have my way some of the time and he has his way some of the time. He says funny things, and we don't fight with each other."
3. The smallest boy in the room picked another relatively short boy "... because he is cute and is a medium height."

When it is inconvenient to interview the entire class, even in a casual way, it is sometimes helpful to have the children write the reasons for their choices. As in the interview situation, older children can often give specific and insightful reasons. A good example is that of an eighth-grade girl who was listing the friends she would like to sit near. The number of selections a student was to make was not designated. She selected four. In listing the reasons for her choices, she displayed a frankness that aided the teacher considerably in understanding her needs and interests. She wrote:

"Abie.... He is a good dancer, and he isnt ashambed of his parents. He is a good sport.

"Rosie.... When I tell her, lets go someplace she doesnt say no. She doesnt flirt with my boyfriend.

"Ferrmin.... He is not rude or embarres me in front of people and he is not stingy with his money.

"Bobbie.... Has very nice manners, he doesnt whistle to other girls when he is walking with you, and he helps me solve my problems."

Children in the lower grades often cannot give very helpful reasons for their choices. Generally, they seem to lack the insight into their motives and interests that will aid the teacher much in understanding their selections. Consequently, the teacher of younger children must rely more upon observation for clues to the needs children are attempting to fulfill by their choices.

Grouping in class

Rather than concentrating on information about the social acceptance or desirability of individuals, some teachers stress the values children derive from groups that result from sociometric choices.

In the past it has often been customary for teachers when arranging their classrooms to separate children who are especially attracted to each other. This practice is based upon the belief that children pay closer attention to schoolwork if they are not near their friends. In at least some cases this belief is probably correct. However, as a general practice the separation of children who like each other may very well be educationally unsound. As Jennings writes (*2:203*):

"Investigation reveals... that better work in general is done when pupils are in close association with other pupils with whom they want to be and with whom they feel most comfortable. Moreover, many other outcomes of such grouping practice make the teacher's work easier and more enjoyable."

Some educators when first introduced to sociometrics assume that one sociogram describes adequately the classroom social structure. However, this is not true. Over a period of time students' choices can change. And, more important, students alter their choices according to the type of question asked. The class social structure, therefore, is more complicated than can be revealed by one sociogram.

Research with sociometrics has shown that two different kinds of choice patterns are often found in classrooms. One pattern, called a *psychegroup,* is the result of students' choosing classmates they generally like to be with for personal reasons. When they select "best friends" or "person to sit near" there is no special group task to be accomplished, and the pupils choose others whose personalities they like. The psychegroup apparently results from psychological needs that are fulfilled simply by being with the chosen friend.

The other social pattern, called a *sociogroup,* is the result of a child's choosing classmates who will best aid him in reaching some common class goal. Examples of sociogroups would be arithmetic study groups or science-experiment committees.

Especially in the lower grades there is a great deal of overlapping between psychegroups and sociogroups. But as pupils mature, and if they have opportunities to make both types of choices in class, they increasingly select the classmates carefully according to the specific occasion.

In some classrooms teachers provide opportunities only for work committees (sociogroups). They do not provide for less formal occasions when the children are left on their own to use their time as they themselves decide. In classrooms providing only work groups the teachers can expect much more overlapping of psychegroup and sociogroup selections (*2*). It appears that children's psychological needs take preference. When they have only work committees available for group contact in the class, they tend to select companions who fulfill their psychological needs, even though such selection may not be the wisest in light of the work to be performed. However, when informal situations are provided to fulfill psychological needs, the pupils seem to be more selective in choosing partners for work projects (*2:219–220*).

It is important, therefore, that the teacher recognize what types of selections will be likely to result from a given sociometric question. Present evidence indicates that with sufficient opportunities for personal relationships during the school day (psychegroups), children will, as they mature, select wisely the classmates with whom they can most profitably work toward common goals (sociogroups).

"GUESS WHO" TECHNIQUE

Another variation of sociometry that is applicable in the elementary or junior high school is termed the "Guess Who" or "Casting Characters" technique. Although it also depends on student rather than teacher opinions of pupils, it supplements the information supplied by the sociogram rather than substituting for the sociometric methods described so far. It enables the teacher to see into what role a child fits in the eyes of his classmates. One form that has proved successful presents a "let's imagine" situation to the class. This is the "Casting Characters" variety of the technique. The teacher instructs the class as follows:

"Let's imagine we wish to put on a class play. On the mimeographed papers I handed to you, you see each character in the play described. At the right on each description of a character, you see a blank. In this blank you are to write the names of one or more students in the class who would be good for that part because they are pretty much like that already."

1. This person is very bashful and has a hard time talking to others.________________
2. This person always likes to be boss and tell the others what to do. ________________
3. This person cries very easily and gets his (or her) feelings hurt easily if somebody finds fault with him (or her).________________

4. This person is a good leader in classroom projects. He (or she) is friendly and others like to work with him (or her). ____________

This list of characters can be expanded to touch upon the type of behavior or characteristics the teacher is interested in.

The "Guess Who" variation of this device puts the students in the position of playing the game of guessing which classmates fit certain characteristics. Usually it is best for the teacher to inform the class that if they think more than one person suits a single description, they are to write more than one name. On the other hand, if no one seems to fit the description very closely, they should leave the item blank.

GUESS WHO

Directions: Read each of the sentences below. Decide which pupil (or pupils) in our class is most like the description in that sentence. Write that pupil's name (or their names) in the space after the sentence. If more than one sentence fits the same pupil, you may write that pupil's name more than once.

Your name ____________ Date ____________

1. Guess who is always smiling and cheerful. ____________
2. Guess who is liked by almost everybody. ____________
3. Guess who isn't very good at outdoor games. ____________
4. Guess who is not liked very much by anybody. ____________
5. Guess who can't mind his (or her) own business and always tries to tell other people how to do things. ____________
6. Guess who says unkind things to others. ____________
7. Guess who plays outdoor games very well. ____________
8. Guess who is very good at schoolwork. ____________
9. Guess who would make the best class president. ____________
10. Guess who gets mad at others very easily. ____________
11. Guess who is very kind to others. ____________
12. Guess who lets others boss him (or her). ____________
13. Guess who doesn't get angry very often. ____________
14. Guess who is often very tired and worn out. ____________
15. Guess who is the hardest worker in class. ____________
16. Guess who is rather lazy. ____________

The teacher can design such a sheet according to characteristics he is interested in investigating, often using two different questions to locate children who, in the eyes of their classmates, show opposite extremes of a given trait, such as: friendly–not friendly, domineering–submissive, skilled–not skilled at sports, etc.

The information from this kind of technique can be used to draw conclusions about why certain choices have been made on sociograms, because the guess-who answers show the impression certain children make on their agemates.

Many teachers prefer not to use such questionnaires because they believe questions of this type focus attention on students who perhaps are already painfully aware of the impression they apparently have made on classmates. *Thus, for the sake of class morale and mental hygiene, these teachers prefer to seek information about the children from their own observations.* The decision about how guess-who questionnaires may affect class morale must be up to the individual teacher, for only he is in a position to estimate the effect on his particular class. The device is best suited for research.

In a research setting guess-who devices have not only been used to show the degree of social acceptance of pupils, but they have yielded information about the values or traits that are important to children at different age-levels and in different socioeconomic circumstances.

OBJECTIVES OF THIS CHAPTER

The effective elementary-school teacher:

1. Constructs sociograms that are easily read (lines not confused, stars and isolates easy to find, and cliques discernible).
2. Uses sociometric results, supported and modified by other evaluation methods and a knowledge of child development, on which to base treatment of children.
3. When deemed appropriate, uses guess-who techniques to determine pupils' characteristics in the eyes of the agemates.

Suggested evaluation techniques for this chapter

1. You teach fifth grade. For a map-making project you wish to divide the class into groups of three. Since you believe they will work better with someone of their choice and also may achieve better social acceptance, you have given the students the following instructions:

   "We are all going to work in groups of three to construct our maps. In order to divide up the class for this work, we will have you take one of these slips of paper and write your name at the top. On the first line below your name write the name of your first choice of a partner on the map committee. On the second line write the name of the second choice for a partner."

Here are the choices the students made. The first choice is the first one listed; the second choice is the second name listed.

Doris chose Sarah and Jane
Sarah chose Molly and Dale
Molly chose Tom and Jane
Lola chose Molly and Sally
Sam chose Tom and Dan
Martin chose Sam and Dan
Pete chose Tom and Dan
Len chose Pete and Tom
Dale chose Sarah and Doris
Jane chose Molly and Sam
Sally chose Sarah and Molly
Tom chose Sam and Martin
Dan chose Tom and Sam
Kenny chose Sam and Tom
Ted chose Len and Pete

Directions: Make a sociogram that shows clearly the relationships among the students of this class in regard to map-making-committee choices. Using the sociogram as a guide, divide the class into committees of three. If you find that you would like more information to do this task adequately, write down *what type* of additional information you would like and *why* you feel you need it.

2. In working on cake baking in her small junior high homemaking class Miss Stalie asks the students to select a partner with whom to work. She also wishes to use these data to learn something more about their social interrelationships. Thus, she asks them: "What girl would you most like to work with during the cake-baking sessions? Since everybody may not be able to get the first partner she selects, you should put a second choice below the first one."

   The choices follow:

   Jill chose Alice and Nancy
   June chose Anna and Kernith
   Betty chose Kernith and Jill
   Alice chose Nancy and Kernith
   Lucy chose Anna and Kernith
   Donna chose Kernith and Nancy
   Kernith chose June and Fran
   Nancy chose Alice and Donna
   Fran chose June and Kernith
   Dolores chose June and Lucy
   Anna chose June and Kernith

   From the following data construct a sociogram. From the sociogram answer the following true-false-with-reasons items. Mark a plus (+) in front of each true statement. Mark a zero (0) in front of each false one. Mark an *N* in front of each statement for which you have insufficient evidence to answer adequately. In the space beside each statement, write the reason for your decision.

   ______(1) In pairing the girls for the unit, it would not be possible for the teacher to give every girl one of her choices.

______(2) It would be a good idea for Miss Stalie to speak to Kernith about making friends with Dolores so that Dolores will have a feeling of being an accepted part of the class.

______(3) Anna was chosen by two girls she apparently likes.

______(4) Kernith was chosen by two girls she apparently likes.

______(5) Betty would probably be accepted better if she were not so aggressive in class.

______(6) Kernith's friendliness and her admired social status in the school (as a result of her family's social position in the community) help account for her being chosen so often as a partner.

SUGGESTED READINGS

1. HORACE MANN-LINCOLN INSTITUTE OF SCHOOL EXPERIMENTATION. *How to Construct a Sociogram*. New York: Bureau of Publications, Teachers College, Columbia University, 1947. A booklet describing simple ways to sketch sociograms.
2. JENNINGS, HELEN. "Sociometric Grouping in Relation to Child Development," in *Fostering Mental Health in Our Schools*. Association for Supervision and Curriculum Development. 1950 Yearbook. Washington, D.C.: National Education Association, 1950. Short, clear examples of sociogram use.
3. JENNINGS, HELEN. *Sociometry in Group Relations*. Washington, D.C.: American Council on Education, 1948.
4. JERSILD, ARTHUR T. *In Search of Self*. New York: Teachers College, Columbia University, 1952.
5. MORENO, J. L. *Who Shall Survive?* New York: Beacon House, 1934. The classic publication that launched sociometry.
6. OLSON, WILLARD C. *Child Development*. Boston: D. C. Heath and Co., 1949. Target chart example: p. 199.

CHAPTER

10

Charting Participation

MR. CORNING'S SEVENTH-GRADE CLASS provides many opportunities for students to participate in class and panel discussions and to work in groups. He says he does this because: "I don't believe people become democratic citizens just because they reach twenty-one. A lot of people of voting age are pretty immature, and I believe people have to learn how to work with each other and be democratic in their everyday lives from the time they are small if they are really going to be good citizens when they grow up. And I don't believe people will speak up in a group unless they have the confidence of knowing how to present their point of view well. People aren't born with this maturity to work with groups and understand others' points of view. I think they have to learn it. Therefore, it's necessary for me as a teacher to give youngsters practice in real group decisions if they are to grow up right."

Mr. Corning realizes that his students must learn gradually, must make mistakes and learn to correct them, before they can work together effectively. To make his teaching aims more specific, he has outlined the following types of student behavior, which are goals toward which the class strives.

"The effective group member:

1. Willingly accepts and carries out fair share of work.
2. Willingly contributes to discussion.
3. Keeps on the topic or problem to be solved; does not digress.
4. Abides by majority decisions.

5. Permits others to express their views on the topic.

The effective group leader:

1. Defines the problem or topic for the group.
2. Encourages each member to contribute to discussion and decisions.
3. Politely directs group toward goal; minimizes digressions.
4. Provides for majority decisions on controversial issues.
5. Ensures a fair division of work on outside research assignments.
6. Plans time and topic or agenda for future meetings."

By defining effective group participation in terms of student behavior, Mr. Corning can better evaluate whether students are reaching the goal or not. If he had not taken the trouble to define what he really wanted from the students, he would have had only the vague term "good group work," which is an elusive criterion by which to judge children's progress, for it does not tell what "good group work" entails.

The problem now is to discover what kinds of evaluation devices will best show how well the students are achieving the goals. The most obvious scheme is for the teacher to sit with a student group and observe how well the chairman handles the situation, who contributes to the discussion, who strays from the topic, and who accepts responsibility readily. By his casual observation, Mr. Corning can secure a "general impression of how things are going." However, he is not satisfied with only a "general impression." He has found that at the end of the day when he stops to think over how well the groups worked, his notion of what part certain students played is often vague or nonexistent. To improve his evaluation of group work, he has adopted a scheme for *charting participation* of the students as he listens in on their committees. His chart gives a much more accurate record than his memory alone would provide of the group dynamics. Each student is accounted for. None is ignored or forgotten.

FORMS FOR CHARTING GROUPS

There are many methods for charting participation. Once a teacher notes the general procedure, he often adds his own improvements to suit the needs of his class best. The techniques suggested below have been found useful.

Probably the simplest method is to record only the number of times each student speaks in the group. If there are five on the committee, the teacher can use a sheet with a square to represent each member's position. During the meeting a tally is marked in the square each time the student speaks. Figure 31 is such a charting of a group meeting of sixth graders planning a bulletin board display on Mexico.

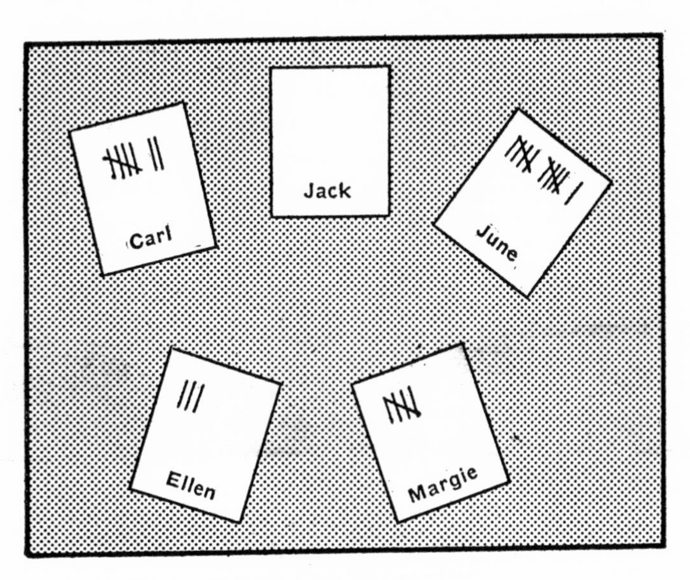

Fig. 31. Simple charting

This chart shows that June spoke most frequently in the group. Carl was next. Margie and Ellen contributed several remarks, and Jack said nothing. Although such a chart is useful, it does not record the comparative value of each student's remarks in making the group effective. This simple diagram does not tell which remarks were important and which were of slight significance. It does not indicate which were digressions, such as jokes or gossip, nor does it tell which students held the floor for a long time and which ones made brief remarks.

Some refinement of the charting system will yield additional worth-while information. For example, in order to show which students kept on the topic the group was discussing, the box representing each person can be separated into upper and lower portions. The observer can place a tally in the upper half when a student makes a remark that is on the subject, and place a tally in the lower half when a student speaks off the topic. In order to record the time each contribution took, the observer can make a long tally for lengthy statements and a short tally for brief ones. The same group meeting recorded in Figure 31 would look like Figure 32 when charted in this more complete manner. Figure 32, therefore,

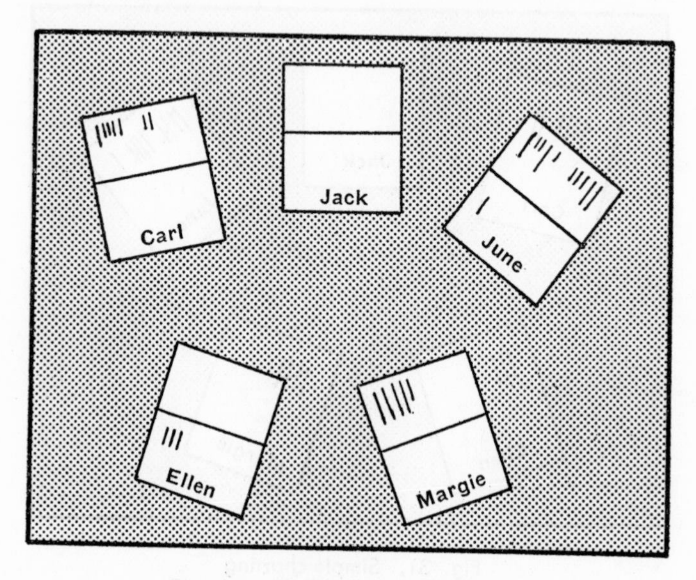

Fig. 32. Charting in double boxes

represents a more sophisticated analysis of the students' participation. Carl's remarks were all brief and on the topic. Some of June's contributions were longer than others; all but one were on the topic. Although Ellen talked three times, she apparently contributed nothing since she was always off the topic. (Actually Ellen's remarks were complaints about what a waste of time such a committee was when she had so much else to do.) Each of Margie's five contributions was of some length and was on the topic. Therefore, this chart is a more helpful picture than was the first one in helping the teacher judge how well students (1) contribute to discussion and (2) pursue the topic or problem to be solved.

Some teachers say, "But such a chart still does not yield as much information as I want. I would like to record not only *whether or not* a student sticks to the topic, but I would also like to show which students make the most important contributions toward reaching the goal and which ones make lesser contributions."

A slight expansion of the device described above enables the teacher to record this additional information. Each box that represents a student can be divided into three horizontal portions. In the top portion the important contributions of the student are tallied. In the middle portion the minor contributions on the topic are tallied. In the bottom portion, remarks that are off the topic are recorded.

Some instructors revise the chart a further step by distinguishing among four categories of student contributions. This becomes a type of rating scale indicating four degrees: (1) major contributions; (2) minor contributions; (3) somewhat passive agreement with group or a contribution of questionable value but still on the topic, and (4) remarks that distract or retard progress; statements that are off the topic.

The types of forms described above for charting group participation are the kinds that seem to be most useful for classroom teachers and for students to use in the upper grades. Samples of other devices for more specialized uses are described in the latter part of the chapter.

THE PROCESS OF CHARTING GROUPS

The teacher, or a student who acts as an observer of a group, listens to the discussion and evaluates each student's remarks as they are being given. When the group member has stopped talking, the observer places a tally in the box that seems most appropriate. This process takes some practice, because the novice tends to become interested in the remarks and forgets to record them. However, after a number of experiences in charting participation, the observer typically finds the charting proceeds easily.

The question is often raised, "If the observer tries to distinguish among three or four degrees of goodness in the remarks of group members, does not the process become complicated?"

It is true that charting demands immediate decisions on the part of the observer. He must decide when a remark represents a major idea or a minor one. Practice enables him to make these decisions more easily. And if his criteria are fairly well defined ahead of time, his task is simplified and his judgments should be more consistent. One teacher will probably chart certain remarks somewhat differently from another. For example, it is sometimes difficult to decide whether a remark was a major or a minor contribution. However, when teachers use the same criteria for deciding where a tally should be placed, *the general pattern of their charts will be the same.*

A record of the actual remarks by students working on a group project in Mr. Corning's seventh grade will indicate how the participation of six students solving a problem was charted. (The reader may wish to chart the group work and compare the result with Mr. Corning's chart at the end of the dialogue.)

The committee was composed of Chuck, Doris, Geraldine, Kent, Lyle, and Margaret. By voting on slips of paper, the group had chosen Chuck as chairman just before the following dialogue began.

CHUCK: Well, now here's what we're supposed to be doing . . . make a plan for showing how our town depends a lot on modern transportation for the way we live.

LYLE: Let's get this straight. Is our committee supposed to do all the work on showing this modern transportation? And how long do we have to do it?

DORIS: The way I understand it, we're supposed to do it all. Just like in that last unit on the town government, every committee had one job.

CHUCK: That's right. And Mr. Corning says this unit's to last about three weeks. Okay?

LYLE: Yeah. But I'm kind of confused about what we're supposed to do.

CHUCK: Well, let's get some different ideas first. Then maybe it'll get clearer what we should do. What do you think would be a good way to show how our town depends on modern transportation?

LYLE: You mean some way to show the rest of the class? A report or something?

DORIS: Of course. That's why we're doing it.

CHUCK: Kent, you have any ideas?

KENT: No.

CHUCK: Gerry. Any ideas about this?

GERALDINE: Well, someway we ought to show all the different kinds of modern transportation . . . like trains and the airfield and cars and trucks.

LYLE: Oh, sure, and bikes and scooters and kiddy-cars. Ha!

CHUCK: Well, Gerry's idea is a start. Margaret, any other ideas?

MARGARET: Gerry's suggestion is all right. The different kinds.

CHUCK: All right, someway we could show all the different kinds of modern transportation. But then that really doesn't show how important transportation is.

DORIS: That's right. Just think what it'd be like if all the cars and trains and trucks and airplanes stopped. What would it be like then?

LYLE: Maybe there's an idea. Maybe we could figure out what would happen if all kinds of transportation stopped. Like she says.

CHUCK: Then put on some kind of thing so the class would understand it?

LYLE: Sure.

GERRY: Thing? You mean a program, like a talk or a committee report?

CHUCK: Well, something like that.

DORIS: Oh, let's not have another report. I get bored by them all the time.

LYLE: Well, we have to do it some way . . . a report or something. We always have to report to the class.

DORIS: Well, I about fall asleep every time some committee gets up there and just talks.

LYLE: Yeah, remember when Harry read that big long thing and we snored in the back of the room?

DORIS: And Corning jumped on you for making so much noise.

LYLE: (loud whisper): Shh. He's right behind you.

(Several in the group giggle.)

CHUCK: Look. We have to give a report, but we don't want it dull. So why don't we make it like a radio program . . . you know, like trucks and trains all stopped and this is a news broadcast?

LYLE: You mean, a war or death rays stop everything. And then we see what our town would be like?

GERRY: That might be all right.

DORIS: Say, I know. You know that microphone and that . . . that big thing they use for the square dances in the gym.

CHUCK: You mean the loudspeaker?

LYLE: That's a public-address system. P-A systems, they call them.

DORIS: Well, maybe we could get that and put it in the other room.

GERRY: What in the other room?

DORIS: The microphone . . . and we'd get in there and broadcast. Then the class wouldn't see us, and they'd hear it just like on the radio here in class.

GERRY: How would they hear us if we're in the other room?

DORIS: You just put the microphone in the other room and then run the cord out and put the loudspeaker in this room.

LYLE: Yeah, those P-A systems have a long cord. That'd work.

CHUCK: That sounds good, Doris. Does everybody agree we should do it like that?

LYLE: Okay by me.

GERRY: Me too.

MARGARET: Yes.

CHUCK: How about you, Kent?

KENT: Sure.

CHUCK: All right, now let's see what we've decided so far. We'll have a radio program and broadcast like news flashes. Have maybe some kind of rays shot down from Mars that stop all transportation. And the news broadcast will tell what it would be like if all modern transportation stopped. Agreed?

(All nod and say Yes.)

(End of Observation)

Mr. Corning, who was listening to the group, charted the members' participation in the following manner:

<table>
<tr><th>Contribution</th><th>Chuck</th><th>Lyle</th><th>Doris</th><th>Gerry</th><th>Margaret</th><th>Kent</th></tr>
<tr><td>Major</td><td>||||| |</td><td>|||</td><td>|||||</td><td>|</td><td></td><td></td></tr>
<tr><td>Minor</td><td>||||| ||</td><td>||</td><td>||||</td><td>|||</td><td></td><td></td></tr>
<tr><td>Passive or Doubtful</td><td>|</td><td>|||||</td><td></td><td>|</td><td>||</td><td>||</td></tr>
<tr><td>Detracting</td><td></td><td>|||</td><td>|</td><td></td><td></td><td></td></tr>
</table>

Fig. 33. Chart of transportation committee

* Major contribution—Introduction of a new idea or significant clarification of the goal.
* Minor contribution—Keeping others on the topic, clarification of ideas already presented, minor addition to idea.
* Passive or doubtful contribution—Passive agreement or statement of dubious value but on topic.
* Detracting contribution—Tends to carry group away from pursuing the goal.

As indicated before, it is expected that another teacher doing the rating would judge certain remarks somewhat differently from the way Mr. Corning did, because distinctions between degrees on this scale are sometimes difficult to make. For example, Mr. Corning rated the following question as a major contribution (category 1):

LYLE: "You mean, war or death rays stop everything. And then we see what our town would be like?"

Another rater might regard this as a minor contribution (category 2). However, it is unlikely another rater would differ from Mr. Corning's more than one degree such as by marking this remark as low as category 3 or 4.

Other remarks that students make more obviously belong in a particular category, such as the following statements which were off the topic and thus tallied in category 4:

LYLE: "Yeah, remember when Harry read that big long thing and we snored in the back of the room?"
DORIS: "And Corning jumped on you for making so much noise."
LYLE: "Ssh. He's right behind you."

Despite slight differences in judgments of raters, the general pattern of their charts should be the same and should lead to the same type of interpretation as the seventh-grade teacher's.

Interpreting what his chart told him, Mr. Corning said:

"Chuck was consistently a fine chairman. He kept the group going and on the topic. He tried to get everyone to contribute. He's a fine group member.

"Lyle was very willing to talk. In some cases his remarks were substantial contributions, but he shows a tendency to talk for the sake of talking oftentimes. He got off the subject occasionally. But he's still fairly good for a seventh grader.

"Doris was one of the main reasons this group worked well and made rapid progress in solving their problem. She contributed freely, and all but one of her remarks helped them toward the goal. She did a fine job.

"Geraldine did not contribute quite so much as some others, but what she did say usually was worth while. She always stayed on the topic.

"Margaret spoke seldom. Her remarks were not off the topic, but neither were they worth while in helping solve the problem. As far as the group progress was concerned, she might as well not have been there at all.

"Kent spoke seldom. His two remarks neither aided nor distracted the group."

USE OF GROUP-WORK CHARTING

There are several ways Mr. Corning can use participation charting in helping the students improve in working with others. These ways include: (1) diagnosing student participation, (2) measuring student growth throughout the year, and (3) aiding students in analyzing their own roles in groups.

Diagnosing student participation

Although teachers typically know which students in their classes talk the most in groups and which ones contribute little, unorganized observation is not as accurate as charting. A teacher may demonstrate the truth of this by charting the contributions of members in class committee work and comparing the results with his former general impressions of the way different students operate in groups. A typical statement by a teacher who has newly learned to plot contributions in class is:

"I could have predicted many of the pupils' actions from my previous impressions. But some of them really surprised me. Now that I look back, I see that I had always felt that several of these students contributed regularly, but in reality they were always silent partners in the group. This chart has also brought out a lot more clearly the distinction between one pupil who talks much but actually *contributes* little and another whose frequent remarks carry the committee steadily toward the goal. Now I believe that occasional charting of group work is really worth while."

After using charting to help analyze how well his students are progressing toward his goals of democratic living, Mr. Corning can decide how he may aid those who are particularly weak in certain skills. At this point there is no general answer that tells exactly how to help students improve once their weaknesses in working with others are diagnosed. It is here that the teacher's understanding of human behavior tells him whether the silent boy in a group needs encouragement or whether he needs to face abruptly the fact that he is consciously shirking a responsibility to the other group members.

Just as the sociogram does not tell *why* a child is not chosen by the others or *what* (if anything) to do about it, so also the participation chart tells only who contributes, how often, and how valuable the contributions are. The chart does not tell what to do about the silent members or the *talkers* who contribute nothing or the *wise guys* who use the group as an arena in which to display their off-the-topic wit. The chart helps spotlight each person's worth in the group. Then the teacher's understanding of child and adolescent psychology tells how to treat each individual to help him progress in an adequate manner toward group work goals.

Measuring growth throughout the year

As suggested above, charting is useful for diagnosing student strengths and weaknesses in working with others so that the teacher can better help individuals improve in weak areas. Charting can also be done in similar situations at various times later in the year, and the several charts can be compared to determine the effectiveness of the teacher's diagnosis and help.

For example, Alvin Kelley was a very poor chairman for a group early in the year. After several students had had opportunities to be chairmen of groups, the class discussed the responsibilities of committee leaders. In addition, Mr. Corning talked with Alvin individually about the steps he should follow and the procedures he should keep in mind as a chairman. Between them they decided that the next time Alvin headed a group he should have these steps written on a card so that he would not forget them. A later charting of Alvin's group helped show how effectively the boy had progressed beyond the first meeting.

Charting groups several times during the year is recommended in order to provide a good sample of the student's typical behavior upon which to judge his general progress and to indicate degrees of improvement throughout the year.

Aiding students in self-analysis

Children in the upper elementary and junior high school grades can effectively chart their own group work patterns. In their beginning group work in the intermediate grades they will necessarily need to use a very simple charting method. However, in the upper grades some students can with practice become accurate observers.

Mr. Corning has taught his students how to chart participation by using a tally system that distinguishes between remarks that are on the subject and those that are off the subject. When they do group work, the students know clearly the responsibilities of good leaders and of good group members, for they have discussed these in class. When each committee organizes, the members usually select three pupils to carry out special duties. One is chairman, another is recorder or secretary, and the third is the observer who charts participation. An observer is not always used in their group work but Mr. Corning has found that:

"Charting draws their attention to the importance of everyone's contributing toward solving the group's problem. The number of students who in the past took the let-George-do-it attitude has been reduced by the fact that definite evidence is available at the end of a meeting to show who did the work."

Mr. Corning was asked, "But doesn't such charting create the wrong kind of motivation for working well in a group? Don't children work well because of the exterior pressure rather than their own desire?"

The seventh-grade teacher said, "That is partly true. But interestingly enough, the chart seems to make the importance of working for the group clear to some students for the first time. And a number of them who probably at first work well to appear satisfactory on the chart actually derive considerable satisfaction from making their group better. So their original desire is self-centered, but in the end they get great pleasure from seeing their increased efficiency in group-planning for a field trip to a factory or in organizing a class project."

Thus, Mr. Corning is one of the teachers who has found that participation charting by students has helped them understand and improve their own roles in working well with others. Such charting can help the school make progress toward this basic goal of effective cooperation.

CHARTING GENERAL CLASS DISCUSSION

For many teachers the charting of the students' roles in general class discussion is even more valuable than charting group work, because in the typical class much more time is spent in general discussion than in groups.

It is common practice in numbers of modern schools to base a portion of the final grade for a pupil on his oral participation. Sometimes class participation makes up a very large proportion of the final grade a student receives. Few teachers formally organize their judgments of how much and how well pupils contribute in class. The judgments are general impressions built up throughout the semester. Some teachers, however, have desired more secure evidence about participation in order to be better prepared to talk with parents and with students and to have more definite evidence for grading. These teachers use some form of charting class discussion to evaluate students better.

Charting classwork presents two problems not faced in charting group work. First, in most class discussions the teacher is the leader and thus is busy as a participant, whereas in group work he is usually a non-participating observer. Leading discussion is itself a challenging task; it allows little opportunity for carrying out an added duty of charting participation. Second, a committee usually is composed of a few members, whereas a class is composed of many. The larger number of students further complicates the problem of charting class discussion.

Despite these problems, teachers have developed ways of securing data about students' oral work in class. Some of these practices are described below.

Roll-book tallies

A simple method of indicating the contributions in a fifth-grade class is followed by Mr. DeLuca who keeps a roll book with him during class discussions. Each time a student contributes, the teacher makes a small tally mark in the book. Although this technique does not provide for reporting the worth of the contribution, it does give more data about class participation than the teacher formerly had. Mr. DeLuca uses the data as a surer basis for talking with parents and marking students in areas where oral work is included.

Charting on a seating plan

Some instructors find it inconvenient to use a roll book or alphabetical list of names for tallying pupils' contributions. They prefer to use a seating chart so that the student's position in the classroom gives the immediate guide to where a tally should be placed on the chart. This is the same system Mr. Corning used with the group work. That is, he made his chart correspond with the seating arrangement of the group members. This eliminates the problem of hunting up and down a list for a particular name. In addition, if the teacher is leading the discussion from his desk or a table, the seating chart can be consulted and tallied rather inconspicuously.

Two objections to this proposal arise: Is it not poor educational practice for the teacher to handle all class discussions from his desk? Would not continual charting of all discussion become an impractical burden?

These are both valid objections. Teachers follow various practices in eliminating such problems. A common method is not to attempt charting participation all of the time but to chart only on certain days, perhaps once a week or once every two weeks, doing it at one time during social studies and another time during science discussions, and so forth. In this way actual samples of children's contributions are charted yet charting does not become a burden.

As teachers become increasingly convinced that pupils *learn by doing,* more class sessions are being led by student panels or by student discussion leaders. During such sessions when the teacher can be seated with the class or in the back of the room their participation can be easily tallied. Figure 34 is such a chart a sixth-grade teacher made when a committee on "Housing Problems in Our Town" was answering questions asked by class members.

Marking after class

Mr. Bunce, who teaches health education in the upper grades, is fortunate in having some free time following each of his health classes. He has made it a practice during this time to rate each student's participation in the previous class. Although he has found it inconvenient during the class to tally each contribution at the time it is made, he is able to pay close attention to who makes contributions and who does not. After class Mr. Bunce writes one of four possible code numbers after each student's name. The four code numbers and their meanings are:

1 = major or frequent, pertinent contributor during class.
2 = minor or fairly frequent, pertinent contributor.
3 = non-participant in discussion.
4 = disrupting factor in discussion; student's activity detracted from class.

In the past Mr. Bunce has counted class participation as one-third of the final grade. However, not until he made a consistent

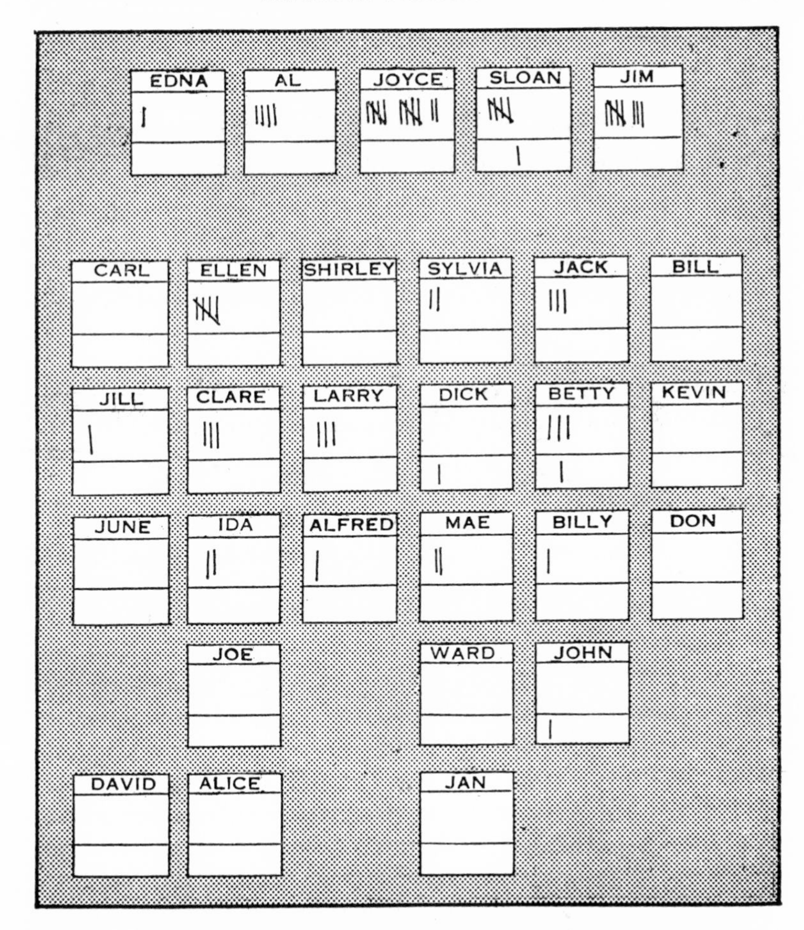

Fig. 34. Chart of class during panel discussion
Tallies above dividing lines indicate pertinent, helpful contributions. Tallies below dividing lines indicate inadequate or off-the-topic contributions.

practice of rating participation after each session did he begin to acquire the data that would ensure more accurate and fair judgments of the students' work. When they understood the rating system and realized the importance of their participation in making the class effective, the pupils took the sessions more seriously. Mr. Bunce says class disturbances and off-the-topic remarks were reduced when the class understood the evaluation plan. As a result, the class became more pleasant and profitable, for effective student-participation had increased.

USES OF CLASSROOM CHARTING

As with smaller groups, charting of general classroom discussions can help the teacher judge growth in participation throughout the year.

In addition it can aid the teacher in evaluating how well students reach subject-matter goals. That is, the effectiveness of student answers in science or social studies discussions can be charted. In this way charting is the record of oral testing.

Charts also provide specific data which the teacher can use in talking with parents about children's class participation.

OTHER CHARTING TECHNIQUES

There are numerous other methods of charting participation within classes and smaller groups. Because they are often complicated and are generally more applicable to research than to daily classroom practice, only two will be mentioned.

Indicating directions of remarks

Some investigators of group dynamics and teachers interested in group work chart not only the numbers of contributions but also indicate at whom the contributions are directed.

One method of doing this is to use circles or squares to represent group members. The observer places a tally in the circle when the speaker makes a remark to the group in general. But when the speaker directs his remark to a particular individual, a line is drawn from the speaker to the one to whom he is talking. The total number of contributions a person makes is the sum of the tallies (remarks to group in general) and the lines from his circle (remarks to individuals).

Such charting may reveal the extent to which a group is operating as a unit or operating as broken segments that communicate only with each other. A teacher might wish to analyze a group for the existence of cliques in it. Otherwise, such a technique probably has little value in most classes.

Figure 35 is such a chart of a committee of sixth graders discussing the entertainment they wish to have at a class Easter party. Obviously, Fran and Shirley carried on an extended discussion which did not include other group members. The discussion was in the form of an argument about the best games to include during the party. These two girls, each of whom strove for leadership, often clashed in group work.

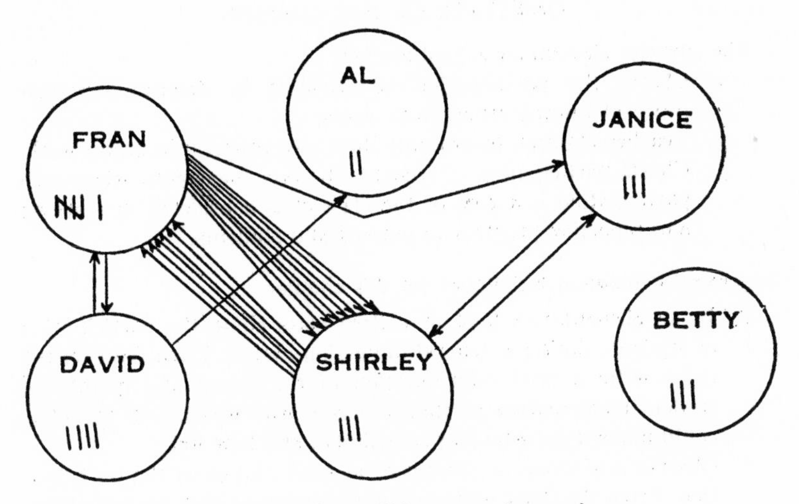

Fig. 35. Chart of direction of remarks

As shown in this chart, the lines indicating the direction of remarks often become complicated if the meeting is an extended one containing many contributions.

Participation symbols

Some observers of group work keep a running account of the participation by listing the speaker's initials followed by a code letter or number which tells the tenor or significance of his remarks. Some typical code letters and their meanings would be:

A = agreement
DK = disagreement in a kindly fashion
DA = disagreement in an antagonistic fashion
N = introduction of new, helpful idea
S = sarcasm or ridicule
O = distracting remark, off topic

Some investigators of group dynamics use many symbols to show subtle distinctions in group participation. Such a list demands much practice for proper use, but the system could contribute significant information about individual children if a teacher were willing to do the work necessary in making such analyses of students' behavior in groups.

OBJECTIVES OF THIS CHAPTER

The effective elementary-school teacher:

1. Charts the participation of students in determining their progress toward group work goals.
2. Teaches children to evaluate their own progress in group work.
3. Charts participation of students in class discussions when such participation is a goal of the class or is considered in marking and reporting progress to parents and students.

Suggested evaluation techniques for this chapter

1. In an elementary-school or college class chart the participation of students during a general discussion period. From data on the chart write a brief interpretation of the extent and quality of student participation so that a person who was not in the class could understand who had contributed and how well.
2. Observe any group or committee at work and chart the participation. From the chart write an interpretation of each person's function in carrying the group toward its goal.
3. The following dialogue is an excerpt from a discussion carried on during a committee meeting of fifth graders who were asked to recommend what they believed would be proper ways of dressing and behaving on a class excursion to a nearby lake to collect science specimens. Group members are Hal, Carol, Nancy, Eleanor, Dick, and Ronald. Chart their participation and write an interpretation of each child's role for this portion of the meeting.

HAL: And school clothes would get ruined.

ELEANOR: How about jeans?

DICK: Yeah, jeans and sneakers. Then if somebody falls in it won't matter.

CAROL: You'll be the first to fall in.

DICK: Not if I push you first.

ELEANOR: What if it rains?

DICK: Let it. What do we care? A little rain won't hurt.

NANCY: Isn't there some place to go if it rains out there?

HAL: Sure, there's a pavilion where you eat and rent boats.

ELEANOR: It still might be a good idea to tell kids to bring raincoats. I've got a plastic one that folds up into nothing. I'm going to bring it.

NANCY: We're supposed to tell how we think our class ought to act out there, too.

DICK: Well, I'm doing what I want when I go.

HAL: Sure, Dick, we all know you're a big shot.

ELEANOR: Let's be serious. We haven't much more time for this. Miss Johnson said we should decide on some rules for the way we act on the bus and out at the lake. What about the bus?

(*End of Excerpt*)

CHAPTER

11

Rating, Checking Student Skills and Products

EACH SPRING CENTRAL SCHOOL dismisses the students for two days in order to hold intensive faculty study sessions in some area of teaching important to the entire school. This spring's topic was "Improving Evaluation."

In preparing for the study sessions, the curriculum director asked teachers to write out evaluation problems with which they would like some help or clarification. He passed these on to the educational psychologist, Dr. Lantz, from a nearby university who had been asked to head up the project.

The psychologist noted that these were some of the more common kinds of evaluation problems the teachers mentioned:

"I would like to know the best ways of marking the products made by students in our junior high industrial arts courses."

"I have more trouble judging and marking students' school citizenship than I have marking their academic work."

"I have been using anecdotal records in evaluating pupils' speech skills, but this takes too much time and it makes the students nervous to see me writing so much while they give talks to the class. Isn't there some more efficient way of doing it?"

"In gym class we teach sportsmanship, but my way of trying to get a definite mark or judgment for each pupil is sometimes pretty hard to explain to a child or parent. I would like a more secure way of making the judgment and explaining it to the child and parents."

While analyzing these problems and similar ones, Dr. Lantz saw that many had this in common: they involved the evaluation of *observable student skills or products.* Thus he suggested to the curriculum director that the two-day session focus on the creation and use of rating scales and check lists, for these devices are often of use in solving such evaluation problems.

The program was organized in this way: The morning of the first day Dr. Lantz explained the general types and uses of scales and check lists. That afternoon and the following day the faculty divided into smaller interest groups. In the subgroups each person developed rating scales or check lists appropriate to some evaluation task he faced with his class. Then the members within the groups completed the work the afternoon of the second day by discussing the advantages and disadvantages of the different devices constructed by the members.

This chapter presents (1) the type of orientation to rating techniques presented by the psychologist and (2) some examples of the kinds of devices constructed by the teachers to help evaluate a variety of skills and products.

CHECK LISTS AND RATING SCALES

Some educators use the terms *check list* and *rating scale* synonymously. However, it is more common to distinguish between them.

A *check list* is usually a list of activities or characteristics that are to be given a check mark if they exist and are to be left blank if they do not exist. A common type of check list for younger children is

Name *Jane Stevens* Date:	1	2	3	4	5	6	7	8	9	10	11	12	13	14	15
1. Washed my hands: before breakfast	X	X	X	X	X	X									
before lunch	X	X	X			X									
before supper	X	X	X	X	X	X									
2. Brushed my teeth after breakfast	X	X	X	X	X	X									
after supper	X	X		X	X	X									
before going to bed	X	X	X	X	X	X									
3. Drank milk at each meal	X	X	X	X	X	X									
4. Had at least 9 hours sleep	X		X	X	X	X									
5. Carried a clean handkerchief or clean tissue	X	X		X		X									

found in the area of health where educators are trying to establish good health practices. The list gives them an opportunity to evaluate, or be evaluated by someone else, on how well they are meeting these health goals. The foregoing form is a portion of such a self-check list for children in the upper primary and the intermediate grades:

The check list, therefore, is useful for "Yes-No" or for "either-or" situations in which only two possibilities exist with no intermediate points between these two possibilities.

The *rating scale,* on the other hand, is used for evaluating situations or characteristics that can be present in varying degrees. The word *scale* indicates a graduated measuring device. Because so many activities and products in life do not merely involve matters of "Yes-No" but are matters of varying degrees, the rating scale is a more widely used and more helpful tool than the check list.

The following items are from a portion of one type of health and safety rating scale used by kindergarten and primary teachers.

Child's Name Jack Schwartz Date Oct. 26 Rater's Name Jensen

Directions: Check the point on each line which best describes the child's behavior.

1. The child puts his fingers in his mouth______

Almost constantly	Much of the time	Occasionally	Very seldom	Never
		X		

2. The child uses tools and play equipment in a way that threatens harm to himself and others or threatens damage to equipment______

Almost constantly	Much of the time	Occasionally	Very seldom	Never
	X			

CREATING RATING SCALES AND CHECK LISTS

As with any evaluation device, the first step in creating a rating scale or check list is to state specifically the characteristics to be judged. If the teacher already has stated his class goals in terms of the desired student behavior, as explained in Chapter 2, the task of constructing a rating device for judging skills is well on its way, because these specific goals form the main elements of the scale or check list.

If a student work product rather than observable skills is to be judged, the teacher begins by stating clearly the characteristics desired in the product.

An example of the criteria for judging a skill and an example of a work product will illustrate this difference:

An eighth-grade teacher wrote down the specific goals or characteristics of good speech skills which she believed the students should exhibit both in casual conversations and in their more formal reports before the class. Effective speech behavior for her class consisted of these.

The student:

1. Enunciates clearly.
2. Does not stammer or stutter.
3. Does not lisp.
4. Pronounces words correctly.
5. Uses acceptable grammar.
6. Relates ideas in a logical order so that his thoughts are easy to follow.
7. Looks at the person or the group to which he is talking.
8. Does not have mannerisms that detract from what he says.

Whereas these speech criteria are in terms of student behavior, the following criteria for judging a work product—student-made maps of South America—are in the form of specific characteristics that a clear, informative map should exhibit.

"An effective political and product map of South America includes:

1. Outlines of the continent and each country in correct proportion and in proper relationship to each other.
2. Clearly defined national boundaries.
3. A legend containing a mileage scale and identification of symbols used (such as a star as the symbol for a national capital).
4. Properly located major cities, rivers, mountain ranges.
5. Easy-to-read labeling of countries, cities, rivers, mountain ranges, and chief products of the countries.
6. Labels whose size is proportionate to the area being identified. That is, countries are in large letters, cities in small letters.

7. Attractive symbols identifying national products.
8. Attractive coloring of countries and ocean areas that makes the map easy to comprehend and pleasant to view."

After these specific characteristics are identified, the second step in planning the rating scale or check list is to decide the most efficient form in which to organize it. There are numbers of ways in which rating devices may be organized. An understanding of these possibilities enables a teacher to choose the one that will be best for a particular evaluation task. Common variations of check lists and scales are illustrated in the following section.

Some common types of check lists

Of the many varieties of check lists available, the following types are among the most useful to teachers in daily classroom evaluation of student work and products.

Skill check list

Often it is helpful for a teacher or a pupil to keep a check list of the skills he has mastered. For the teacher it may well be a chart which shows where each pupil stands in relation to the tasks attempted, such as the intermediate-grade list below.

ARITHMETIC SKILLS CHECK LIST

Grade 3 Semester 2	Names of Students					
Check skill when desired mastery is achieved.	Dael K.	Marty	Sally R.	Rob T.	Jim S.	Lisa T.
NUMBERS: Count, Read, Write						
Reads, writes numbers to 1000.	✓	✓	✓	✓	✓	✓
...to 10,000		✓		✓	✓	
Reads, writes dollars and cents through $20	✓	✓	✓	✓	✓	✓
Reads, writes fractions: ½, ¼, ¾, ⅓, ⅔		✓	✓	✓	✓	✓
Counts by 2's, 5's, and 10's	✓	✓	✓	✓	✓	✓

Grade 3 Semester 2	Names of Students					
Check skill when desired mastery is achieved	Darl K.	Marty	Sally R.	Rob T.	Jim S.	Lina T.
ADDITION, SUBTRACTION						
Immediate recall of addition, subtraction facts		✓	✓	✓		✓
Adds two columns with carrying		✓		✓	✓	
Adds three columns with carrying		✓		✓	✓	
Does three-order subtraction with borrowing				✓		
Makes change within limit of $1		✓		✓	✓	
Makes change within limit of $5				✓		

This type of chart can be adapted for use in recording skills in many areas, such as reading, physical education, art, music, writing, health and safety, and classroom citizenship.

Problem or difficulty-analysis check list

Often it is a teacher's desire to analyze problems or difficulties which students develop in their pursuit of skills. A check list may focus the teacher's and the student's attention on the specific difficulties and thus more readily alert them to subskills with which the pupil needs help. The following inventory of reading difficulties is suitable for use with primary and intermediate-grade pupils.

This reading-difficulty inventory can be made more diagnostic and yield more sophisticated results if the check mark is replaced by the following kinds of symbols, which in fact turn it into a kind of scale:

Symbol	*Meaning*
N	= no difficulty
O	= occasional difficulty
F	= frequent difficulty

INFORMAL INVENTORY OF READING DIFFICULTIES

Check each difficulty that is a common one for the pupil.	Names of Pupils			
	Clara	Bill G.	John F.	Debbie D.
SILENT READING				
1. Comprehension Unable to state main idea				
Unable to recall details				X
Unable to recall idea sequence	X			X
2. Visual habits Frowns	X			
Blinks				
Squints	X			
Rubs eyes				
Shades eyes		X		
Book too close				
Book too far away				
Book at angle				X
3. Vocalization Whispering				X
Silent lip movement	X			X
4. Finger following		X		X
ORAL READING				
1. Comprehension Unable to state main idea				
Unable to recall details				X
Unable to recall idea sequence	X			X

Check each difficulty that is a common one for the pupil.	Names of Pupils			
	Clara	Bill G.	John F.	Debbie D.
2. Word recognition Repetition of words	X			X
Omission of words				X
Reversal of letters				
Reversal of word sequence				
Meaningful substitutions of words	X			X
Meaningless substitutions of words	X			X
Confusion of initial consonants				X
Confusion of final consonants				X
Overdependence on picture clues				X
3. Rhythm Ignores punctuation	X			
Word-by-word reading	X	X		X
Hesitates	X			
4. Rate Too fast				
Too slow				X
Halting	X			X

Check lists of the same variety can be created for analyzing pupil difficulties in such activities as working with tools in industrial arts, speaking before a group, writing compositions, working with others on group projects, playing games, demonstrating posture in sitting and walking positions, singing or playing an instrument, getting along with classmates in social situations, and exhibiting study habits in various kinds of schoolwork.

Check lists that convert to scores

It is possible to list many behaviors a person might exhibit and place these on a check list. Then for each item checked the person receives a certain number of points which, when they are totaled, give an over-all score on the general characteristic being judged.

The best-known list of this type is the *Vineland Social Maturity Scale* (3) which is designed to estimate the level of a child's social development. It consists of items relating to communication, self-direction, socialization, and such. The items describe behavior that is typical of children at various ages, and norms have been established according to when a given item usually appears as a child's social behavior. Someone who knows the child well fills out the check list, and the checked items convert to a score which can be interpreted by a table of norms. Thus you can find developmental age equivalents for a child's score and can compute a developmental quotient that reflects the child's rate of progress toward self-sufficiency. Here are a few sample items selected from the Vineland Scale.

Item No.	*Age-Level* (years, not months)	*Item*
6	0-1	Reaches for nearby objects
11	0-1	Drinks from cup assisted
15	0-1	Stands alone
28	1-2	Eats with spoon
34	1-2	Talks in short sentences
40	2-3	Dries own hands
44	2-3	Relates experiences
51	4-5	Cares for self at toilet
68	7-8	Disavows literal Santa Claus
70	7-8	Combs or brushes hair
78	10-11	Writes occasional short letters
80	10-11	Does small remunerative work

The Vineland Scale has been used with considerable success. However, as will be pointed out later, only certain types of check lists or scales lend themselves to yielding a meaningful score. There is a danger in trying to derive scores for many kinds of check lists or scales.

Some common types of rating scales

The following descriptions of rating scales illustrate some of the most common varieties useful to teachers and point out ways of constructing them.

Scales utilizing simple code letters or numbers

Many report cards are actually rating scales that utilize code letters or numbers to represent degrees of goodness of performance over a period of weeks or months. We might use A for excellent performance, B for good, C for average, D for below average, and E for very low. The health and safety rating scale illustrated earlier in the chapter could be changed into one using code numbers if it were recast in the following manner:

Directions: In the blank at the left of each statement, place the code number which best represents a description of the child's behavior.

Code Numbers	*Meaning of Code*
1	Never
2	Very seldom
3	Occasionally
4	Much of the time
5	Almost constantly

_____1. The child puts his fingers in his mouth.

_____2. The child uses tools and play equipment in a way that threatens harm to himself and others or threatens damage to equipment.

Graphic scale

Another popular variety consists of (1) a statement of the characteristic (usually called the *dimension*) to be rated and (2) a horizontal line beneath the statement, one end of which represents "good" and the other end "poor." Or perhaps one end represents "always" and the other end "never."

This variety is no more precise than the code-number type. It is merely the same idea in a different form. If this variety were used for scaling some of the speech skills mentioned earlier in the chapter, it might look like this:

Directions: Make a check mark on each line at the point that best describes the student's standing on the numbered characteristic above the line.

1. Enunciation

Very good	Good	Average	Poor	Very poor

2. Stammering or stuttering

Very good	Good	Average	Poor	Very poor

This type of scale is said to have *constant alternatives* because the descriptions from which the rater may choose are the same for each of the numbered items, that is, the same terms (good, very good, and so forth) are used beneath each line.

Such a scale as this has the advantage of being easily constructed, for it necessitates only a listing of the characteristics and a line beneath each. However, critics of this form say that it is too simple to be most diagnostic. They ask:

"What does 'very good' or 'average' really mean when you are talking about stammering? Admittedly these words are somewhat helpful so that we do have a *general* idea of how to rate a person on enunciation or stammering. But isn't it likely that one rater carries in his mind a rather different idea of 'average enunciation' than does another rater? Thus they would mark the same student at different points on the scale. So we would be able to get more agreement among raters if there were *more specific behavioral descriptions* than 'good' and 'poor' for each dimension."

Scales involving more specific descriptions of characteristics

The disadvantages of the *constant-alternatives* type of scale often can be corrected if the descriptions written beneath each line can be *descriptions of types of behavior applicable specifically to the characteristic being judged,* such as descriptions applicable to enunciation in particular or to stammering in particular. This form, using different specific descriptions for each characteristic, is often called *changing alternatives* to contrast it with the *constant-alternatives* type shown above. By using this plan, we might recast the first two dimensions on the speech scale this way:

1. Enunciation:

All words understood easily.	Some words not understood or difficult to understand.	Mumbles. Most words incoherent.

2. Stammering or stuttering:

Smooth flow of speech. Does not hesitate in attempt to say any word. Does not repeat syllables.	Hesitates occasionally in attempt to say words. Occasionally may repeat syllables.	Repeats syllables many times on many words. Hesitates continually in attempt to speak.

Sometimes the teacher who constructs such a scale will place behavioral descriptions at five points rather than three in order to give a more specific guide in observing and rating students' behavior. On page 292 there is a completed speech scale with five alternatives described for each dimension. In addition, a space is provided below each dimension for a comment which the teacher might wish to write about a particular child. Consequently, any anecdote the teacher wishes to keep is written beneath the proper dimension and need not be "kept in mind" or written on another sheet.

Assigning ranks and percentages

In the case of a school class, the teacher knows all the people to be rated. Hence, since he can compare each of them with all the others in his mind, it is usually reasonable to expect that he can rank them on the characteristic to be considered. For instance, under the title *school citizenship* we may have a list of behavioral characteristics that include the following:

1. Works diligently, even when not watched.
2. Completes assigned work on time.
3. Keeps work area neat.

For each of these characteristics the teacher can think of which children are best and which are poorest in relation to each other. He ranks them from the top to bottom on the criteria. This ranking

RATING SCALE FOR SPEECH Student Claire Tyson Date 12/3 Rater Gaines

Directions: On each of the scales below, check the point on the line which best describes the speech behavior of the student. Use the space below each line to write any comments which help evaluate the student's speech.

Situation: (Check One)
Informal conversation ______
Report or Panel ______
General Class Discussion ______

1. Enunciation

✓ (at "Most words understood easily")

All words understood easily.	Most words understood easily. Occasional word not clear.	Some words not understood.	Mumbles. Many words not clear.	Continually mumbles. Words completely incoherent.

2. Stammering or stuttering

✓ (at "Usually smooth speech")

Smooth flow of speech. No hesitation in trying to say any word. Does not repeat syllables.	Usually smooth speech. Rarely hesitates trying to say words.	Hesitates sometimes trying to say words. Occasionally repeats syllables.	Frequently stops in attempt to say words. Repeats numerous syllables.	Repeats syllables many times on many words. Hesitates continually in trying to say words.

3. Lisping

✓ (at "All "s" sounds in words said clearly")

All "s" sounds in words said clearly.	Most "s" sounds clear. Few given slight "th" sound.	Several "s" sounds given slight "th" sound.	Many "s" sounds made like "th." Other sounds clear.	All "s" sounds like "th." Many other sounds improperly "thick."

4. Pronunciation

✓ (at "Rarely mispronounces a word")

All words pronounced correctly.	Rarely mispronounces a word.	Several words mispronounced.	Numerous words mispronounced.	Great many words mispronounced.

"winner" for "winter"

5. Grammar

Always uses grammar accepted as standard for class.	✓ One or two instances of improper grammar. "He don't"	Several instances of improper grammar.	Numerous instances of improper grammar.	Continually makes mistakes in grammar.

6. Logical sequence of thought

Talk moves easily from one idea to another. No ideas left out or misplaced in sequence.	Logic usually understood. Rarely omits important elements or mixes sequence of ideas.	✓ Occasionally neglects to include all ideas needed for listener to understand adequately. Sometimes *wanders* from topic.	Often relates ideas in mixed-up sequence. Often wanders off topic. Spends time on insignificant details.	Continually begins at illogical place. Omits many important ideas. Completely off topic much of the time.

7. Eye-contact with listener or audience

Always looks at eyes of listener or looks from one to another of audience.	Rarely looks away from listeners. May glance at notes.	✓ Spends about half the time looking at listeners. Notes	Occasionally looks at eyes of listeners. Most of time looks at notes or other objects.	Never looks at listeners. Reads from notes or looks around room.

8. Mannerisms and gestures

Gestures emphasize speech well; no distracting mannerisms.	✓ Rarely hand or face movements distract from speech.	Occasionally hand, face, body movements draw attention from speech. fingers locket	Often hand, face movements distract from speech.	Hands play with objects. Posture awkward. Face movements continually distract listener from speech.

technique forces the teacher to distinguish between the pupils' skills, whereas when the teacher just marks a spot on a line, as with the *graphic scale* discussed earlier, he may mark every student at about the same place on the dimension, thus not reflecting the real differences that exist within the class. With the ranking system, somebody must be first and somebody last, whether the pupils are marked by a strict, hardheaded rater who normally doesn't think anyone deserves a high rating or by a very kindly, softhearted soul who would otherwise give every pupil a high rating on a graphic scale.

This ranking system can be used with work products as well as with student skills. In the junior high art class that has completed posters, the products can be ranked according to over-all effectiveness or according to many specific characteristics, such as legibility of lettering, attention-getting value, and suitability of the design to the poster theme.

A variation of this ranking system occurs when the teacher is rating one or two children on some characteristic, not the entire class. In this case, the teacher estimates which quartile or which decile the child would fall into compared with his classmates. Thus the teacher may estimate that on the characteristic of *Uses materials without wasting them* Carl Jones would be in the top quarter of his class. Darcy MacTaggert, on the other hand, would be in the quarter just below the middle of the class, that is, between the twenty-fifth and fiftieth percentiles.

These ranking systems often do not give as clear a verbal description of the child's standing on a dimension as the speech scale on pages 292-93 does, but they do force the teacher to decide how a child compares with his age group, and this information is often useful to have.

The problem of totaling numbers on scales

Some educators say, "The trouble with rating scales is that in order to interpret what a student is like after he has been rated, you have to inspect every line or dimension on the scale. And when some scales have as many as 20 or 25 characteristics to be judged, this job of inspection can be complicated. Why not give a student a score for the rating he receives on each dimension, and then total up these individual scores to get an over-all score that tells what he is like in general?"

This attempt to change many ratings into one over-all score has resulted in the creation of scales involving numbers and weighting schemes. One of these types, the *Vineland Social Maturity Scale,* has already been illustrated. With the Vineland Scale the pupil receives points for each of the characteristics he exhibits that are on the check list.

But another kind of score is derived from graphic scales that have numbers along each dimension. The numbers begin at the less desirable end of the dimension and increase to the more desirable end. The student is given a score on each dimension. These are totaled to yield an over-all number that represents the student's general ability or success in the area covered by the scales. Here is an example of the first two dimensions on a work-habits scale.

WORK-HABITS RATING SCALE

Directions: Circle the number on the line that best reflects the pupil's behavior. Then, in the blank at the right, write the circled number. After rating each study habit, total the numbers in the right column to derive the student's study-habit score.

1. Persistence in work

Score

1 2 3 4 5 6 7 8 9 10 ____

Almost never completes a task on his own. Easily distracted by others or by even minor problems met in work.	Usually continues at task unless real difficulties are met or companions persist in bothering him.	Always completes work, despite difficulty of task or outside distractions.

2. Effective use of time

1 2 3 4 5 6 7 8 9 10 ____

When through with one task, does not begin another. Fools around a lot.	Works fairly steadily, but sometimes stops to chat. Sometimes voluntarily begins new task upon completion of a job.	Schedules work ahead of time. When one task is completed, voluntarily begins another. Never wastes time fooling around.

Although at first glance this may appear to be an efficient method of evaluating, such practices should be handled sparingly and applied with wisdom or the results can be very misleading. Let us see what happened when the speech scale on pages 292-93 was changed so that each dimension became a ten-point scale, and the numbers a student received on the dimensions were totaled to yield an over-all speech score. Two eighth-grade students rated in speech were Jane and Carol. Jane was slightly better than the middle of the dimension on all eight scales. Her total score out of the 80 possible points was 52.

Carol's enunciation, pronunciation, eye-contact, and freedom from distracting mannerisms were superior. She received ratings of 9 or 10 on each of these. On only one dimension, that of logical thought, was she low. Her talk to the class was so poorly organized and rambled off the topic so much that the teacher rated her 2 on logical thought. When her scores on all dimensions were summed, her total was 66.

Comparing the two girls' total scores, we conclude that Carol was considerably more effective as a speaker. In reality, however, her speech was less effective than Jane's in communicating information to the class. Carol's fine enunciation and her effective use of gestures could not make up for her lack of such an essential element as logical sequence of ideas. Though it was enunciated well, her report served to confuse the class because she left out important facts and spent time on unimportant details.

Jane, on the other hand, had mispronounced three words and once or twice had not spoken clearly enough. She had fingered a pencil while talking, which was somewhat distracting, and she did not look at the class all the time. Her talk, however, was rather well organized and her ideas were easy to follow. In general, her speech was more effective than Carol's, although the total scores did not reflect this fact.

In the cases of Carol's and Jane's speeches, totaling the individual dimensions did not improve the evaluation. Instead, it misled. This is often true when a rating sheet contains *varied characteristics, each of which is essential to success*. If a person is very low or fails on only one of these essential characteristics, he is not successful even though he may possess a high degree of the other traits which would give him a high total score.

A few years ago a college supervisor of student teachers made this mistake of ignoring essential characteristics when trying to derive a total score from a rating scale. He designed a scale to mark such characteristics of student teachers as: appearance, lesson preparation, speech, use of teaching aids, rapport with other staff members, knowledge of subject, and classroom control. An established number of points was possible on each of these dimensions. The total points possible was 90. One diligent and pretty girl received a total of 78 because she had the highest or nearly the highest possible scores on all dimensions except the last one, classroom control, on which she received no points in a possible 10. The supervisor then realized that something was wrong with the process of totaling scale points to derive an over-all score representing the student teacher's general ability. This girl, with one of the highest totals of all the student teachers, had no discipline in her class at all. Therefore, with no control of the class, she was really no teacher at all. Other student teachers, with totals in the 60's and 70's were either adequate or good teachers. As a result of this experience, the supervisor abandoned the practice of giving numerical scores on the dimensions and totaling them. The rating scale itself was retained, and student teachers were thereafter judged on their strong and weak areas, through a process of inspecting the individual elements of the scale.

The above examples illustrate the possible invalidity of the practice of totaling points on rating devices. Some authors of scales have attempted to derive valid total scores by awarding more points for important characteristics and giving less weight to less essential ones. However, even this weighting procedure is not proper to use when judging certain types of skills or characteristics. When contemplating the use or construction of a scale that would yield a total score, the teacher should ask himself, "Will a total from this material make good sense? Could a person receive a relatively high total and actually be very inadequate because he was so low on one essential element?" If the answer to the first question is *no,* and to the second *yes,* then totals should not be computed.

Haggerty-Olson-Wickman Scales

As noted in the discussion of the Vineland Scale, not all attempts to secure numerical scores from rating devices have been unsatisfactory. Another example of successful uses of scoring is furnished by the Haggerty-Olson-Wickman Behavior Rating Scales, Schedules A and B. Much research has gone into the development of these scales, which are designed to locate maladjusted children in school. Schedule A is composed of a list of fifteen behavior problems common among school children. The problems range from acts such as stealing to minor matters such as lack of interest in schoolwork. Schedule B is used for graphically rating 35 physical, mental, social, and emotional characteristics. Items on the scales are given numerical values which can be added up to yield a so-called "problem-tendency" score for each schedule. Studies of large numbers of children over a period of years have indicated that the higher a child's problem-tendency score the more likely he will become a behavior problem and will in later years come to the attention of a child-guidance clinic or the police. Unlike the total scores of teacher-made scales, total scores from the Haggerty-Olson-Wickman Schedules have been validated by research (*6:238–245*). The typical rating scale created and used by teachers probably should not be converted into a total-score variety.

The way the Haggerty-Olson-Wickman Schedules are organized to yield scores is illustrated by the following two examples from Schedules A and B[1]:

SCHEDULE A EXCERPTS

Behavior Problem	*Frequency of occurrence*			
	Has never occurred	Has occurred once or twice but no more	Occasional occurrence	Frequent occurrence
Disinterest in schoolwork	0	4	6	7
Truancy	0	12	18	21

SCHEDULE B EXCERPTS

25. Is he even-tempered or moody?

Stolid. Rare changes of mood. (3)	Generally very even-tempered. (1)	Is happy or depressed as conditions warrant. (2)	Strong and frequent changes of mood. (4)	Has periods of extreme elations or depressions. (5)	*Score*

[1] M. E. Haggerty; W. C. Olson; and E. K. Wickman, *Haggerty-Olson-Wickman Behavior Rating Schedules, Manual of Directions*. Yonkers, N.Y.: World Book Co., 1930.

27. Is he generally depressed or cheerful?

Dejected. Melancholic. In the dumps. (3)	Generally dispirited. (4)	Usually in good humor. (1)	Cheerful. Animated. Chirping. (2)	Hilarious. (5)

In Schedule B the number beneath each degree on the dimension is the score given the child who fits the behavior description. Note that the higher the number the less desirable the behavior. This scale is a good example of the type in which the two extremes on the dimension do not necessarily represent the most and the least desirable behavior.

COMBATING THE HALO EFFECT

When judging a student, a teacher frequently finds himself prejudiced in each new evaluation situation by the student's past performance. On objective tests a teacher's bias either in favor of a pupil or against him has little or no effect, for an objective item is specifically right or wrong in most cases. Personal opinion does not enter into the scoring. But in using other evaluation devices, such as correcting essay tests or writing anecdotal records, a previous opinion of a student may affect the way the teacher marks current work. This tendency to be influenced by a student's past performance when judging him is termed the *halo effect*. Rating scales have been cited as being especially susceptible to halo effect.

The way a rater judges a student on one characteristic, such as enunciation or eye-contact, should not influence his marking of other characteristics, such as pronunciation or logical thought. And the rater's general impression of the student should not determine or influence his marking of specific elements, such as use of gestures in giving a speech. However, many people who use rating scales mark them hurriedly. If they have a generally good opinion of the student, they will check each of the dimensions at the high end. If they have a generally poor opinion, they will check all dimensions at the low end. Other raters do not seem to like to make decisions about other people, so they tend to check nearly everybody around the average or middle portion of the scale. Efficient use of rating devices demands that the halo effect be reduced to a minimum and that the student be judged carefully on each characteristic.

Three main methods are used to reduce halo effect: (1) using behavioral descriptions, (2) mixing the direction of the *good* and *poor* ends of the scales, and (3) educating raters to guard against prejudice. The first two of these are concerns for creators of scales. The third is a concern of everyone who uses scales.

Behavioral descriptions

By using actual descriptions of students' behavior under several points on each dimension (as in the example on page 292), the rater can compare the behavior he sees in class with these specific descriptions and can better mark the proper point on the line. However, if no specific behaviors are described and the scale line has only numbers along it or general terms like *good, average,* or *poor,* the rater's general impression of the student is more likely to influence the marking of all dimensions.

Random scale directions

On the speech rating scale illustrated earlier, the more desirable end of each dimension was at the left. That is, the student who has all the finest speech characteristics will be checked on the left side of every scale. Experts in evaluation have observed that placing the more desirable end of each dimension always in the same direction may tend to increase halo effects. They believe that a typical teacher or administrator who has a generally good impression of a student may tend to mark the student rather rapidly down the *good* side of the scales if the *good* end is always in the same direction. To reduce such halo influences and to force raters to read each dimension carefully, some creators of scales mix the direction of the more desirable end of the dimensions. For example, the *good* end of dimensions 1 and 2 might be at the left, but dimension 3 might be switched so that the desirable end is at the right. The subsequent dimensions would be mixed in random order, making it necessary for the rater to read each carefully before marking it.

The Haggerty-Olson-Wickman Schedule B is a good example of a device with scales whose graduated steps do not necessarily reflect desirable behaviors at one end, contrasting with undesirable ones at the other. To mark these scales, the rater must read each description carefully and cannot depend on his general impression of the child for hurriedly checking the schedule.

In some cases, however, constructors of scales purposely place the *good* end of all dimensions in the same direction so that the check marks on each line can be connected with each other to form an over-all profile of the student's characteristics. In the case of the speech rating scale, the teacher who connects the individual rating marks to form a profile can show the student a better over-all impression of his combined speech skills when he talks with the student individually.

Therefore, switching the ends of dimensions in a random manner probably helps reduce the halo effect, but if this is done the scale sheet cannot be used for drawing a meaningful profile of the student's general success.

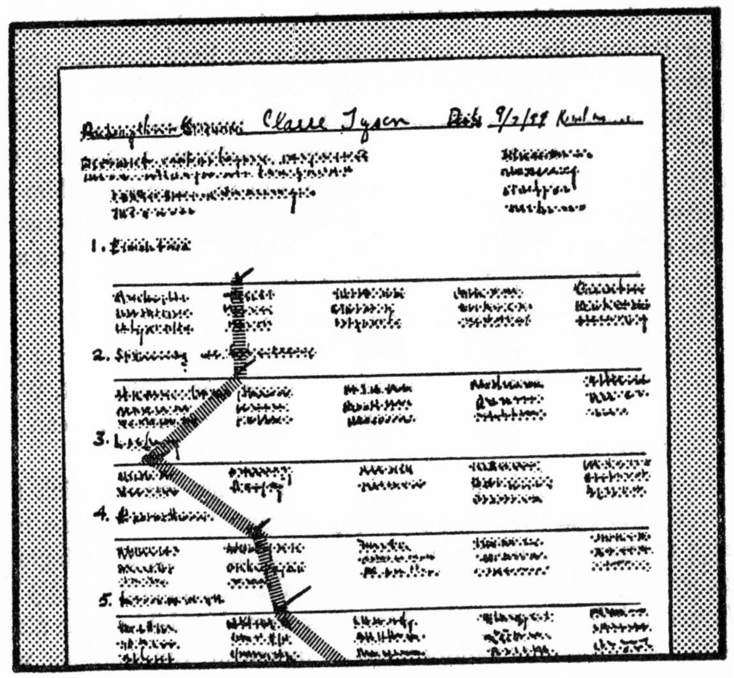

Fig. 36. Profile on rating scale

Awareness of halo effect

The teacher who is aware that his general impression of his students may unconsciously influence his ratings of their present work can guard against the halo effect. He can judge his students' progress in a fairer manner because he carefully compares their present actions with the actual descriptions of behavior on the scale. Thus, awareness of the possibility of prejudice can help reduce the halo effect.

USING RATING SCALES

After check lists or scales have been created, the teacher pays attention to ways he can (1) mark the scales most accurately and (2) use data from the scales in judging and guiding students' progress.

Accurate marking of rating devices

Errors in marking check lists and rating scales usually occur either because the rating scale itself does not have specific enough characteristics to guide the rater effectively or something is wrong with the rater's own observation skills or personality. By saying something is wrong with the rater's personality, we mean that the nature of his personal outlook on the world tends to make him an inaccurate evaluator. If we look more closely at these characteristics of the rater we can see more clearly what his specific errors are and what can be done to reduce or eliminate them.

The inexperienced rater may err because:

1. He does not observe carefully. Many people fail to hear or see everything significant in a child's behavior or a work product. With more experience and guidance, this shortcoming usually can be ameliorated.

Often there may be a dimension on a rating device which the rater cannot mark accurately simply because he has seen no evidence upon which to base a judgment. For instance, a sixth-grade teacher marking school citizenship faced the item *Sportsmanship on Playground.* Since the teacher had never seen this child on the playground, she could not validly record a judgment. But since she was supposed to fill out all of the scale, she made a guess. What she should have done instead was to write "no evidence" on that dimension and leave it unchecked. Or, better yet, the creator of the scale might have foreseen this problem and have given such teachers guidance in filling out the device by including in the directions a statement of this type:

"If you believe that you have not enough evidence to mark this child accurately on one of the listed characteristics, write the letters IE (insufficient evidence) in the left margin beside that item, and leave that scale unchecked."

2. *He avoids extremes in ratings.* That is, he tends to rank low traits higher than they deserve and rate superior traits or qualities lower than they really are. This may result if the rater is inexperienced or is not a careful observer of people; or he may be personally insecure and does not like to risk extreme ratings for fear he will not show enough agreement with others who also might rate the same children. This tendency to rate extremes too close to the middle may also occur if the observer does not feel competent to judge the particular characteristic accurately, so he stays near the safe "average" ratings which he feels will not overvalue or undervalue the pupil too much.

3. *He commits the generosity error.* That is, when the rater is not sure about the meaning of a dimension or the degree of it exhibited by the pupil, he may rate that particular item rather high to give the pupil the benefit of the doubt. (*8:166–167*)

If it is because of some basic personality characteristic that the judge makes errors 2 and 3 above, there is nothing much we can do about it. But if inexperience is the cause, the rater can learn to mark scales more accurately by being aware of these sources of error and by practicing observing children and rating them on a variety of characteristics. It is most helpful for several teachers to rate the same children on a scale, then compare their ratings and discuss the reasons for any lack of agreement they may have shown in their judgments.

USES FOR RATING DEVICES AND CHECK LISTS

As indicated earlier, rating scales and check lists are best suited to evaluating *behavior or products that are easily observable and demand little from the rater in terms of interpretation.*

After much experience with rating techniques, Olson wrote:

"When persons have observed children over a period of time, they tend to form some distinct impressions, even though they have neither recorded their observations nor arranged controlled situations. Students of childhood have utilized these general impressions by the construction of rating scales for standardized reporting. It has been demonstrated that such impressions can be reliably reported under proper conditions and have a valid basis in terms of other criteria." [2]

Questions that sometimes bother teachers when they consider using rating techniques are:

"When should I fill out a rating scale? As the child carries out the activity or behavior? After the child leaves? Or should I wait until after several incidents and then rate him on my over-all impression of the several incidents?"

The answer depends upon both the children's reaction to being rated and the way the teacher subsequently wants to use the data from the scale.

For example, an eighth-grade teacher wanted to secure data about students' speech in front of class as well as in their less formal discussions and their conversations in the classroom. Consequently, she used her scale in more than one way. As she sat at the back of the class during panel discussons or during reports, she usually checked a rating sheet on each student's speech. Since she could not effectively check such a scale when she was leading class discussions, every three weeks or so she took some time after school to rate several students' speech as she remembered it from class discussions. By doing only several students at a time, she found that the task did not become a burden and she did a more conscientious job. Thus, she used her speech rating scale two ways: (1) to evaluate one specific performance of a student by marking his characteristics as the speech progressed and (2) to sum up many casual observations and impressions of a student's speech habits over a period of time.

Frequently, a teacher who uses a rating scale as a method of summing up casual observations is aided by other evaluation techniques in deciding which point on the scale best describes a student's behavior. For instance, in his seventh grade Mr. Corning uses the following scale to sum up his observations of students' progress toward group-work goals. Charts of participation in group work which he and student observers have made provide much specific data for accurate marking of this scale. He completes such a scale on each pupil every six weeks.

In some cases teachers wish to evaluate a specific situation, such as a child's singing or speaking, but they do not wish to fill out the scale while the child is performing for fear it will embarrass him.

[2] Willard C. Olson, *Child Development* (Boston: D. C. Heath and Co., 1949), p. 7. Quoted by permission of the publisher.

GROUP-WORK SCALE

The effective group member:

1. Accepts and carries out fair share of work:

Always volunteers for at least own share of work. Always completes it without complaint and on time.	Accepts work when assigned, but may do so reluctantly. Seldom volunteers. Tries to secure easy task.	Tries to shirk responsibilities. Accepts work only after teacher insists. Job usually late or not completed.

2. Contributes to discussion:

Speaks freely without urging. Talks almost all the time.	Speaks an amount which would be average for size of group.	Never speaks unless urged. Then makes very brief remark or indicates has nothing to say.

3. Keeps to topic:

May joke, gossip, talk on other subjects. Wanders from topic most of the time.	Usually on topic. Sometimes discusses ideas distantly allied to topic. Sometimes jokes, gossips, wanders from subject.	Always on topic. May urge others to get back to subject if they digress.

4. Abides by majority decisions:

Always does what group decides by vote. Never complains about decision when he voted with minority.	On most matters does what group votes. May complain some but remains in group if he voted with minority.	Always complains if majority decides against his view. Quits or obstructs group action when he is in minority.

5. Permits others to express their views:

Frequently interrupts others. Ridicules their views.	Occasionally interrupts others. Usually lets them speak. Rarely makes fun of others' views.	Waits turn to talk. Allows or urges others to give their ideas, whether they agree with his or not.

The teacher keeps in mind the dimensions on the scale and as soon after the performance as feasible he marks the scale.

Thus, the answer to "When should I do the rating?" depends partly on whether it is a rating of one incident or a summary of several and partly on how the teacher thinks the child will feel about knowing he is being rated as he performs. Generally, the sooner the rating of an incident can take place after the incident the more accurate the teacher's memory will be.

After the teacher has filled out his rating sheets and check lists, he must answer the question, "How are these data best used?" At elementary and junior high levels, they are most valuable in aiding the teacher to (1) diagnose pupils' strengths and weaknesses, (2) help students understand and personally accept goals of the school, (3) help students evaluate their own growth, and (4) report student progress to the students, their parents, and administrators.

Diagnosis and guidance

Here are four examples of the way rating devices helped teachers to diagnose weak areas in students' development and to provide guidance in strengthening these areas.

The speech rating scale illustrated earlier aided the the eighth-grade teacher in showing clearly that the student Carol was strong in all areas except in the organization of her talk. Consequently, Carol was given special help in outlining her reports before presenting them. The rating of another student, Karl, showed that he consistently said, "She don't," and that he looked out the window as he spoke during a panel discussion. He was given aid in correcting these weaknesses.

A second-grade teacher used a *Reading Difficulties Check List* once a month as she listened to each pupil read in the small-group reading sessions. She preferred using the check list periodically, for it ensured that she paid attention to each specific reading characteristic of each child, which her daily casual observation did not ensure. On the basis of these check lists she formed special afternoon reading groups to enable children having similar difficulties to work together on special exercises she provided, such as to aid those having trouble with initial consonants or word reversals or reading with expression.

A sixth-grade teacher in discussion with her students constructed a check sheet for judging the graphs they had drawn to picture the trends in the prices of products in their local community. As the teacher and students used the list in judging each graph, they not only saw what aspects the entire class should improve in their next graph-making session, but each pupil had a record of the aspects he himself needed to correct the next time.

A school citizenship scale was checked for each pupil by a fourth-grade teacher. Then each pupil was asked to check a similar scale as a self-judgment. Later the teacher compared her own rating of a child with the child's self-rating. This also gave her a chance to talk over with a child any discrepancies in ratings between teacher and pupil.

Informing students of goals

In an eighth grade the teacher, Miss Gaines, led a class discussion early in the semester on "What kinds of speech habits will make me the best kind of person?" The students talked about the kinds of adults who, they believed, "make the best sense when they talk and are the most interesting and the easiest to listen to." They listed characteristics on the board. Miss Gaines suggested some characteristics of her own. The eighth graders showed that they seriously wished to become more effective in both informal and formal speech situations. Then Miss Gaines passed a copy of her scale (pp. 292-93) to each student and explained:

"Here are some goals I thought you might like to work toward. As you see, most of these are the same as the ones you suggested. We will add the others you mentioned. This semester you will have a chance to decide where you might stand on such a scale. And you may wish to select one or two of these goals which you want to stress this year. I'll try to help you judge your progress, and you and I will have chances to talk it over. Remember, you aren't competing with your classmates on this. You are competing with yourself. You are trying to see how much you can grow in better speech compared to where you stand now."

By using such a procedure, the students in Miss Gaines's class were not only aware of the specific goals toward which they were working, but the class discussion enabled them to present their own reasons for working toward improved speech. They wanted to become better, and the specific behaviors described on the rating sheet helped them to see how they could actually do so. This *wanting to improve* is the kind of motivation that leads to effective learning.

Thus, a well-organized rating scale can be used to inform a class of specific goals toward which they can work. It can at the same time be *used by the students for self-evaluation*, keeping them constantly aware of their goals and progress.

Reports to parents.

Methods of reporting students' progress to parents and to administrators are discussed at length in chapters 14 and 15. However, it is proper to indicate here that data from rating scales are helpful for such reporting.

The teacher who discusses with a parent a child's social behavior or progress in speech or skill in group work is usually on more secure ground when using information from such devices as rating scales than when using only memory of casual observations.

In lower grades, where it is common practice for the teacher to write letters to parents in reporting children's success in school, the teacher will find the task of letter writing considerably simplified if rating scales have been used to judge certain types of child behavior. Too often letters to parents are so general that they mean nothing to the parent. However, if the teacher uses rating scales with specific behavioral descriptions printed under each line, those specific descriptions that best describe a particular child's behavior can become phrases used in the letter to tell what the child is like in school.

THREE MORE RATING DEVICES

Throughout this chapter we have inspected a variety of check lists and rating scales useful in the elementary and junior high grades. To conclude the chapter we offer three additional types of devices which teachers may wish to adapt for their own use. These are designed to help in evaluating (1) hearing difficulties, (2) singing ability, and (3) written reports.

HEARING DIFFICULTY CHECK SHEET

Child's Name *Peggy Phillips* Birthdate *12/7/54*

Rater *Landale* Class *1* Date *Nov. 17*

At the right of each item, check the blank which you think best represents this child's status in regard to the symptom.

Symptoms of Possible Hearing Difficulties	Pupil shows this behavior: *Never*	*Rarely*	*Occasionally*	*Very often*	*Rater had insufficient chance to observe*
Hearing Ability					
1. Strains to listen			X		
2. Unable to hear questions or instructions first time		X			
3. Speaks in monotone	X				
4. Speech unusually loud	X				
5. Speaks very softly				X	
6. Uses gestures instead of words		X			
7. Ignores oral instructions			X		
8. Watches speakers' lips intently					X
9. Apparently confused		X			
10. Has faulty speech			X		
11. Speech difficult or impossible to understand		X			
12. Apparently daydreams		X			
Ear Troubles					
13. Has dizzy spells	X				
14. Reports noises in ears	X				
15. Has excess wax in ears	X				
16. Ears discharge	X				
17. Reports earaches	X				
18. Has had mastoid operation					X

Additional Comment: Intradental lisp. When tries to listen, may cock head to left a bit.

The following combination check list and rating scale can aid the teacher in focusing on simple but significant aspects of a child's singing ability at the elementary or junior high level.

CHECK LIST FOR SINGING PERFORMANCE—INDIVIDUAL

Name *Peter O'Hara* Date *May 6* Class or Occasion *6th grade*

Directions: Check each item that is characteristic of this pupil's singing. If you have had insufficient opportunity to observe a characteristic, write o beside the item.

---

1. *Voice Quality*

____ Nasal
____ Thin
____ Strained
____ Pleasant, full
_X_ Breathy
____ Hoarse, husky

2. *Music Reading Skill*

____ Cannot read time or tone changes
_X_ Reads time values
____ Can tell when tone goes up or down
_X_ Can read tone changes that move by steps
____ Can read tone changes that move by steps or skips

3. *Voice Range*

_X_ More than octave
____ Less than octave
____ Nearly monotone

4. *Breath Control*

____ Often gasps for breath
_X_ Cannot sustain tones, chops them off
____ Sustains tones well. Breathing inconspicuous

5. *Ability to Stay in Tune*

____ Tends to sing sharp
____ Tends to sing flat
_X_ Usually on pitch
____ Always on pitch
____ Tends to slip into wrong key

6. *Posture*

____ Stiff
_X_ Straight but relaxed
____ Slumps
____ Head down
_X_ Shifts, wiggles *(some)*

7. *Volume*

____ Always loud
____ Always soft
_X_ Soft or loud, as song requires

8. *Memory for Lyrics*

____ Often forgets words
_X_ Rarely misses a word
____ Always knows words

9. *General Appearance*

____ Enthusiastic, obviously likes singing
____ Tense, frightened
____ Bored
____ Uncomfortable, worried, unenthusiastic
_X_ Impassive, sings mechanically

The rating scale below, designed for use in the sixth grade and above, permits the teacher to total the points on the scales to derive an over-all score from which he can assign a mark, if he desires. Note that by setting a limit on how low a student's score may be on "crucial dimensions," the scale-maker has tried to solve the problem of having a student fail completely on an important characteristic and still receive an acceptable final score.

SCALE FOR RATING WRITTEN REPORTS

Student *Ralph Vodarski* Assignment *Biography*
Date *March 19* Class *Grade 7, Core* Rater *L. Mattera*

Directions: For each of the seven scales, circle the number above the statement that best describes the student's paper. To derive an overall score, write the circled numbers in the right column and total the column. *Important:* If a student receives a score of 2 or less on one of the *crucial characteristics* (identified by asterisk *), no total score should be computed, for such failure on crucial elements usually means the paper is a general failure, despite the student's success with other characteristics.

---

1. *Choice of Topic* (*)

7	6	(5)	4	3	2	1	*Score*
Very well suited to class goals.			Related to class goals, but more suitable topic might have been chosen.		Off the subject. Not aimed at proper goals.		*5*

2. *Coverage of Topic* (*)

1	2	3	(4)	5	6	7	
Very incomplete or spotty coverage. Insignificant aspects overstressed and/or important aspects missed.			Most significant aspects treated, but some too briefly.		All important aspects included, kept in good balance.		*4*

3. *Organization of Paper* (*)

1	2	3	(4)	5	6	7	
Rambles from one thing to another without apparent plan. Orangization very confusing.			Fairly understandable plan, but a few ideas seem misplaced.		Ideas move in logical, interesting sequence. Plan of paper easily understood.		*4*

4. *Accuracy of Facts* (*)

7	(6)	5	4	3	2	1	6
Good command of facts and use of accurate sources.			Most facts fairly accurate. Some misstatements.		Many inaccurate statements. Personal student opinion given as fact.		

5. *Writing Style*

7	6	(5)	4	3	2	1	5
Simple, direct sentences. Statistics, examples all clear. Few or no usage errors.			Fairly easy to follow, but some clumsy sentences and usage errors.		Very fancy, complex, overwritten sentences and/or many clumsy, confusing sentences. Frequent usage errors.		

6. *Neatness*

5	(4)	3	2	1	4
Neat, clean handwriting easy to read, margins neat.		Fairly neat, a few smudges, some words hard to make out.		Smudged paper, irregular margins, handwriting very difficult to read.	

7. *Spelling Errors*

1	(2)	3	4	5	2
More than 6 per page	5 or 6 per page	3 or 4 per page	1 or 2 per page	None	

Total Score 30

In the foregoing scale the author of the device attempted to reduce halo effect by alternating the desirable end of the dimensions in a random fashion. Note that the last two items, which were not considered quite as important as the first five, were given a lower top score (5) than the earlier dimensions (7). In this way it was possible for the scale-constructor to weight the dimensions he thought should be more influential in determining the final score.

OBJECTIVES OF THIS CHAPTER

The effective elementary or junior high teacher:

1. Tries to observe as accurately as possible, and conscientiously guards against *halo effect* and *generosity error*.
2. Creates rating devices which consist of carefully defined, specific, observable behaviors or of specific characteristics of work products.
3. Uses rating instruments for diagnosing and improving areas of weakness in student development and for reporting progress to students, parents, and administrators.

Suggested evaluation techniques for this chapter

1. Use the speech scale on page 292 to rate a person's speech in a formal situation such as presenting a class report or taking part in a panel discussion. Use the same scale to rate a person's speech characteristics in a more informal situation such as general class discussion or casual conversation. Write a brief conclusion or analysis of the results of your ratings.
2. Secure three written reports of junior high students and evaluate them on the rating scale reproduced on pages 311-12. Ask a friend to do the same. Then compare your ratings.
3. State five kinds of skills or work products in your field of teaching for which check lists or rating scales might profitably be used. Construct a scale or check list for one of these.
4. You are an elementary-school teacher. The physical education instructor in your school says that one of the main functions of physical education programs is to help pupils to become good sports. This goal of good sportsmanship, which is listed under *character education* in the school's curriculum plan, has been defined by the instructor in the following terms.

The good sport:

1. Willingly plays within the rules of the game.
2. Accepts the umpire's or referee's decisions.
3. Plays hard whether winning or losing.
4. Is friendly toward other players, including opponents.
5. Places the good of the team above personal glory.
6. Does not brag about winning; does not tease the losers.
7. Accepts defeat without alibis and without attacks on opponents or officials.

Your Problem: Construct a rating device that will help the physical education instructor do an efficient job of judging how well the students are progressing toward these types of sportsmanlike behavior. If you believe more characteristics than the seven he listed above should be included in such a scale, add these when constructing the instrument.

SUGGESTED READINGS

1. BARON, DENIS, and BERNARD, HAROLD W. *Evaluation Techniques for Classroom Teachers*. New York: McGraw-Hill Book Co., 1958. Chapter 11: Rating techniques in pupil evaluation.
2. CRONBACH, L. J. *Essentials of Psychological Testing*. New York: Harper and Bros., 1949. Chapter 18: Values and limitations of ratings.
3. DOLL, E. A. *Measurement of Social Competence*. Minneapolis: Educational Test Bureau, Educational Publishers, Inc., 1953. Vineland Scale.
4. GREENE, E. B. *Measurements of Human Behavior*. New York: Odyssey Press, 1952. Chapter 16: Discusses rating methods and devices.
5. GREENE, HARRY A.; JORGENSEN, ALBERT N.; and GERBERICH, J. RAYMOND. *Measurment and Evaluation in the Elementary School*. New York: Longmans, Green and Co., 1953. Sample rating devices: pp. 294-96.
6. OLSON, WILLARD C. *Child Development*. Boston: D. C. Heath and Co., 1949. Pp. 7-8, 238-45, 289-91, 380-86.
7. REMMERS, H. H., and GAGE, N. L. *Educational Measurement and Evaluation*. New York: Harper and Bros., 1955. Chapter 12.
8. SCHWARTZ, ALFRED, and TIEDEMAN, STUART C. *Evaluating Student Progress in the Secondary School*. New York: Longmans, Green and Co., 1957. Chapter 9: Clear discussion of check lists and rating devices.
9. THORNDIKE, ROBERT L., and HAGEN, ELIZABETH. *Measurement and Evaluation in Psychology and Education*. New York: John Wiley and Sons, 1955. Chapter 13: Good overview of rating methods and ways to improve them.

PART III

Organizing and Using Evaluation Data

ALTHOUGH NUMEROUS USES OF EVALUATION DEVICES HAVE BEEN discussed so far, the over-all organization of evaluation data and their use in marking and reporting student progress have yet to be inspected. In Part III these matters are developed in some detail.

CHAPTER

12

Organizing Records

EACH CENTRAL ELEMENTARY TEACHER received a note from the principal saying:

"Monday's faculty meeting will be used for deciding whether a pupil's cumulative-record folder should be kept by his current teacher and passed on to his next teacher in the fall or whether it should be kept in the main office. Please be prepared to aid in this decision."

This note precipitated a discussion at the faculty lunch table. Mr. Long, a sixth-grade teacher, said, "I think the teachers ought to have the records in their rooms. A good cumulative record really does show how a child develops through the years."

Miss O'Connel, a third-grade teacher, had a much different view: "I think records handed on from one teacher to the next are a menace. I think such records should be kept at a minimum . . . no more than a health record and the school marks of the child. And even these marks ought to be kept in the main office."

MR. LONG: "You can't be serious."

MISS O'CONNEL: "Very serious. I've seen cumulative records full of test scores and anecdotes in other schools. I know how they're often made up and used. I don't want a folder full of prejudiced observations about children handed to me by the children's lower grade teachers who half the time couldn't make an unbiased, accurate report of a child's behavior if their lives depended on it."

MR. LONG: "I think you are unduly pessimistic. I've found reports to be accurate and helpful."

MISS O'CONNEL: "Maybe I'm making it a bit strong. But I've seen records used to children's disadvantage. For example, the school gives a non-verbal group test to first graders. It's supposed to measure school ability. But many teachers don't realize that a single test, especially a non-verbal group test with little children, usually isn't thoroughly accurate in predicting all future school success. So a naive teacher takes this test result as gospel, then records an IQ score in the book. This score follows the child through school. He's branded for life as an 82 IQ. No matter what kind of good work he does later, his teachers who accept the original IQ score as infallible say, 'He can't do as well as he is doing on arithmetic with such a low IQ. He must be getting improper help on his homework.' "

MR. LONG: "I'll grant that in some cases there has been a misuse of test scores that were passed along. But I think you're taking too dim a view of it."

MISS O'CONNEL: "All right, take children's marks. I know of teachers who keep a child's past year's marks in a folder. They study these marks at the beginning of the year. Then if a child does poorly in spelling or reading but had high grades last year, the teacher tends to raise the child's mark this year because she thinks it looks bad for her if her marks are inconsistent with those the last teacher gave. And the opposite kind of prejudice can affect the child who is now doing well but received low grades last year."

MR. LONG: "What if a teacher is well trained to write accurate anecdotes and to interpret tests correctly? Don't you agree that a collection of information about a child over a period of time can aid the teacher in helping him more?"

MISS O'CONNEL: "Yes, but that certainly is a big *if*."

She turned to Miss Solski, fourth-grade instructor, and asked, "What do you think?"

Miss Solski admitted that she did not know much about record systems other than her own method of keeping grades in a roll book. She said she would "have to do some reading on the topic before I can be of any help in the faculty meeting."

Her investigation led to the following information about (1) methods teachers use for organizing evaluation data and keeping records throughout a year, (2) cumulative records, and (3) case studies.

TEACHERS' CLASS RECORDS

Teachers follow a variety of practices in organizing data about children's progress.

Roll book

Probably the most common procedure is using a roll book in which to keep all the information about a class. The book typically provides small spaces where attendance is noted and where marks on tests or projects are recorded. The roll book has the advantage of being easily handled. Information is concise and readily recorded. However, it usually does not provide space for the teacher's personal observations about a child such as anecdotes, rating scales, or conclusions derived from sociograms or participation charts.

A roll book containing attendance, test scores, and marks on projects is often supplemented by a notebook in which anecdotal records are kept. In this case, a page in the notebook is dedicated to each child, and pertinent incidents are recorded in diary form. This notebook is sometimes called a behavior diary.

Individual folder

Other teachers prefer to keep a manila folder for each child. In the folder they place anecdotes, rating scales, summaries of interviews with parents, and samples of the pupil's work. The material one teacher keeps in the folder may be meager; for another it may be extensive. The folder may contain all the data about the child's progress, or it may be used to supplement a roll book in which test scores and marks are kept.

For the instructor who maintains folders, the process of evaluation will be much simplified if a standard *face sheet* or *summary sheet* is developed. This sheet provides for rapid recording and rapid reading of data the teacher keeps about every child.

Following is one type of summary sheet for use in a fourth grade. The teacher mimeographed it and stapled the sheet inside the cover of the folder. Class attendance was kept in a regular roll book.

Name ______________________ Birth Date ______________
Address ______________________ Telephone ______________
Parents ______________________ ______________
Address (es) ______________________ ______________
Occupations ______________________ ______________
Psychological Exam Score __________ Reading Test Grade Level
Speed __________
Comprehension __________

Class Quiz Scores

Date	*Test*	*Score*	*Points Possible*	*Rank in Class of 30*

Get-acquainted card

A technique some teachers use to obtain immediate data about pupils when they first enter a new grade is the *get-acquainted card.* It is appropriate for middle-grade and upper-grade pupils, for it demands some ability to write. For younger children the same data are usually secured from parents or in an interview with the child.

This is the way the card is commonly developed. On the first day of class when the teacher is greeting the students, he tells them that in order for him to become better acquainted with them in a brief time, he would appreciate their filling out an information card. A five-by-eight-inch card or a sheet of paper may be effective for such data as indicated on the sample card shown on the next page.

As the pupils fill out the cards, the teacher answers questions or explains items.

A factual sheet such as this yields information that often is valuable to the teacher in understanding a child. For example, the

Name ________________ Age ______ Birthday ________
Address ________________________ Telephone ________
Father's Name ________________________________
His Address ________________ His Work ________
Mother's Name ________________________________
Her Address ________________ Her Work ________

Brothers and Sisters: Name	*Age*	*Work or School*

(Front of Card)

Books or magazines you have read and liked this past year:

________________ ________________
________________ ________________
________________ ________________

Games you like: ________________________________
____

Your hobbies: ________________________________
____

(Back of Card)

child's address may indicate the socioeconomic level of his family. Parents' addresses or names not consistent with the pupil's often reveal a broken home. The number of brothers and sisters and their ages may help provide clues to the child's behavior in school. A knowledge of the books he has read and the hobbies he pursues are valuable to the teacher who tries to fit schoolwork to a child's individual needs and interests.

Thus, a get-acquainted card may become an easily compiled and valuable portion of the summary material in a child's folder.

Work samples

Many teachers keep occasional samples of pupils' work in their folders. Here are examples of the kinds of materials often kept:

In the third grade where children are changing from manuscript writing (printing) to cursive writing, samples of each pupil's work at various times during the year give a good picture of his growth in this area.

An illustrated book report by a seventh grader might be kept in his folder.

An autobiography written by each fifth grader could be valuable in showing ability in written composition as well as in giving indications of the child's conception of himself.

Summary

The records teachers keep about their students differ in form and amount. They vary from a roll book containing attendance and test scores to a folder containing a summary sheet of personal data and test scores, anecdotal records, rating scales, notes about parent-teacher interviews, and samples of student work.

CUMULATIVE RECORDS

A cumulative record is a collection of information about a child over a period of time, usually several years. Typically, it includes many kinds of information which in some schools is passed from teacher to teacher as the child advances through the grades. In other schools the record is kept in the main office or in the guidance director's files, and the child's current teacher is asked to consult and to contribute to the record. These records often follow the pupil as he graduates from elementary school into high school.

The only type of data about students kept by all schools from year to year is marks in academic work. Many also keep attendance records and health reports. However, school systems are increasingly adding more information to the cumulative data. The more complete records contain information about health, family, school success, aptitudes, and apparent social adjustment.

A student's cumulative record usually is kept in a folder that contains a *front sheet* (*face* or *summary sheet*) for summarizing data such as test scores, health reports, attendance, marks, schools attended, and family information so that they can be easily read. The rest of the folder is for important anecdotes, teachers' summaries of the student's success in their classes, samples of student work, and miscellaneous information.

Some school systems do not keep anecdotal material or student work samples. Rather, they develop or adopt a *cumulative record card,* which typically is a large card (12 x 12 inches or so) with spaces on both sides for particular information.[1] Other schools use separate summary cards for medical and dental reports, school grades, information about home, and attendance.

In a school where teachers at various grade levels keep frequent anecdotes, much information has been collected about a pupil by the time he is in sixth or seventh grade. To include all of these anecdotes, rating scales, and samples of student work in the cumulative folder would make it excessively bulky. For this reason, teachers may at the end of the year write a summary profile of each student's progress throughout the year. This eliminates the bulk of material that often discourages the potential user of a cumulative record, and also it organizes the teacher's records in a concise, understandable form. To write this profile takes time. But if the teacher has built up data gradually throughout the year, the task of summarizing it is not unduly burdensome, and the results can be rewarding. Such a summary, or at least portions of it, may also function as a report of progress to the child's parents.

The following example of such a summary of a half year's records was written by a kindergarten teacher. The material in this summary was based primarily upon frequent anecdotes of specific events and upon unrecorded observation. The summary statements include some interpretation, usually supported by sample incidents or phrases from the actual anecdotes to make the explanation clearer. As you read this summary, decide whether you would want to have this information if you were to be Billy's first-grade teacher. Or would you rather meet Billy without any data from his kindergarten teacher? Do you think this summary tells you things about Billy that might help you understand him and aid him in being a happier, more successful first grader? Is there anything in this

[1] Reprinted through the courtesy of the Educational Records Bureau.

NAME Lewis, Paul R. BIRTHDATE 12-29-38

YEAR	1949-50	1950-1951	1951-1952	1952-1953	1953-1954	1954-1955
SCHOOL	Hawthorne					
GRADE	6 6	7 7	8 8	9 9	10 10	11 11
MENTAL AGE	15-0	16-6				
CHRON AGE	11	12	13	14	15	16

SUBJECTS, GRADES AND CREDITS

1949-50 Subject	1st Sem	2nd Sem	1950-1951 Subject	1st Sem	2nd Sem	1951-1952 Subject	1st Sem	2nd Sem
Eng.	A	A	Eng.	A	A	Eng.	A	A
Arith.	B	A	Arith.	A	A	Lit.	B	A
Sci.	A	A	Sci.	A	B	Lat.	B	B
Soc. Stud.	A	A	Soc. Stud.	A	A	Arith.	A	A
Art	S	S	Music	S	S	Sci.	A	A
						Soc. Stud.	A	B

1952-1953 Subject	1st Sem	2nd Sem	1953-1954 Subject	1st Sem	2nd Sem	1954-1955 Subject	1st Sem	2nd Sem
Eng. I	A	A	Eng. II	A	B	Eng. III	B	A
Fr. I	A	A	Fr. II	A	A	Fr. III	A	B
Alg. I	B	A	Pl. Geom.	A	A	Alg. II	B	A
Anc. Hist.	A	A	Wld. Hist.	A	A	Phys.	A	A

ACADEMIC APTITUDE AND READING

Year	Test	Score M.A.	I.Q.	%ile
1949-50	Kuhlmann-Anderson	15-0	138	86 / 90
1950-1951	Calif. Ment. Mat. Adv.-Tot. Ment. Fact.	16-6	140	57 / 92
1950-1951	Traxler Sil. Read. - 4	139		97
1951-1952	S.E.B. Jr. Sch. Apt.-DR Verb. / Num.	647 / 639		96 / 91
1951-1952	Traxler Sil. Read. - 1	147		95
1952-1953	Amer. Council Psych.-1952	126		96
1953-1954	Amer. Council Psych.-1949	147		98
1954-1955	Amer. Council Psych.-1954	133		93

ACHIEVEMENT TEST SCORES AND PERCENTILES

1949-50 Test	Score E.A.	%ile	1950-1951 Test	Score E.A.	%ile	1951-1952 Test	Score E.A.	%ile
Stan. Ach.-Adv. D-Tot. Av.	Gr. Pl. 11.0	95	Stan. Ach.-Adv. F-Tot. Av.	Gr. Pl. 12.9	96	Stan. Ach.-Adv. H-Tot. Av.	Gr. Pl. 14.1	98
Av. Read.	12.0	94	Av. Read.	13.3	95	Av. Read.	13.7	96
Lang. Us.	12.3	94	Lang. Us.	14.4	93	Lang. Us.	14.4+	96
Av. Arith.	9.9	91	Av. Arith.	13.0	93	Av. Arith.	14.2	94
Lit.	13.5	95	Lit.	13.8	87	Lit.	14.4+	98
Av. Soc. St.	12.2	96	Av. Soc. St.	13.6	98	Av. Soc. St.	14.4	99
Elem. Sci.	13.5	97	Elem. Sci.	13.8	99	Elem. Sci.	14.1	98
Spell.	11.0	95	Spell.	13.5	97	Spell.	14.4+	99
			Math 7&8-Coop. RO	66	94	Lat. Coop. Q-Gr. 8-1 yr. Elem. Tot.	54	86
						Read.	53	78
						Vocab.	50	88
						Gram.	57	84

1952-1953 Test	Score E.A.	%ile	1953-1954 Test	Score E.A.	%ile	1954-1955 Test	Score E.A.	%ile
Eng.-Coop. Z			Eng.-Coop. Y			Eng.-Coop. RX		
A-Mech. of Exp.	52	63	A-Mech. of Exp.	68	97	H-Mech. of Exp.	78	99
C1-Read. Comp.	76	93	C2-Read. Comp.	66	88	C2-Read. Comp.	75	93
Vocab.	63	88	Vocab.	69	95	Vocab.	73	95
Speed	69	84	Speed	66	83	Speed	72	87
Level	86	99	Level	60	71	Level	77	94
Fr. Coop. P-Gr. 9-1 yr. Elem. Tot.	64	96	Fr. Coop. R-Gr. 10-2 yrs. Adv. Tot.	87	99	Fr. Coop. Q-Gr. 11-3 yrs. Adv. Tot.	88	92
Read.	62	97	Read.	83	97	Read.	90	90
Vocab.	66	94	Vocab.	89	100	Vocab.	83	88
Gram.	60	90	Gram.	79	99	Gram.	79	91
Elem. Alg.-Coop. Y	64	70	Pl. Geom.-Coop. Z	70	91	Int. Alg.-Coop. T	70	94
Anc. Hist.-Coop. P	73	92	Cum. Wld. Hist.-AM	133	97	Phys. Coop. ERB-SX	58	91

○ SCHOOL GRADES — TEST PERCENTILES: ● INDEPENDENT SCHOOL ⊕ LOCAL ○ PUBLIC

GR | %ile: 99, 98, 96, 93, 89, 84, 77, 69, 60, 50, 40, 31, 23, 16, 11, 7, 4, 2, 1

Months: Jy Au S O N D Ja F M A My Je (each year)

(front)

	M. F.	BIRTHDATE—PLACE	GEN'L HEALTH	RELIGION	RACE OR NAT'L'TY	OCCUPATION	ADDRESS
NAME Lewis, Paul R.		12-20-38 Chicago Ill.	Good	Episc.	American	Student	5925 Maryland Avenue, Chicago, Ill.
FATHER Lewis, George D.		6-19-10 Buffalo N.Y.	Excellent	"	"	Public Accountant	RES. 5925 Maryland Avenue, Chicago, Ill. BUS. 254 N. LaSalle Street, Chicago, Ill.
MOTHER Lewis, Josephine Ward		8-23-14 Springfield Mo.	Good	"	"	Housewife	RES. 5925 Maryland Avenue, Chicago, Ill. BUS.
STEP-PARENT OR GUARDIAN							RES. BUS.

LANGUAGE SPOKEN IN HOME BEFORE 10— English AFTER 10— English

TYPE OF COMMUNITY BEFORE 10—Residential-City homes & apts. AFTER 10— Residential

IF PARENTS SEPARATED GIVE DATE

YEAR AND AGE	1949-50 11	1950-51 12	1951-52 13	1952-53 14	1953-54 15	1954-55 16
ADVISER	Dabney	Dabney	Winslow	Winslow	Goff	Goff
ATTENDANCE	A Regular T	A Absent 5 days with colds T	A Regular attendance T	A Out three weeks with pneumonia T	A Regular attendance T	A Regular T
DISCIPLINE	Good	Fair - Inclined to be noisy	Good	Excellent	Good	Excellent
HOME INFLUENCES AND COOPERATION	Parents interested and cooperative	Very good	Fine home background	Always willing to cooperate	Interested in helping Paul plan his future	Superior
MENTAL AND EMOTIONAL	Very intelligent and dependable Inclined to be nervous Gets so excited in class he stutters at times	Still somewhat excitable and high strung but is developing good self-control	Very bright An all-round good student	Intelligent and emotionally stable	Splendid ability Material for a good college	Intelligent and well-balanced
PHYSICAL AND ATHLETIC	Health generally good Slightly over-active thyroid Wears glasses	Good health except for occasional colds Interested in baseball	Good A little nearsighted but vision normal with glasses	Had a setback with pneumonia in middle of year but made quick recovery	Very good Rapid physical development this year Out for basketball and track team	Good Is active in basketball, track & golf Rifle club
EXTRA-CURRICULAR ACTIVITIES AND INTERESTS	Builds model ships Collects stamps Reads many books Has ducks and rabbits for pets	Makes model ships and planes Interested in military history and history of the airplane	Building models illustrating stages in development of airplane Reading military and naval history	Model planes and ships Extensive reading in history and science Summer camp	Boat building Overhauling and rebuilding automobile engine Summer camp	Boat building Sailing Mountain climbing Counselor in summer camp
NOTABLE ACCOMPLISHMENTS AND EXPERIENCES	One of the leaders in his class Very popular	Leads the class in general ability Took trip to Mexico City last summer	Winning personality makes him a leader Organized club of boys interested in model ships & planes	Vice-president of his class	Class president Elected to student council	Student council Rifle clubteam
EDUCATIONAL PLANS	No definite plans	Plans to take college preparatory course	Interested in Naval Academy	Thinks he prefers small to medium sized college for men	Is considering Hamilton, Lehigh, Amherst and several other colleges	Will apply to Amherst College Plans to major in social science
PERSONALITY RATINGS +2	A boy of excellent promise	Popular & a natural leader	Ability to work, organize, cooperate,	Splendid personal qualities	Cooperation, leadership	Outstanding personality
+1						
0						
−1						
−2						

REMARKS An outstanding boy in every way. Should be a real asset to his college. Vocational aim is not yet definite, but will decide during senior year of high school. Is thinking of graduate degree in political science and then some aspect of diplomatic service.

(back)

Fig. 37. Cumulative record card

Smith, John William

LAST NAME FIRST NAME

RESIDENCE SEX: M. ✓ F.

576 Ninth St. L.A.

LOS ANGELES CITY SCHOOL DISTRICTS
HEALTH RECORD

SCHOOL

Washington Elementary

V YEAR	T YEAR	M RESULT YEAR
52	51	Neg. 50

BIRTH: MO. 4 DAY 2 YR. 45 — BORN CALIF. ✓

RM. NO. OR GYM. PER.

SYMBOLS—Λ NEEDS ATTENTION GRADE URGENCY 1, 2, 3, OR 4 — A RECEIVED ATTENTION — F FURTHER EXAM. NEEDED — O OVER

PHYSICAL EXAMINATION

Date of Examination	Name of Examiner	Grade	NUTRITION			EYES			EARS			NOSE & THROAT			TEETH				HEART		LUNGS	Orthopedic		Nervous System	Speech	SKIN	Endocrine	Misc.	GYM
				Wgt.	Hgt.	Vision R	Vision L	Pathology	Hearing R	Hearing L	Pathology	Pathology	Tonsils	Adenoids	Decay	Cleaning	Gums	Orthodontia	Organic	Functional		Posture	Feet						
10-7-53	H.S.	B4	Λ	46	50¼	20/30	20/30		N	N			A	A	Λ(3)	Λ			Λ			Λ(2)							

Form 34-EH-6 THIS CARD MUST BE TRANSFERRED WITH OTHER RECORD CARDS. EVERY CHILD MUST HAVE A HEALTH CARD OR AN EXCUSE CARD. 50M—4-52

(*front*)

PERSONAL HISTORY Date 10/2/53 Family Physician D. D. Blank, M.D.

Allergy: Asthma ___ Hayfever ___ Eczema ___ Diph. ___ Heart D. ✓ Hernia ___

Polio ___ Pneumonia ___ Rheum. F. ✓ Scarlet F. ___ Tb. (self or family) ___

Upper Respiratory: Frequent Colds ___ Cough ___ Sore Throat ✓ Ear Infection ___

Operations ___ Accidents ___ Other serious illness ___

Symptoms occurring frequently: Headaches ___ Fatigue ✓ Fainting ___ Nose Bleeds ___ Growing Pains ✓

Family status: F. ___ M. ___ Bro. ___ Sis. ___

Immunizations: Smallpox ___ Diph. ___ Tetanus ___ Wh. Cough ___

Health Habits:	Adequate diet	Elem.	Jr. Hi.	Sr. Hi.	Daily Breakfast	Elem.	Jr. Hi.	Sr. Hi.	Bedtime hr.	Elem.	Jr. Hi.	Sr. Hi.
		?								9		

DENTAL RECORD						
Date Examined	Name of Examiner	TEETH				
		Decay	Cleaning	Gums	Orthodontia	
11/4/53	J.B.	3	∧			

Date	
10/7/53	Cardiac II
	Recommend Heart Board appointment. No strenuous play activities. Daily rest period. Attention to diet. Dental care urgent. Fatigue posture. H. S.
10/9/53	Conference with parent. Heart Board appointment arranged. J. Wright, P.H.N.

Tests: Tb. Mantoux Neg. Sept. '50 Audiometer Normal Hearing

(*back*)

Fig. 38. Health record

Health records are one important part of cumulative records.

summary that you believe should be omitted from a cumulative record?

Name: William Henry Carlton (called Billy)
Age: 5-1 in September Parents: Mr. and Mrs. George Carlton

Physical Appearance and Activities. Billy is slightly taller and heavier than the average kindergarten child. His hair is light brown, his cheeks rosy. At school he usually wears blue, brown, or maroon corduroy overalls with matching T-shirt.

He is husky and appears to be above average in motor skills. He runs, climbs, jumps, pushes, pulls, and swings himself well. He seems to have little or no fear of attempting motor tasks that other children his size often shy away from. He has many tricks he appears to enjoy doing on the monkey ladder. He climbs the ladder with ease, jumps to the ground from the third step up, and hangs from the horizontal ladder upside down. Though sometimes he falls when doing a new trick, Billy seems to be unaffected emotionally by the falls, but jumps up to try the stunt again or goes off about his business, apparently unconcerned.

He spends much time on the swings, especially since he learned to pump standing up. He swings higher than his schoolmates. When he fell last week while trying to alight from the speeding swing, he cried a moment, then sobbed, "Nothing's wrong," and went back immediately to conquer the trick of alighting from the swing without falling. In the school yard Billy is active most of the time. He appears to have a lot of energy.

In handling such finger materials as clay, sand, and finger paints, Billy seems to have at least average skill. Though he shows little or no interest in easel painting, he does enjoy handling clay to form simple objects, especially if an adult is working with the class. The only time I saw him use easel paints was when he wanted to paint some clay Easter-eggs he had made.

Billy's use of language is quite advanced. He speaks clearly, though oftentimes in a high-pitched and possibly strained voice. He seems to enjoy books. On two occasions when he ran out of the school yard, the only thing that brought him back was the promise of "reading a story." When an adult reads a story to the group, Billy sits close, listens intently, and is usually the last to leave. He follows the story (though many of the others are easily distracted) and asks frequent questions about the plot as well as the meanings of words, such as "What does 'clumsy' mean? Where is Washington?"

In addition to asking questions during the story to gain information, Billy asks many questions during the school day to gain attention, especially from adults. The most common term in Billy's vocabulary seems to be "Know what?" He uses "Know what?" to attract the attention of others so that he can tell a story or past experience. Sometimes the "Know what?" is a preface to an obvious untruth that Billy tells an adult. For example, one day he said, "Know what? My daddy's a fireman. No, he's a pilot."

Social and Emotional Relations. Billy seems to have definite social problems in kindergarten. When I first observed him I thought he got along quite well with the others. But after seeing him in a number of situations, I realized that in group play he is *with* the group but not an intimate *part of* the group. He tries to be accepted by the other children but he always ends up on the outside of group activities in which children are the controllers. For example, one day the children were playing train with a large box. Billy was allowed to help put sand (they called it coal) in the engine. But when the other four children decided to get into the engine and ride away, Billy was told he had to stay out.

He does not seem to be able to make close friendships. Other children can tease and hit each other and still be liked and accepted. But Billy does things that cause him to be rejected. An example of this was seen the day the children were playing with a tub of water. Billy insisted on being one of the first to play in the tub. When the others came around, he squirted them liberally and swung a muddy stick at the girls, making a few of them cry. From time to time he will be accepted by someone for a short period, but the relationship usually ends with an aggressive attack by Billy.

Sometimes he uses his superior physical ability to gain the attention of the group. One day he hauled a big board to the monkey ladder and made a slide. The others in the play yard were fascinated by this invention and gathered around. Billy showed the braver ones how to slide down. But their interest soon lagged, and they went back to their own groups, leaving him alone again.

Billy has different reactions toward different children. He is in awe of most of the first graders who sometimes play in the same yard as the kindergarten group. He readily gives up the swings or toys to any first grader who asks for or demands them.

Among the children his own age, Billy shows respect for the demands of Chris Jones and Robin Teller. But when either Chris or Robin is not looking, Billy may make a hit-and-run attack. After incidents of this type the other children often call him a naughty boy, and Billy again will go back to his more solitary activities, such as making cupcakes out of sand. But he soon tries to get back into the group again.

Instead of carrying out a solitary activity, Billy may join a group that is listening to a story. Frequently, after he has had a fight or has done something the others call bad, he tugs at his lower lip and frowns.

Thus, in his social relations Billy attempts to be a leader, but many of his playmates call him a bad boy. That he feels this ostracism was shown to some extent by his answer to an adult who asked him whom he liked best among the children: "I hate them all."

Family Background. The family lives in a bungalow in what is regarded as a middle-class section of town. Billy lives with his father, mother, and baby sister (nine-months old). Mr. Carlton is a pharmacist. Mrs. Carlton is a housewife.

Billy's mother says he is often "naughty" at home. She says, "His little sister is so cute and good compared to him. I'm afraid he's jealous of the attention other people pay her. But you can't blame them, when she's so good and he's naughty so often." Mrs. Carlton says that Billy runs away from home frequently, and she has to set out to find him playing (usually by himself) someplace else in the neighborhood. His real feeling toward his home could be determined accurately only after more information about his home relationships.

Billy says he likes school very much and frequently comes to school long before it opens and tries to stay after it closes. When he wants to frighten another child into doing something, Billy often says, "I'll tell the teacher, and she won't let you come to school any more. Then you'll be sorry."

The above summary is quite an extended one. A more common type of summary is one composed of brief generalizations not supported by specific examples. Such a summary of Billy's half year in kindergarten might be:

"Billy Carlton (William Henry Carlton) is above average in physical and mental abilities. At present, he seems to be at a rather disturbed, insecure stage of his life. He is physically brave, but is unsure of himself in social situations. Because of his inability to be accepted by his more desirable schoolmates, he is left outside their social groups. This obviously disturbs him, because he continually wants to be with the group. Billy handles his emotional disturbances by hitting or by running away. He appears most happy when he is listening to stories or is having success in some physical activity. But generally he appears to be a somewhat unhappy boy."

Case study

A *case study* is a thorough investigation of a pupil's family history, home environment, medical history, school record, social environment, and personal reactions. Such a study usually is made in an attempt to discover factors relevant to a student's maladjustment. Typically, only children who are marked deviants warrant a real case study by a psychologist, psychiatrist, social case worker, or teacher. However, a teacher's records or good cumulative records actually are to a degree case studies in that many factors of students' lives are reflected in them. The rather complete summary of Billy Carlton's kindergarten experiences could be considered one type of case study.

Although a teacher may not often find it necessary to compile a thorough case study of a maladjusted child, he may be requested by a psychologist or social worker to contribute material on school adjustment to such a study. The practices of being specific and unbiased in reporting the child's life in school should be followed in providing such information. To the teacher's data, the professional worker will add facts gathered through medical examinations, projective testing and intelligence testing, and through interviews with the child, his family, his associates, and church or club workers.

The case study is primarily a clinical method to be used in determining the probable causes for a child's maladjustment and in suggesting ways of helping him make better adjustment.

THE DECISION ABOUT CUMULATIVE RECORDS

At the Central School faculty meeting arguments were voiced on both sides of the question of who should keep the cumulative record folders.

Those who thought the teachers should keep the records stated that:

1. All data possible that indicates the individual problems and abilities of a child should be immediately available to the teacher who is trying to help that child develop.
2. Records in a central office are too much trouble for teachers to use; therefore they are ignored, fill up space, and gather dust.
3. Teachers will be more likely to develop worth-while material for such records if they realize the material is actually used.

Those who thought the cumulative records should be kept in the main office said that:

1. Teachers may be prejudiced against a child by having information about him before the child has had an opportunity to prove himself in that particular grade.

2. Even when they have records in their own rooms, teachers often do not use them.
3. Records should be in the main office where everyone, teachers and guidance workers alike, may inspect them.

Following the discussion, Mr. Long suggested that since records had formerly been kept in the main office, they might now experiment with the plan of keeping them in the classrooms. Teachers who did not wish to inspect a child's record before the child proved himself in the class would not have to do so. He further suggested that two or three faculty meetings be dedicated to the study of proper ways to write records and interpret them. This, he said, might help counteract the criticism that some teachers used records improperly. By vote the faculty adopted Mr. Long's proposal.

The Central Elementary plan might work in some schools but not in others. The system that will be best for a given school system depends upon such factors as size of school, ability of teachers in using records, facilities for keeping records in main office, and the number of different teachers who work with a child during a school week.

OBJECTIVES OF THIS CHAPTER

The effective elementary or junior high teacher:

1. Organizes the evaluation data about each child in a form that includes numerous kinds of information and is easily understood.
2. Contributes accurate, unbiased information to cumulative records and case studies.
3. Takes advantage of cumulative data to understand better the unique needs, problems, and abilities of each pupil.
4. Interprets material in cumulative records with caution and due regard for personal bias that may have influenced the contributions.

Suggested evaluation technique for this chapter

1. Observe a child or youth over a period of time. Write anecdotes about the individual, and collect all possible data from other sources that would add to the picture of this person. Compile this information into a brief case study, including at the end a summary and tentative interpretation of what the person's problems, strengths, and weaknesses appear to be in his adjustment.

SUGGESTED READINGS

1. SCHWARTZ, ALFRED, and TIEDEMAN, STUART C. *Evaluating Student Progress in the Secondary School.* New York: Longmans, Green and Co., 1957. Chapter 12: Material on case study applicable to elementary and junior high schools.
2. TRAXLER, A. E. "A Cumulative Record Form for the Elementary School," *Elementary School Journal,* September, 1939, pp. 45-54.
3. TRAXLER, A. E. *How to Use Cumulative Records.* Chicago: Science Research Associates, 1947. Simple, helpful explanation of the many uses of cumulative records.
4. WRIGHTSTONE, J. WAYNE; JUSTMAN, JOSEPH; and ROBBINS, IRVING. *Evaluation in Modern Education.* New York: American Book Co., 1956. Chapter 12: Case studies. Chapter 13: Cumulative records.

CHAPTER

13

Marking Student Progress

BEFORE THE FIRST MARKING PERIOD of the school year two teachers from the departmentalized junior high grades of Central School asked to talk with their supervisor. Both instructors, Mr. MacDonald and Miss Leong, were in their first year of teaching. At lunch they had been talking together about the marks they planned to give their pupils. As they compared the marking systems they were using, and as they noted the way the marks probably would come out by the end of the school year, they foresaw possible troubles. They came to the supervisor to compare their marking procedures with the systems other teachers in the school were using.

Mr. MacDonald explained his grading this way:

"To keep personal opinion out of marking in my social studies classes, I grade on the curve. The trouble is, in two of the classes some of the pupils who are set to fail, really don't seem that bad. But, according to the statistical curve, 10 per cent are to fail, so that's the way I'm doing it. And in another class, more than 10 per cent really deserve to fail, I think, but according to the curve some of these inadequate students will pass. Maybe I should combine the classes for computing the marks. What's the policy here?"

Before the supervisor answered this question, she listened as Miss Leong explained:

"I don't use a curve as Jim does. I realize that he has to use some type of relative scale in a less precise area like social studies. But as an arithmetic and mathematics teacher, I can use a definite percentage scale that is really exact. Each pupil is scored on the basis of the per cent of problems he gets correct during the marking period. I follow the standard marking procedure: 90 to 100 per cent is *excellent,* 80 to 90 per cent is *good,* 70 to 80 is *average,* 60 to 70 is *below average* but still passing, and below 60 is *failing.* But I find in my classes here there are many, many failures this first grading period. What I would like to ask is whether it's common in Central School for so many of the seventh and eighth graders to be so poor in arithmetic that they can't pass? I foresee many failing at the end of the year unless they reform rapidly."

The first thing that struck the supervisor about these questions was that Central School had neglected to orient the new teachers properly to the marking system at the time they had begun in September. She suggested that they call all the new teachers together for several sessions to clarify the entire matter of grading. During the ensuing series of discussions, the following questions were investigated:

1. How do you grade "scientifically"? That is, how can you eliminate personal opinions and judgments from marking so that the process is really objective?
2. What are the purposes or uses of marks in elementary and junior high schools?
3. What are some methods of improving marking procedures?

ELIMINATING PERSONAL JUDGMENTS FROM MARKING

Both Mr. MacDonald and Miss Leong had felt they were grading "scientifically" and eliminating their own personal opinions in marking. However, as we analyze the assumptions underlying their practices, we see that subjectivity was certainly there. It was hiding behind such terms as *statistical curve, percentage scale, really exact,* and *standard marking procedure.*

For instance, the *statistical curve* that Mr. MacDonald referred to was one he had read about in an older evaluation book. But Mr. MacDonald did not realize that in using a normal-distribution curve as a basis for marking he tacitly *assumed* that:

1. For the skill or knowledge he was judging (such as knowledge of local government structure), the bulk of the students bunched together around an average score, and the number of students achieving scores above and below the average diminished gradually in a precise manner. That is, he had to assume that the scores never

tended to bunch more toward the higher ones or toward the lower ones if he expected to use normal curve data.

2. He had measured the students very accurately, making few if any errors in constructing tests, marking tests, judging compositions, and rating pupil skills in order to arrive at the final score or mark.

3. Every class he taught had the same percentage of bright, average, and slow students as every other one. This assumption was necessary if he planned to apply the same statistical decisions equally to all classes.

But Mr. MacDonald faces two principal difficulties here. First, rarely if ever could he support these assumptions with convincing evidence or arguments. And, second, after he has made such assumptions he still has not decided "scientifically" who should pass and who should fail. It is true that he had read in a book that 10 per cent should fail. But he did not wonder, "How does the author know?" Instead, he took this as a truth. If he had looked in some other measurement texts he might have seen that other authors recommend different percentages that should fail "according to the curve." Some say 5 per cent, others 12. Still others say 15 per cent should get below-average marks, and of these 15 per cent the very lowest few should fail. Mr. MacDonald failed to realize that he had accepted an author's personal opinion as a fact.

Miss Leong's marking system, she said, used "a definite percentage scale that is really exact." Her procedure differed from Mr. MacDonald's. His method passed or failed a certain *percentage of students,* so his scale slid up and down with the abilities of the particular class he was judging. Miss Leong, on the other hand, judged pupils on the *percentage of problems* they got right or wrong on tests. If a test consisted of 50 problems and one student got 43 correct, he received a score of 86 because he had marked 86 per cent of the problems correctly. This score, in Miss Leong's system, put the student in the *very good* range (80-90). With her scheme, all the students could fail, because all might get less than 60 per cent of the problems correct if the problems were difficult or the students were very poorly prepared. Likewise, all might be judged excellent if the problems were very easy ones so that everyone could get more than 90 per cent correct.

Miss Leong believed her method eliminated personal judgments. But when we analyze it we see that opinion entered at several crucial points. In the first place, the "standard marking procedure" she mentioned is not standard at all, even for those teachers who use a type of percent-of-problems scale. Some consider 95 to 100 per cent *excellent* or grade A work, 87 to 95 *very good* or grade B work, and so on down the line to a failing point of 70 or, perhaps, 65. Still other teachers use different cutting points in determining grades. Thus Miss Leong was simply accepting someone's personal opinion that students getting less than 60 per cent of the problems correct should repeat the course. Perhaps even more important, her personal judgment entered in when she made up the test items. By creating very difficult questions or wording them badly, she could fail most of the class. By creating easy items, she could pass them all. She also affected the final totals by the way she decided to score the answers. For instance, did she give no credit if the answer was almost correct but not quite? Or did she give partial credit if the student had used the proper arithmetical reasoning but had made a careless mistake in computation?

It should be apparent, then, that using statistics does not take the human judgment factor out of marking. For that is just what a mark is: *a judgment of a student's progress.* Often this judgment is summed up as a symbol, such as a letter (A or B) or a number (92 or 81) or a word (superior or average). Statistics can only help you organize the data and summarize individual judgments in a more precise way. They do not make the judgments for you.

PURPOSES AND USES OF MARKS

After they recognized that their marks were really personal judgments, Mr. MacDonald and Miss Leong were ready to analyze the purposes of making these judgments. It is necessary to understand the uses to which you are putting your grades before you can decide accurately what form of marks to give and what evidence to base them on.

At the elementary and junior high levels, marks are typically used for (1) determining which students are to be promoted to the next grade and which are to be retained another year or eliminated from a class, (2) motivating pupils to work hard, (3) guiding the planning of a student's current schoolwork, (4) guiding plans for future education, (5) providing records for the school, and (6) providing reports of pupil progress for the parents and the child.

Determining promotion and retention

This matter of promotion or failure of students was uppermost in Mr. MacDonald's and Miss Leong's minds when they brought their grading problems to the supervisor. Without knowing it, the two teachers were using marking systems that conflicted with the basic purposes of their school. They were basing their marking practices on a set of assumptions best suited to grading students in advanced professional schools, not in the elementary school.

Today in America public elementary and junior high education is for all children, not for only a selected few. The guiding principle underlying these schools of basic education might be stated as: *Help each child become the best person he is capable of being, regardless of the natural abilities and socioeconomic background he brings with him.* At these lower levels of schooling it is not the purpose of education to establish set standards of performance, and then to eliminate from the school the children who have not met the standards as soon as some of their agemates have. Instead, the school recognizes the wide range in abilities of children and tries to adapt its program to provide education appropriate for pupils of all levels of skill. It tries to give each child a chance to learn at his own rate. The focus, then, is on each pupil's optimum growth, not on set standards which a child must reach if he is to be allowed to progress with new work.

Educators and laymen alike often confuse this purpose of the elementary school with the quite different purpose of a professional school, like a teachers' college, law school, or medical college. The main objective of professional schools is to produce skilled people to fulfill an important function in society. The main focus of the professional school is on society's need rather than on the needs of the individual student. Therefore, unlike the elementary school, the professional college has a screening or eliminating function in addition to a teaching function. Students who are liable to become clumsy surgeons or badly informed teachers need to be screened out of the program. The school manages this by setting standards for competence in the profession, and students who do not reach the competency level in their classwork receive failing grades and are eliminated from entering the profession. A society cannot long thrive if it does not set standards for people who are to fill crucial jobs.

So it is seen that Miss Leong was using a marking system which tended to screen out students who had not met her standards. And, from her remarks about the number of failures, we suspect that her standards were unrealistically high or that her teaching methods were so poor that the students failed to learn much. Her general approach was better suited to the university than to a modern concept of the purpose of elementary and junior high education. In a slightly different way, Mr. MacDonald's approach also was better suited to higher education, though even at a university level the way he interpreted the "normal curve" was unfortunately rigid.

Our best guide to what our promotion policy should be at the elementary and junior high levels comes from the wealth of research on the problem. Most important are the studies that compare the subsequent success of the slow student who has been retained another year in the grade with the success of the slow student who has been allowed to progress with his classmates. As a general policy, it has been found best to promote the less adequate scholar with his class, for he will usually do better scholastically than if he is held back to repeat the grade. (This policy is not recommended as "soft pedagogy" or "softheartedness" or "softheadedness" on the part of educators. It is recommended because research shows that it usually works.)

But in some cases it is more desirable for the student to be retained in a grade, or it is desirable for the gifted pupil to be accelerated beyond his agemates. Hence, we are not recommending regular "automatic" promotion each year for each child. Instead, we are suggesting that the key question to ask at the elementary and junior high levels is: "What will be best for this student?" When a student is considerably behind or ahead of the others, the teacher should look carefully at his case. The following procedure is recommended for handling the deviate when a decision is to be made about whether he should be retained, promoted, or accelerated:

1. Carefully evaluate the pupil's achievement in all areas of schoolwork, his mental ability, his chronological age, his size, his social adjustment, and his ambitions and attitudes when deciding what is best for him.
2. Be sure you have the cooperation and sincere consent of the student, his parents, and the school administration, so that all of them feel that retardation, or acceleration, is for the pupil's benefit.

This was the kind of recommendation the Central School supervisor offered to the new teachers. A final mark for a student which serves as a summary of his test scores, ratings, and observations does not itself dictate his promotion or retention. The decision about promotion is not statistical. It is a careful weighing of all factors by the teacher in cooperation with parents, the child, and school officials.

Motivating pupils

Teachers and parents use a variety of techniques to stimulate pupils to learn. One of the most popular has been school marks. The student is promised a high mark if he succeeds in school and is threatened with a low one if he does not.

Some students react quite differently from others to these promises and threats of marks. For instance, a child from a lower-class home, where school success is not considered important, may pay little or no attention to the prospect of a low grade. On the other hand, for a middle-class child, whose parents consider school success vital to "getting ahead in the world," the fear of a low mark and consequent parent disapproval may cause the pupil to exert great effort to do well.

The way a pupil's motivation is affected by marks can vary according to (1) the standard that his performance is compared with, (2) parents' and friends' attitudes toward marks, and (3) the teacher's emphasis on marks. A brief inspection of each of these variables can often help us to understand better the ways our own students are likely to react to our grading systems.

The standard of comparison

As noted earlier, a mark is a judgment of a student's progress compared with some standard. There are three principal kinds of standards. First, a student can be compared with his classmates. (Mr. MacDonald used one variety of this approach.) Second, he may be compared with some level of performance the teacher has in mind. (Miss Leong used a form of this approach.) As a third possibility, the pupil's present success can be compared with his own past performance, regardless of the level of work being done by his classmates.

The first two of these standards have been the most popular. The third is gaining adherents, especially in the elementary grades.

Sometimes a teacher uses more than one of these approaches. Pupils' motivation can be affected by the particular standard the teacher chooses to use. We cannot predict accurately how children in general will react to each of these kinds of standards, because other factors also influence the pupils' behavior. But we can suggest a few of the possible student reactions which a teacher can keep in mind as he tries to analyze the way his own grading practices stimulate or depress the desires of his own pupils to work hard.

Comparing the pupil with his classmates. We are not sure what kind of student thrives best under this system. But it is probable that the somewhat above-average pupil (though not necessarily the most capable one in class) is stimulated to work well when he is being rated against the others' performances. We might estimate also that this pupil is from a home and social-class level that puts stress on competing strongly and using education as a ladder for improving one's lot. Under this system it is often possible for the most capable student in class to stay at or near the top without exerting very much effort. If he can easily outstride the pack, he is not likely to be stimulated to work up to his potential. On the other hand, the least capable pupils inevitably show up poorly. Many of them, though they once may have tried hard to learn, stop striving after they recognize time and again that even with great efforts they still end up trailing far behind.

In addition to these possible reactions to being compared with their classmates, we will find numbers of others, such as the low-achieving pupil who continually works hard in the face of very low-level success. This may be because he and his parents aspire only to a barely passing mark. And if he barely passes, though he is poor in relation to the others, he still considers this worth trying for. Or there is the very bright, very diligent student who is never satisfied with being nearly the best or just barely the best, but aspires to being far above the rest of the crowd, so he continually is anxious about his grades and he works very hard. And we find many other varieties of student attitudes toward being judged against the performance of classmates.

Comparing the pupil with a teacher-set standard. How pupils react to this system also depends upon many factors, including how high the teacher sets his standards. Student motivation is affected differently in a class where it is known the teacher gives all high grades and in a class with a tradition of mostly low grades.

Comparing the pupil with his own apparent ability. This approach has become increasingly popular in elementary schools as educators recognize the wide differences in ability of the children within a single classroom. In its ideal state this system does not allow the bright student to become lazy. Instead, he is held by the teacher to a high standard of performance commensurate with his talent. The marks he receives reflect how well he measures up to his potential. Likewise, the slow student's progress is measured against his own talents, which are lesser. If he is working along well within the limitations of his abilities he can receive quite a satisfactory mark, though his performance is poor in comparison with his classmates'. This system, then, is aimed at adjusting the grade to what realistically can be expected of the pupil.

It is difficult to say for sure who is happiest under such an arrangement as this. But in most cases it probably is the poorer student, for the system gives him more opportunities to receive commendation for his efforts in the form of a satisfactory mark.

In theory at least this method of grading is the best, for it suits the mark to student ability. But in practice its potential advantages are usually reduced somewhat by influences arising from tradition and human nature. For instance, our school systems in the past have been geared to judging the student against his classmates or against the teacher's standard. With this tradition, it is often hard for the bright pupil who may be a bit lazy to accept a lower mark than that received by the slow but diligent classmate who obviously does not know as much as the bright one. The slow student, too, recognizes that he is not nearly so capable as his better endowed classmates, so that he may regard his own high mark with some suspicion.

When using this system the teacher also faces the problem of deciding what the fair basis for judging each student should be. He must make his estimate of the student's potential ability on the basis either of past schoolwork or of aptitude-test scores. When he uses past school performance as his base, he may expect too little of a potentially bright pupil who has always worked much below his own capabilities. Likewise, the teacher may err in expecting too much of an intellectually limited but extremely hard-working pupil who has managed to perform about as well as the average of his class only because he has strained to do his utmost at all times.

These, then, are some of the possible ways student motivation can be affected by the kinds of standards the teacher uses in marking.

Parents' and friends' attitudes

Children usually try to do those things which will get them praise and approval from the people who are important to them, especially their parents and their friends. If parents consider school marks important, they will encourage the child to work for high grades. They will praise and reward high grades—often with money or presents—and will scorn and punish low ones. Similar pressures may be exerted by agemates if they are the kind who admire school success. When this is the child's psychological atmosphere, as is often true in middle-class and parts of upper-class American society, a high mark becomes the equivalent of parental approval. We expect a child from such a family will usually strive for grades. But sometimes the opposite is true. Parental stress on grades can reduce motivation if a child highly resents parental domination. In this case the child, either purposely or subconsciously, does poorly in school so that his resulting poor marks will be a punishment to his parents.

In families which do not consider school success very important, as is often true in the bottom stratum of social classes, the pupil feels no pressure from home or from agemates to work for high grades. In fact, the student who applies himself and does well in school is often looked upon with suspicion by siblings and the street-corner gang which his agemates hang around with.

Therefore, the extent to which grades motivate the pupil is governed partially by the attitudes toward grades of the people he considers most important in his life.

The teacher's emphasis on marks

The teacher, too, by his daily actions can focus more or less attention on marks. Some instructors, probably found less frequently in elementary grades, use the promise or threat of a final mark as their prime motivating device. Their daily remarks to the class are liberally sprinkled with such comments as: "The grade you get on this composition counts toward the mark on your report card. Don't forget that."

Without doubt, keeping the prospect of a final mark in front of the class stimulates some children to greater effort. This is probably more true in the upper than in the lower grades, because the older children have had several years of such conditioning and are adjusted to equating a high mark with adult approval.

But placing great stress on the mark is accompanied by some noteworthy dangers. Chief among these is that the child focuses on getting a grade rather than acquiring learning that will really improve his life. The learning has thus become a mere concomitant of getting the desired mark. Such learning is often rote, not meaningful. It is often only temporary, for it was not sought as something worth while that would be used in the student's life. In addition, this striving only for a grade sometimes encourages the student to cheat or to become unduly competitive, so he does things like purposely passing misinformation to classmates before a test to make them do poorly on it.

Fortunately, at elementary and junior high levels the teacher has other methods of stimulating pupils to work and does not need to depend on the threat of a final mark. Here, briefly, are some of these motivating techniques:

1. *Demonstrating to the students that the learning they are pursuing will really improve their lives and fulfill their needs.* For instance, to stimulate work on the use of resource books, the teacher takes a current interest or problem of the pupils and shows them how to locate books that will answer their questions about the problem.

2. *Appealing to students' curiosity.* That is, the teacher may begin a new phase of study by asking intriguing questions about the new topic. Their interest thus excited, the pupils seek answers to the puzzling questions.

3. *Appealing to a desire for adult and peer approval.* In many situations verbal approval—not the final grade—can be given by the teacher as a desirable type of motivation. It can help define for the child the ways of fulfilling needs that are most acceptable and rewarded in his society. Unlike formal report-card marks, it is not limited to approving success in academic subjects but can be used to commend behavior in any area of living. When students strive for long-range goals, like learning to read well or compute well, it is often difficult for them to maintain motivation. But a word of approval from time to time along the way provides the psychological fuel needed to keep them striving toward the long-term goal. In addition, verbal approval is not for the very talented students alone, but it can be adjusted to the minor success achieved by the child of little talent as well.

Verbal approval or censure is not, however, a desirable motivating device when the adult bases his approval or lack of it on standards that are much too high for the child.

4. *Providing constant opportunities for the child to evaluate his own progress.* Children's progress should be evaluated constantly, not just at the end of a unit of work or the end of a marking period. On each of these appraisal occasions the student sees his present progress and can plan his next steps to improve. The continual, immediate evaluation serves constantly to stimulate students to work. It is doubtful that the threat or promise of a final grade adds much motivation to this. In schools that have done away with traditional forms of marking, there is no evidence that the problems of motivating students are any greater than in schools which continue to stress periodic grades.

From this discussion of the relation of marks and motivation, we conclude that:

1. A teacher should be alert to the ways standards for grading and the opinions of parents and friends affect pupils' motivation. An awareness of these factors may enable him to analyze how different children in his own classes react to marks and to adjust his practices when the reactions are undesirable ones.
2. A stress on a periodic final grade is not necessary or, in many cases, desirable for motivating learning when there are better techniques at hand for stimulating pupils to work hard.

Planning current schoolwork

The marks pupils receive at the six-week or nine-week grading period are of some aid in planning current schoolwork, for these marks reflect the areas in which a pupil is strong or weak. But even more important for helping the teacher design classwork for the students' particular abilities are the day-by-day evaluations on class quizzes, rating scales, anecdotal records, and unrecorded observations by the teacher. These daily appraisals are more useful guides than the six-week mark, for the daily judgments analyze student skills into their specific components. Thus you see in detail the precise areas of misunderstanding as well as the areas of strength in the pupils' learning. As a result, new learning experiences can be created to fit the particular needs and developmental level of the students.

Guiding plans for future education

Despite the many shortcomings of the "final grade," it often functions as a useful predictor of future success in school. In general, the person who has achieved high grades in a particular area of learning in the past can be expected to do relatively well in that area in the future. Likewise, a person who has done very poorly in an area of learning in the past, such as in arithmetic, may be expected to be poor in the subject when he meets it again.

These relationships are not invariably true, but they are consistent enough to make past school marks quite useful to counselors at the junior high level where plans for differentiated high-school education are being laid. Of course, numbers of other factors need to be considered in the educational counseling situation, such as test scores and student interests, but school marks should form part of the data used in guiding pupils' plans for future schoolwork.

It should be noted here that the kinds of marks which compare the student with his classmates are more useful in predicting future success than are marks comparing the pupil's progress with his own apparent abilities.

The literature of educational psychology abounds in studies which correlate school grades with later success in different subject-matter areas and with different vocations. The counselor who helps plan pupils' courses should become familiar with these studies in journals and in volumes on educational-vocational guidance.

Providing records for the school

Because this function of grades was inspected in Chapter 12, it does not warrant much further attention here.

However, one point is worth mentioning in relation to the kinds of standards teachers use in marking their pupils. Although many elementary schools use report cards containing only marks of the child's progress in relation to his own talents, these schools usually also wish to have records of marks which compare the child's progress with his classmates' performance. Such records help school officials in transferring pupils from one district or city to another, and they help counselors plan future courses for the students. In such schools teachers must keep two sets of marks: ones comparing the child with his own potential, and others comparing his work with his classmates'.

Providing reports for parents

This use of marks is not discussed here because Chapters 14 and 15 consider it in detail.

Summary

From the foregoing inspection of the purposes of marks, we conclude that:

1. A statistically derived mark should not determine promotion or retention of a child. Instead, the decision about promotion should be made only after careful consideration of many factors that can affect the child's future success.
2. For motivation purposes it is much better to count on continual evaluation of daily work to stimulate student efforts than to stress the goal of a final mark.
3. Plans for adapting current schoolwork to a child's needs and abilities are sounder if based on specific daily evaluations of progress rather than on a six-week or semester mark like a "C in literature" or "A in science."
4. Final marks are useful in predicting success in future schoolwork, especially at the junior high and high school levels.
5. It is desirable to have some form of mark as a school record. A pair of marks, one comparing the pupil with himself and the other comparing him with classmates, probably is most useful for office records.

WAYS TO IMPROVE MARKING PROCEDURES

So far in this chapter we have been talking about the summarizing mark, such as one given each six weeks, each semester, or at the end of the school year. It is our purpose in this final section to discuss some ways of arriving at the final mark. In doing this, we shall inspect (1) steps in determining what a mark means, and (2) ways of combining daily judgments of a student to arrive at a final grade.

Determining the meaning of a mark

As noted earlier, a variety of different symobls for marking are used by different school systems. Some schools use numbers, others letters. Some use per cents, others verbal descriptions. But it should be clear that, whatever the scheme, the symbols themselves have no inherent meaning. The meaning is assigned to a mark by the people who use it.

Unfortunately within many school systems the staff has reached no really specific agreement about the meanings of the marks they use, so the mark given by one teacher (such as a B) does not mean the same at all as the identical mark given by another. It is most desirable within a school for the staff to establish as much agreement as possible concerning the meanings of the marks. If the mark is a letter or number grade intended to compare the child's progress with that of his classmates, the agreement can take the form of a description of the quality of work and the kind of pupil that is represented by each mark. For example, here is the description for the meaning of the mark of C in a junior high school:

A pupil receives C when he:

Is generally cooperative and reliable.

Does quite acceptable work, but requires frequent guidance from the teacher, because he cannot work independently for any length of time.

Gets along with classmates and teacher with little friction most of the time.

Tries to do his assigned part in group work but does not take a leadership role or offer many fruitful ideas.

Has only minimum interest in the subject, so does not pursue it beyond bare required work.

Usually fulfills assignments.

It is obvious that the above description is a general one, intended to be applied to a range of grades and a variety of kinds of classes. Such descriptions are even more useful if they are stated in a way that applies them more specifically to the objectives of a particular grade (such as sixth) and specific subject matter (such as social studies or health education).

In upper grades in which a student is compared with classmates, the school staff may not create such descriptions as that above, but may define marks in terms of the quarter or half of the class the pupil falls into on the basis of the quality of his work. Here is one such description:

The mark of 1 means: The student succeeds as well as the top 25 per cent of his classmates.

The mark of 2 means: The student succeeds as well as the middle 50 per cent of his classmates. That is, his work is better than the lower quarter of the class, but not so effective as the top quarter of the class.

The mark of **3** means: The student's work is of the same quality as the lowest 25 per cent of his classmates.

Such descriptions in terms of quarters do not commit any particular per cent of the class to fail, as in the case of Mr. MacDonald's normal curve. Whether any of the pupils in the bottom quarter of the class are retained in the grade depends on decisions concerning what will be best for each child in his individual case.

If, however, the mark is based on a comparison of the child with his own apparent abilities, descriptions of the meanings of marks will take a different form. For example, for intermediate-grade classes the marks might be defined in such terms as these:

The H pupil: Always strives hard, always does his best at every task. We could not expect more progress for a person of his ability.

The S pupil: Usually work up to his ability, but on some tasks does not do as well as he is capable of doing. Work is satisfactory, but might be improved.

The L pupil: Usually seems content to perform at a level somewhat below his ability. Makes progress, but is likely to quit or reduce effort when he meets any difficulties.

The U pupil: Makes little progress. Level of performance is far below capabilities. Needs much more effort or help in order to progress at a level equal to his potential.

These, then, are a few of the ways marks can be made more specific and understandable for the school staff. Other examples are found in Chapter 14: Reporting Student Progress.

Summarizing daily evaluations

When the school has decided what standards to base grades on and how to define each mark, the teacher faces the task of summarizing daily evaluations of pupil progress to arrive at the final mark. How this summarizing is done depends partly upon the kinds of daily records the teacher keeps and upon the way he weights each assignment. The following examples serve to illustrate these points.

When daily marks are letters. Perhaps the commonest way in which teachers grade students' daily assignments and quizzes is by marking each assignment with a letter grade. At the end of the marking period the teacher averages the daily grades to find the final mark. But with this system the teacher faces the problems of (1) averaging the letter grades accurately and (2) weighting assignments fairly.

For instance, over an eight-week period a seventh-grade language-arts teacher collected 21 marks on daily work for each pupil. Here is the list of grades for just one student: F, C, C, D, B, C, C, C+, B−, A−, B, C−, C, B, B+, B, C+, B, B−, B−, B.

If you were the teacher, what final grade would you give? There are several approaches to this problem. One is to inspect the letters and estimate the average. Another way is to arrange them in graduated order and choose the middle mark, which is the median, or B−.

Still another method involves changing each letter to a number (A = 4, B = 3, C = 2, D = 1, F = 0). These numbers are added and the total divided by 21, which yields a mean of 2.4. This would convert back to a letter grade of C+, for it is closer to C than B. (We obviously have ignored + and − values of the original daily marks. To account for these, we would need to use a scheme that includes a certain amount for + and subtracts an amount for −.)

But even if we use such averaging schemes, we still have not accounted for the fact that one assignment may be more important than another and thus should receive more weight in the final summary. For instance, in the first assignment above the student received F because he failed to hand in a clipping from a magazine advertisement illustrating the use of emotionalized language. The A− mark was for a comprehensive test on English usage. If the teacher assigned weightings to these two according to their importance, she might consider the test three times as important as the magazine clipping. Hence, the A would be weighted three times (4 × 3) in compiling the final total score. Then the final total would not be divided by 21 but would be divided by the total weighting (such as a weight of 1 for the magazine clipping, a weight of 3 for the test, etc.). Hence, the resulting average would assign proper importance to each letter mark.

This procedure we have just described illustrates a method of finding a final mark in a class where each pupil's success is judged in comparison with his classmates' performance. But the same general procedure may be used in a class where the pupil's performance is compared with his own apparent ability.

When daily marks are numbers. One way to simplify the procedure described above is to give marks on daily work and tests in the form of numbers instead of letters. In this way the teacher can weight each assignment as it is corrected and recorded. At the end of the marking period he simply totals each pupil's daily marks. These totals are then made into a distribution or tally sheet, and the teacher by inspecting the sheet assigns letter grades in accordance with the school's marking policy. Thus, with this system the teacher of language arts may have decided that the test on language usage was worth 35 points. So the pupils' papers would be marked with 35 as the top possible number. But in the teacher's opinion the magazine clipping was worth only 8 points as the top possible score, so each pupil's work was marked in relation to 8 points as the best mark. And so it would be with every other assignment. Each time the students' papers were handed back to them, they would find the mark in terms of a fraction at the top of the paper rather than a letter mark. The numerator would be the number of points the student earned, and the denominator would show the top number possible on that assignment. Letter grades would be assigned only at the end of the marking period on the basis of the distribution of students' total scores.

In some schools daily marks are all in terms of 100 as the top possible score. If each assignment is equal in importance, these daily marks can be totaled, then averaged to find the final mark. But if they are not all equally important, they need to be weighted before they are totaled. That is, more important assignments should be weighted twice or three times as much as less important ones.

When daily marks are in a variety of forms. Often a teacher has daily evaluations in a variety of forms: test scores, rating scales, anecdotal records, student compositions, student work products. It is then a problem of combining these in a meaningful way to arrive at a final grade.

There are several ways of trying to solve this problem. One is to attempt to assign a fair letter or number grade to each kind of evaluation, even though some of the evaluations in the form of ratings and anecdotes may not always seem readily marked in this manner. Another way is not to depend just on one single mark at the end for summarizing the student's success but to include marks on different phases of classwork and perhaps a brief written explanation of the student's progress. Further solutions to these problems of trying to lump a number of different kinds of evaluations of different objectives into a single mark are suggested in the following chapter on reporting pupil progress.

OBJECTIVES OF THIS CHAPTER

The effective elementary-school teacher:

1. Explains ways that personal judgments of the teacher and school staff affect marking procedures.
2. Explains relationships that exist between marking procedures and:
   a. Policies of promotion and retention of pupils.
   b. Student motivation.
   c. The guidance of pupils' current schoolwork.
   d. The guidance of pupils' educational plans.
   e. School record keeping.
3. Combines daily marks in such a manner that the final mark reflects as accurately as possible the pupil's over-all success during the grading period.

Suggested evaluation techniques for this chapter

1. Interview three elementary or junior high teachers to discover: (*a*) whether they compare a student with classmates, with a preconceived standard, with the student's own apparent ability, or with a combination of these; (*b*) how they keep their records of marks, and (*c*) how they summarize daily marks to determine a final mark or final judgment. Compare the results of your interviews with those of your own classmates.
2. At a local school, inquire about the method the school uses for orienting new teachers to the marking policy. What oral instructions are given new teachers, and by whom? What written policy concerning marking and standards is provided? Write your own appraisal of the probable effectiveness of this orientation procedure.
3. Interview a school principal or supervisor to discover what the policy is concerning the promotion, acceleration, or retention of students. Does the slow student fail automatically upon receiving a low mark, or does the low mark merely alert the school authorities, teachers, and parents to inspect what should be done with the child so that he will gain most from school?

SUGGESTED READINGS

1. BURTON, WILLIAM H. *The Guidance of Learning Activities.* New York: Appleton-Century-Crofts, 1952. Chapter 21.

2. CRONBACH, LEE J. *Educational Psychology.* New York: Harcourt, Brace and Co., 1954. Pp. 477-83 treat competition and marking.
3. THORNDIKE, ROBERT L., and HAGEN, ELIZABETH. *Measurement and Evaluation in Psychology and Education.* New York: Wiley and Sons, 1955. Chapter 17: Marking and Reporting.
4. WANDT, EDWIN, and BROWN, GERALD W. *Essentials of Educational Evaluation.* New York: Henry Holt and Co., 1957. Chapter 6.
5. WRINKLE, WILLIAM L. *Improving Marking and Reporting Practices.* New York: Rinehart and Co., 1947.

CHAPTER

14

Reporting Student Progress

In many schools there is widespread dissatisfaction with the currently used grading and reporting methods. This dissatisfaction is experienced by both students and faculty. The students often feel that they have been misjudged. The teachers say, "I like teaching, but I hate to make out those report cards. The main trouble is that I'm never quite sure if I have been fair or accurate in marking. There are so many things to take into consideration."

An undercurrent of dissatisfaction about grading and reporting was felt in the Central School System. Mr. Harris, the curriculum director, was seeking a good method for bringing to sharp focus the need for an improved reporting system in the school. He wished the faculty to become sufficiently aroused to work actively together in developing a better system. It was in Dr. William Wrinkle's excellent little book, *Improving Marking and Reporting Practices,* that he discovered the method which would draw the teacher's attention to the problem. In his book Dr. Wrinkle describes an experiment by E. C. Bolmeier in which Mr. Bolmeier demonstrated some of the fallacies of conventional marking systems. The experimenter had a group of P.T.A. officers mark a number of children according to fairly detailed descriptions of the children's behavior in school. Mr. Bolmeier found that the P.T.A. officers, like teachers, differed rather markedly among themselves on exactly what letter-grade a student deserved.

Adopting the same general technique used in the experiment, the curriculum director mimeographed the descriptions of four fifth-grade pupils. In faculty meeting he handed these descriptions to the teachers and asked them to fill out a report card for each of the four students.

The Central-Elementary report card and the descriptions of the students are given here so that the reader may also mark the fifth graders and compare his judgments with those of the faculty.

Report Card____Central Elementary School
End-of-Semester Report

Name __________________________________ Date __________

Grade __________

Subject	*Mark*	*Explanation of Marks:*
Arithmetic	____	
Art	____	
English	____	A—Superior
Music	____	B—Above Average
Physical Education	____	C—Average
Science	____	D—Below Average
Social Science	____	F—Failure

Remarks ____

____

Teacher ________________________

Fig. 39. Report card—Central Elementary School

The fifth-grade students

1. Ralph has an IQ of about 135, according to group intelligence tests given in the third and fifth grades. He gets along well with the other students, probably because he is friendly, jolly, and a good athlete. His work in school has been somewhat erratic. Usually he will not work unless prodded continually or unless he is faced with some type of penalty that especially concerns him, such as having to miss baseball or football at noon or after school.

Sometimes he tends to be sassy with the teacher. He will talk back or make a sarcastic remark when the teacher gives directions or suggestions. However, at other times he is polite and cooperative.

He reads a good deal, mostly books about history, adventure, and science. His handwriting is quite poor, almost illegible, and he does not seem to try to improve. His written ideas are usually clear and in good sequence. He always scores at or near the top of the class in social studies, literature, spelling, and science tests. He does not do homework assignments unless they particularly interest him, such as making illustrated maps or reading history books. His work in arithmetic is very good on the tests but very poor and messy on the homework. He has been found copying arithmetic and social studies homework and class exercises from another student just before class or else trying to complete his homework in class when he has other duties to carry out. Although he has been warned, he continues to copy. When the teacher speaks to him about doing his own work, he always denies having copied, although there is clear evidence that he has done so. Recently he has been reading whenever possible during arithmetic period and then copying the answers to the problems he was to complete.

Ralph turns out large amounts of artwork of high quality. The art period is about the only time he really pays consistent attention to his own work and does not bother others.

Although he can lead well in group work and see that the committee gets the job done when he wants to, he may turn a meeting into a wise-crack-and-laugh session. He leads well on the play field, although he occasionally teases younger or less capable boys.

When singing, Ralph continually slips off key. He is, however, interested in rhythms and keeps them well. He is one of the best square-dancers in class.

Ralph speaks clearly, but his class reports have not gone over very well because he does not think them out ahead of time. Consequently, his thoughts often ramble.

2. Caroline is a pretty little girl who is very quiet in class. She never volunteers an answer or question. Even when she is called on she often answers only in monosyllables or says that she does not know, although in written work she usually has adequate answers. She spends much of her time reading, both during class time and during free time when she might be playing outside or talking

with the other girls. She does not seem to have any real friends. The others do not seem to dislike her actively. Rather, they appear to neglect her as a nonentity.

In arithmetic she completes her work hurriedly and then reads a storybook, even though her arithmetic answers are frequently wrong. On the arithmetic tests she is third or fourth from the bottom of the class.

In science Caroline is better on the book work than on field trips or demonstrations, which she avoids when possible. In social studies she writes good analyses of the topics studied. She works better alone than in a group. Since the class involves considerable group work and frequent panel discussions or reports in social studies, she does not show up as well as if the work were all reading. When she talks before the class she looks at her hands and mumbles her speech. After the first six weeks in the grade she talked freely and clearly with the teacher at noon or after school, but she speaks poorly during class sessions.

Caroline says she does not like to paint or draw, but she likes to work with clay and to do weaving. During a recent unit on Indians she wove five small blankets on a cardboard loom that the class had learned to construct.

She does not enter into the singing or dancing when she can avoid it, although she can sing well and read music better than most of her classmates. She plays the piano, although she would not do so before the class.

It is not uncommon for Caroline to complain of a headache about the time the class is ready for gym period. In the gym or outside she plays the games as adequately as most of her classmates, but she tries to avoid playing at all.

3. Kenneth is the boy the teacher calls "the most serious-minded pupil in the class." He never fails to have his home assignments or class assignments completed, although it usually takes him longer than the others to finish. In school he works diligently at each task, and only rarely does the teacher need to speak to him about attending to work. All school time is spent on schoolwork. He does not engage in horseplay with the other boys. On the playground he works seriously to do an adequate job in the game.

Despite his diligence, Kenneth usually experiences less success than any of his classmates in learning and remembering about the social studies or science topics. He reads typical second-grade material fairly well but is usually overwhelmed by the reading that most of his classmates can do. He pronounces words properly when he reads aloud, but rarely can he answer questions accurately about the meaning of the passages he reads. In arithmetic tests Kenneth is almost always at or near the bottom of the class.

The grammar and sentence structure he uses in speaking are adequate. However, in writing he has difficulty organizing his thoughts into a sequence.

Kenneth applies himself as seriously to art and music as he does to his other studies. When working with clay or drawing he continually asks the teacher, "How do you want me to do it? No, I don't want to think up my way to do it. I want to do it right. I want to do it the way you show me. Show me how you want me to do it." Unless the teacher demonstrates, Kenneth will not try to draw or model, or else he will copy the work of another student whom the teacher has complimented. In music he takes longer than most of his classmates to learn songs. He forgets the melody and creates his own.

Although his work in general is in many areas inferior to that of his classmates, Kenneth has shown improvement in all areas compared to his level of achievement when he entered the grade. He wishes very much to succeed, as is evidenced by his frequent questioning of the teacher: "I won't fail, will I? I just can't fail. I'm trying hard, you know."

Kenneth's parents have said they wish him to be a dentist like his father. One day in February when the class was discussing Abraham Lincoln and his struggle as a youth, the teacher asked Kenneth what he liked best about Lincoln. Kenneth said, "I liked him because he tried hard. My father always says you try hard and you can do anything. He says if you don't do good it's 'cause you don't try."

4. Betty's work has shown the most notable change during the semester. After some initial difficulty with understanding addition and subtraction of fractions, she has demonstrated an adequate mastery of fifth-grade arithmetic.

During the first half of the semester Betty did very poorly in science when the class studied electricity and weather. But throughout the health units the last part of the semester, she contributed more than most of the pupils in class discussion and did very well on tests.

In social studies she developed much the same as in science. During the first two units on the "Development of Our Community" and "Industry in Our Community" she did not complete her portions of class projects and she scored low on tests. However, after the teacher and Betty's parents gave her extra help and apparent incentive at mid-semester, she scored increasingly higher on written work and carried out her part in group work well.

In the literature program Betty also did little during the first weeks but read numerous books during the last weeks of the term.

Despite a slight lisp, she speaks as clearly as most students. Her talks in front of the class are ordinarily well organized, although she occasionally gets off the topic. It is not uncommon for Betty to giggle during her own speech or when others are talking before the group.

She writes her thoughts in an orderly manner and makes few grammar errors. Her spelling, however, is rather poor for a fifth grader.

Betty plays games as well as many girls her age. She has never been selected as team captain or leader when the students have done the choosing. However, she is usually selected as a team member fairly early in the choosing process.

The type of artwork Betty prefers is drawing costumes. Her drawings look much like those of the other fifth graders.

Although she learns the songs along with the others, she does not sing with much enthusiasm. She frequently looks out the window while singing along with the group. When the group listens to records, she must be cautioned occasionally not to giggle and disturb the class.

After the Central School faculty had marked the fifth graders, they reported by a show of hands what marks they had given. Mr. Harris recorded these results on the blackboard in the manner shown on the next page. The numbers show how many teachers gave a particular letter-grade in each subject listed on the report card.

As Mr. Harris had imagined, the chart precipitated a lively discussion among the teachers. There was general amazement at the variance among marks given by different teachers on the basis of the same evidence. These were typical remarks:

RALPH	A+	A	A–	B+	B	B–	C+	C	C–	D+	D	D–	F
Arithmetic		5	1	1	8	1	3	19			1		
Art	1	32			4								
English		4		1	14	2	3	11			2		
Music		4		5	11		3	13	1		1		
Physical Ed.	3	14			16	1	1	1					
Science		8	1	2	21	3		2					
Social Science		9		4	19			5					

CAROLINE	A+	A	A–	B+	B	B–	C+	C	C–	D+	D	D–	F
Arithmetic								1	2	1	28	1	4
Art		2			17	1	2	14			1		1
English					5	2	2	20	3		2		
Music		2		1	13	1	1	17	1		1		
Physical Ed.					2	1		24	3		7		
Science					6	1	1	27	2				
Social Science					14	1	4	16	1		1		

KENNETH	A+	A	A–	B+	B	B–	C+	C	C–	D+	D	D–	F
Arithmetic					1		2	12	4	2	16		
Art					1		2	31	1		2		
English				1	4	1	3	20	3	1	4		
Music					5		1	24	1		6		
Physical Ed.	1				10	1	2	22					
Science					2	2	2	23	5	1	2		
Social Science					3	1	3	22	5	1	2		

BETTY	A+	A	A–	B+	B	B–	C+	C	C–	D+	D	D–	F
Arithmetic		4	1	2	20		6	4					
Art		1		2	8		3	23					
English		1			8		5	23					
Music				1		2		22	4		8		
Physical Ed.		4		2	14	1	3	12	1				
Science		4	1	4	19		1	8					
Social Science		2		5	17		1	12					

"There's no way on the report card to show differences of attainment within a subject. English should be broken down into reading, spelling, handwriting, and so forth. The same is true of social studies. Is group work to be considered social studies here?"

"I don't see how you could give Ralph an A. He cheated. He copied."

"I think you should consider most what a student is doing by the end of the term. It's not fair to average Betty's work for the semester when she was doing so well at the end."

"It seems to me we should decide on some philosophy of marking students. That would reduce this inconsistency in our marking."

"There certainly must be better ways of reporting students' work than this. No wonder the students and parents get confused when we don't even agree on how these cards should be marked ourselves."

All of the teachers wished to express their views, but the curriculum director suggested that a committee of teachers aid him and the principal in studying and proposing a way of revising the reporting system. Being especially disturbed about their experience in marking the fifth graders, the faculty heartily agreed, and a committee was selected. In their study they learned the following about reporting systems.

PURPOSES OF MARKING AND REPORTING

Marks and reports have two mains purposes:

1. To tell the student and his parents how well he is progressing toward the school's goals.
2. To provide the school with information about the student's progress for purposes of promotion, grade placement, and transfer to other schools.

TRADITIONAL REPORTS

The traditional report cards usually do not fulfill these purposes well. By *traditional report card* we mean the Central-Elementary form which, with slight variations, is typical of those used in many elementary and junior high grades, although it is being altered or replaced in more schools each year.

This type of card has two notable characteristics:

1. It is composed of a short list of from four to eight *broad subject fields,* and there may be one space for remarks by the teacher or for a grade in *citizenship, deportment,* or *discipline.*

2. The quality of a student's work in each subject field is marked by a symbol, usually a letter or a number.

In discussing the traditional card we will begin with this second characteristic. The A-B-C-D-F system used on the Central-Elementary card probably is the most common. In some schools an H is added to represent "honors," a mark higher than A. In other instances different letters are used or a number system of 1-2-3-4-5 is used in place of letters. Some schools still mark by per cents. Like the letter grades, these per cents are usually translated into general qualitative terms to help parents and students interpret their meanings. For example, in some districts 95-100 means *superior,* 90-94 means *very good,* 85-89 means *above average,* 80-84 means *average,* 75-79 means *lowest passing mark,* and below 75 means *failure.* The fact that the interpretation of such per cent marks is not standardized occasionally causes confusion. In some schools the lowest passing mark is 75, in others it is 70, while in still other districts it is 65 or 60. Such confusion is possibly experienced most in districts where per cents are used from kindergarten through high school, but the high school maintains 60 as the lowest passing mark and the elementary school maintains 70 as the minimum.

As mentioned above, the traditional report card is composed of a short list of broad subject fields. In schools where the students remain in one room all day, the teacher marks the student in each subject. In a departmentalized system each teacher gives the student one grade to represent the student's success in the particular subject.

The fact that a pupil receives a *single mark in a broad subject field* is one of the most obvious disadvantages of this traditional card. For example, we would assume that included under the subject of English on the Central-Elementary card would be such diverse behaviors as textbook reading, literature, speech, handwriting, spelling, and written composition. In marking a fifth grader, the teacher must try to average together the student's success in these different behaviors and come up with a single mark. It is somewhat like trying to average shoes, ships, and sealing wax. This mark for English is seen by the student and his parents. But what does a single mark in English mean to the parents? Take the case of Ralph, one of the fifth graders described earlier. His teacher has given him a mark of B− in English. What does this tell Ralph or his parents or the school administrators or his next-year's teacher about his success? Translated from the card it means *Above Average* (but with reservations, as indicated by the minus sign) in *English* (and what behaviors go to make up *English* is not always clear to parents). The B—, then, was the teacher's attempt to average several quite varied skills. It does not differentiate these important elements that went into the average—elements that, when listed singly, mean much more than the single letter-grade.

Ralph reads well and frequently. He writes fairly well, as far as composition is concerned. His speech is quite clear, but he does not organize his thoughts before giving a talk to the class. His handwriting is the worst in the class. He scores very high on literature tests. He spells well. He copies other people's homework.

It is little wonder that the Central School System staff showed such differences of opinion when they graded the four fifth graders. The teachers had different ideas about how much weight the various elements should carry in determining the final mark.

If a single mark in each broad subject field often does not provide accurate information about a pupil's progress, what type of reporting would be better? Chapter 2 of this book outlined a method of stating the numerous specific objectives toward which pupils in a given grade work. Thus, when the school wishes to provide the pupil and his parents with a *complete* report of his progress, it seems logical that the report consist of a *list of all the specific objectives with the teacher's judgment of the pupil's progress toward each.* Such an approach would indeed be thorough. But it would also be impractical. Teachers have neither the time nor the patience to write for parents reports of children's progress toward every specific goal. In addition, it is doubtful that many parents would make a careful study of such a report card, which would be several pages long. Consequently, modern elementary schools are developing reporting systems that are compromises between the two methods discussed above: (1) the single mark in broad fields and (2) the extended list of all the specific objectives of a grade-level.

CURRENT VARIETIES OF REPORTS

In attempting to improve marking and reporting, schools throughout the country have developed a variety of methods and forms. It would be extremely difficult if not impossible to decide which of these methods and forms is the best. Each has advantages and disadvantages. Some are better suited to a particular kind of community than are others. All of them appear to be improvements over the traditional type discussed earlier. A survey of some of these departures from the more traditional types will demonstrate the values and limitations of these practices. Such a survey may provide suggestions for teachers and school systems which are developing reporting methods that accurately tell pupils, their parents, and the school administration of the pupils' progress.

Parent-teacher conferences

Various practices are being followed in utilizing parent-teacher conferences for reporting pupil growth.

In most schools the conference is not the chief reporting technique, but it is used with those parents who are particularly interested or are concerned with the report-card results. Or it is used when the teacher believes an interview would be specially profitable. As a result, the conference usually is held only when a child's progress is disappointing to either the school or the parent. In a statement printed on the report card, many schools invite mothers and fathers to visit classes and talk with the teacher. Some school districts, such as San Francisco, provide a space at the bottom of the card which says: "A check (in this space) means that a conference with the home will be helpful and is requested."

Other school systems go to considerable effort to bring about more home-school cooperation, especially for the child who is not doing as well as expected. L. C. Bain, Chief of the Bureau of Child Accounting in Cleveland, explains the purpose and procedure in a typical program of this type:

"In the Cleveland schools much emphasis is placed on conferences with parents. In the Primary Division especially the principals make an effort to arrange conferences with the parents of pupils who are not getting along well. This plan brings to the attention of the parents early in the school life of a child difficulties that may hinder the progress of the child. These may be physical, mental, social, or emotional. The schools may be represented at the conferences not only by the principal but also by the teachers, psychologist, speech therapist, school doctor, dentist, or nurse.

"The individual records (cumulative records and pertinent evaluation data) of the children help to make conferences with the parents objective."

A smaller number of schools have adopted a program of interviews which eliminates any report cards. The way in which one school system evolved such a program is outlined by Ernest F. Weinrich, Assistant Superintendent of Schenectady (N. Y.) Schools:

"We no longer use a written report card form in the elementary grades in Schenectady. The whole procedure of reporting to parents is done through parent-teacher conferences. There is a scheduled conference between parent and teacher in the fall and another one in the spring, although additional conferences can be arranged at the request of either teacher or parent. Tuesday has been chosen as our planned parent-teacher conference day, and on that afternoon school dismisses about a half hour earlier, which enables the teacher to do a portion of her conferencing on school time. The process of moving over to parent-teacher interviews began about 1945, and in the early stages we did have a parent-teacher conference and in addition an informal written card. About four years ago, however, principals recommended the present plan of two scheduled parent-teacher conferences and the abandonment of the informal card, which in many cases got to be quite routine and meaningless.

"With the influx of many new elementary teachers the problem of helping teachers to improve their conferencing technique is an ongoing one. It is our feeling in Schenectady that although we know that parent-teacher conferences can be improved, we are also confident that it is the best method of reporting the whole progress of the child to the parent."

In some schools, such as the Berkeley (Calif.) system, interviews of the type described above are used at the kindergarten level, and report cards are used in the grades.

The advantages of the interview as a reporting technique are indicated in the foregoing statements. In a conference the teacher can be specific about the actions of the child in school, the particular strengths and weaknesses of his work. In addition, the parent can ask questions, can understand better the school program, and can, with the teacher, plan for the child's future growth in a more realistic manner. (Actual techniques for carrying on such interviews are described in Chapter 15, Talking with Parents and Students.)

There are a number of disadvantages to the conference plan that account for its limited use in schools as the single method for reporting progress. The conference demands considerable time. Parents are frequently unwilling or unable to arrange appointments. Unless the teacher takes notes about the conference there may be no record of the child's progress for the school office. And the interview plan does not work in departmentalized systems where a child has several teachers (a typical situation in many seventh and eighth grades). (7)

Letters home

If the teacher cannot report personally to parents, he can write specific judgments of a child's development for the parent to read. Like an interview, a letter is well suited for discussing the particular facts of a child's progress. The factors that make the pupil different from all the others can be noted, for the teacher is not controlled by a limited list of school subjects upon which the child is to be given a number or letter grade.

Letters or notes sent home, like conferences, take many forms, ranging from a blank sheet which the teacher is to fill to a small space on the report card marked "Teacher Comments."

An example of the type of letter that functions as the complete report is the one used in New Rochelle (N. Y.) It consists of three sheets. The first is titled *Social Growth,* the second *Growth in Skills and Understandings,* and the third *Parent's Comment.* There are no subheadings on any of the sheets. The lack of definite subtopics allows the teacher to fit the comments to the particular child's work.

Another style of letter is used for the kindergarten and primary grades of Seattle. A report card is used which provides descriptions of the specific types of behavior the student is working toward, such as "shows interest in reading" and "exhibits independence." These descriptions are organized into three areas: social adjustment, physical development and growth, and mental development. Following the descriptions, the teacher has a page on which to write a letter treating the individual's progress toward the goals. A space is also provided, as on many such report cards, for parents' comments. The two pages of behavioral descriptions not only define for the parent what the child is learning, but also aid the teacher in keeping these specific goals in mind when writing the report.

In the Tucson (Ariz.) system two pages of questions about child growth are used as guides for teachers to write meaningful letters that are used as the progress reports in the primary grades.

The Dallas Public Schools' report form used in the primary department is a folder consisting of five identical sections, one to be used at each of the five marking periods. The form provides some organization for the teacher's report yet allows for remarks applying to the individual child. (See Fig. 40.)

DEAR PATRON:
Your child is making__________ progress in__________

______ needs to improve in__________

______ conduct generally is__________

Additional remarks:__________

Grade______ School______ Teacher______
Parent's comment:__________

Parent's Signature__________ Date______

For the Fifth Period Ending______

Fig. 40. Partially organized letter—Dallas Public Schools

A capable teacher who writes lucidly can create an interesting and very useful letter for parents. However, some teachers either do not express themselves well in writing or do not keep adequate evaluation data to form a specific report of the pupil's progress. Consequently, letters home can become stereotyped and meaningless, such as the following:

"George has entered into the third-grade activities throughout the year. He has been a pleasant student to have in class. His progress in the various subjects has generally been adequate. He appears to have been purposeful most of the time in his activities. In general, he is developing relatively at an expected rate in social growth."

To increase the meaningfulness of letters home, some school systems which prefer this type of report have organized in-service workshops during which letter-writing is discussed and analyzed. Others (7) have developed extensive lists of commonly used (but meaningful) statements around which to build letters that describe accurately how well individual children are meeting the behavioral goals of the school. Examples of such statements are:

"(child's name) listens well when others are speaking."

"(child's name) usually listens well but sometimes interrupts when others are speaking."

"(child's name) finds it difficult to remain quiet when others are speaking."

"(child's name) is reading books on numerous new topics."

"(child's name) is making slow but steady progress in learning number facts."

From such lists of statements, which are usually organized according to grade level, the teacher selects ones appropriate to each child and builds a letter to the parents around these statements.

As mentioned earlier, many schools do not rely solely upon letters to parents for the complete report. Instead, they use a printed report-card form which includes, in addition to marks on various skills and traits, space for teacher comments. In some cases this space is of considerable size, and a short letter home is generally expected. When writing such letters or comments it is especially helpful for the teacher to have sufficient data about each child's specific behavior to create an individualized report. It is here, at reporting time, that the effective elementary-school instructor is especially glad that he made anecdotal records and checked rating scales throughout the semester. Statements from rating scales (See Chapter 11) can function in exactly the same ways as the lists of commonly used statements mentioned above in providing material for letters and comments.

Guidance in helping teachers determine the topics about which they can make specific comments is sometimes given during faculty meetings or in the form of printed suggestions. An example of the latter type is the section on "Specific Comments in Curricular Fields" which is included in the six-page booklet of *Directions for Use of Progress Record* given to elementary teachers in Philadelphia:

"The following sub-headings should prove valuable to teachers as a source of expressions to be used in the informal comments.

"SPEAKING AND LISTENING: Speaks distinctly and uses pleasant voice; speaks correctly; expresses thoughts clearly; listens attentively; uses good vocabulary.

"READING: Understands what is read; reads at satisfactory speed; masters new words independently; interests the group when reading orally; can locate information independently.

"WRITING: Writes sentences correctly; organizes work; expresses ideas well.

"SOCIAL STUDIES (History, Geography, Civics, Science): Uses globes, maps, books, collections, and other source materials effectively; contributes appropriate materials; contributes to group discussions; completes assignments well; gives careful attention to facts.

"ARITHMETIC: Has clear number concepts and sees number relationships; knows the basic number combinations; can do the fundamental operations; deals with problem situations efficiently."

Aside from the regularly scheduled reports to parents, numerous school districts make a practice of writing occasional notes containing information believed to be of interest to mothers and fathers. The printed form used in the Minneapolis and Cincinnati systems is typical. The title is *Exchange of Information between Home and School.* Above the space for the note is this printed introduction:

"To Parents: We hope the information below will be of value to you. We in turn shall be pleased if you will give us any information which can be used in helping your child get the most out of school."

The note is signed by teacher and principal. Another space on the note is provided with this introduction:

"To Parents: Please use space below for any information or suggestions which you believe would be helpful. If you think it would be helpful for us to talk together, we shall be glad to arrange a time that will be convenient to both of us."

Report cards—in terms of behavior and more detailed

Earlier in this chapter we saw the faculty of Central Elementary School wrestling with the problems of an inadequate reporting system. Their more traditional report card consisted of a list of school subjects, and it was assumed that parents were accurately informed of their child's success when a number- or a letter-grade was placed beside each subject. However, when even the Central Elementary teachers could not agree upon how to grade four typical fifth graders, it became obvious that such a report did not adequately reflect a child's development. A more detailed, specific type of report appeared desirable.

As suggested in Chapter 2, we often understand more clearly what we are trying to do as teachers if we define our objectives in terms of how the student should act as a result of his learning. Consequently, we not only can plan our classes better and judge children's growth more accurately, but we can make our reports to parents much more understandable. The effective teacher-parent conference and the well-written letter do this task. The suggestions listed above, which are provided for Philadelphia's elementary-school teachers, are more detailed behaviors toward which the schools are working than are provided on the report cards. Thus, in that school system it is recommended that teachers' written comments also help parents understand their children's growth.

Increasingly, schools throughout the country are revising their report cards so that they are more detailed and are stated in terms of the skills children show. These newer cards or progress reports are becoming the chief means of informing parents of their children's growth toward the school's goals.

Report cards that vary with grade level

In the past there has been a tendency for the same report-card form to be used throughout the entire school, or at least from the kindergarten through the eighth grade. It contained a list of general subject-matter areas common to all levels. However, when we move to reporting more specific behaviors, we realize that goals in the lower grades are not the same as those in the upper grades. This has resulted in the development of separate report cards to fit the particular programs at the different levels. As a result, parents are receiving information that makes considerably more sense. They know more precisely the skills and activities developed in the school and their children's progress toward each of these.

An example of this newer approach is the series created in the Niagara Falls Public Schools. (See Fig. 41, 42, 43, 44, 45.) In this case separate report cards are used to cover the elementary grades: (1) kindergarten, (2) first grade, (3) second and third grades, (4) fourth, fifth, and sixth grades, and (5) seventh and eighth grades. Other schools that have developed cards appropriate to varied levels divide the grades differently. For example, the Columbus (Ohio) cards are for (1) kindergarten and first, (2) second and third, (3) fourth and fifth, and (4) sixth. In St. Louis three separate cards are provided for these levels: (1) kindergarten and transition unit, (2) first through third, and (3) fourth through eighth.

While inspecting the report cards gathered from many school systems, one cannot fail to be impressed by how much more in-

Kindergarten Report Card

Niagara Falls Public Schools

Tomorrow

I saw tomorrow marching by on little children's feet,
Within their forms and faces read her prophecy complete.
I saw tomorrow look at me from little children's eyes,
And thought how carefully we'd teach if we were wise.

Pupil's name ______________________

School ______________________

School year ______________________

Teacher ______________________

Principal ______________________

Department of Education
Niagara Falls New York

William J. Small
Superintendent of Schools

Fig. 41. Niagara Falls Kindergarten Report Form
(continued on next three pages)

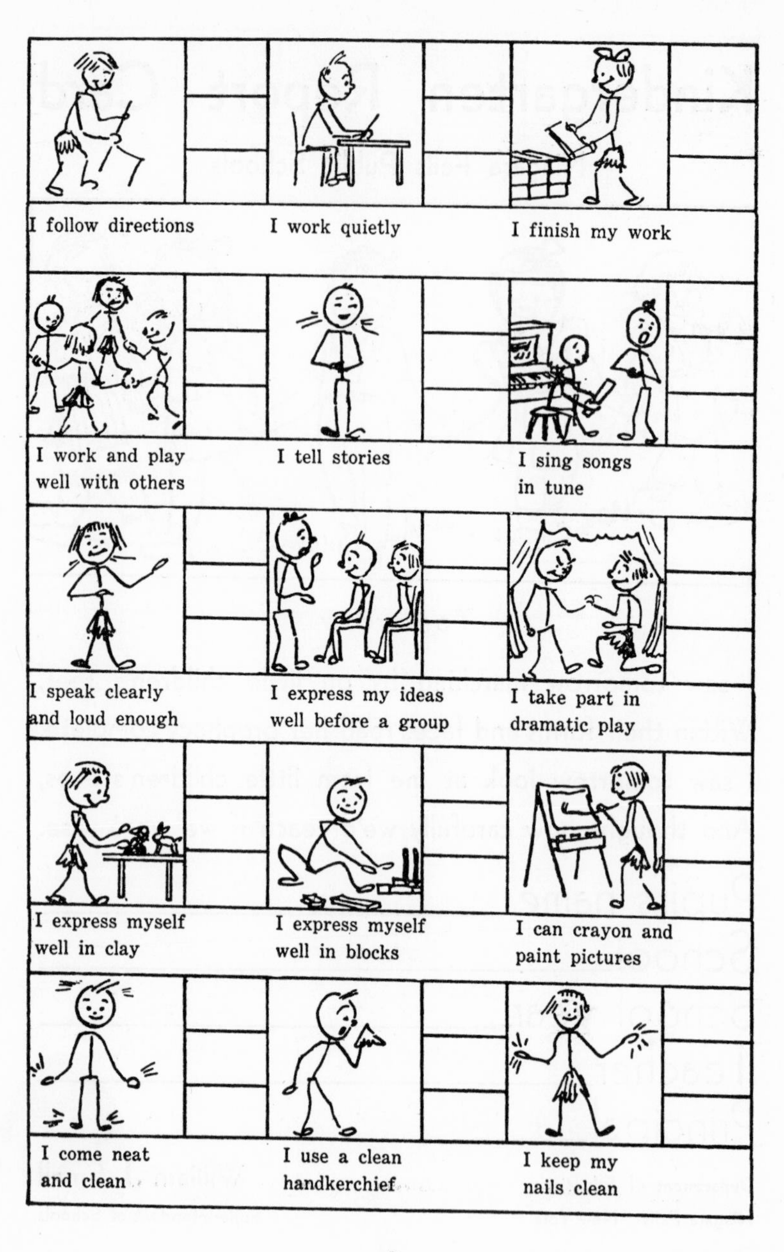
I follow directions
I work quietly
I finish my work
I work and play well with others
I tell stories
I sing songs in tune
I speak clearly and loud enough
I express my ideas well before a group
I take part in dramatic play
I express myself well in clay
I express myself well in blocks
I can crayon and paint pictures
I come neat and clean
I use a clean handkerchief
I keep my nails clean

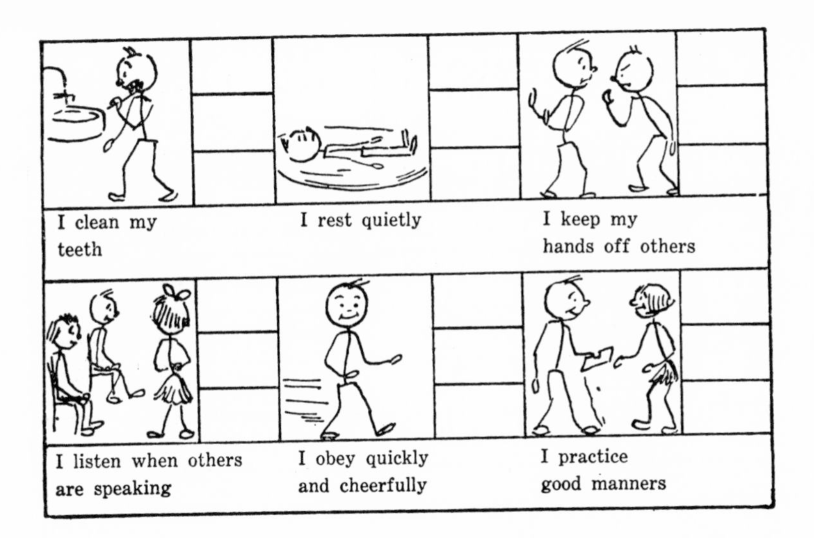
I clean my teeth
I rest quietly
I keep my hands off others
I listen when others are speaking
I obey quickly and cheerfully
I practice good manners

Attendance	10	20	30	40
Half Days Absent				
Times Tardy				

Explanation of Marks

U - Usually

P - Part of the time

S - Seldom - Occasionally

N - Not Yet

Marked after 20, 30 and 40 Week Period

Other Goals To Be Attained

	Can skip		Ties shoe strings
	Can hop		Puts on rubbers
	Can march		Puts on wraps
	Repeats rhymes		Knows full name
	Knows standard colors		Knows address
	Knows right and left		Knows age

Parent's Signature

20 wk. ____________________

30 wk. ____________________

Recommended Placement

____________________ is assigned to ________ grade, room no. ______ beginning in September 19 ____

Teacher ____________________

Principal ____________________

Superintendent of Schools William J. Small

M-7

Department of Education

Niagara Falls, New York

PROGRESS REPORT

PRIMARY - FIRST GRADE

Last Name ____ First Name ____ Grade ____

School ____ School Year ____

Teacher ____ Principal ____

A MESSAGE TO PARENTS

We believe that schools should prepare children to live in a democracy.

We recognize that children are unlike in many ways and develop at different rates.

The Elementary Schools of Niagara Falls are helping your child to grow in taking responsibilities.

Mentally——To learn and use the 3 R's.

Physically——To be a healthy child.

Emotionally—To be a happy child.

Morally——To decide what is right and live accordingly.

Socially——To acquire habits and skills to interest and serve other people.

To understand and appreciate other people.

We hope that this report card will tell you how your child is getting along on the basis of his own abilities, and also where he is in relation to his classmates. Occasionally comments will be enclosed on a separate sheet. Please feel free to visit your school at any time. We are always glad to plan a personal conference with you.

William J. Small, Superintendent of Schools

Fig. 42. Niagara Falls First-Grade Report Form
(continued on next three pages)

THIS CARD SHOWS THE PROGRESS

Individual Progress for your child (Based upon the child's own abilities)

Marking Key

C	Commendable	Very good. Makes a wholehearted effort.
S	Satisfactory	Makes a good effort. Tries to do what is expected.
N	Needs improvement	Effort not up to ability.

Page three to be marked at end of twenty weeks.

HABITS AND ATTITUDES

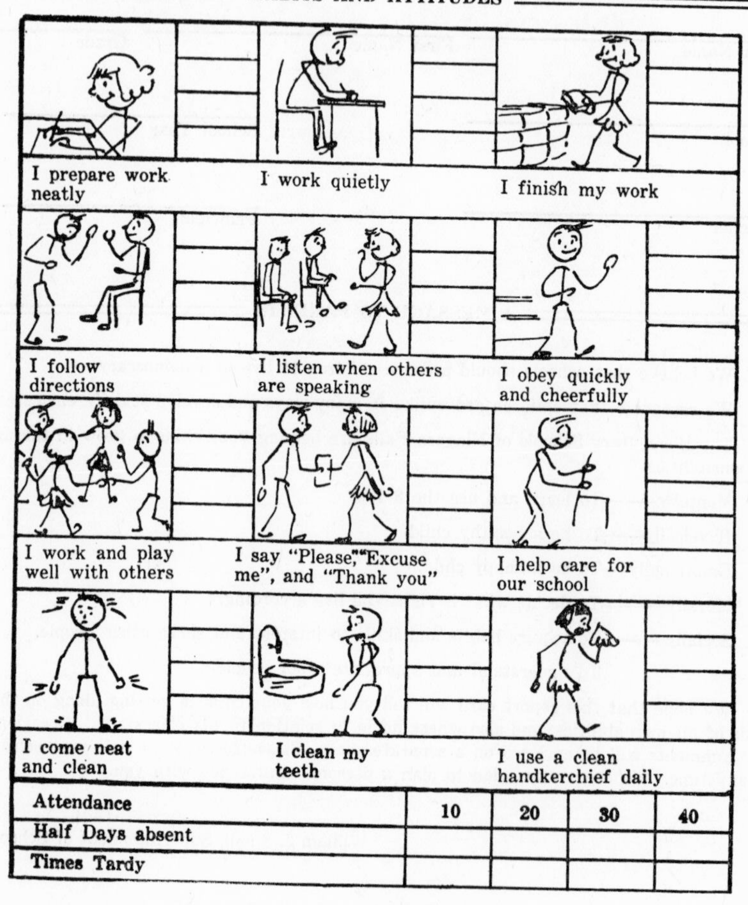

I prepare work neatly
I work quietly
I finish my work
I follow directions
I listen when others are speaking
I obey quickly and cheerfully
I work and play well with others
I say "Please," "Excuse me", and "Thank you"
I help care for our school
I come neat and clean
I clean my teeth
I use a clean handkerchief daily

Attendance	10	20	30	40
Half Days absent				
Times Tardy				

OF ______________________________
Last Name   First Name

PROGRESS IN SUBJECTS

Achievement Level . . (Based upon your child's position within his class group as judged by standardized tests, teacher made tests, and careful teacher observation.)

Marking Key

1. . . . . Above average for grade.
2. . . . . . . Average for grade.
3. . . . . Below average for grade.

Minor items under the main headings in PROGRESS IN SUBJECTS are marked + or — to show areas in which your child has shown exceptional progress or has had difficulties. Minor items not marked may be presumed to be satisfactory.

Individual Progress 20	30	40		Achievement Level 20	30	40
			READING			
			Is gaining skills needed to read			
			Learns and uses sounds			
			Reads well orally			
			Understands what he reads			
			LANGUAGE			
			Speaks distinctly			
			Speaks in sentences			
			Tells a simple story			
			Takes part in dramatic play			
			NUMBERS			
			Recognizes numbers			
			Knows number facts			
			Knows meaning of numbers			
			SOCIAL STUDIES			
			Has knowledge of environment and people in it			
			Shows growth in solving problems			
			Shows growth in getting along with others			
			SCIENCE			
			MUSIC			
			ART			

READING LEVEL (Based on daily work and tests)

Reading Readiness ____________
Pre-primer ____________
Primer ____________
1st Reader ____________

ITEMS TO BE CONSIDERED BY PARENTS

IF YOUR CHILD DOES WELL ON THIS PROGRESS REPORT, commend him. If his marks indicate that he needs help, please come to the school and discuss his problems with the teacher and principal.

Please remember that your child's teachers and principal are making a sincere effort to know your child better. We attempt to teach skills and provide experiences which help the child to develop into a happy, wholesome, interesting personality.

With cooperation and understanding, such a goal is possible. Let's work together.

EMOTIONAL DEVELOPMENT IS IMPORTANT

A happy child is one who is not timid and fearful.
A child should be encouraged to face reality.
A well adjusted child does not cry easily and frequently.
A contented child is not easily excited.
A sense of humor is necessary for a good personality.
A healthy child finds joy and satisfaction in work and play.

PARENT'S SIGNATURE

Please sign this progress report each quarter and return it to school with your child.

10 wk. ____________________

20 wk. ____________________

30 wk. ____________________

RECOMMENDED PLACEMENT

____________________ is assigned to ______________ grade

Room no. __________ beginning in September 19 ______________

Principal ____________________ Teacher ____________________

William J. Small, Superintendent of Schools

M-7A

formative are those used in the elementary school than are those commonly used in the junior high and high school. Even in school systems which have developed clear, descriptive cards for the lower grades there is frequently a marked change at the end of the sixth grade. From seventh through twelfth the more traditional and less-informative type predominates. This situation probably exists for several reasons. Beginning in the seventh grade, many schools are departmentalized, making it difficult (at least with the inadequate evaluation techniques frequently used) for teachers to judge certain traits because they see so many different pupils each day. However, the fact that numbers of secondary schools have improved their reporting systems makes departmentalization appear to be an insufficient excuse for the plain subject-matter card in many districts. Perhaps, as some educators have observed, many of the better educational practices originate in the lower grades but take time to work into the secondary schools.

Among the exceptions to this observation about a break in the quality of report cards between grades six and seven is the report form used in St. Louis for grades four through eight. Although it includes the usual subject-matter divisions, skills within each division are specified so that the parent knows where the student's particular strengths and weaknesses lie.

Attitude reflected by card

Magazine and newspaper cartoons consistently present us with a stereotyped view of report cards, a view possibly shared by much of the population—that report cards are fearsome things to children and depressing and ominous things to parents. Since the report card is often a main link between school and home, it is important for us to inspect its probable effect as an instrument of public relations.

Consider yourself a parent of an elementary-school child. Do you think the card in Figure 47 (currently used through the twelve grades of an Eastern central school) would make a better impression on you than would one of the cards from Niagara Falls or St. Louis? (See Figs. 41 through 46.)

The card that immediately flashes *Danger* or *Warning* at the child or parent seems to justify the stereotyped notion that report cards are ominous judgments and fearsome things.

On the other hand, the idea that school is interesting and that reports to the home are nothing to be feared appears to be conveyed

THIS CARD SHOWS THE PROGRESS

Individual Progress for your child (Based upon the child's own abilities).

Marking Key

C	Commendable	Very good. Makes a wholehearted effort.
S	Satisfactory	Makes a good effort Tries to do what is expected.
N	Needs improvement	Effort not up to ability.

Minor items under the main headings in both HABITS AND ATTITUDES and PROGRESS IN SUBJECTS are marked + or — to show areas in which your child has shown exceptional progress or has had difficulties. Minor items not marked may be presumed to be satisfactory.

HABITS AND ATTITUDES

Work Habits	10	20	30	40
Is prompt in beginning and finishing work				
Works well with others				
Follows directions				
Prepares work neatly				
Uses unassigned time wisely				
Uses books and materials carefully				
Shows initiative				
Works quietly				

Social Attitudes				
Pays attention when others are speaking				
Shows good sportsmanship				
Is courteous in speech and manner				
Understands and obeys school rules				
Shows qualities of leadership				
Takes responsibility in caring for the appearance of rooms, buildings and grounds				

Health Habits				
Sits, stands, walks correctly				
Keeps face, hands, fingernails and clothing clean				
Makes use of handkerchief				
Brushes teeth regularly				
Keeps head and hair neat and clean				

Attendance	10	20	30	40
Half-days absent				
Times tardy				

2

Fig. 43. Niagara Falls Report Form—Grades 2–3
Pages 1 and 4 are the same as on First-Grade Form.

OF ______________________ ______________________
Last Name First Name

PROGRESS IN SUBJECTS

Achievement Level . . (Based upon your child's position within his class group as judged by standardized tests, teacher made tests, and careful teacher observation.)

Marking Key

1. . . . . Above average for grade.
2. . . . . Average for grade.
3. . . . . Below average for grade.

Individual Progress — **Achievement Level**

10	20	30	40		10	20	30	40
				READING				
				Oral				
				Silent				
				Learns and uses sounds				
				LANGUAGE ARTS				
				Tells main points of a simple story				
				Writes simple sentences correctly				
				WRITING				
				Writes carefully and neatly				
				SPELLING				
				Spells assigned lessons				
				Uses correct spelling in written work				
				NUMBER				
				Knows number facts				
				Uses numbers in every day problems				
				SOCIAL STUDIES				
				Knows about community life				
				Contributes to activities and discussions				
				Accepts responsibilities of good citizenship				
				SCIENCE				
				MUSIC				
				ART				

READING LEVEL

Reading readiness ______________
Pre-primer ______________
Primer ______________
1st Reader ______________
2nd Reader ______________
3rd Reader ______________

THIS CARD SHOWS THE PROGRES

Individual Progress for your child (Based upon the child's own abilities).

Marking Key

C	Commendable	Very good. Makes a wholehearted effort.
S	Satisfactory	Makes a good effort. Tries to do what is expected.
N	Needs improvement	Effort not up to ability.

Minor items under the main headings in both HABITS AND ATTITUDES and PROGRESS IN SUBJECTS are marked + or — to show areas in which your child has shown exceptional progress or has had difficulties. Minor items not marked may be presumed to be satisfactory.

HABITS AND ATTITUDES

Work Habits	10	20	30	40
Is prompt in beginning and finishing work				
Works well with others				
Follows directions				
Prepares work neatly				
Uses unassigned time wisely				
Uses books and materials carefully				
Shows initiative				
Works quietly				

Social Attitudes				
Pays attention when others are speaking				
Shows good sportsmanship				
Is courteous in speech and manner				
Understands and obeys school rules				
Shows qualities of leadership				
Takes responsibility in caring for the appearance of rooms, buildings and grounds				

Health Habits				
Sits, stands, walks correctly				
Keeps face, hands, fingernails and clothing clean				
Makes use of handkerchief				
Brushes teeth regularly				
Keeps head and hair neat and clean				

Attendance	10	20	30	40
Half-days absent				
Times tardy				

2

Fig. 44. Niagara Falls Report Form—Grades 4—5—6
Pages 1 and 4 are similar to First-Grade Form.

OF ______________________ ______________________
Last Name First Name

PROGRESS IN SUBJECTS

Achievement Level . . (**Based upon your child's position within his class group as judged by standardized tests, teacher made tests, and careful teacher observation.**)

Marking Key

1. . . . . Above average for grade.
2. . . . . Average for grade.
3. . . . . Below average for grade.

Individual Progress ——— **Achievement Level**

Individual Progress (10 / 20 / 30 / 40)	Subject	Achievement Level (10 / 20 / 30 / 40)
	READING	
	Reads with understanding	
	Finds and uses new words	
	Shows interest in independent reading	
	SOCIAL STUDIES	
	Shows growth in knowledge of facts	
	Shows growth in using and sharing materials	
	Shows growth in understanding and respecting how other people live and feel	
	LANGUAGE ARTS	
	Speaks well before group	
	Uses clear speech	
	Shows growth in clear language usage	
	Shows growth in orderly arrangement of thought in written work	
	SPELLING	
	Spells assigned words	
	Spells correctly in written work	
	WRITING	
	Writes legibly and neatly	
	ARITHMETIC	
	Has knowledge of arithmetic facts	
	Applies arithmetic in practical situations	
	Works accurately	
	SCIENCE	
	Shows growth in power of observation	
	Shows growth in scientific concepts	
	MUSIC	
	ART	
	HOMEMAKING	
	INDUSTRIAL ARTS	

Pupil's Name .... R. C. Room..........

The circle O indicates the student's mark and the class distribution shows the number of pupils who received the mark indicated.

Class Distribution	Subject Grade				Subject Grade				Subject Grade				Subject Grade			
	Teacher				Teacher				Teacher				Teacher			
	10 Wks	20 Wks	30 Wks	40 Wks	10 Wks	20 Wks	30 Wks	40 Wks	10 Wks	20 Wks	30 Wks	40 Wks	10 Wks	20 Wks	30 Wks	40 Wks
95																
90																
85																
80																
75																
70																
P																
F																
Citizenship																
Work Habits																

Class Distribution	Subject Grade				Subject Grade				Subject Grade				Subject Grade			
	Teacher				Teacher				Teacher				Teacher			
	10 Wks	20 Wks	30 Wks	40 Wks	10 Wks	20 Wks	30 Wks	40 Wks	10 Wks	20 Wks	30 Wks	40 Wks	10 Wks	20 Wks	30 Wks	40 Wks
95																
90																
85																
80																
75																
70																
P																
F																
Citizenship																
Work Habits																

INTERPRETATION OF MARKS AND LETTERS

90-100—Honor
80-85 —Good
70-75 —Fair

P—Passing on Effort
F—Failure

C—Commendable
S—Satisfactory
U—Unsatisfactory

Fig. 45. Niagara Falls Report Form—Grades 7—8

SUBJECTS WITHOUT CLASS DISTRIBUTION

	Subject Grade				Subject Grade				Subject Grade				Subject Grade			
	Teacher				Teacher				Teacher				Teacher			
	10 Wks	20 Wks	30 Wks	40 Wks	10 Wks	20 Wks	30 Wks	40 Wks	10 Wks	20 Wks	30 Wks	40 Wks	10 Wks	20 Wks	30 Wks	40 Wks
Mark																
Citizen-ship																
Work Habits																
	Subject Grade				Subject Grade				Subject Grade				Subject Grade			
	Teacher				Teacher				Teacher				Teacher			
	10 Wks	20 Wks	30 Wks	40 Wks	10 Wks	20 Wks	30 Wks	40 Wks	10 Wks	20 Wks	30 Wks	40 Wks	10 Wks	20 Wks	30 Wks	40 Wks
Mark																
Citizen-ship																
Work Habits																

WORK HABITS:

Has necessary materials at hand.
Follows plans and directions accurately.
Makes good use of time and materials.
Prepares assignments on time.
Turns in neat and well organized work.

CITIZENSHIP:

Gets along well with others.
Takes an active part in group activities.
Demonstrates desirable character traits.
Respects authority and school regulations.
Takes good care of school materials and equipment.

Teacher	Date	Comments

BOARD OF EDUCATION
of the
CITY OF ST. LOUIS

School____

GRADES 4 - 8

School Year 19____ 19____

PROGRESS REPORT OF

____

To Parents: Grade__________________

This report is intended to describe the growth and development of your child and is to be used as a guide in helping him make as rapid progress as is consistent with his own abilities.

Many goals are listed in this progress report that a child should achieve to get along well in school and outside of school. Your child's growth toward these goals is shown by a check in one of the descriptive columns.

A check in the column entitled "Needs More Time or Effort to Develop" indicates that the child is not making sufficient progress in that phase of development. Among the reasons for this may be the following:

1. The child's attendance may not be regular.
2. The child may be disturbed over something which is happening at home or at school.
3. The child may find the school work difficult.
4. The child may not be in good physical condition.
5. The child may not put forth enough effort.

A child makes his best progress when the home and school work together. Please discuss this report with your child. You are invited to use the space provided for any comments you care to make and to visit the school to confer with the principal regarding your child's development.

PHILIP J. HICKEY,
Superintendent of Instruction.

Form S-38 July '52 50M

Fig. 46. St. Louis Report Form—Grades 4–8

Pages 2, 3, 4 follow on the next three pages. Two additional pages are provided for teacher and parent comments.

EXPLANATION OF TERMS

Outstanding Development: Indicates exceptional ability, originality, and accomplishment.

Satisfactory Development: Indicates that the child is making the growth expected of him.

Needs More Time or Effort to Develop: Indicates the child is not making sufficient progress for advancement.

CHECK MARKS (✓) ARE USED TO INDICATE DEGREE OF PROGRESS	FIRST SEMESTER						SECOND SEMESTER					
	First Ten Weeks			Second Ten Weeks			First Ten Weeks			Second Ten Weeks		
	Outstanding Development	Satisfactory Development	Needs more time or effort to develop	Outstanding Development	Satisfactory Development	Needs more time or effort to develop	Outstanding Development	Satisfactory Development	Needs more time or effort to develop	Outstanding Development	Satisfactory Development	Needs more time or effort to develop
LANGUAGE ARTS												
Reading												
Shows an interest in reading												
Works out new words for himself												
Reads grade level material												
Oral and Written Expression												
Uses language skills in written expression (capitals, punctuation, etc.)												
Strives for correct speech												
Expresses ideas well												
Spelling												
Spells well in written work												
Learns words at grade level												
Writing												
Writes plainly and neatly												
SCIENCE												
Shows an active interest in science												
Understands scientific facts and principles												
SOCIAL STUDIES												
Geography												
Shows an understanding of people and places												
Knows how to use maps, graphs, references, etc.												

CHECK MARKS (√) ARE USED TO INDICATE DEGREE OF PROGRESS	FIRST SEMESTER						SECOND SEMESTER					
	First Ten Weeks			Second Ten Weeks			First Ten Weeks			Second Ten Weeks		
	Outstanding Development	Satisfactory Development	Needs more time or effort to develop	Outstanding Development	Satisfactory Development	Needs more time or effort to develop	Outstanding Development	Satisfactory Development	Needs more time or effort to develop	Outstanding Development	Satisfactory Development	Needs more time or effort to develop
History												
Is learning to consider both sides of problems—past and present												
Understands American history												
Understands the functions of government (Local, State, National) (Gr. 7-8 only)												
Human Values in Democratic Living												
Social and Spiritual Growth												
Gets along well with others												
Assumes responsibility												
Observes school and group rules												
Shows respect for property												
Listens attentively												
Work Habits												
Follows directions												
Makes good use of spare time												
Begins and finishes work on time												
Keeps materials orderly												
Prepares neat and careful papers												
ARITHMETIC												
Knows number facts and processes												
Is able to solve problems												
FINE ARTS												
Music												
Seems to enjoy music												
Participates in music activities												
Art												
Shows progress in the use of art materials												
Expresses own ideas												

CHECK MARKS (✓) ARE USED TO INDICATE DEGREE OF PROGRESS	FIRST SEMESTER						SECOND SEMESTER					
	First Ten Weeks			Second Ten Weeks			First Ten Weeks			Second Ten Weeks		
	Outstanding Development	Satisfactory Development	Needs more time or effort to develop	Outstanding Development	Satisfactory Development	Needs more time or effort to develop	Outstanding Development	Satisfactory Development	Needs more time or effort to develop	Outstanding Development	Satisfactory Development	Needs more time or effort to develop
PRACTICAL ARTS Shows growth in handicraft or home-making skills												
PHYSICAL WELL BEING **Health and Safety** Takes pride in personal appearance												
Knows and practices health and safety												
Physical Education Takes part in physical activities												
Shows good sportsmanship												

ATTENDANCE

Normal progress in school cannot be attained if your child does not attend regularly and on time.

	FIRST SEMESTER		SECOND SEMESTER	
	First Ten Weeks	Second Ten Weeks	First Ten Weeks	Second Ten Weeks
Days Absent				
Times Tardy				

The one item checked below gives an overall appraisal of your child's development in all areas of learning.

	FIRST SEMESTER		SECOND SEMESTER	
	First Ten Weeks	Second Ten Weeks	First Ten Weeks	Second Ten Weeks
Is showing outstanding development (PASSING)				
Is showing satisfactory development (PASSING)				
Is making progress but is capable of doing better (PASSING)				
May need to spend more time in present grade (PASSING DOUBTFUL)				
Must spend more time in present grade (NOT PASSING)				

Assigned to Grade________________, effective January, 19_____

Assigned to Grade________________, effective September, 19_____

____

Principal

much better by many cards being developed in all parts of the country. It is common for the better reports to be colored and, especially at the primary level, to have a cartoon or sketch on the front. Numerous report forms show that excellent modern typographical

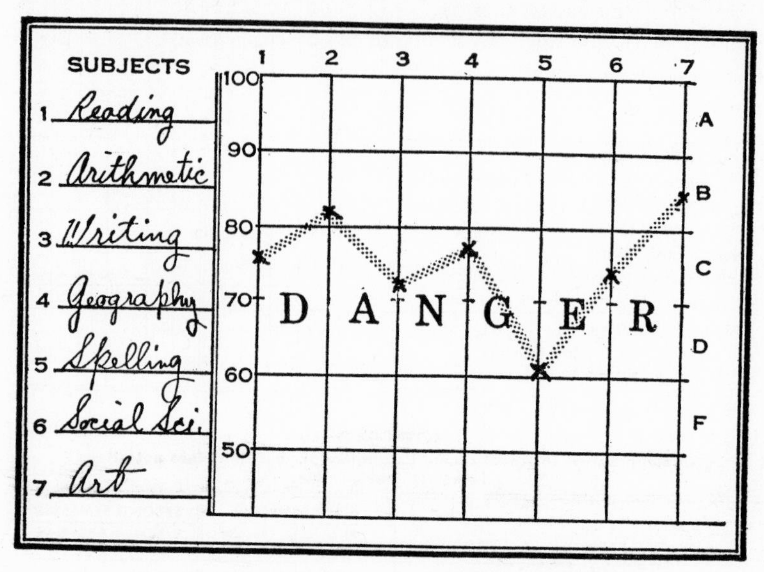

Fig. 47. Report forms reflect attitudes of school

On the opposite side of this card the following statement is included with the explanation of marks to the parent or guardian: "A grade of 65 per cent is the passing mark for high-school subjects and a grade of 75 per cent is passing in elementary subjects. However, in the first three grades we consider any mark below 85 per cent as questionable. When a grade ever falls near or below the DANGER line, there is cause for alarm concerning your child's work."

design and attractive colors make the "Progress Report" a pleasant-appearing folder. Increasingly, the message to the parent on the front of the progress report is friendly and mature. All this appears to bring school and home closer together for the child's benefit.

The Pittsburgh Public Schools have developed an extensive series of brief, illustrated brochures, each describing some phase of the school program about which parents commonly ask questions. Some typical pamphlets are: *Your Child Learns To Read, Health Teamwork, Homework?—Yes,* and *The Art Program in the Pittsburgh*

Schools. An appropriate pamphlet is often sent home with the progress report to provide better parent understanding of the schools.

A point of philosophy—self versus classmates

In reporting current progress, should the teacher compare the student with his own past achievement and ability or with his classmates? Or should he be compared *both* with himself and his classmates?

These questions pose a basic problem in educational philosophy that plagues the teacher each time a student is tested, rated, judged, or marked. What is the function of the elementary school? To see that children reach certain standards in each grade and to mark them according to their relative excellence when compared with one another? Or to see that each child has opportunities to do as well as he is able, recognizing that children vary so much in abilities that they reach the goals in different degrees at different times?

Defenders of the viewpoint that children's marks should reflect their relative standing in a class say that:

1. Children must learn realistically what their abilities are.
2. Children must learn to recognize their areas of low ability, where they receive low or failing marks, and where they need additional work.
3. If a student's records are inspected by a college or an employer following his school career, marks comparing him with his classmates will give the college or employer a better estimate of his ability.
4. If a student realizes in school what his abilities are, he will be realistic and not expect to be successful in areas in which he has little or no ability.

Defenders of the viewpoint that children's marks should reflect the progress they have made in relation to their individual abilities say that:

1. The elementary school does not have the function of comparing children with each other or eliminating the less apt, but it operates to provide opportunities for each to learn to the best of his ability, despite what that ability is.
2. Constant defeats for a child, as shown by consistently low marks when he is compared with others, are damaging to his personality and do not give him the supposed *realistic*

and healthy attitude toward his abilities that proponents of competitive grading claim.

3. When individuals, as older youths or adults, are being trained for particular vocations, such as medicine or teaching or engineering, comparative marking may be appropriate to distinguish the more able from the less able. But vocational selection is not the function of an elementary school in a democracy. Instead, the elementary school should provide for all ability levels.

Other educators take a compromise view. They desire that children be compared both with their own apparent abilities and with the achievement of their classmates.

Which of these points of view is the *correct* one or the *best* one is a philosophical matter that each school system must decide for itself. All three philosophies are reflected in report forms from various parts of the country. In recent years, as more information about individual differences among children and mental hygiene principles has been developed, there has been a noticeable trend toward comparing the child with himself, at least in the lower grades. For example, report cards at all elementary-school levels in the Minneapolis Public Schools contain this message to parents:

"Marks for your child are based upon the child's own abilities insofar as the teacher can judge from standard tests, teacher-made tests and observation. These marks do not indicate his standing in relation to the group. If you wish to know where your child stands in his group, make arrangements to discuss this with his teacher."

This statement is similar to those found on many cards in current use.

The Niagara Falls progress reports (Figures 42 through 45) above kindergarten illustrate the type that utilizes two comparisons: with self and with others.

Symbols or marks used

The philosophy of marking also affects the types of symbols or statements used on report cards.

For example, the explanation of marks on the Niagara Falls kindergarten form reflects an up-to-date understanding of maturation in young children. (The symbols are: U—Usually, P—Part of the time, S—Seldom—Occasionally, N—Not Yet.) That is, almost all children achieve the goals listed for the kindergarten, but some achieve them sooner than others, and there should be no stigma nor parental pressure attached to the slow maturer's progress. The use of *Not Yet* instead of *Never* is in indication of this understanding of individual differences in maturation rate.

The St. Louis kindergarten report indicates this same understanding of maturation. A child may receive one of two possible marks for each skill or type of behavior: (1) *shows satisfactory development* or (2) *needs more time and help to develop.* In grades above kindergarten the St. Louis cards provide three possible marks: (1) *outstanding development,* (2) *satisfactory development,* or (3) *needs more time or effort to develop.* This last category is explained further for the parent on the front of the card. (See Figure 46.)

A great variety of other symbols are used by schools. The percents, letters (A,B,C,D,F) and numbers (1,2,3,4,5) mentioned earlier are common. A sample of three others will be given here to indicate that practices differ considerably and that the symbols sometimes mirror the apparent philosophy of marking in the school system.

School 1.	S—Satisfactory progress U—Unsatisfactory progress E—Effort and interest shown but progress is slow O—Outstanding achievement +—Better than average growth ——Special attention needed
School 2.	(lower grade) S –I do very well U –I need to do better I—I am improving
School 3.	T—In top quarter of class M—In middle half of class L—In lowest quarter of class

Usually only a brief statement is used to explain the meaning of these symbols. However, occasionally a more complete definition is provided for parents. Such a definition is illustrated by the following descriptions of letter grades that appear on the junior high report form used in Seattle:

"The following definitions are given in order that the full meaning of the grades may be clear. In grading pupils, teachers attempt to judge the results in the classroom. These definitions specify the qualities that constitute successful school work and therefore set up definite goals for effort.

"The A Pupil

Is careful, thorough, and prompt in the preparation of all required work.

Is quick and resourceful in utilizing suggestions for supplementary activities.

Works independently and has sufficient interest and initiative to undertake original projects beyond the assigned work.

Uses his time well.

Does not guess.

Is careful to express thought clearly and accurately.

Shows leadership in classroom activities.

Has excellent self-control and effective study habits.

"The B Pupil

Prepares all assignments carefully.

Is conscientious and dependable.

Requires no urging to have work done on time.

Shows consistent interest.

Responds readily when called upon.

Makes a practice of doing all the work assigned and makes some use of suggestions for supplementary work.

Has good study habits of routine assignments.

Is loyal, dependable, and helpful in class activities.

"The C Pupil

Does good work, but requires considerable direction and stimulation from the teacher.

Is usually dependable and cooperative.

Has good intentions, though interest is not always keen.

Does not show a great deal of concern in following his subject beyond minimum requirements.

Responds to encouragement and guidance, though sometimes inclined to be careless or slow in accomplishment.

Needs to be prompted by frequent questions in reports or discussions before the class.

Should develop more independent habits of study.

"The D Pupil

Does work regarded as passable according to minimum requirements for course.

Lacks in concentration in study.
Fails frequently to respond in recitation or prepared work.
Requires special help and encouragement constantly.
Shows some improvement in study habits during the semester, and sufficient mastery of fundamental work to warrant the opinion that he will grow more through advancement than through repetition of the subject.
Lacks sense of responsibility.
Is too easily diverted from any task.
Is decidedly irregular in his attention and application.

"The S Pupil

Finds subject difficult but has made progress.
Accomplishes less than the fundamental minimum essentials necessary for a 'D.'
Is loyal, dependable, and helpful in class activities.
Shows consistent effort to work to capacity.
Repetition of subject does not appear advisable.
Does not show sufficient accomplishment to warrant reporting credit in the subject for college entrance.

"The E Pupil

Fails to accomplish the fundamental minimum essentials necessary for success in the course.
Needs to spend more time on the subject.
Has study habits that are poor and ineffective.
May lack adaptability for a specific subject.
Either will not, or cannot hold his attention to his work.

"NOTE: The definitions of grades given above do not apply to music and physical education. The only grades given in these subjects are: 'S' satisfactory, or 'E' the failure grade."

Thus, it is seen that a variety of symbols have been adopted by schools throughout the nation. What symbols will be best for a particular school system depends upon: (1) the marking philosophy of that system, that is, comparing children to themselves or to their classmates or both, and (2) the kinds of symbols the faculty believe will give parents a true reflection of children's progress.

Developing an effective reporting system

A survey of reporting practices throughout the country at any given time shows that numerous schools are revising their current practices. The question arises, "How should a school proceed in developing an effective reporting system?" Various approaches are used.

In some cases the staff of administrators and supervisors in the central office revise practices after informally consulting a few teachers.

Other school systems organize faculty workshops in which teachers and administrators participate to debate their philosophies of marking and to develop more adequate reporting techniques. Usually consultants from neighboring schools, colleges, and county or state education departments are invited to aid in such workshops.

Another plan that features a wider range of participation is illustrated by that used in Indianapolis to develop the progress reports that recently were put in use. Paul I. Miller, Assistant Superintendent of the Indianapolis Public Schools, explains that:

"The committees working on the cards included parents, teachers, principals, supervisors, and central office personnel. In addition, in many schools children were consulted concerning reports. Parents participating on the various committees were very helpful in working out the present report forms."

A similar plan is described by Mrs. Martha K. McIntosh of the San Diego Public Schools where report forms "... were developed by a committee on which were represented teachers, parents, and principals. After survey and study of many types of reports a tentative form was developed.

"The tentative form was used on an experimental basis for a year. All parents were then sent a questionnaire to survey their reactions to and evaluation of the card. Responses indicated overwhelming acceptance of the card. After a few minor revisions, it was reprinted for ..." current use.

This newer approach to developing report forms, which includes administrators, teachers, parents, and children, has generally resulted in more constructive inspection of the school reports and school goals in a community. In some cases the plan has resulted in the children as well as the teachers filling out the marks on the progress report. In such instances the child may indicate the mark he believes he deserves in an area and then may discuss with the teacher the way he has marked himself compared to the way the teacher has marked him. A rarer report plan provides spaces for marks by (1) teacher, (2) child, and (3) parent.

An effective guide for any school to use in revising its reporting system is Wrinkle's *Improving Marking and Reporting Practices.* This book has direct and simple methods for teachers to determine their philosophy of marking and for developing practices best suited to the individual school's needs.

Summary

Among schools in the United States there is no uniform method of marking students and reporting their progress to parents. The most common technique of reporting is the *report card,* a term which is gradually being supplanted by *progress report.* However, even among report cards there is marked variation from one school district to another. The following appear to be trends in the current development of reports.

A change from:	*To the practice of:*
1. Listing only broad subject fields. In each a student receives a single mark.	Explaining in terms of student behavior the activities that compose each subject-matter field as well as character traits. Thus, the progress report is more detailed, more specific.
2. Including only school *subjects* and perhaps a single item titled *character* or *deportment.*	Including numerous objectives under such titles as *social adjustment, personal development,* and *work habits.*
3. Using a single report form for the entire school.	Developing forms suited specifically to the goals of individual grades or levels, such as kindergarten, primary, intermediate, and upper divisions.
4. Comparing all children with a set standard or with their classmates.	Comparing each student's progress with his own apparent ability (especially in lower grades) or with himself as well as with others.
5. Using per cent or letter grades, which are sometimes defined in such terms as *excellent, good, fair,* and *failure.*	Developing additional symbols or statements, which tend to reflect a more modern understanding of child development (such as *needs more time and help*).
6 Using a relatively small card, printed black on white.	Using a larger folder in color with newer typographical design and

	friendly explanations to parents. Pictures or cartoons on the card are common at the primary level.
7. Providing a line for a teacher comment and a line for the parent's signature.	Providing more space for both teacher and parent comments.
8. Having the central supervisory staff, with possible suggestions from a few teachers, develop the report card.	Organizing committees including teachers, supervisors, parents, and students to improve reporting practices.

Rather than use a report *card,* a smaller number of schools prefer the informal letter to parents or the parent-teacher conference for reporting pupils' progress. These two techniques can provide more individualized descriptions of a child's behavior but also demand considerably more teacher time.

CENTRAL SCHOOL'S COMMITTEE REPORT

At the beginning of this chapter we saw the Central School System faculty create a committee to recommend revisions in the reporting system. After the committee studied the progress reports used in different sections of the country, they brought the following report back to the faculty:

"We believe that some changes should be made in our method of reporting students' progress. When we first were appointed to this committee, we imagined that we would return to you with a specific new plan for you to put into effect. However, our study of the experiences of other schools has convinced us that the best reporting system will be developed if more people than the committee members work on it. Consequently, we make the following recommendations:

"1. Several entire faculty meetings should be devoted to a workshop in which we will discuss different philosophies and forms of reporting. Our committee, which has learned a great deal about practices in other schools, will act as a consultant and directive body to provide efficiency in the discussions.

"2. A representative committee of parents should be selected to meet with us and present the parent's view of what he wants in a report from the school.

"3. Students should also be consulted, probably by teachers discussing pertinent problems of report cards in classes.

"4. Central Elementary should develop the form of report that will be best suited to the stage of understanding of our community and faculty. It would be possible for our committee or for the principal to issue a detailed and very pioneering card for us to use. However, other school systems have discovered that when teachers are not thoroughly convinced that the system is worth while, they do not do a conscientious job of using it accurately, As a result, the desirable aspects of the *form* are lost in the *misuse* of the card. We do not believe the proper use of a new reporting practice can be dictated to the teachers by a committee or administrator. Instead, the new form is used best when each teacher is wholeheartedly convinced that such a practice means fairer judgments of student progress. Consequently, we believe that if the entire faculty have some part in the planning and are present when the issues are debated, we will develop a reporting system that will be used wholeheartedly by all of us."

The committee report came somewhat as a surprise to the faculty members who had expected a specific new report card to result from the group's study. However, the proposed workshop sounded like a profitable approach, even though it would take a longer time. The administration and teachers, therefore, agreed to the plan. Rather than adopt a card used in another school, they developed a series of progress reports suited specifically to Central School's philosophy and community.

OBJECTIVES OF THIS CHAPTER

The effective elementary or junior high teacher:

1. Explains advantages and disadvantages of various practices of reporting students' progress.
2. Writes specific and accurate letters or comments to parents concerning a child's progress.
3. Aids in developing progress reports that are best suited to the goals of the school and to a particular community.
4. Secures data from many sources and with a variety of evaluation techniques in order to report students' progress adequately.

Suggested evaluation techniques for this chapter

1. Using the description of one of the fifth-grade students mentioned in the chapter, develop a *letter to the parents* that would act as an effective report of the child's progress. Do you think your

letter would be more meaningful than the original report-card form used in Central School?

2. Some of the main goals of the Central Elementary School fifth grade are reflected in the descriptions of the four fifth-grade students in this chapter. Develop a report form that you believe would be an effective one in this fifth grade. Mark each of the four students on the progress report you have created. Compare the meaningfulness of the marks on your report form with those on the original Central Elementary report card.
3. Obtain a report card from a nearby elementary school. Try to estimate the philosophy of marking students as reflected by the report card.
4. Get report cards from the elementary, junior-high, and high-school levels in the same school system. Try to estimate the differences, if any, in the philosophy of marking students among these grade levels as reflected by the progress-report forms. Which form do you think provides the best information for parents?

SUGGESTED READINGS

1. HARRIS, FRED E. "Three Persistent Educational Problems: Grading, Promoting, and Reporting to Parents," *Bulletin of the Bureau of School Service,* XXVI. Lexington, Ky.: University of Kentucky, September, 1953.
2. "Reporting Pupil Progress," *The National Elementary Principal,* Department of Elementary School Principals, N.E.A., Vol. XXXI, No. 6 (June, 1952). Explanations of newer reporting systems by staff members from schools in various sections of the nation.
3. STRANG, RUTH. *How to Report Pupil Progress.* Chicago: Science Research Associates, 1955. Booklet on newer ways of reporting to parents.
4. WRINKLE, WILLIAM L. *Improving Marking and Reporting Practices.* New York: Rinehart and Co., 1947. Direct, simple methods for teachers to determine their philosophy of marking and for developing reporting practices best suited to individual schools' needs.

CHAPTER

15

Talking with Parents and Students

AT THE COUNTY TEACHERS' INSTITUTE an expert in techniques of counseling and interviewing spoke on "Concepts behind Non-Directive Counseling."

It was during this speech that Miss Langworthy began wondering about the effectiveness of her methods of talking with students and parents. Several questions bothered her: "Do I give a child too much advice when we have a conference? Are children capable of figuring out the right thing to do without my telling them? When parents come, should I show them the records I keep? Should I tell a parent directly that his child has low ability if I believe it is true? How should I talk with a child who begins to tell me about something usually regarded as improper? When I am convinced that a child's problems are primarily caused by the way his parents treat him, how should I talk about it with his parents?"

Miss Langworthy's concern over these daily teaching problems led her to talk with the counseling expert after his speech. He suggested a number of books and pamphlets for her to read. From her study about techniques of interviewing, she learned the following:

A FOCUS FOR DISCUSSION

In recent years considerable controversy has revolved around the question of what types of counseling procedures are best.

Some experts have recommended a very active role on the part of the counselor who attempts to determine the cause of the client's problem and often makes specific suggestions about ways the client might solve it. This approach has been termed a type of "directive" counseling because of the therapist's prominent part as an active problem-solver.

Other experts have recommended a less active role on the counselor's part. Instead, they would have him function more as a sounding board for the client's problems. Here the therapist tends to reflect the client's views and feelings about the problem so that the client can see his own situation in better perspective and as a result solve the problem himself. With this approach, termed a "nondirective" technique, the counselor is more a bystander than an adviser.

The discussions about directive and nondirective techniques have been carried on primarily by psychologists, psychiatrists, and guidance workers, because interview methods are the chief tools of their daily work. These therapists, through a series of talks with clients, try to evaluate what causes the individuals' disturbances and try to aid them toward better adjustment. It is not normally a teacher's job to pursue involved problems through interviews. However, an understanding of the principles behind various counseling techniques is valuable, for in their talks with parents and students teachers must continually make decisions about when to listen and when and how to talk. By using the directive-nondirective controversy as a focal point, we may discuss interview methods and hope to aid teachers in deciding the best ways to handle parent and student interviews.

DIRECTIVE AND NONDIRECTIVE INTERVIEWING

In professional journals which discuss these approaches to counseling, it is sometimes easy for the reader to gain the impression that a counseling interview is *either* directive *or* nondirective. This impression can result from the authors' attempts to delineate clearly their point of view by contrasting it with the opposite point of view. However, in actual practice most counseling interviews are neither completely directive nor completely nondirective but are some compromise between the two. For discussion purposes these techniques may be regarded as on two ends of a continuous scale. The characteristics of these extreme ends of the scale are listed in the chart below. However, in a given situation most interviewers are not at an extreme end. Rather, they adjust their technique to the particular problem and particular person with whom they are working. As will be seen later, the teacher should adjust his talks with parents and students in the same way. Sometimes he will be more directive. At other times he will use an indirect approach in accomplishing his purpose.

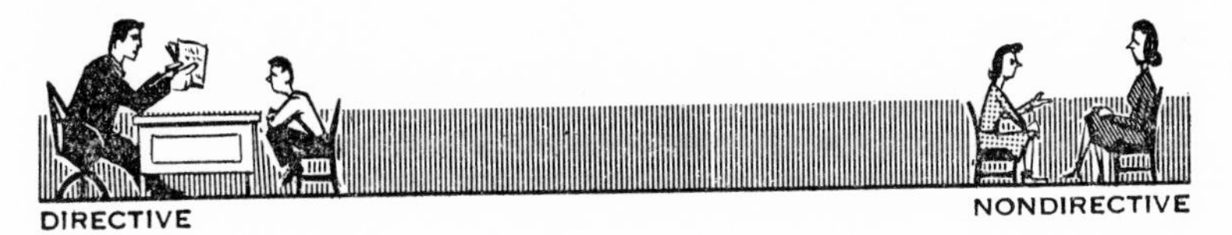

Fig. 48

Comparison of Directive and Nondirective Views

Directive	*Nondirective*
FOCUS OF SITUATION	
Counselor-centered. Concerned chiefly with a specific *problem* of client. Counselor investigates and handles cause and treatment of this one, specific problem.	Client-centered. Concerned mainly with helping client develop ability to achieve satisfactory adjustment in any situation rather than in only the specific problem situation that brought him to the therapist.
BASIC ASSUMPTION	
Counselor should select desirable, socially approved goal client should reach and help client reach it. Counselor is an experienced, mature individual who can make more adequate decisions about this problem than can client.	Client has right to select own life goals, even though they may not be compatible with society's or counselor's goals. Counselor is not to impose his goals and ideals on client. Goals that are right for one person may not be appropriate for another.
SUITED FOR	
People who need information. People not able to solve their own problems because of emotional, social, cultural, economic, physical, mental, or hereditary limitations.	People who have enough ability to understand their situation. Not suited for those with borderline intelligence nor for psychotics or persons much over 50 years old. Not suited for *very young* children.

INTERVIEW INITIATED

Either client comes freely to counselor or is sent for by counselor.	Client comes freely to counselor.

ATMOSPHERE

More authoritarian because counselor is authority who is trained in helping solve people's problems.	More permissive because counselor is person to whom client can talk as he solves his own problem in his own way.

ROLE OF CLIENT

Relies more directly on counselor and listens to counselor's interpretation ot problem's causes and possible solutions.	Relies more directly on self with counselor acting as a reflector of client's feelings and as a "side-line assistant" for client. Client is required to act more mature.

TECHNIQUES OF COUNSELOR

May use ordering, forbidding, exhortation, suggestions, questioning, criticism, reassurance, encouragement, advice, or persuasion, or give information. More participation on part of counselor.	Listens permissively and when he does talk he tries to reflect the client's feelings. Counselor exhibits amoral attitude and accepts client for what he is without condemning, acting shocked, or praising. Client does most of the talking.

CENTRAL RESULT

Solve client's problem. Intellectual analysis and interpretation by counselor of the particular problem, its causes and probable solution.	Self-understanding, release of feelings, and achievement of insight into reasons for these feelings and reactions. This results primarily through client's own efforts.

AMOUNT OF TIME USUALLY NEEDED

Relatively quick. Many cases can often be handled.	Long, drawn-out treatment.

The difference in actual practice between these two approaches may become clearer if we inspect a particular student's problem and analyze how it might be handled first directively and then nondirectively. Our student will be Carl Johnston, a seventh grader in a junior high school.

Directive situation

Carl has been called to the boys' adviser's office. The adviser begins:

"Carl, the gym teacher reports that you said you had a cold and couldn't change into gym clothes with the rest of the boys. Is that right?"

CARL: "Yes."

ADVISER: "Then he said a few days later, after he had told you that you needed a medical excuse if you were to miss gym again, you brought him this excuse which was supposedly written by your doctor. Is that right?"

CARL: "Yes."

ADVISER: "But doctors usually don't write excuses on plain paper. They use their prescription pads. So the gym teacher suspected that this note . . . reading 'Carl Johnston has an ailment. He should not take gym' . . . was not written by the doctor. He phoned your mother and your doctor and they don't know anything about such a note. Do you have an explanation?"

CARL: "No."

ADVISER: "What do you think about such a situation?"

CARL: (pause) "Nothing."

ADVISER: "Look, Carl, we're here to help you. And we mean that honestly. I know that lots of times boys and girls don't want to take gym for various reasons. Perhaps it's because they're embarrassed because they don't want to undress near the others, or they feel embarrassed wearing shorts. Other times it's because they feel they can't play games as well as the others, and if they don't take gym they won't show up poorly in games. Isn't that true?"

CARL: "I don't know. I guess so."

ADVISER: "Do you know why you wanted to get out of gym badly enough to write a note like this? You must have had some reason."

This initial portion of the interview indicates the tone of a type of directive interview process. It evidences some of the directive counseling features presented in the chart. In handling Carl's case the adviser questions the boy about his motives and secures information about his background from cumulative records. After studying the boy's reactions and his past record, the adviser concludes that it is likely the gym problem is caused by a combination of embarrassment over undressing in the locker room and a lack of skill in games. The adviser concludes that the situation can probably best be treated by:

1. Advising Carl that "frequently in life we have to do some things that embarrass us at first and aren't easy to do. But we find that as soon as we show courage and face the unpleasant task and do it, we begin to lose our fear of it. This leads to more confidence in ourselves, and we feel better about it. You try it in gym and just see how successfully it works."
2. Reassuring Carl that many students feel the same way and conquer it.
3. Complimenting the boy from time to time for doing a good job in adapting to the gym class.
4. Having the gym teacher spend a little extra time with Carl to aid him in game skills.

The question is now appropriate: "Would such counseling help solve Carl's problem?" The answer is not definite. Some students of human behavior say it would. Others say it would not. Critics of such directive techniques contend that:

"The immediate problem of the gym class is not the issue. That problem just brought the boy to the adviser's attention. Thus the gym class was the *precipitating* problem. Underlying this precipitating incident is a disturbance that cannot be solved merely by advising the boy to 'be brave and everything will turn out all right.' Such an approach makes him defensive, and he will not learn to stand on his own. The boy must establish a new concept of himself and must develop feelings toward himself and others that will enable him to face such situations as the gym class with confidence. Such a transformation means change in his personality, and that demands time and a different approach."

Defenders of the more directive approach say that there is not sufficient time for a long, drawn-out therapy. They can point to cases in which such an approach as the above appears to have worked.

Nondirective situation

Let us see how Carl might appear in a situation with a teacher-counselor using a nondirective interview technique. The boy's social-studies teacher, Mr. Barth, is a part-time counselor in the junior high school. The teacher has been friendly with the students and has let them know that any time they wish they can chat with him. Carl has asked if he can stop and talk during one of Mr. Barth's free periods (two set aside for counseling). Mr. Barth has made the afternoon appointment. Carl enters the room.

MR. BARTH: "Hello, Carl. Won't you sit down?"

CARL: "Unhunh."

MR. BARTH: "You wanted to chat?"

CARL: "Yes. I . . . uh . . . I wondered how I'm doing in social studies."

Mr. Barth looks at his records and gives the boy information about his progress which he realizes Carl already knew before he came for the interview.

MR. BARTH: "And I think that's pretty much the way it stands, Carl."

There is a pause for a few moments. Carl draws circles on the back of his notebook, then—"Uh . . . a couple weeks ago you said we could talk to you about anything . . . and . . . well, and you wouldn't think we were funny or kind of crazy no matter what we said."

MR. BARTH: "Yes, that's right."

CARL: "Well . . . uh . . . uh . . . do you . . . uh . . . (long pause) . . . I never had to change clothes and . . . I mean . . . well, in gym in grade school we never had to take showers. (Pause) I mean, don't you think people who catch colds easy shouldn't have to take showers? I mean, doctors say that's a way to catch cold."

MR. BARTH: "You find this junior high gym setup pretty new."

CARL: "Yes, that's right. I mean, I catch colds easy. Well, I guess the gym teachers ought to know what they're doing, but . . . course, cold weather's coming along, and . . . I don't want to be missing school like when I was little . . . I mean by getting colds after showers."

MR. BARTH: "Then you feel that this regulation about showers after gym may cause you to get sick and miss school."

CARL: "But it isn't just that. They make us run around in shorts on pretty cold days, you know."

In such a vein the conversation continues. During the interview Mr. Barth listens as Carl skirts around his problem of not wishing to take gym. Mr. Barth speaks occasionally, attempting to reflect and clarify the way Carl feels about the situation. The counselor refrains from showing approval or disapproval of the boy's feelings or statements. The information that comes slowly from the interview is that Carl told the gym teacher he could not take gym. The teacher had said the boy needed a doctor's excuse, and Carl tells Mr. Barth:

"Well, I know the doctor wouldn't want me catching cold, but I didn't want my folks to have to pay for a doctor's visit, so I wrote a note myself. And . . . well, Mr. Barth . . . you got to protect yourself when they don't understand you. And now I'm supposed to go see the assistant principal after school . . . and I'm afraid I'm in for it. . . . Gym teachers are supposed to know about health and all that. How come our gym teacher doesn't understand things like getting colds?"

At the end of forty minutes Mr. Barth indicates that he has another appointment. He invites Carl to come back to talk another day if he wishes. Carl says he thinks he will.

Proponents of this nondirective counseling, who say that the gym problem is only a symptom of a more general maladjustment, indicate that any changes that are made in the boy's personality must come from him through his own efforts. Thus, advice given to him in a short session or two, even though it is accurate advice, may merely make him defend his present condition. However, they say, if he has an opportunity to express his disturbed emotions and talk through his problems in the presence of a sympathetic counselor, he can gradually come to face himself and the inevitable adjustments he must make if he is to develop confidence and the ability to fulfill his responsibilities. By talking out his conflicts (achieving emotional catharsis), the boy can relieve himself of guilt feelings and can take steps toward his own goal which he has decided upon himself. The nondirective counselors believe that not only does the boy solve the immediate problem, but, more important, he grows in his ability to solve future problems by himself.

The critics of this approach ask, "But what if the boy chooses his own goal and that goal is contrary to society's pattern of adequate behavior? What if his particular solution does not eventuate in his being able to adjust to the gym situation? Is that really a solution? What if he does not want to face himself as he really is but would prefer to rationalize his behavior or escape difficult situations?"

These critics also point out that such a nondirective approach takes much time, a commodity that teachers or school counselors do not have in abundance.

Defenders of nondirective therapy point to records of cases (usually those of college students) in which the technique has apparently been successful.

Compromises somewhere along the line between complete directive and thoroughgoing nondirective interviewing are very common. Probably most counselors today utilize techniques of both approaches. Their decision about the degree of directiveness or nondirectiveness that should be used depends upon the particular person they are counseling and the problem involved.

THE TEACHER AS AN INTERVIEWER

What bearing does the preceding discussion of counseling and interviewing have on evaluation in the elementary school?

The foregoing brief introduction to viewpoints toward counseling has been included to show that there is more than one possible interviewing technique. Recognizing this and understanding different techniques, a teacher is more likely to attempt to utilize the approach that appears most appropriate in a given situation.

When does the teacher need interview techniques in judging and reporting students' progress?

There are numerous evaluation situations that call for a talk between the teacher and a student or his parents. Some of the common interviews with parents concern:

1. Reporting a child's progress.
2. Securing data about the pupil's home and his parents' attitudes toward him.
3. Securing evidence about how much school learning carries over into behavior at home.

Some of the common interviews relating to evaluation situations with children concern:

1. Reporting the pupil's progress to him.
2. Securing data about the way he feels toward school, home, and peers, or toward the problems he faces.
3. Securing evidence of the extent to which he has reached the specific objectives of the class.

As each type of interview situation is discussed, it should prove helpful for the reader to estimate the degree of directiveness or nondirectiveness that would probably be most profitable in that case.

TALKING WITH PARENTS

Reporting children's progress to parents

In the lower grades of many schools the parent-teacher conference has become the chief means of reporting children's progress. The principal reporting technique in upper grades is rarely the parent-teacher conference. However, parents of upper-grade pupils commonly discuss their children's work when they attend the Parent-Teacher Association "open-house" or "parent visiting night." In other instances a parent who is disturbed about his child's progress visits the school to talk it over.

The nature of this type of interview makes it more *directive* because the teacher must give information. The teacher tells the parent how well the child is progressing toward the objectives the school is helping him to reach. However, it is not enough simply to say that the teacher gives information. When the reporting job has been done most effectively, the parent also *accepts* the teacher's report as a valid judgment of the child's progress and *plans* with the teacher the most efficient ways for school and home to cooperate in promoting the child's future growth. The teacher-parent conference that leaves the parent angry at the school and desirous of "getting even" or "making trouble" or "getting our girl out of there" has not been the most effective interview. Therefore, it is necessary for the teacher in reporting a child's progress to fit the interview technique to the particular situation so that the parents will accept the report and cooperate in further plans for the child.

How may some typical interview situations best be handled?

The cases of children who are doing very well in all areas of schoolwork rarely present problems of reporting. The conference between parent and teacher is pleasant. The teacher reports directly the evidence of the universal success the child has shown, and the parent is satisfied because the child has lived up to family expectations.

The cases of children who are not doing so well as parents wish provide the interviewing problems for teachers. There are various techniques for handling them. During the interview the teacher usually is given clues by the parents' statements to what their feelings are concerning the report they are receiving. These clues help the teacher decide whether to present more evidence to them, whether to suggest ways the child might be aided, or whether to let the parents talk out their complaints about the school and thus release their negative feelings.

As much as we all would like parents to be objective and face the facts in life without becoming emotional, we must remember that in most parents' eyes their children's inadequacies are also their own inadequacies. And when the children appear to be failures, it is natural for parents to be somewhat disturbed. Thus, when the child does not do so well as expected, it is not uncommon for parents to blame the teacher or the school for being inaccurate. In doing so the parents defend their children, and consequently themselves, from exhibiting shortcomings in arithmetic, reading, or social relationships with other children.

When a parent first learns that his child has been judged lower on some skill or characteristic than the parent wished, he may well question or attack the teacher's methods of measuring progress. "What makes you say Jimmy doesn't cooperate in groups as well as most of the others?" In many cases the teacher at this point must say, "Well, I've observed his general behavior, and that's the way he is." Sometimes such an answer may convince the parent. However, he is much more likely to be convinced if the teacher can show more evidence than only general observation. If the teacher has a folder containing information about the child, and if a participation chart or rating scale with data about "cooperating in groups" can be shown to the parent, the judgment of Jimmy's progress is much more likely to be accepted. Parents typically do not know the variety of evaluation devices used by the efficient, modern teacher. Explaining a little about some of these techniques to the parent as the verbal report of the child's progress is being given helps convince the parent of the accuracy of the teacher's judgments.

Consequently, by having available evidence collected by a variety of techniques throughout the year, the teacher can usually present a more convincing picture of the child's growth. If the teacher can present no evidence but must always rely on "I've observed that . . ." the parent's conviction that the school is inaccurate or unfair will appear to have foundation.

When they see carefully collected data about their child, many parents become less defensive and say, "Oh, I see. Well, what do you think we could do to help?" This is a desirable state, for then the parents and teacher can plan together the ways in which they can help the child to grow.

In other instances, however, the teacher's carefully collected data about a child does not convince the parents. Adults who have so few inner resources that they cannot face and accept any hint of weakness in themselves or their children may attack the school despite the actual evaluation evidence the teacher can produce about the child. They may say:

"I don't care. What are tests? What are statistics? Statistics can lie. I'll tell you one thing, Helen hasn't had decent treatment since she's been in this school. It's been the same in every grade. The other kids have gotten preference and extra help every time."

When the teacher sees that parents for personality reasons cannot accept the evaluation, he probably will find a nondirect approach more profitable. Giving advice to "face the facts" to an emotionally disturbed parent is usually folly. In most cases if he is going to "face the facts," it will probably be a result of his wrestling with the idea that he has previously expected too much of his child. The teacher's or principal's direct advice to the parent is likely to increase the parent's resistance to the school which is presenting him with a disappointing picture of his child. On the other hand, if the teacher or principal presents the evidence without accompanying advice or apparent censure, the parent may be better able to struggle with the emotional problem and reach a more satisfactory conclusion. The following typical example indicates how the guidance worker in a school was first directive (that is, gave information) and then shifted to a more nondirective approach to allow the parent to work through the problem of readjusting her expectation level for her son.

During his first six months in first grade Charles Knox, a seven-year-old, demonstrated great difficulty in learning skills that most of his classmates learned rather easily. His teacher recommended psychological testing, to which the parents agreed. After the testing (Stanford-Binet and Goodenough Draw-A-Man tests) the school's guidance director invited the mother for a conference.

Mother: "Now, exactly what kind of tests did you give Charles? And what did you find out?"

Director: "Well, these tests are mostly questions and answers or little tasks for the child to do, pictures to talk about or draw . . . things like that. The tests are usually a fairly good indication of how a child compares with other children in ability to learn those things that we teach in school."

MOTHER: "What did you find out?"

DIRECTOR: "On the tasks he did for us, he performed about the way an average five-year-old boy would. On some tasks he did a little better; on others he did not do so well. Generally, however, his performance was about like a five-year-old."

MOTHER: "Why, that sounds silly. He's seven."

DIRECTOR: "Yes, I know."

MOTHER: "Who gives these tests?"

DIRECTOR: "I was the one."

MOTHER: "Of course, you were strange to Charles. He certainly would do better for someone he knows."

DIRECTOR: "That's possible. But I felt he was rather at ease. The tests are actually games to the children. He appeared rather engrossed in the tasks. He talked a lot and didn't want to leave at the end of the session."

MOTHER: "Why . . . I can't understand that. Are these tests really good?"

DIRECTOR: "They've been developed carefully with thousands of children at all ages in many parts of the country."

MOTHER: "Well, I don't know. . . ."

DIRECTOR: "Charles has an older sister, does he not?"

MOTHER: "Yes, Doris is ten."

DIRECTOR: "How would you say Charles' behavior now compares with the things Doris could do at seven?"

MOTHER: "Oh, of course Doris always has been quick. Things have come pretty easily to her. But you see, she concentrates better than the boy. She puts her mind to things. I've tried to work with him to get him to put his mind to things, but he's . . . well, he's smart enough, but he just . . . (pause) Of course, she could read some by the middle of first grade. But I guess most of the children do, too?"

DIRECTOR: "Well, many of them do."

MOTHER: "Now Charles has been something of a . . . oh, not a problem really, but he . . . well, he just can't get his mind on things."

DIRECTOR: "This has worried you?"

MOTHER: "Well . . . of course, I . . . Well, it's things like not talking very plain. When Doris was little she talked very well. I've tried to work with Charles. We all have."

DIRECTOR: "And he hasn't responded very well to your aid. That naturally causes parents concern."

MOTHER: "That's right. Sometimes I think it's because he doesn't really try. But . . . well, I guess he really does. Like the reading. We've tried to help him. He seems to know a word, but when he comes to it again, he's forgotten. . . . Would that be natural for a five-year-old?"

DIRECTOR: "Yes, that would be natural."

This excerpt from the beginning of the interview shows the guidance director's role in providing realistic information and in functioning then as a sounding board for the mother's emotional reaction to a problem she did not wish to face but apparently suspected. The fact that during this initial portion of the interview the mother appears to be taking steps toward accepting the reality of Charles' limited ability indicates that she actually has been aware of the situation but had hoped it was not true.

In her excellent discussion of "Interpreting Mental Retardation to Parents," Harriet L. Rheingold has outlined a procedure for helping parents accept the limited ability of their children. Although her article is directed mainly to psychologists who handle mentally retarded children, the general principles she outlines provide the teacher with a point of view that can be profitable in numerous interviews concerning children whose abilities are among the lowest in school.

"The interview, to be successful, should resemble closely any other therapeutic interview in which the gaining of insight is the objective. This means that the psychologist should not be, and should not allow himself to be, forced into the role of an authoritative person whose sole function is to give advice. As in all therapeutic interviews both persons — here psychologist and patient — must play active roles. The parent should feel not that he is being forced to accept what he has been told, but that he has worked in equal measure with the psychologist toward a solution of his problem. At least he should feel that having obtained a basis for action he can carry on independently.

"This interview differs in some respects from the typical therapeutic interview. The psychologist possesses information which the parent needs. This means that the parent's questions cannot be turned back upon himself at every point, although at many points they need to be. The psychologist's role is therefore the more active one. Throughout the interview he should help the parent to clarify his own feelings about his problem, but if asked a question concerning test findings, private schools, and so forth, he should give a direct answer. The attitude of the psychologist should be that of any psychotherapeutic worker—interested, sympathetic, understanding."[1]

It should be stressed that the teacher should *not* picture himself as a "therapeutic worker" like a clinical psychologist who helps markedly maladjusted persons work through their problems. However, the principles underlying the psychologist's interview techniques can aid the teacher in reporting children's progress.

Revealing IQ scores

A question that teachers constantly ask is:

"Should I tell a parent the child's IQ score? Should I show the parent such data in my folder as anecdotal records and rating scales?"

Some educators say that since the teacher is a servant of the parents and hired by them, the parents have a right to any information about their children that the school secures. Many others, however, state that parents often lack the training necessary for a proper understanding of test scores. They also contend that a parent's emotional involvement with his child can cause him to attack material gathered by the school as infringement on personal rights. These educators, therefore, feel that parents should not be handed all evaluation data about a child.

Perhaps this controversy can be placed in its proper perspective when we ask the questions that should underlie all of a teacher's decisions: *"What am I doing to this child? How will my actions affect his growth toward maturity?"* Viewed in this manner, the problem becomes not one of *parents' rights* but one of *child's rights.* The school exists for the child's good and development. Information given out by the teacher should be presented primarily in the light of its effect upon the pupil. Such a philosophy enables a teacher or administrator to decide how and when to pass on certain data to parents.

For example, a fourth-grade girl has taken a group "academic intelligence" test composed mostly of word definitions and analogies. Her score when converted to an IQ is 97. The question now is whether in the teacher-parent conference this information should

[1] Harriet L. Rheingold, "Interpreting Mental Retardation to Parents," *Journal of Consulting Psychology,* 9 (1945), 143-44. Quoted by permission of the American Psychological Association.

be given to the parent. And if so, what procedure should be followed. The teacher who understands intelligence tests knows that:

1. Group tests are usually not as valid as individual tests.
2. Such an "intelligence" test does not measure abilities in all areas of a child's personality, but, if the test is valid, will tend to measure ability to do academic schoolwork.
3. The score the girl received may change somewhat on subsequent tests and in subsequent years depending upon the girl's motivation, the test's reliability and validity, and environmental changes.

Thus, the 97 IQ the girl received is not an infallible measure of her ability to do all life tasks. Actually, it is a measure of her apparent present ability to do verbal school tasks. If this information is to be passed on to the parents, the teacher must convey its meaning in the fairest manner so that the data will not be used to the child's disadvantage.

In addition to considering what the test score means, the teacher must estimate what the parents' use of this information might be. One parent who misinterprets an IQ of 97 as being "higher than I thought . . . almost 100 per cent" may well put undue pressure on the child to do "top-notch work rather than just mediocre like she's been doing." Another parent who hears that 100 IQ is average may feel that the girl is below average and may attempt to "raise her IQ by not letting her be so lazy." A third parent, who has previously expected a great deal from the fourth grader, may realize now that the girl is really of only average academic ability and as a result the parent may more often praise the daughter's average attainments and gradually become accustomed to the idea that an average daughter is not less worthy of approval than a superior one.

In the cases of the first two parents, the teacher's report of the IQ score was detrimental to the child. In the third case, the report resulted in better parental attitudes. Consequently, when reporting information to parents, the principal or teacher must adjust the amount of data and the way it is presented to the particular parent. What the parent's attitude is toward the child and how the information will be likely to be used by the parent can often be estimated by the teacher from cumulative records and from remarks during the conference.

How might a teacher report a child's apparent ability to a typical parent who, we judge, will not misuse the information? It might be presented this way:

"From our tests and the work Carol has been doing, she is in the average range of ability for her age. When I say *ability*, I mean reasoning and reading in the fields of social studies and such. These tests are not intended to measure musical or mechanical or art abilities. Nor do they tell anything about social relationships. They just give us an estimate in the more academic types of schoolwork. In our fourth grade she has been working up to her apparent ability."

Note that the term "IQ of 97" was not mentioned. Instead, the interpretation was in language parents can understand; there was no chance for them to misinterpret a psychological term, *intelligence quotient*, and a number, 97.

Resenting evaluation data

In addition to their possibly using test results inappropriately, some parents may resent certain types of evaluation data the school collects. These data include anecdotal records that reflect a child's negative feelings for the parent, information about the home that indicates unwise handling of a child, or ratings of a child's behavior that parents would regard as a personal affront. Such information is valuable for the teacher in helping children grow toward maturity and happiness, but mothers and fathers may not want such information collected about their children. At a P.T.A. meeting on "Child Study," parents can listen with interest to the case of some child in a city remote from them and can agree that "All the material possible should be gathered to help such a boy." However, in the case of their own children, their views are understandably not so objective. Consequently, the school should keep such data confidential if the children are to be aided as much as possible and if the school is to avoid unjust criticism.

Summary

During interviews with parents, teachers commonly report student's abilities and progress in school. The teacher's aim in such interviews is not merely to report facts, but also to help the parent *accept* the report and *make plans* for the best ways school and home can aid the child's future development.

In order to carry out these tasks, the effective teacher adjusts his interview techniques to the particular parent with whom he is talking. He presents evaluation data in language that will be readily understood by a person not trained in statistics or educational procedures. He recognizes that a parent whose child is not living up to parental hopes may express negative feelings toward the school, teacher, or child. The teacher allows opportunities for such an emotionally involved mother or father to talk out such negative feelings in facing disturbing facts about the child's progress.

In deciding what types of material to report to parents and how to report them, the teacher keeps in mind: "Will this help the child grow toward maturity? Or will it cause him harm?"

Securing information about parents' attitudes

The teacher's job as an evaluator is not restricted to securing information about student progress toward school goals. He also gathers data that help him understand the interests, feelings, and problems of the pupil, for all of these affect the way the child learns. They help the teacher know the uniqueness of each pupil. This is part of what is commonly termed *understanding individual differences.*

During conferences with parents, the alert teacher can gather significant clues about the child's home life, his parents' feelings toward him, and their expectations for him. This is done best when the teacher lets parents do most of the talking. Some teachers have a distorted idea of what a parent-teacher *conference* means. They believe that if they themselves do not spend most of the conference time giving information or advice, they are not fulfilling their responsibilities as teachers. However, some of the most profitable results of a conference come from the father's or mother's talking and the teacher's listening.

Many parents will talk freely about their children. Others are shy and will need to be asked questions before they will discuss much about the pupil. Obviously, direct questions about a mother's feelings toward her daughter, such as, "Do you get angry at Mary very often?" may readily erect a barrier between teacher and mother. Other friendlier questions will usually yield indirect information about parental expectations and feelings. Each teacher will wish to develop his own stock of interview questions or remarks. The following, however, are indicative of the type that can act as a starting point for parents to discuss their children.

1. "Mrs. Smith, at home how does Harold seem to feel about his schoolwork?"
2. "Is there any way you think we could be of more help to Jane?"
3. "Mr. Kelley, we try to get parents' ideas on ways we can improve school offerings for the children. Would you have any suggestions about the kinds of things Clara is studying here and the work she has to do?"
4. "At school we are interested in what hobbies or jobs pupils carry on outside of school. Does Frank have anything special he does after school or on Saturdays?"
5. "There has been some discussion about our giving the seventh graders homework. How do you feel about homework for James?"
6. "As Phyllis is beginning first grade, we want to know as much as we can about her so that we can be of the most help. Is there anything else besides this information we've already taken down that you think we should know? About her skills or about things she has trouble with? Her likes and dislikes? What makes her especially happy or sad?"

Checking progress toward school goals

Parents often have better opportunities than teachers to observe how well pupils are succeeding in reaching certain goals of the school. Consequently, in conferences with parents the teacher may wish to ask questions concerning what changes in behavior the child shows at home as a result of schoolwork. Interviewing for this purpose is usually directive questioning, and clues to the parent's feeling toward the child are often a valuable by-product of this questioning.

Miss Solski uses conferences to help evaluate progress toward some of the goals of her fourth grade. She has chosen only four objectives about which to ask each of the parents she interviews. In terms of student behavior, these are the goals:

During or after the first semester's work the student:

1. Carries on a hobby related to a topic studied in science.
2. Reads more books and magazines than in third grade; reads a wider variety of material.
3. Uses acceptable manners. (Especially, introduces friends, asks pardon when he disturbs others.)

4. Discusses the election of local officials with a knowledge of of who is running for principal offices.

Typical questions Miss Solski asks are these:

"Mrs. Sorenson, does Ralph have any hobby such as growing plants, working with magnets, caring for fish or other pets?"

"Mrs. Mitchell, we are interested in the children's reading interests. Does Grace read much at home? What types of stories or books does she like best?"

"We have been talking in school about manners, and we would like to know if this work has any effect on the way the boys and girls act outside of school. Of course, we realize they learn manners at home, too. But have you noticed anything about Jim's asking to be excused or introducing his friends that might have resulted from our practice in school?"

"Does Janice ever talk about the local elections that are coming up next month?"

Through such questions the teacher may discover to some extent the carry-over into home life of school learning.

Although the interview is an aid in judging children's progress toward specific goals, it should not be a major element in the total evaluation program, at least in the upper grades. There are several reasons why the teacher should not count heavily on conferences for evaluating progress.

First, except in the primary grades, the teacher does not talk with the majority of parents. Even in so-called *enlightened* and *intellectual* communities where parents know the value of close school-home contact, mothers and fathers do not generally confer with teachers. (*13:54*) Consequently, the teacher is able to learn of pupil behavior at home from only some parents, not all.

Second, the teacher can confer with parents about only a few of the school's goals. Limitations of time and parent patience makes this necessary.

Third, parents may be fallible observers. Not knowing what behavior the teacher will be interested in, parents do not pay attention to, or remember, actions the teacher will ask about. In addition, the mother who is highly ambitious for her son to succeed may, either purposely or subconsciously, exaggerate or report progress that does not take place. To mark the children heavily on data reported by parents during conferences would appear to be an invalid procedure.

As a result, the teacher should use conference material only as supporting information in evaluating pupils' growth.

Summary

Teachers may use conferences with parents to carry out three tasks related to evaluation:

1. Report pupils' progress.
2. Secure data about home background and parents' attitudes toward a child.
3. Secure evidence of school learning influencing a pupil's home activities.

During a given interview the teacher may do any or all of these tasks. The amount of directiveness or nondirectiveness assumed by the teacher will depend upon which of these tasks he is carrying out, the parent's attitude, and the teacher's own interviewing ability. Much conference time can well be spent with the teacher as listener. Keeping his interviewing purposes clearly in mind should enable the teacher to derive the most from talks with parents instead of allowing the time to be wasted in rambling chatter, often unrelated to the child's welfare.

TALKING WITH STUDENTS

Reporting a student's progress to him

Most of the remarks made earlier about techniques of reporting to parents apply also in reporting to pupils. As with parents, it is not enough to report the extent of his progress to a child, but if the report is to aid him in his future growth, the student should accept it and use it in making subsequent plans. Thus, the spirit of the teacher's interview with the student should, in most cases, be a friendly one. The student usually is more likely to make adequate use of the report if he is not antagonistic toward the teacher. If the child can blame any apparent deficiencies in his progress on the teacher rather than accepting them himself, he is more likely to be satisfied with his present stage of development and not try to improve. (This assumes that the teacher actually uses appropriate methods of teaching children and of evaluating their growth. Unfortunately, it is sometimes true that the child is correct in blaming the teacher.) On the other hand, if the pupil can accept the teacher as a friend who is trying to help him develop, the report of his progress can be a useful steppingstone for their planning together his next experiences.

Although the friendly interview atmosphere probably brings about the best results in most cases, there is evidence to indicate that resistance on the part of a student does not necessarily mean that the report has failed to aid him.

"When a learning situation arouses resistance and causes discomfort because it calls upon the child to correct or to change a pose, an unrealistic idea about himself or his relationships with others which he treasures and regards as important in his total self picture, it does not mean that the learner is being perverse. Any circumstance which threatens to expose a false and unhealthy self picture is anxiety-producing. The learner will be sensitive and resistant to anything which might penetrate his false pride. He cannot help it." (*4:114*)

Thus, the resistance may be an indication that an accurate interview report is causing the student to see himself in a clearer light. The resistance may be the necessary precursor to his accepting himself and his limitations in a healthier, more realistic manner. In any case, it is well for the teacher to *try* to meet the pupil on friendly terms, although sometimes this may be made impossible by the student's need to blame the teacher or the school in attempting to defend his own deficiencies, which he is unable to face.

The progress-report interview can take various forms. The following example demonstrates one approach which, at least with some pupils, helps them regard the teacher more as a friendly but firm helper than as a bitter taskmaster. The interview concerns a fifth-grade pupil's progress in organizing a report and presenting it to the class. His latest talk before the group had been given the previous day. The interview is held while the rest of the class is doing silent recreational reading.

TEACHER: "Well, Bill, how did you feel about your talk yesterday compared to the ones you have given before? What do you think were the strong parts of your talk? Were there any things you think you would want to do differently another time?"

BILL: "Oh, I don't know exactly."

TEACHER: "Well, try to think how the talk probably went over with the other students in the class. What were some of the things you thought went well?"

BILL: "Oh . . . I was prepared. I mean, I'd looked up what I was to talk about, and I could answer the questions they asked at the end."

TEACHER: "Yes, I felt the same way about it. You knew your topic well. Anything else?"

BILL: "I didn't have to look too much at my notes. I've been trying to do that better . . . not just read it."

TEACHER: "I noticed that, too. And I noticed that you stood better. Remember how you had slouched against the blackboard before?"

BILL: "Well, I was trying to stand up straighter."

TEACHER: "Yes, it made a much better appearance for the listeners. Those were all definite improvements. You are making good progress. Now, was there anything you noticed that you would like to make further improvement with?"

BILL: "Oh . . . I don't know exactly. Well, maybe saying 'and-a.' Did I say 'and-a'?"

TEACHER: "Yes, that is one thing that you might work on next time I did notice you hooked many sentences together with 'and-a' instead of stopping one sentence, then starting the next. But that will come gradually. Perhaps you could pay special attention to that next time. Anything else?"

BILL: (pause) "No, I can't think of anything. But I guess there must have been some bad things."

TEACHER: "Oh, I wouldn't say 'bad' ones. Generally your talk was successful . . . considerable improvement over other times. There is one thing, though, which might help your next report. You might start it off by a question to challenge the class or an interesting incident to catch their attention. They weren't paying very close attention at first, although they listened well after you got into the body of your report. What incident or point was most interesting to you? If you had been sitting in the class, what part might have caught your interest first?"

BILL: "Well, the part I liked best was where the trappers made those different kinds of traps and the way they caught the different animals."

TEACHER: "Yes, I think the whole class liked that."

BILL: "But I wouldn't want to start the report like that. I wanted to tell it later."

TEACHER: "I think that's right. But is there any way you might have asked a question or given a hint at the beginning so that the class would have looked forward to that part and been interested all the way through?"

BILL: "A question?"

TEACHER: "Before you read the material, did you know how to trap a beaver or a bear?"

BILL: "No."

TEACHER: "Could you begin by asking the class some question like that, and then have them listen to your report to hear the way the frontiersmen did it?"

BILL: "Oh, you mean like . . . a . . . say, 'What kind of way would you trap a beaver or a bear . . . or a deer or a skunk? I'll tell you how it's done.' You mean like that?"

TEACHER: "Exactly. That's a very good start. With your next report, think about the beginning in the same way."

In this interview the teacher has reported the boy's progress by first having him try to evaluate himself. The instructor has done this through questioning. She compliments his improvements and, by questions, helps him discover ways he can develop the weaker areas of his talk. The interview becomes not only a report of progress but also a positive teaching technique for building the next step in the student's growth. This approach stresses self-analysis on the student's part, not teacher criticism only.

Progress-report interviews with children can be used fairly frequently for talking over students' work in specific areas, such as reading, speaking, writing, and arithmetic. Or interviews can come at the end of the term and cover all areas. The teacher's time and purposes determine how the interviews should be used.

It is well to note that the interview as a technique of reporting a student's growth to him has three strong points in its favor:

1. It provides him with an opportunity for self-analysis with the teacher's aid. This practice of accurate self-evaluation will, we hope, become a part of the pupil's life pattern and enable him to recognize his strong points and improve his weak ones in activities outside of school as well.
2. It not only informs him of his present stage of achievement but also provides an immediate opportunity for planning the next steps toward future achievement. Too often the report card is regarded as *the end,* and future plans are not built upon it. The interview should answer both questions: *Where am I?* and *What should I do about it?*
3. It provides a personal contact between student and teacher which is often lost in the impersonal printed report card that has been checked off and sent home. There is value in the student's knowing that the teacher is concerned about him as an individual. This concern and attitude of friendly help is often

conveyed in an interview where the student has an opportunity to express his ideas also.

Securing data about the student's feelings and problems

Much evidence has been collected by psychologists to indicate that a student's emotions and his problems greatly affect what he learns and how well he learns it. It is therefore part of the teacher's daily job to discover as much as possible of each pupil's unique problems and his feelings toward school, his peers, and his home. This is an evaluation task toward which the interview can contribute much.

Many of the problems and feelings that affect the child's school adjustment and progress are ones that he cannot easily talk about to others. These problems are commonly tinged with feelings of shame, guilt, and personal inferiority. In the child's efforts to appear adequate to the outside world, he has to suppress and hide these feelings under masks of bravado, wisecracks, silliness, shyness, or sneering aggression. Frequently, the underlying problems and distressing emotions could be ameliorated if unmasked and recognized in their true light. Knowing of the problems within a child, teachers can better fit their treatment and methods to the unique personality with which they deal. Thus, the teacher's jobs include learning of the often-hidden concerns that affect student progress.

Since pupils erect defenses to prevent others from recognizing weaknesses they feel within themselves, it is important that teachers follow several general rules of interviewing in order to learn of student problems and be of most help toward understanding and solving them. From the writer's observation, the teacher who best carries out this evaluation task fulfills the following criteria:

1. *He informs the students,* through discussions in class and through his conduct, that they may talk freely with him in private, that they may tell him any confidences and *he will not be shocked* and *will not tell* these confidences.
2. *He provides other types of interview situations,* such as those concerning school progress, where personal matters may also arise and be discussed without the other students in the class knowing that "Sally went into talk with Miss Benning... alone, too. She must have some problem." The student with the problem often is the one who, because of feelings of in-

adequacy, must assume the façade of a self-confident person completely able to care for himself. If the only time the teacher has student conferences is when students come with personal problems, all the rest of their classmates know of it. More data about children will be gained if no stigma is placed on talking with the teacher.

Bits of information and clues to children's feelings also can be gathered in informal discussions that accompany the day-by-day activities of the class. Conversations with the teacher as they work on the puppet show, the aquarium, the miniature frontier village, and the relief map of Britain can provide these clues.

3. *He is unshockable.* Often teachers are not tolerant of many varieties of human behavior. They have been criticized for having a too-narrow view of life and of being shocked too readily by the experiences some children have had or the feelings some children express. If the teacher is to learn innermost feelings and ideas that bother a child, he must demonstrate by his actions that he accepts the child and is not shocked by anything that is told to him. If a pupil admits being connected with the basketball-stealing episode or having masturbated in his father's garage, it is usually an indication that he has great confidence in the teacher as a true friend who can be a help. In order to divulge these hidden problems, the student has had to put aside the mask behind which he usually faces the world. If the teacher is disturbed by this view of the student's self, the mask surely will be assumed immediately and probably never lowered again in the teacher's presence. The teacher, by such behavior, can cause the student to feel: "She tricked me into telling. Then she thought I was bad. I won't get caught again like that. You can't trust teachers."
4. *He does not laugh at students' feelings and problems.* To an adult, the concerns of childhood and youth are often amusing. The problems that young people take seriously are, the adult realizes, many times ephemeral or are youthful misconceptions, not problems at all in the eyes of the world. Acne of adolescence, not being chosen on the first team, the disapproval of a teacher, *puppy love,* a feeling of being "all wrong inside" when menstruation appears early, wearing glasses, not

being invited to a picnic: all these and many other situations can become major problems for pupils. When an adult takes them lightly, the child is less apt to confide in the adult. Because the child is worried over the matter, the teacher should not laugh but should regard the child's concern seriously and help him talk through and view the matter in a more realistic manner.

5. *He encourages the pupil to talk.* Since, from the evaluation standpoint, the teacher can learn little from the student unless the student does most of the talking, a more nondirective approach is stressed.
6. *He recognizes his limitations.* The teacher is not a psychiatrist or clinical psychologist and consequently should not try to handle difficult personality problems. Often, however, the emotions and problems that concern pupils are within the normal range, and the pupils require mainly an understanding friend with whom they can talk out this difficulty. It is important that the teacher be able to function as such a friend: serious yet pleasant, unshockable, and one who can be trusted not to divulge confidences.

In cases where the teacher senses marked disturbance or a major problem, it is proper to "divulge confidences" to the proper authorities, such as the county psychologist or the school guidance director. The principle governing the proper time to tell confidential matters is found in the questions: "What will this do to the child? Will this help him become more mature and happier in the long run?"

Obviously, most of the gossip about their pupils that some teachers spread among their colleagues or people in the community is inexcusable. Such student confidences as are broadcast over a community rumor network can do much damage to the students.

Checking progress toward school goals

Interviews are commonly used by teachers for judging pupils' growth toward specific objectives, such as the ability to discuss a recreational-reading book or to speak clearly in conversation. The nature of such interviews makes them teacher-directed. Usually the student answers questions that are asked to sample the student's ability. For this type of interview to yield the most useful information, it is well for the teacher to have questions prepared ahead of time and to have a method of recording the results. The method of recording may vary from a check list or rating scale of the pupil's performance to an anecdotal record of his success. Whether the check list is used during the interview or whether it is not marked until later depends upon the effect the teacher believes such a grading device would have on the pupil's feelings and performance.

Summary

Teachers use the interview as a technique in evaluation with the student when they:

1. Report his progress to the student.
2. Secure information about the way he feels toward himself, his home, his peers, and the school.
3. Secure evidence of the extent to which he has reached particular school goals.

During a single interview more than one of these tasks may be performed. Informal and spontaneous conversations before or after school, during work on class projects, on field trips, or during art periods may function as interviews through which valuable data about the student may be secured.

OBJECTIVES OF THIS CHAPTER

The effective elementary or junior high teacher:

1. Uses the interview for reporting student progress to parents and the student.
2. Uses the interview with parents to secure information about their attitudes toward, and their treatment of, children.
3. Uses the interview with students for securing information concerning their problems and feelings about themselves, their families, their peers, and the school.
4. Uses the interview with parents for securing data about the extent to which school learning is carried over into behavior at home.
5. Uses the interview with students for judging how well they have reached school goals.
6. Adopts the degree of directiveness or nondirectiveness that appears most appropriate to each interview situation.

Suggested evaluation technique for this chapter

1. Worth-while practice in interviewing can be secured by the use of sociodramas. One person can play the role of the teacher, another can be the parent or student. They should first define

the problem around which the interview is developed or the type of evaluation function the teacher intends the interview to play. The parent or student should define the role or point-of-view he will take toward the school and teacher at the beginning of the conference. Then the sociodrama interview begins. Each participant must take the situation seriously and try to play the role defined for his particular character. When taken seriously, the sociodrama interview yields worth-while results. When regarded as a silly procedure, the sociodrama becomes a farce, signifying nothing. The following are suggested situations around which such make-believe interviews may develop.

a. At a P.T.A. parents' night the mother and father of Jane Latimore talk with Jane's third-grade teacher. The parents are disturbed about the girl's grade of C in science. They believe her notebook on nature study was very well done at home. They contend that a neighbor boy who received B had help with his notebook "and still it wasn't as good." The teacher wishes to show that the grade was not based entirely on the notebook.
b. Larry Carpenter, an eighth grader, had been doing satisfactory work until midyear, at which time he neglected to complete assignments and he often read comic books when other work was to be done. The teacher, who has been discussing each student's work with him in a personal interview, has now come around to Larry. The interview takes place during the lunch period.
c. Mrs. Klein has come to school to talk with Janice's fifth-grade teacher about "these achievement tests she says she took last week." Mrs. Klein indicates that she is a college graduate and thus knows something about tests. Her daughter, Janice, has made the following percentile scores (compared with the other 114 fifth graders in the school):

Arithmetic Computation	58
Arithmetic Reasoning	41
Reading Comprehension	43
Reading Speed	51
Social Studies Facts	46

Mrs. Klein is a mother who expects her children to do quite well in school because "they have a good background."

After performing such sociodramas as suggested above, it is well for the participants and audience (if there is one) to evaluate the strong and weak elements of the interviews.

SUGGESTED READINGS

1. DAVIS, FRANK G., and NORRIS, PEARLE S. *Guidance Handbook for Teachers.* New York: McGraw-Hill Book Co., Inc. 1949.
2. ERICKSON, CLIFFORD E. *The Counseling Interview.* New York: Prentice-Hall, Inc., 1950.
3. FENTON, NORMAN. *The Counselor's Interview with the Student.* Stanford, Calif.: Stanford University Press, 1943.
4. JERSILD, ARTHUR T. *In Search of Self.* New York: Teachers College, Columbia University, 1952.
5. RHEINGOLD, HARRIET L. "Interpreting Mental Retardation to Parents," in Robert I. Watson, ed., *Readings in the Clinical Method in Psychology.* New York: Harper and Brothers, 1949.
6. ROGERS, CARL R. *Counseling and Psychotherapy.* Boston: Houghton Mifflin Co., 1942.
7. SNYDER, WILLIAM U. "A Short-Term Nondirective Treatment of an Adult," in Robert I. Watson, ed., *Readings in the Clinical Method in Psychology.* New York: Harper and Brothers, 1949.
8. SNYDER, WILLIAM U. "Dr. Thorne's Critique of Nondirective Psychotherapy," in Robert I. Watson, ed., *Readings in the Clinical Method in Psychology.* New York: Harper and Brothers, 1949.
9. STRANG, RUTH. *The Role of the Teacher in Personnel Work.* New York: Teachers College, Columbia University, 1946.
10. THORNE, FREDERICK C. "A Critique of Nondirective Methods of Psychotherapy," in Robert I. Watson, ed., *Readings in the Clinical Method in Psychology.* New York: Harper and Brothers, 1949.
11. WILLCUTT, GLADYS. "Informal Talks with Children and Parents," in *Fostering Mental Health in Our Schools.* Association for Supervision and Curriculum Development. 1950 Yearbook. Washington, D. C.: National Education Association, 1950.
12. WITMER, HELEN LELAND, ed. *Psychiatric Interviews with Children.* New York: The Commonwealth Fund, 1946.
13. WRINKLE, WILLIAM L. *Improving Marking and Reporting Practices.* New York: Rinehart and Co., 1947.

PART IV

Seeing the Over-all Program

PART IV CONSIDERS THE OVER-ALL EVALUATION PROGRAM FROM TWO viewpoints. First, the students' part in evaluation is inspected in Chapter 16. Then the entire year's program, viewed in relation to objectives and teaching methods, is inspected for three typical grade levels and classrooms in Chapter 17.

CHAPTER

16

Developing Students' Evaluation Skills

By spending one entire day visiting Mr. Payne's fifth-grade class, we are able to see pupils involved in the following evaluation activities:

During arithmetic study the pupils work textbook problems in subtracting fractions. The teacher circulates around the room to observe any mistakes they are making and to help them correct misunderstandings and errors in computing. The students who finish early are asked to create problems involving addition or subtraction of fractions. These problems are to be ones that could occur in their own lives. Later some are read to the rest of the class, and everyone works them out.

In recent weeks most of the class's social-studies and science learnings have centered around a study of transportation, past and present. Since they are nearing the completion of this study, the pupils are involved in a number of activities that summarize their learning. One consists of preparing for a test over (1) the ways inventions have changed transportation and (2) the ways changes in methods of transportation have altered people's ways of living. Yesterday the teacher and students listed on the blackboard the main objectives and subject matter this test would cover. Each group of objectives was assigned to a different group of students, who worked individually in creating questions aimed at these learnings. Today the class is using these questions to review for the test the teacher will give early next week. Each student reads two of his questions for his classmates to answer. In this way they have organized the review to be somewhat like a television quiz program, but with the audience volunteering the answers. An occasional argument arises about an ambiguous question or about whether a question is truly aimed at one of the objectives. However, rather than detracting from the learning situation, these disagreements seem to focus student interest more sharply on the objectives of the coming test and on distinctions between good and poor answers.

Another summarizing activity is the creation of a time-line mural tracing the growth of transportation over the past three centuries. The mural is to be painted with poster colors on a long roll of wide newsprint and hung in the corridor outside the classroom. Several days ago the teacher led a class discussion during which the pupils decided what type of mural they might have and what its contents would be. Two students were commissioned to prepare a plan for the mural. Before school today they sketched the general outlines of their plan on the side blackboard. During the middle of the morning they explain their plan, and it is revised in light of suggestions made by other class members. The revisions concern (1) which groups of students will be assigned to paint different sections, (2) how air, land, and sea transportation should be separated on the painting, and (3) what legend should accompany the mural. After this evaluation of the plan, student committees are selected to work later on different sections of the time line.

For fifteen minutes the class takes a final spelling test over words they have studied during the week. On tryout tests earlier in the week the pupils corrected their own papers, but for the final test they hand their papers in to be corrected by the teacher.

The day's music activity consists of the class's singing "The Erie Canal," a song learned during their study of the development of transportation. The teacher first has the class sing it through once while he tape-records it. Then, before playing the recording, he leads a discussion during which he helps the pupils list criteria they can use for judging ways they might improve their presentation of the song. These criteria include: "Sing in tune, everyone start and stop together, sing the words clearly, and make interesting variations in the loudness and speed." After they listen to the recording and make suggestions for improvement, the students practice the song twice more and then record it in the improved version.

Several days ago each pupil completed a story about a travel adventure involving one of the forms of transportation they have been studying. Mr. Payne had collected these fiction adventures to see how successful they had been. Today he asks several students to read their tales aloud so that their classmates can enjoy what they have created. He suggests that after each pupil's story the others may wish to make comments. He indicates that the comments should not be faultfinding, because when people have created stories they might be embarrassed by others saying uncomplimentary things about them. In this way the teacher tries to stress making comments which draw attention to strong elements of the stories, such as the way a student author has included much action to make his story interesting. The teacher has set these ground rules because he believes that negative remarks, even when true, soon kill the creative attempts of the budding author.

After several stories have been read, Mr. Payne passes all the tales back to their owners. He says that he feels today is a good time for everybody to inspect his own handwriting and to decide in what ways he has improved recently and in what ways he still needs to improve. He suggests this plan: After lunch each pupil is to underline the letters in his story that he thinks cannot be read easily. Then he is to consult a neighboring student to see if his neighbor agrees with his selection of illegible letters and to see if the neighbor can find additional letters that are difficult to read. Then each pupil is to practice writing the words containing these letters until he and his partner agree they are easily read. A chart of sample handwriting at the side of the room serves as a guide to improve legibility. As this activity continues, the teacher moves around the room, offering encouragement and suggestions about posture or about the position of the paper on the desk. Students who need little or no improvement can read or complete unfinished work.

Sometimes the class has reading experiences in the morning, but today they are reading early in the afternoon. While the teacher meets with about a third of the class which has not advanced as rapidly as the others in reading, the rest of the students read a story individually. After the individuals have finished their reading they are to make up questions about the content of the story and select a nearby classmate who is expected to answer these questions. Thus by the end of the lesson the individual readers have become whispering pairs that quiz each other over the story.

Meanwhile, Mr. Payne is working with the group of less advanced readers near the front of the room. For today's work they have three principal objectives: (1) to comprehend the main ideas and details of their story, (2) to locate new words and look them up in the dictionary, selecting from the meanings there the one that best fits in this story, and (3) to remember the meanings of the new words. In beginning the work, Mr. Payne writes on the blackboard sentences containing the words he thinks might be strange to the students, and asks for opinions about their meanings. Some students offer ideas. Then each one uses a dictionary to locate the words and to decide which meaning (if more than one is given) best fits in the sentence. In this way the teacher evaluates the pupils' present knowledge of word meanings and also observes their abilities in using dictionaries. After reading the story, the pupils answer Mr. Payne's questions about people and events in it. Thus he learns something of their reading comprehension. Then he asks everyone to write a series of sentences, each sentence using one or more of the new words. This gives them additional practice with the new terms and also helps measure their understanding of the words. While these pupils work on the sentences, the teacher visits briefly with each of the students who have been reading individually. In this way he learns how well their whispered quizzing has worked out. And he adds a few questions of his own about the story.

Later in the afternoon, during physical education, the boys play kickball while the girls learn relay games. In both of these situations the physical education instructors observe the students' performance and offer encouragement and suggestions for improving their skills.

THE STUDENT'S ROLE IN EVALUATING

As suggested by the example of Mr. Payne's pupils, in a typical class many kinds of evaluation can be used each day to improve the quality of teaching and learning. We have observed here that teaching method and evaluation go hand in hand. We have also seen that evaluating student progress is not a task for the teacher alone but is best carried out by both teacher and students. Sometimes the teacher can most efficiently do the judging himself, but at other times it is best to include the students so that they will become better able to appraise their own work and constantly be aware of their own progress.

It is the purpose of this chapter to inspect more closely the role students can play in evaluating their own progress and that of their class. Our discussion will treat ways that pupils can take part in (1) *defining goals*, (2) *constructing* evaluation devices, (3) *using* evaluation techniques, and (4) appraising the effectiveness of *teaching methods* and the *teacher himself*.

STUDENTS HELP DEFINE GOALS

Among today's educators there is no complete agreement about what role, if any, students should play in setting school learning objectives. Some people think the teacher or the school should set all goals. Others, at the opposite extreme, apparently believe the students should set the goals. Many other people hold an opinion somewhere between these two poles. But we should not assume that most educators stand on a middle ground on this issue. After observing many classrooms in operation, you see that most teachers in practice are at or near the "teacher-determines-objectives" end. Only a rare few will, in actual practice, be at the Rousseauan "child-determines-objectives" end.

Arguments for and against students defining goals

The strongest argument in favor of student participation in goal setting is that *people work hardest toward their own goals*. It is commonly agreed among psychologists that the driving forces behind human actions are human needs, such as needs for food, affection, or recognition. The goals a person chooses to strive for are the ones he thinks will satisfy his needs. Often, in order to reach an objective he must learn a new skill or acquire new information. He will go to the bother of learning only if he is convinced the effort will pay off in satisfaction. The school, in guiding pupils' learning, must recognize these psychological truths. The teaching-learning situation in a classroom is a most happy one when the teacher's goals are identical with the students'. Of course, this is not always the case. Teacher and students can be aiming in different directions. When this is the case the teacher has several choices of action, namely:

1. to convince the pupil that the learning the teacher proposes will actually improve the pupil's life and meet important needs;
2. to entice the pupil with other rewards (such as getting out of homework or receiving a gold star) if the pupil learns what the teacher wants him to learn;
3. to threaten the pupil with a punishment (like staying after school) if he does not learn what the teacher wishes;

4. to postpone striving for the teacher's objective until the pupil is mature enough to see its worth and will voluntarily work toward it;
5. to abandon the teacher's goal and adopt one that the pupil himself selects, or
6. to teach away, and let the student sink or swim.

In cases where the teacher entices or threatens the pupil, the resulting learning may be only temporary, may not ever be used in the pupil's life, or may be so tainted with strong antagonistic feelings that its intended worth is destroyed.

Supporters of student participation in goal setting also state that by taking part in defining the aims pupils are much *more likely to understand where they are headed* than when the teacher determines the goals alone. In addition, they argue, *pupils may suggest very desirable objectives* that had not occurred to the teacher.

On the opposite side of this issue, critics of student participation in goal setting marshal the following support for their stand:

1. *Pupils are too immature for such responsibility.* The reason children need schooling is because they lack the maturity, experience, knowledge, and skills of an adult. How, then, can they be expected to make wise decisions about so complex a problem as what it is best to learn? How can they decide for themselves the best ways to meet their complex needs and responsibilities in a very complicated world?

2. *Education focuses not only on meeting the pupil's present needs but also on his future ones.* Since they understand little of the past and of cause and effect, children cannot predict the future well. And even when they can set up desirable long-range aims, it is often difficult for them voluntarily to work hard on currently difficult tasks for the sake of the far-distant reward. They need adults to set future goals and provide intermediate rewards that keep them striving toward the ultimate objective.

3. *A roomful of children, each setting his own goals, is difficult to direct.* Working with one child who designs his own objectives is something of a challenge, but a teacher with thirty-five with somewhat different goals in mind has the possibility of chaos at hand.

4. *Students seek orientation to their complex world. They seek stimulus from adults.* Children's interests are not limited to projects of their own creation. They seek stimuli from outside. After a science

teacher demonstrated how to make a simple electric motor and a radio, his students exhibited appetites for more of these kinds of activities. If the teacher had not chosen the goals in this instance, the possibilities of building motors and radios might never have occurred to the class.

It is apparent that there is virtue on both sides of this issue of student-participation-in-goal-setting. Each teacher must decide what his own practice will be in his own classroom. By looking at the following examples we will see the extent to which four teachers included pupils in this first step of the evaluation process: stating objectives.

FOUR INSTANCES OF GOAL SETTING

Speech and arithmetic in first grade

Each morning shortly after class begins, pupils in a first-grade class gather in a semicircle around the teacher and take turns standing before the group to talk briefly. The teacher does not select the topics the children bring up. Instead, each pupil tells his classmates about anything that has interested him: a trip with his family, a pet rabbit, a new dress his mother bought, a funny dream, a television show, or Uncle Fred's error of sitting on a lady's lap in the dark movie theater. The teacher uses this "circle-time" to help children (1) speak with confidence before a group, (2) tell incidents in an understandable sequence, (3) enunciate clearly, and (4) (for the listeners) listen to others tell an incident and be able to ask pertinent questions about it. Because these speech objectives can be realized despite the topic the child talks about, the pupils are free to select their own subjects.

However, the same is not true of the children's arithmetic study. Here the teacher judges that it is most profitable for her to choose not only the skill goals (ability to count, to write numbers, to remember simple addition and subtraction facts) but also for her to select which number facts they study on a given day.

Hence the children are less free in choosing arithmetic topics than they are in choosing speech topics. The teacher believes children are mature enough to select incidents they might talk about. But she thinks they do not understand enough about the learning of arithmetic to choose wisely which combinations are easiest to learn first or to know how it is best to learn the relationship between adding and subtracting.

Year's goals in a fifth grade

At the beginning of school in September a fifth-grade teacher talked with the class about things they would be learning during the year. She described briefly, and listed on the board, some of the skills and kinds of information that the school had planned for fifth graders to learn. Then she suggested that, in addition to these objectives, the students themselves probably had ways in which they would like to improve and things they would like to learn about. In this discussion several other aims arose, some shared by many pupils and others more specific to the interests of individuals. For example, one goal many shared was a desire to learn some folk dances which the pupils had seen upper-grade students perform in an assembly program. One boy wanted to learn about stamp collecting, an interest shared by only a few. The teacher added these to the list on the blackboard. Then each pupil copied the goals shared by everyone on a page of his notebook and added aims more specifically his own. Periodically during the year the pupils would pause to judge their progress toward each objective.

The teacher thought this procedure had three desirable features: (1) it enabled everyone to discuss and better understand the directions in which they would be headed during the year, (2) it enabled pupils to suggest some objectives for the class and for themselves individually, and (3) it gave pupils a basis for later evaluating their own school progress.

Two general-science classes

In an eighth-grade class the teacher began the school year by talking with the students about different kinds of questions that science helps people answer, such as: When did dinosaurs live? Why does an airplane fly? How can you make water run uphill? What kinds of meals are best for athletes?

Then he had the students themselves spend a day locating other science questions that especially interested them. During a class discussion they combined these lists of problems into groups of questions that were related to each other. For instance, questions relating to fire or combustion were placed in one group, those relating to weather in another, and so forth. By vote they determined which group of questions interested them most, which next, and so on until they had made a priority list of the groups. In this way the students themselves, with only general guidance from the teacher, selected the subject-matter goals they would work toward.

The next step consisted of a class discussion during which they attacked the first group of questions. They tried to suggest methods they might use to find good answers. When he thought the pupils were being too limited in suggesting only that they look in books, the teacher offered some ideas about experiments and observations they might carry out. Then the labor was divided up so that some class members read in library books and took notes to report to the class, others did simple experiments at home to report later, and still others worked with the teacher in performing demonstrations and experiments in class. After their reading and experimenting, the class tried to draw conclusions about what they had learned, to judge the strengths and weaknesses of their methods of investigation, and to suggest practical applications of what they had learned.

Four beliefs underlay this teacher's plan to give students opportunities to choose what they would study in science: (1) The chief goal of the class is not to learn specific lists of facts but is: "The students learn scientific methods of investigating and how to draw appropriate conclusions from investigations." (2) The actual subject matter the students study does not matter so much as their learning methods of science that can be applied to any kind of problem. (3) By the end of the year student interests will naturally have ranged over so many areas of science that a true *general*-science course will have been covered despite the lack of prescribed topics. (4) Students will be more interested in questions they themselves conceive than in questions the teacher might pose.

In contrast with this class, a second general-science teacher outlined the subject matter that would be covered each week, so that by the end of the year the class had learned something about each of a specified variety of fields, such as electricity, levers, space travel, and so forth. He did not have the students choose the areas they would study, because he did not want to take a chance on their missing out on learning something about each prescribed area. Although in this class the pupils did simple experiments and talked some about scientific methods, the course consisted chiefly of learning facts that already had been discovered by scientists and published in textbooks, rather than stressing methods of investigation and ways of appraising these methods.

From time to time, however, students would bring up science questions that had been precipitated by something in their daily lives and were not related to the topic the class was currently studying. The teacher usually took some class time to discuss these, but generally they concentrated on the preplanned topics. To this limited extent, students presented some of the goals.

Summary of goal setting

In the examples above we have seen how four teachers determined the teacher-student relationship in goal setting. In each case the teacher allotted as much responsibility to pupils as he thought was appropriate for the maturity of the students, the kinds of objectives the class was to pursue, and the teacher's ideas about the ways people learn efficiently in school.

STUDENTS DEVELOP EVALUATION TECHNIQUES

Although it is chiefly the job of the teacher, not the pupils, to develop appraisal techniques, students often can make some contribution in this area. For instance, they can help decide what methods are best for evaluating their current learning. They can help develop test items, rating scales, and check lists. They can judge their own work and write self-analyses.

There are three principal advantages to such student participation. It helps focus their attention more precisely on the objectives they are to pursue. It helps them develop ways of evaluating themselves so that they can learn to make better judgments to their own progress without the aid of teacher or parents. It sometimes provides the teacher with new ideas for evaluating pupils' work.

In Mr. Payne's class at the beginning of the chapter we saw students involved in creating and using several different evaluation devices. In some cases they developed these techniques *on their own* with only general direction from the teacher, such as:

1. The faster workers in arithmetic created problems to show their understanding of life applications of arithmetic and to test their classmates' understanding.
2. All class members made up questions to review what they had learned about transportation.
3. During a reading session the students who worked individually made up questions to ask a partner about the content of the story.

In other cases the *pupils and teacher worked together* in developing and using an evaluation technique, such as:

1. Through discussion they appraised the mural plan submitted by two students.
2. They devised criteria for an effective presentation of "The Erie Canal" and used these for judging the recording of their singing.
3. Students judged their own and each other's handwriting, using legibility and the samples on the handwriting chart as their standards. The teacher also aided in this evaluation.
4. Students were encouraged to comment on their classmates' short stories.

(Still other techniques of appraisal were administered *primarily by the teacher*. Students were involved only as the objects of the appraisal, such as with the spelling test, the oral questions of the group's reading, observations of students' use of the dictionary, the assignment of sentences to write involving newly learned words, and observations by the physical education teachers to appraise the pupils' kickball and relay skills.)

Examples of student participation

The ways pupils can take part in these kinds of evaluation activities at levels other than the fifth grade may become clearer when we inspect the following examples:

Student-created tests

Students usually are not skilled enough in constructing tests to do a good job of contributing many valid items for a formal type of examination, such as a mimeographed arithmetic quiz in the fourth grade or a history test in the junior high. But often their test items are good for review purposes. Even when the items are not sufficiently clear or well enough directed at the desired goals, the questions precipitate desirable discussion that focuses attention on the real goals and on appropriate answers. Here are two further instances of the use of student-created questions.

In a second grade during the introduction of number facts ($4 + 6$, $10 - 4$, and $10 - 6$) the pupils first worked problems with the aid of beads on a string. Then they tried oral problems that the teacher posed, like: "If I have ten pencils in this box, and each of these four children borrows a pencil, how many are left?" After trying a few of these, pupils took turns at the front of the room making up other lifelike examples of these facts and ones learned on preceding days. After each child presented his problem and a classmate answered it, the classmate had a turn to present a problem.

A seventh-grade class was divided into committees to study the main contributions that people of different nations had made to American culture. Each committee was responsible for one or more nations. After a week's study, the groups reported their findings to their classmates. Following its report, each committee asked twenty true-false or fill-in questions which their classmates wrote answers for and then discussed. This served as a summary of the report, as an additional stimulus for the class to listen well, and as a method for each student to appraise immediately his understanding of the report.

Personal reports

As the year progresses, it is possible for upper-grade students to inspect a list of the behavioral goals they have been striving toward. For each goal, a pupil can write a brief statement of what progress, or lack of progress, he thinks he has made. Later, in an interview with the teacher, the student's report can be compared with the teacher's own evaluation of his progress toward these goals. This interview can become a session for pupil-teacher planning of the most desirable steps for the student to take next in improving himself.

In the lower grades, where the children cannot write out self-analyses, the teacher may wish only to call each child aside privately and chat with him while the rest of the pupils are working on individual tasks at their seats. In this case, the children are told ahead of time what the conference is about, and the goals they have been pursuing are listed on the board or on a chart so they can think about each one before talking with the teacher.

Rating scales and check lists

Especially in the upper grades, pupils can help develop check lists or rating scales for self-analysis. By creating the scale through class discussion, the students are well aware of the meaning of each item on the scale because each has been talked over thoroughly. Topics appropriate for such student-teacher planning of scales and check lists include (1) fair play or good sportsmanship, (2) school citizenship, (3) skill in presenting a report to the class, (4) oral reading skill, (5) arithmetic number facts already mastered, (6) balanced diets, (7) oral storytelling, (8) group projects such as skits, bulletin-board displays, murals, model displays, (9) participation in group work, (10) posture and personal grooming, and (11) individual work products such as models, tools, or machines created as industrial art activities, or collections and displays of such things as rocks, insects, stamps, or postmarks.

To open a discussion aimed at planning these evaluation devices, the teacher often will find this kind of approach successful: "Now we've decided that each of our five committees will build a model of a different type of Indian village to show how Indians made different kinds of homes depending on their surroundings and the part of the country they lived in. Before we start the models, let's think of the ways we finally will judge whether each of the villages is well built or not. That is, what's the difference between a well-built model and a poorly built one?"

If the students do not immediately understand how to suggest criteria, the teacher may start them off with one, such as: "The people, buildings, trees, and fences should be made about the right proportion to each other—so people should not be larger than their tepees." Other ideas will then likely come from the class, such as criteria focusing on authenticity of the village layout, appropriate labeling of the display, use of modeling materials that simulate the actual life material (like twigs for logs, a piece of glass with blue paper under it for a lake). These criteria then can be organized into a check list which guides the students' planning of their models and can be used by the groups at the end of the project for judging their villages.

Participation charts

For group discussions in upper grades, one pupil can be assigned to chart the contributions of his fellow group members. He should not be expected to be an active participant, for the charting is usually enough of a task itself. After the meeting each student can look at the chart and understand more clearly the part he has played in the group.

STUDENTS USE READY-MADE INSTRUMENTS

In addition to helping develop appraisal techniques, students may also use instruments provided by the teacher. These may be teacher-made or ones from the central school office or from a commercial publisher. Here are some examples:

Workbooks and textbooks often have self-test items which pupils complete on their own and then correct themselves.

More individualized spelling work may be carried on in upper grades when one student quizzes a partner over a list of words which the partner, with the teacher's aid, has collected as his own special spelling stumbling blocks.

When standardized test batteries are administered at the beginning of the year in upper grades, it is sometimes profitable for each student, with teacher help, to develop a test-result profile that shows his status in various areas. This provides a basis for individual pupil-teacher planning of the kinds of stress the student's efforts may need that year. Then at the end of the semester or year, if the student takes a comparable form of the same test he can superimpose the year-end results on the sheet to form a new profile indicating his year's progress in the tested skills. (Needless to say, before embarking on such a plan, the teacher must be able to estimate the way pupils will be affected by seeing their test results on the profile. In light of this estimate he must determine whether the plan would do more mental health harm than good for some of the students—particularly the less apt. In addition, it must be clear before this is attempted that the achievement test is a valid one for the particular class.)

Students can also judge themselves on check lists and rating scales provided by the teacher.

Some teachers find it desirable to give each student a copy of the school report-card form (perhaps only a mimeographed version) which the pupil fills out as a judgment of his own progress during the past reporting period. The teacher then compares the student's self-judgment with his own, and they talk over any marked discrepancies.

STUDENTS JUDGE THE TEACHER AND HIS METHODS

There is a good deal of disagreement about whether students are capable of making valid judgments of their teacher's worth. On one side of the argument are educators who do not trust student opinion, and to support their stand they recall a teacher in their own childhood who "was tough on us and I didn't like her at the time, but now I realize that I learned a lot in her class." On the other side we hear supporters of student evaluations say, "Who knows better than the pupils how effective a teacher is? They sit in judgment several hours a day. And they usually know whether they are progressing or not."

Since no answer is completely convincing to all teachers, each must make his own decision about the value of student opinions. He must base his practice on an estimate of how mature his students are, how much information they have about the question at hand, and how brave he himself is.

Although elementary and junior high pupils are not able to offer as careful insights as the university student, many teachers have found that they too can give helpful answers to certain kinds of questions. Here are three approaches to soliciting student opinions in middle and upper grades.

Questions about method

In a fifth-grade class at the end of a month's study of *The Earth and Its Surface,* the teacher asked:

"What activities did you like best during this study?" After pupils expressed opinions and told why they preferred certain activities, the teacher continued the discussion with these queries: "What activity did you think you learned most from? It could be the one you liked best, or perhaps it was some other. If we were to start over again to study about the earth, how do you think we might change our activities so we would learn more or enjoy it more?"

With this approach the class focused on the methods, not directly on the teacher. Thus they could be franker and more objective in their evaluations than if they recognized that negative comments were really criticisms of the teacher. The teacher, in the role of methodologist, was therefore being appraised in a slightly indirect, face-saving way.

Open-ended questions

A second approach suitable for the junior high involves writing three or four general questions on the blackboard: "What have you liked about this class? What have you disliked about it? What would you like to have changed? What have you not learned so far that you would like to learn soon?"

The students are asked to write answers to each question. They are told not to sign their names, for the teacher does not want them to be afraid to put down their real opinions. The papers pupils turn in typically contain opinions covering a variety of aspects of the class, including the room lighting, a bothersome classmate, an activity that was especially enjoyable, the teacher's manner, the testing and report-card systems, and the difficulties pupils have reading the textbooks. Therefore, the teacher gains information about the social atmosphere of the class, teaching materials, and his evaluation techniques as well as about himself personally.

The teacher's report card

A third approach suited to upper-grade levels consists of the teacher's asking for a direct judgment of her as an individual. She may introduce the proposal in this manner:

"Each nine weeks I make out a report card for you. Part of the reason is to help you understand yourself better. Often we can see our own strong points and weak points better when somebody else gives us a carefully thought-out opinion of us. I would like you to help me understand myself and my way of teaching better by learning what you think. So I have mimeographed a little check list here which I hope you will read carefully. Then put an X in the space beside any opinion you agree with. Don't write your name on it. But if you have any other opinions besides the ones you mark, please write them on the back. Please do it carefully so it will be a real help to me."

Obviously, it takes a more daring soul to launch this scheme than it does to use the first approach mentioned above. But it can provide some helpful insights for the instructor. For instance, one eighth-grade teacher was trying a new technique for stimulating better critical thinking on controversial topics. Often, when a student gave an opinion in class, the teacher pursued the student with a series of questions that probed the weak spots in the argument. In this way the instructor hoped to make pupils more careful in marshaling evidence to support their opinions. But it was not until he had the students fill out anonymous evaluations of him that he learned that his new approach was interpreted by them as biting sarcasm. Numbers of students who had formerly liked the class now dreaded coming to be pinned down with sarcastic questions. This evaluation surprised and disturbed the instructor. But he was convinced the criticism was a valid one, since so many pupils had written it. As a result, he explained to the class what his intentions had been, said he was sorry he had been misunderstood, and thereafter adopted a more kindly approach to probing weaknesses in students' statements.

But not all student evaluations offer negative opinions. Many consist of compliments that encourage the teacher to continue his current practices.

OBJECTIVES OF THIS CHAPTER

The effective elementary or junior high teacher:

1. Encourages students to help state objectives when the teacher judges such an activity will enhance their learning.
2. Encourages students to evaluate their own progress by using appraisal techniques developed by themselves and the teacher, such as: tests, rating scales, autobiographies, participation charts, report cards, and interviews with the teacher.
3. Encourages students to evaluate the teaching-learning methods and materials used by the class.

Suggested evaluation techniques for this chapter

1. Construct a rating scale or check list which students might use to evaluate their own progress in: (*a*) health practices in the home, (*b*) school citizenship, or (*c*) personal work habits in school.
2. Develop a set of criteria which a student committee might use for judging a bulletin board it has constructed. Describe how this scale or these criteria would be used.
3. Interview three elementary or junior high teachers to discover what role students play in evaluating their progress in these teachers' classrooms. Compare your results with those of others who have made a similar survey.

CHAPTER

17

Planning the Year Realistically

IN VIEWING SPECIFIC EVALUATION DEVICES closely, as has been done in Chapters 3 through 14, there is the danger that the over-all plan and purpose of an evaluation program can be lost among the details of techniques. Consequently, the purpose of this final chapter is to show how specific techniques are organized to form an effective over-all judgment of students' progress throughout the school year.

Three representative grade levels have been chosen: grades 1, 4, and 7. For each of these grades we have outlined goals that are typically chosen for children to work toward. Then the general methods the teacher plans to use during the year to help children reach these goals are indicated. Finally, the evaluation techniques which the teacher feels are most *efficient* and *practical* for judging the students' growth are listed. By having such a general outline at the beginning of the year, the teacher can know ahead of time what types of data to collect throughout the year so as best to aid the children and report their success accurately.

The goals selected for these three sample grades are called *typical* ones. They do not represent any particular *traditional* or any special *pioneering* educational philosophy. They are the types found in most schools today. Such middle-of-the-road objectives have been selected because the intention here is to demonstrate how modern evaluation techniques can aid the teacher in the typical American classroom.

In the form indicated here, some of the objectives are more specific than others. For example, in the first-grade list under "Social Living and Health," the goal of "listens when it is time for others to speak" is more specific than "complies with school safety rules." In actual use, the school rules would have to be spelled out more specifically. It is seen, therefore, that these sample lists of objectives for the three grades are not definitive.

The objectives also differ in their degree of importance in a child's development, and they differ in the amount of time a teacher would spend helping children reach them. For instance, in the first grade "works and plays well with others" is a more complex and more important objective than "washes hands before eating." In evaluating a child's growth, the teacher would wish to spend more time in securing a complete appraisal of the former objective.

The question of individual differences among children in their abilities to reach the objectives naturally arises when lists of goals for specific grade levels are proposed. Consequently, in examining the following sample objectives we must realize that they are stated as *typical* ones for average children in those grades. Because of their varied talents and varied maturational speeds, children will succeed to different degrees in reaching these goals. The goals will be expanded for the more capable. The less capable will often be working on objectives their classmates have already met. Just because goals are stated for a grade does not mean that all children must achieve them at the same time or on the same level in order to be worthy class members. Instead, it means that these are goals or developmental tasks children ordinarily work toward at these age levels. The evaluation devices are used to tell teacher, child, and parents the extent of the pupil's progress. It is expected that teachers and parents will interpret the child's progress according to his own abilities and opportunities to succeed.

Before we inspect the chart of objectives, a question posed in Chapter 2 should again be asked: "Is this chart supposed to be the teacher's plan for the year?"

Yes, it is a general overview of the teacher's job for the year. But, *no,* the chart is not a statement of the *sequence* in which the teacher will take up the year's work. The chart is a method of stating clearly (1) objectives in terms of student behavior, (2) general methods to be used, and (3) the types of evaluation devices desired.

For convenience, objectives within the chart have been divided into several areas, such as reading, arithmetic, and social living.

These are arbitrary divisions. It is understood that learning, like our daily lives, is not separated into several categories. Therefore, even though the goals are separated here for convenience, we realize that in the classroom work they overlap and intertwine.

A YEAR'S PLAN IN FIRST GRADE

OBJECTIVES After his experiences in first grade the child:	METHODS The teacher:	EVALUATION Techniques used for judging progress toward objectives:
LANGUAGE ARTS—READING		
Reads simple material silently and answers questions about it.	Divides class into 3 groups according to reading-readiness. Has children in each group read twice daily, progressing from readiness books to preprimers and primers.	Reading-readiness tests. Oral questions that result in anecdotal records.
Begins to use such tools as picture clues, phonetic analysis, structural analysis, and verbal context to identify strange words.	Aids in learning word-attack tools during daily reading. Places titles under pictures on bulletin board.	Oral questions that result in anecdotal records or rating scales.
Recognizes familiar words readily in various settings and combinations.	Develops experience charts with children; places titles under bulletin-board pictures; writes notes and announcements on board; uses basic and supplementary reading books in reading groups.	Observation that results in anecdotes or rating scales. Workbook, teacher-made exercises, and simple tests.
Reads silently with little if any vocalization or lip movement.	Has children read silently.	Observation that results in anecdotes or rating scales.
Reads increasingly wider variety of material.	Introduces supplementary reading in reading groups. Introduces class to classroom library or reading table. Suggests particular books to individual children according to their abilities.	List of books or material read by each child.

Reads increasingly longer units of material.	Introduces longer units in reading groups. Suggests longer units in books for leisure-time reading. Has such units available on reading table.	Anecdotal records or list of material read by each child.
Reads aloud smoothly rather than jolting from word to word.	Has children read aloud daily in reading groups. Suggests ways of learning to read more smoothly.	Observation that results in anecdotes or rating scale.

LANGUAGE ARTS—SPEAKING

Speaks clearly and loudly enough to individuals and the group.	Provides "conference time" each day during which each child is asked to tell an experience or something that is interesting. Provides numerous opportunities for discussion during reading, social studies, art, music, and arithmetic sessions. Corrects child's errors according to child's apparent ability to profit from such correction. Talks individually with children about their work and experiences. Provides dramatics.	Observation that results in anecdotes or rating scale.
Tells experiences and stories understandably with occurrences in proper sequence. Does not omit important elements. Does not spend time on unimportant details.	Provides "conference time" and opportunities for describing occurrences relating to science, social studies, and reading experiences.	Observation that results in anecdotes or rating scale.

LANGUAGE ARTS—HANDWRITING

Does clear manuscript writing (printing).	Teaches letter forms. Provides opportunities for writing words and copying short messages developed by the class during discussions.	Observation. Samples of writing.

SOCIAL STUDIES—HOME AND COMMUNITY STUDIES

Describes what his parents and parents of other children in room do for a living.	Stimulates children to describe parents' work.	Oral questions and observation resulting in anecdotes.
Describes ways he might help at home.	Leads discussions. Helps children develop chart about *helping at home.*	Oral questions resulting in anecdotes. Parent-teacher conference.
Describes his home and the purposes of various rooms and implements in home.	Leads discussions. Stimulates children to bring magazine pictures for bulletin board and scrapbook. Leads planning of living room or kitchen in corner of classroom.	Oral questions resulting in anecdotes or check list.
Describes purposes and general functions of "community helpers": postman, fireman, policeman, grocer, baker, auto mechanic, service-station operator, farmer, milkman, plumber, druggist.	Organizes field trips into community. Invites "community helpers" to speak to class and be interviewed. Provides stories to be read by children. Reads stories or tells them to class. Stimulates children to draw or paint murals of community scenes as they interpret the community.	Observation resulting in anecdotes.

SCIENCE—PLANTS, ANIMALS, EARTH, STARS

Seeks evidence for happenings in physical world.	During discussions of occurrences in physical-biological world, asks class to estimate "why it happened." Asks for their reasons or evidence for their answers. Points out evidence for phenomena they can understand.	Observation resulting in anecdotes or rating scale.
Observes and reports happenings accurately.	On field trips asks what they see. Asks what they observe outdoors, in classroom aquarium, terrarium, and pet corner. Discusses their observations with class.	Observation.
Explains how animals live all around us, eat different foods, and have different ways of moving about.	Leads discussions and field trips. Reads and tells stories in class. Has class read simple tales. Leads class in writing experience charts of their	Observation. Oral questions. Few simple written tests latter half of year.

Explains that most plants cannot move about as animals do.	observations and field trips. Shows movies, film strips, bulletin-board pictures brought by teacher and pupils.	Same as above.
Explains that our earth is made up of air, water, and land.		Same as above.
Describes sun, moon, and stars.	Same as above.	Same as above.
Explains how and why animals and plants are active in spring.	Same as above.	Same as above.
Explains how we get food from animals and plants.	Same as above.	Same as above.

SOCIAL LIVING AND HEALTH

Follows directions.	Gives directions in conducting daily classwork.	Observation resulting in rating scale or anecdotes.
Takes turns and shares willingly in group activities.	Explains and enforces principles of fair play in group activities.	
Listens when it is time for others to speak.	Discusses need for taking turns in talking. Enforces in friendly manner "raising hand to talk."	Observation.
Complies with school safety rules.	Has children practice fire drills and act out and discuss the ways they should conduct themselves on playground, crossing streets, in halls, and using equipment such as hammers.	Observation resulting in anecdotes, rating scale, or check list. Reports from school safety patrol.
Comes to school neat and clean. Washes hands before eating. Uses clean handkerchief or tissue. Keeps teeth clean.	Discusses cleanliness as related to appearance and health. Reads stories, teaches songs about health practices.	Observation resulting in anecdotes, rating scale, or check list.
Rests quietly.	Supervises rest period.	Same as above.
Says, "Thank you," "please," and "I'm sorry" at appropriate times.	Leads discussion of manners. Has children act out situations with appropriate manners.	Same as above.

ARITHMETIC

Counts, reads, writes numbers meaningfully from 1 to 100.	Has children count objects, identify oral and written symbols for numbers of objects.	Observation. Sample number sheets created by each child. Oral questions.
Makes simple comparisons, as larger-smaller, older-younger, longer-shorter.	Provides opportunities to compare objects, people, and distances.	Oral questions. Observation.
Adds, subtracts simple amounts using concrete objects.	Provides concrete objects to handle. Asks questions about how many result if added to or taken-away from groups of objects.	Oral questions. Simple written problems near end of year.
Reads calendar.	Asks different child each day to read date and day of week from calendar.	Observation.

ART

Expresses ideas and feelings with poster paint, finger paint, crayons, and clay.	Provides materials and stimulates children to express their feelings in art about particular events and experiences.	Observation. Samples of art products.

MUSIC

Sings songs by rote. Remembers words and tune. Stays on key.	Presents songs. Encourages children to bring songs for class. Encourages them to sing alone and in groups and to create own songs.	Observation.
Beats time or moves body to rhythm.	Creates class rhythm band. Has class march, dance, skip, hop, swing bodies to rhythm.	Observation.

PHYSICAL EDUCATION

Runs, jumps, skips, hops, throws ball, catches ball. Plays simple circle games in which each child takes turns.	Provides simple games and exercises involving basic skills. Provides free play time outdoors and indoors.	Check list or rating scale.

Summary of first-grade evaluation techniques

As the outline for the first grade indicates, the teacher at this primary level depends most heavily upon oral questions and personal observation which result in anecdotal records and rating scales or check lists. For this reason, the primary-grade teacher should develop efficient ways of recording her observations of children's progress. (See Chapters 8 and 12.) By developing rating scales and check lists for certain objectives (such as social living and health), the primary teacher can do an effective job of evaluation and still save much time that would otherwise be used in less organized note-taking about children's activities.

Some workbook exercises or very simple tests (multiple-choice) are also used effectively in first-grade classrooms. In general, however, such evaluation devices are limited by the children's lack of reading ability.

Work products, such as drawings and paintings or handwriting samples, can be collected at different intervals throughout the year and can reflect the type of progress being made by a child.

First-grade report

We do not wish to overstress report-card systems compared to such functions of evaluation as discovering children's weaknesses and strengths and judging the effectiveness of the teacher's methods. However, the present chapter, as an overview of a year's evaluation program, provides a good opportunity to show how the type of report-form or conference used by a teacher should be a logical reflection of the goals of the specific class. Consequently, a sample progress report for this particular first-grade program is included here. In this example the child's marks compare him with his apparent ability (as judged by aptitude tests and the teacher's observation) rather than with the rest of the class.

Explanation of Marks:

S—I do well. O—I do especially well. N—I need more time or effort.

Area of Growth	*Marking Period*					
SOCIAL LIVING AND HEALTH	1	2	3	4	5	6
I follow directions.						
I work and play well with others.						
I listen when others speak.						
I follow safety rules.						
I come to school neat and clean.						
I use a handkerchief or tissue.						
I rest quietly.						
I say *Thank you, Please,* and *I'm sorry* at proper times.						
READING, SPEAKING, AND WRITING						
I am getting ready to read.						
I understand what I read.						
I discover new words myself.						
I read aloud clearly.						
I speak clearly.						
I tell stories and happenings well.						
I write my letters clearly.						
COMMUNITY STUDY AND SCIENCE						
I tell about my town and the work people do.						
I plan ways to help at home.						
I observe happenings in nature.						
I tell about plants and animals around us.						

NUMBER WORK I can count.						
I write numbers properly.						
I read numbers well.						
I compare sizes, shapes, distances.						
I read the calendar.						
ART AND MUSIC I sing with the group.						
I move to the rhythms.						
I express my ideas with paint and clay.						
PHYSICAL ACTIVITIES I run, jump, skip, hop.						
I throw and catch a ball.						
I play games with others.						

Following these descriptions, substantial space is provided for comments by the teacher and comments by the parent who receives the progress report.

Comparing the general outline of the year's work with the progress-report form, we see that every phase of the year's work has been reported to the parents but not in minute detail. The intention is to have the report differentiate clearly among the areas in which the child has worked, yet not be so detailed as to be cumbersome for the teacher to mark or boring for the parents to read.

AN INTERMEDIATE GRADE

The following chart presents a typical kind of program for an intermediate grade.

A YEAR'S PLAN IN FOURTH GRADE

OBJECTIVES After his experiences in fourth grade the pupil:	METHODS The teacher:	EVALUATION Techniques used for judging progress toward objectives:
LANGUAGE ARTS—READING		
Adapts silent reading speed to difficulty of material.	Discusses adapting speed to material. Presents varied materials; has children time themselves. Discusses methods of skimming, reading thoroughly. Gives exercises in these skills.	Timed reading exercises and tests.
Independently works out pronunciation of strange words by context, word analysis, and dictionary.	Helps students use word-attack skills. Gives them exercises for practicing skills.	Oral and written tests. Observation resulting in anecdotes.
Readily recognizes familiar words in almost any situation.	Provides numerous types of reading experiences and materials. Discusses word meanings with class. Provides exercises for practice.	Oral and written questions. Observation.
Uses various techniques (such as verbal context, interpretation of figures of speech, punctuation, chart and map interpretation) to secure meaning from difficult reading.	Provides exercises developed from class's social studies and science reading to give practice in these specific skills.	Oral and written questions. Observation.
Begins the following reading-study jobs: 1. Locates information pertinent to problem, question, or topic.	Provides exercises developed from class's social studies and science problems to give practice in using index and table of contents of book, using	Oral and written problems. Observation.

	library, and using reference books.	
2. Evaluates pertinent information according to its importance to purpose in mind and according to its probable validity.	Leads discussions about pertinence and validity of data class members collect. Provides exercises developed around social studies, science, literature, and arts to give practice in these skills.	Oral and written problems. Observation.
3. Organizes important and valid information according to purpose in mind.	Gives class practice in taking notes and outlining. Provides opportunities for writing reports, giving talks on topics about which class desires information.	Students' written and oral reports. Exercises and tests on note-taking and outlining.
Reads more widely in both fiction and nonfiction.	Makes bulletin-board displays of book jackets and pictures suggesting variety of books. Reads portions of books to class. Places variety of books on reading table in classroom. Invites students to tell about books they have liked. Takes class to browse in library.	List of books students read. Observation resulting in anecdotes.
Reads aloud in a more fluent, interesting manner.	Provides frequent opportunities for oral reading in reading groups. Has children take turns with teacher in reading portions of stories to entire class. Leads discussion of effective reading techniques.	Teacher - made rating scale and anecdotes.
LANGUAGE ARTS—HANDWRITING		
Writes in both manuscript (printing) and cursive (script) styles that are legible and composed of proper letter forms.	Provides specific practice in cursive writing according to class needs. Provides frequent opportunities for students to write stories, verses, and reports.	Samples of written work.
LANGUAGE ARTS—SPELLING		
Accurately spells words he uses in writing and and ones common for grade level.	Provides regular spelling practice, utilizing words common to grade and words misspelled frequently by individual children in written work.	Spelling tests. Written work.

LANGUAGE ARTS—SPEAKING

Speaks clearly before group. Enunciates and pronounces words correctly. Relates events or stories with details in proper sequence. Does not omit important details nor stress unimportant ones.	Directs frequent class discussions. Provides opportunities for children to tell their experiences, tell stories, read aloud, act in plays, and report their findings on topics of interest to class.	Rating scale. Anecdotes.
Acts in plays (both preplanned and spontaneous) in a manner that interprets characters accurately.	Organizes sociodramas about problems students might face or wish to understand. Directs plays planned by class or selected from books.	Observation.

LANGUAGE ARTS—WRITING

Writes reports of what he has read or seen. Uses increasingly clearer sentence structure and punctuation.	Provides situations in social studies, science, literature, and arts studies for children to write reports of what they have read or observed.	Students' compositions.
Writes friendly letters with increasingly clearer sentence structure and punctuation.	Provides real opportunities for children to write letters to friends, parents, brothers, and sisters.	Students' letters.
Expresses own ideas and interpretations of his world in short stories, poems, and articles.	Reads stories and poems that illustrate ways different people express ideas and feelings. Stimulates students to express their experiences, ideas, feelings.	Students' stories, poems, articles.

SOCIAL STUDIES—LOCAL HISTORY AND FOREIGN LANDS

Describes the ways of living and working in the local community today, in colonial or pioneer times, and in Indian times (including celebrations and festivals enjoyed during each period).	Organizes units of study which include reading in texts and reference books, student reports, teacher-led discussions, field trips, film strips, student projects such as historical plays and model communities.	Oral questions. Written tests. Observation of student reports. Student projects.
Describes the ways of living and working in	Throughout the school year has students choose specific	Oral questions. Written tests. Observation of

one country of each of these areas: Southeastern Asia, Africa, South America, Southern Europe, Scandinavia. Explains how, in relation to above areas: 1. All people are much alike. 2. The type of food, clothing, and shelter that people need is conditioned largely by the environment in which they live. 3. It is to man's own advantage to conserve the resources of nature. 4. Men's customs, habits, and manners today are different in many respects from what they were in earlier times. 5. Men are learning ways of controlling their environment. 6. Climate tends to determine man's needs. Differences of living caused by climate are somewhat modified by invention, transportation, and communication.	country to study from each of these geographical areas. Organizes units to include reading in texts, reference books, magazines, and newspapers. Utilizes student reports, films, visiting speakers, discussions, and student projects such as murals, dressed-up dolls, plays, miniature villages, and realia.	student reports. Student projects.

SOCIAL LIVING AND HEALTH

Works progressively better with others.	Provides opportunities for group work and cooperative activities. Provides team games.	Participation charting. Anecdotes. Sociograms.
Is better able to help plan group action and carry it through.	Provides opportunities for leadership and responsibility in group work.	Participation charting. Anecdotes.
Willingly obeys classroom rules.	Has class help state appropriate classroom rules. Enforces rules.	Anecdotal records or rating scale.

Keeps hands, face, teeth, and clothing clean.	Leads discussion of health and social reasons for cleanliness and neatness. Shows health films.	Rating scale or check list.
Behaves in a progressively safer manner: 1. On streets and highways.	Draws model streets and crosswalks on board. Has students show how they would act in problem situations.	Written test. Report of safety patrol.
2. In school.	Leads discussions of behavior.	Observation. Safety patrol.
3. In outdoor play.	Directs playground activities. Leads discussions of proper play behavior.	Observation. Safety patrol.
4. At home in relation to fire and electricity.	Develops unit on fire and electricity safety to include reading, reports, discussions, demonstrations, and talks by firemen.	Oral questions. Written tests. Parent - teacher conference.

SCIENCE—PLANTS, ANIMALS, ELECTRICITY, LIGHT, THE MOON

Seeks evidence to explain happenings in physical - biological world. Alters hypotheses in light of new data.	During discussions of occurrences in physical-biological world, asks class to estimate "why it happened." Asks for their reasons or evidence for their answers. Asks where they can find evidence. Stimulates them to form hypotheses and support or alter hypotheses in light of new data.	Oral questions. Written tests. Student reports.
Observes and reports happenings accurately.	Asks them to observe and report happenings such as actions of fish in aquarium, growth of flowers in class window box, and weather phenomena. Leads discussion of accuracy of their observations.	Oral questions. Written tests. Student reports.
Explains how: 1. Some plants and animals live in communities.	Provides reading materials and field trips. Leads discussions. Helps class organize ant	Oral questions. Written tests. Student oral and written reports. Ob-

	communities in glass jars. Helps develop terrarium. Provides films.	servation of student work on projects.
2. Plants and animals have lived on the earth a long time.	Provides reading materials. Leads discussions. Organizes groups that create drawings, murals, clay models.	Oral questions. Written tests. Student reports. Observation of work on projects.
3. We can get electricity in several ways.	Provides reading, demonstrations, discussions, experiments to be done by students.	Oral questions. Written tests.
4. Light enables us to see things.	Same as above.	Same as above.
5. The moon is the nearest heavenly body.	Provides reading, bulletin-board displays, opportunity to view moon through telescope in night session.	Same as above.
6. Flowers are necessary to produce seeds.	Provides reading, discussions, student - conducted experiments, and collections of seeds. Has each student keep experiment notebook.	Oral questions. Written tests. Notebooks. Observation of experiments.
7. Plants and animals depend upon each other.	Leads discussions of student observations. Provides reading. Organizes individual picture-projects of animals and plants that depend on each other.	Student picture - projects. Oral questions. Written tests.
ARITHMETIC		
Reads and writes numbers to 10,000 and some Roman numerals.	Provides exercises and lifelike problems plus frequent questions at appropriate points in social studies and science discussions and in classroom business sessions.	Oral questions. Written exercises and tests.
Extends column addition to whole number and money types used in school and home life. Extends subtraction for home and school situations. Makes change.	Same as above, plus situations such as grocery and post office.	Same as above.

Increases speed and accuracy in addition and subtraction.	Provides computational exercises, both oral and written.	Same as above.
Extends facility in meaningful (not rote) way with basic multiplication and division combinations.	Provides lifelike problems and computational practice plus problems arising from other classwork, such as social studies, physical education, and science.	Same as above.
Extends concepts of value and size of measures formerly used.	Demonstrates and has children use actual measures and values in class, on playground, at home. Provides lifelike problems to solve in class situations and in books.	Observation. Oral questions. Written exercises and tests.
ART AND MUSIC		
Expresses own ideas, feelings, interpretations of his world through painting, drawing with chalk or crayon, clay modeling, and stenciling.	Stimulates class to experiment with varied media in expressing their ideas. Provides opportunities for individual and group work on art projects.	Observation of student activity. Sample art products.
Creates designs by weaving fabrics on homemade loom.	Demonstrates weaving techniques and method of making cardboard or wooden loom.	Observation. Art product.
Sings many songs.	Provides frequent opportunities for singing. Songs include ones related to holidays, seasons, and social-studies and science units.	Observation.
Sings in tune.	Provides opportunities to sing alone as well as with group. Provides training in listening to pitch, then trying to sing on pitch.	Listens to individual pupils. Rating scale.
Keeps appropriate rhythm.	Provides frequent opportunities for singing and beating rhythms or moving body to rhythms and dances.	Observation.

Begins to read music notation.	Provides music books and teaches concepts of rise and fall of tone and of note value.	Observation. Oral questions.
Identifies instruments heard on records.	Demonstrates basic instruments such as violin, trumpet, snare drum, and clarinet or has them demonstrated. Plays recorded music that features instruments being studied.	Oral and written questions while listening to records.
Voluntarily listens to music, sings, or plays an instrument.	Provides records and record player in classroom to be used by pupils during free time.	Anecdotal records. Parent-teacher conference.
PHYSICAL EDUCATION		
Takes part in races of various types.	Organizes individual and relay races utilizing running, hopping, jumping, skipping, throwing, and catching.	Rating scale.
Plays team games of fairly low degree of organization. Games utilize throwing, kicking, and catching a ball as well as running.	Organizes, teaches, and supervises team games.	Rating scale.
Engages in elementary folk dances and rhythmic games.	Demonstrates and organizes folk dances, *acting* to music, and rhythmic games.	Rating scale. Anecdotal records.

(In the chart above, when the term *observation* was used it was assumed that the teacher's observation of the students' progress would subsequently be recorded as either an anecdote, a rating on a scale, or a mark on a check list. The form of recording would depend upon the teacher's preference and time available for evaluation of that particular behavior.)

Summary of fourth-grade evaluation techniques

Compared to the primary grades, evaluation in the intermediate grades can depend more upon simple written tests and exercises and upon written reports. Despite the availability of these techniques, the teacher who judges children's development adequately also depends considerably upon anecdotal records, teacher-made rating scales and check lists, samples of student work (projects, art products), participation charts, and, to a lesser extent, sociograms.

Fourth-grade report

Educational psychologists indicate that we usually learn skills best when we *learn by doing* and that we evaluate best when we judge the actual behavior we are working toward. Thus, it is suggested that the reader, in order to learn and to judge his own ability to develop a report form, use the chart above to construct a type of progress report that would yield a true, but not too lengthy, reflection of a child's success in this fourth-grade program. In carrying through this task, the reader's own philosophy of marking will determine whether the report form he develops will compare the child with himself (his estimated ability) or with his classmates or both.

AN UPPER GRADE

An outline of a complete year's program for an upper-elementary grade at this point would probably be unprofitable for the reader, because it would include much repetition, though at a more advanced level, of the types of goals and activities outlined for the fourth grade. Instead of a complete year's outline, we shall inspect some of the ways objectives and evaluation devices in a typical seventh-grade class should differ from those at the fourth-grade level.

Seventh-grade goals and evaluation

Seventh graders advance in reading skills along the same lines outlined for fourth graders but at a higher level of proficiency. They use more complicated words, handle more complex ideas, read longer passages, read a greater variety of material, and develop to a higher degree the reading-study skills (locating, evaluating, and organizing information). Because seventh graders can write better, the teacher can utilize more written types of evaluation devices: student reports, written exercises, and objective and essay tests (both teacher-made and standardized). However, the teacher still judges pupils' progress in reading by student contributions in discussions, individual interviews, and lists of books and magazines read.

The seventh-grade speech goals are likewise an extension of objectives of the intermediate grades. Growth is expected in students' ease before a group, in clear speech, in organization of ideas, and in the interest of the talk. Better interpretation is expected in situations requiring acting or expression, such as dramatics or oral reading. Observation that results in anecdotal or rating-scale records is an effective evaluation technique.

Similar advances, related to each child's abilities, are expected in spelling and written composition. Additional functional grammar is included at this higher level.

In the area of social living these pupils, now entering early adolescence, are expected to be establishing appropriate relationships with their peers of both sexes. They are also working toward taking responsibility when adults are not around, leading a group in working on projects, and directing a meeting in an orderly, democratic manner. The seventh-grade teacher will find participation charts, sociograms, rating scales, and anecdotal records useful for estimating pupil progress in these areas.

Tests and written exercises, along with some class discussion and oral questioning, form the most efficient devices for measuring growth toward arithmetic goals in this grade. Observation also aids the teacher in estimating how well pupils apply their knowledge of whole numbers, fractions, decimals, percents, and types of measures to everyday problems they meet in social studies, science, physical education, and art.

In judging seventh graders' understanding of the social studies units (such as "The Development of Our State" or "Contributions of Other Countries to America") and science units, the teacher can utilize more complicated forms of written tests than those used in the intermediate grades. However, in the upper grades evidence of students' progress also arises in class discussions and is produced in students' written and oral reports. Pictures, magazine cutouts, and scientific gadgets built at home that the pupils bring to school are additional evidence of their growth in awareness and understanding of the topics. In the upper grades, pupils are more capable of creating projects, such as building models of modes of transportation or making maps of the state showing the outstanding products for each area. The projects provide indications of growth that should be noted in an anecdote or on a rating scale.

By seventh grade the pupils are learning to sing in parts and perhaps play an instrument. Observation of the student's performance (according to his apparent ability) and the degree of cooperation in the group musical effort usually comprise the evaluation of his work in this area. Sometimes tests covering technical aspects of musical notation or names of composers and their works are used in appraising pupil progress. Whether such tests are proper in the area of music appreciation must be decided by each instructor in light of his philosophy of music education.

Techniques of evaluating students' growth in art and art appreciation are similar to those used in music. The teacher has the pupils' art products available to judge. His main problem is to decide the criteria he is to use for marking them. That is, to be most effective he must decide specifically what objectives the students are to reach. These objectives are commonly very evanescent in the cases of art teachers or classroom teachers who handle upper-grade art programs. As a result, such teachers may be evasive when asked about their bases for evaluating students in art. Until they state their objectives clearly, teachers appear to have little defense for their judgments. As soon as the instructor can state the objectives in terms of student behavior, the proper techniques for evaluation become more obvious. In the upper grades these objectives vary from a simple requirement in one class that the student complete a given number of drawings for a mark of *satisfactory* to complex requirements in another class concerning the use of line, form, space, and color to achieve particular effects of composition.

By the seventh grade, students are engaging in a wide variety of physical activities, including complex team sports (basketball, softball, touch football) and folk dancing that is leading into adult forms of social dancing. Teacher-made rating scales can be efficient devices for judging how well students are reaching these goals.

OBJECTIVES OF THIS CHAPTER

Chapter 2 of this book, titled "Stating Goals," was designed to aid the reader in achieving skills important to the effective elementary-school teacher. The writer assumed that the behavioral objectives of Chapter 2 would not actually be *reached* by the end of that chapter. Instead, it was hoped that some first steps would be made toward these objectives. However, at the present point in this book it is hoped that more progress has been made by the new teacher toward these goals, which are the core of effective teaching. The goals stated at the end of

Chapter 2 are, therefore, the over-all goals of the entire book and of this final summary chapter:

The effective elementary or junior high teacher:

1. Writes educational objectives in terms of student behavior.
2. Bases teaching methods upon stated objectives.
3. Evaluates students' progress by judging how closely they approach the behaviors outlined in the objectives.
4. Whenever possible judges student behavior *directly*. When this is not feasible, judges on the *planning* or *understanding* levels.
5. Does not use one type of evaluation device exclusively but suits the evaluation device to the particular objective being measured.

(A sixth goal has been added for this final chapter.)

6. Utilizes a system of reporting to parents and students that is a true and relatively detailed reflection of the students' progress toward the variety of goals of the particular class.

Suggested evaluation techniques for this chapter

1. Develop a report card for a fourth grade as suggested in the body of the chapter.
2. Listed below are several topics of units which are commonly the cores around which worth-while learning experiences are developed for children. Using one of these topics, or one of your own, as a starting point, create a unit of study which would continue at least several days. In planning this unit, use these steps:
   a. State in terms of student behavior the goals you wish to reach. (Note: Goals of a unit usually are not in only one subject-matter area, such as social studies, but cross subject-matter lines to include such areas as reading, speech, social studies, art, social living, etc.)
   b. Outline methods which might enable children to reach each objective.
   c. Indicate evaluation devices by which children's progress toward each goal might be measured.
   d. Create one or more of the actual evaluation devices you would use, such as a rating scale, written test, situational test, check list, or technique for judging projects.

These are the suggested unit topics:

Primary Grades (K-3)

1. How Plants and Animals Get Ready for Winter.
2. Folk Stories and Legends of Many Lands.
3. How Cowboys Live.

Intermediate Grades (4-6)

1. How Climate Affects the Kinds of Work, Clothing, and Houses of People around the World.
2. The National Parks of the United States. My State and Town Parks.
3. Growth of Transportation.

Upper Grades (7-8)

1. Importance of National Resources to Our Nation.
2. The American Revolution.
3. Branches of U. S. Government and Their Functions.

SUGGESTED READINGS

1. Blough, Glenn O., and Huggett, Albert J. *Elementary-School Science and How to Teach It.* New York: Dryden Press, 1951.
2. *Community Living in the Days of the Early Settlers,* A Resource Unit for Teachers. Albany: New York State Education Department, 1949.
3. *Exploring the Environment.* University of the State of New York Bulletin 1250. Albany: New York State Education Department, 1943.
4. *Living and Working in Indian Communities,* A Resource Unit for Teachers. Albany: New York State Education Department, 1949.
5. *Mathematics for Boys and Girls.* University of the State of New York Bulletin 1385. Albany: New York State Education Department, 1950.
6. McKee, Paul. *The Teaching of Reading.* Boston: Houghton Mifflin Co., 1948.
7. *Science, A Program for Elementary Schools.* University of the State of New York Bulletin 1224. Albany: New York State Education Department, 1941.
8. Wesley, Edgar Bruce, and Adams, Mary A. *Teaching Social Studies in Elementary Schools.* Boston: D. C. Heath and Co., 1952.

Appendix A

Standardized Tests and Test Publishers

THIS APPENDIX IS DIVIDED into four sections: (1) achievement batteries for elementary and junior high grades, (2) reading tests, (3) general intelligence tests for group administration, and (4) publishers of the tests listed in the first three sections.

SECTION 1: ACHIEVEMENT TEST BATTERIES

The following are the more modern and more useful achievement test batteries suited to elementary and junior high pupils. The publisher's name is listed in the parentheses below the test title. Publishers' addresses appear in Section 4.

American School Achievement Tests

(Public School Publishing Company)

Suited for grades 1 to 9.

Primary Battery I, grade 1 (35-50 minutes). Tests cover Reading (word recognition, word meaning), Arithmetic (numbers).

Primary Battery II, grades 2 and 3 (85-105 minutes). Tests cover Reading (sentence and word meaning, paragraph meaning), Arithmetic (computation, problems), Language (language, spelling).

Intermediate Battery, grades 4 to 6 (127-147 minutes). Tests same areas as Primary II.

Advanced Battery, grades 7 to 9 (127-147 minutes). Tests same areas as Primary II.

California Achievement Tests (formerly Progressive Achievement Tests)
(California Test Bureau)
Suited for grades 1 through 9.

Primary Battery, grades 1 through 4 (90-110 minutes). Tests cover Reading Vocabulary (word form, word recognition, meaning of opposites), Reading Comprehension (following directions, directly stated facts, interpretations), Arithmetic Reasoning (number and sequence, money, number and time, signs and symbols, problems), Arithmetic Fundamentals (addition, subtraction, multiplication, problems), Language—Mechanics of English (capitalization, punctuation), Spelling.

Elementary Battery, grades 4 through 6 (120-135 minutes). Tests cover Reading Vocabulary (word form, word recognition, meaning of opposites, meaning of similarities), Reading Comprehension (following directions, interpretations, reference skills), Arithmetic Reasoning (signs and symbols, problems, number concept), Arithmetic Fundamentals (addition, subtraction, multiplication, division), Language—Mechanics of English (capitalization, punctuation, words and sentences), Spelling.

Intermediate Battery, grades 7 through 9 (150-165 minutes). Tests cover Reading Vocabulary (mathematics, science, general), Reading Comprehension (following directions, interpretations, reference skills), Arithmetic Reasoning (problems, number concept, symbols and rules, numbers and equations), Arithmetic Fundamentals (addition, subtraction, multiplication, division), Language—Mechanics of English (capitalization, punctuation, words and sentences, parts of speech), Spelling.

Cooperative Achievement Tests
(Educational Testing Service)
Suited for grades 7 through 9 (360 minutes).

Tests cover English (grammatical usage, punctuation and capitalization, spelling, sentence structure and style, diction, organization), Reading (vocabulary, speed of comprehension, level of comprehension), Mathematics (skills, facts, terms, concepts, applications, appreciation), Science (informational background, terms and concepts, comprehension and interpretation), Social Studies (informational background, terms and concepts, comprehension and interpretation).

Coordinated Scales of Attainment
(Educational Test Bureau)
Suited for grades 1 through 8 with separate form for each grade-level.
Battery 1, grade 1 (90 minutes). Tests cover Reading (picture-word association, word-picture association, vocabulary recognition, reading comprehension), Arithmetic (arithmetic experience, number skills, arithmetic computation, arithmetic problem reasoning).
Battery 2, grade 2 (110 minutes). Tests cover same as grade 1 form plus spelling.
Battery 3, grade 3 (100 minutes). Tests cover same reading areas as grade 1 form plus: Arithmetic (arithmetic computation, arithmetic problem reasoning), Spelling.
Batteries 4-8, one for each grade 4 through 8 (each battery about 256 minutes). Tests cover Reading (reading, reading experience or literature), Arithmetic (arithmetic computation, arithmetic problem reasoning), Language (spelling, punctuation, capitalization, usage), Social Studies (history, geography), Elementary Science.

Gray-Votaw-Rogers General Achievement Tests
(Steck Co.)
Suited for grades 1 through 9.
Primary Battery, grades 1 through 3 (50-62 minutes). Tests cover Reading (comprehension, vocabulary), Arithmetic (computation, reasoning), Spelling.
Intermediate Battery, grades 4 through 6 (135 minutes). Tests cover same areas as Primary Battery plus: Literature, Language, Social Studies, Elementary Science, Health and Safety.
Advanced Battery, grades 7 through 9 (135 minutes). Tests cover same areas as Intermediate Battery.

Iowa Every-Pupil Tests of Basic Skills
(Houghton Mifflin Co.)
Suited for grades 3 through 9.
Elementary Battery, grades 3 through 5 (196-230 minutes). Tests cover Silent Reading Comprehension (reading comprehension, vocabulary), Work-Study Skills (map reading, use of references, use of index, use of dictionary, alphabetization), Basic Language Skills (punctuation, capitalization, usage, spelling, sen-

tence sense), Basic Arithmetic Skills (vocabulary and fundamental knowledge, fundamental operations, problems).

Advanced Battery, grades 5 through 9 (263-325 minutes). Tests cover same areas as Elementary Battery, except that the reading of graphs, charts, and tables is substituted for alphabetization in the Study Skills portion, and the sentence-sense part is omitted from the Language section.

Metropolitan Achievement Tests
(World Book Co.)

Suited for grades 1 through 9.

Primary Battery I, grades 1-2 (45-60 minutes). Tests cover Reading (word picture, word recognition, word meaning), Arithmetic (numbers).

Primary Battery II, grades 2-3 (85-100 minutes). Tests cover Reading (reading, word meaning), Arithmetic (fundamentals, problems), Spelling.

Elementary Battery, grades 3 through 5 (135-150 minutes). Tests cover Reading (vocabulary, reading), Arithmetic (fundamentals, problems), Language (spelling, language usage).

Intermediate Battery, grades 5 through 7 (220-240 minutes). Tests cover Reading (reading, vocabulary, literature), Arithmetic (fundamentals, problems), Language (spelling, English), Social Studies (history, geography), Science.

Advanced Battery, grades 7 through 9 (220-240 minutes). Tests cover same areas as Intermediate Battery.

Stanford Achievement Tests
(World Book Co.)

Suited for grades 2 through 9.

Primary Battery, grades 2-3 (80 minutes). Tests cover Language Arts (paragraph meaning, word meaning, spelling), Arithmetic (computation, reasoning).

Elementary Battery, grades 3-4 (145 minutes). Tests cover same areas as Primary Battery plus a Language portion.

Intermediate Battery, grades 5 through 7 (232 minutes). Tests cover same areas as Elementary Battery plus: Social Studies, Science, and Study Skills.

Advanced Battery, grades 7 through 9 (232 minutes). Tests cover same areas as Intermediate Battery.

SECTION 2: READING TESTS

The following reading tests are among the most popular at elementary and junior high levels. Some are actually subtests of one of the batteries reviewed in Section 1, but the reading portion may be purchased alone.

California Reading Test (Subtest of California Achievement Tests)
(California Test Bureau)
Suited for grades 1 through 9 (35-55 minutes). Forms for primary (grades 1-4), elementary (grades 4-6), and intermediate (grades 7-9). Test covers reading vocabulary and comprehension. Most suitable for surveying class reading rather than diagnosing individual problems.

Durrell-Sullivan Reading Capacity and Achievement Tests
(World Book Co.)
Suited for grades 2 through 6 (45 minutes). Forms for primary (grades 2-4) and intermediate (grades 3-6). Yields information on word meaning, paragraph meaning, spelling, and written recall skills.

Gates Primary Reading Tests and Gates Advanced Primary Reading Tests
(Bureau of Publications, Teachers College)
Suited for grades 1-2 (Primary Tests) (25-30 minutes) and grades 2-3 (Advanced Primary) (40-50 minutes). Both tests yield word recognition and paragraph reading scores, with the former test also yielding a sentence reading score.

Gates Basic Reading Tests
(Bureau of Publications, Teachers College)
Suited for grades 3 through 8 (60 minutes). Test covers reading to appreciate general significance, reading to predict outcome of given events, reading to understand precise directions, and reading to note details. Best suited to intermediate grades.

Iowa Silent Reading Test: Elementary Form
(World Book Co.)
Suited for grades 4 to 8 (50-60 minutes). Test covers rate and comprehension, word meaning, paragraph comprehension, directed reading, sentence meaning, and location of information.

Iowa Every-Pupil Silent Reading Comprehension (Subtest of battery)
(Houghton Mifflin Co.)

Suited for grades 3 through 5 (Elementary Form) and 5 through 9 (Advanced Form) (60-85 minutes). Tests cover vocabulary and reading comprehension.

Stanford Achievement Test: Reading (Subtest of battery)
(World Book Co.)

Suited for grades 2 through 3 (Primary Form), grades 3 through 4 (Elementary Form), grades 5 through 6 (Intermediate Form), grades 7 through 9 (Advanced Form) (30-40 minutes). Tests cover paragraph meaning and word meaning.

SECTION 3: GROUP INTELLIGENCE TESTS

California Short Form Test of Mental Maturity
(California Test Bureau)

Suited for kindergarten through grade 1 (Pre-Primary Form), grades 1 through 3 (Primary Form), grades 4 through 8 (Elementary Form), grades 7 through 10 (Intermediate Form) (40-60 minutes). Yields scores on verbal, non-verbal, and total IQ.

California Test of Mental Maturity

Suited for same levels as California Short Form (90-110 minutes). Tests cover memory, spatial relations, logical reasoning, numerical reasoning, vocabulary, total language score, total non-language score, and total over-all mental factors.

Chicago Non-Verbal Examination
(Psychological Corporation)

Suited for age 7 to adult (40 minutes). Tests designed to measure non-verbal aspects of intelligence, consists of ten subtests. Most useful with children who have reading, speech, and hearing difficulties.

Kuhlmann-Anderson Intelligence Tests
(Personnel Press, Inc.)

Suited for kindergarten through grade 8 (advanced form for grades 9-12). Separate forms for each grade to 7 (30-45 minutes). Yields over-all IQ score.

Lorge-Thorndike Intelligence Tests
(Houghton Mifflin Co.)
Suited for kindergarten through grade 9 (advanced forms go higher). Separate forms for grades: kindergarten-1, 2-3, 4-6, 7-9. Both verbal and non-verbal material at grade 4 and above.

Otis Quick-Scoring Mental Ability Tests
(World Book Co.)
Suited for grades 1 through 9 (advanced form goes higher) (20-35 minutes). **Alpha Form** for grades 1-4, **Beta Form** for grades 4-9. Tests aimed primarily at verbal ability and yield over-all IQ score.

Pintner General Ability Tests: Non-Language
(World Book Co.)
Suited for grades 4 through 9 (50-60 minutes). Best for children with reading or hearing difficulties in intermediate grades.

Pintner General Ability Tests: Verbal
(World Book Co.)
Suited for grades 4 through 9 (45-55 minutes). **Primary Form** for kindergarten through grade 2, **Elementary Form** for grades 2-4, **Intermediate Form** for grades 4-9. Verbal Counterpart of **Pintner Non-Language Tests**, yields five ways to interpret scores.

Terman-McNemar Test of Mental Ability
(World Book Co.)
Suited for grades 7 through 12 (40-45 minutes). Yields single IQ from highly verbal contents.

SECTION 4: TEST PUBLISHERS

Following are the addresses of the publishers referred to in the three previous sections. Teachers and school administrators will find it helpful to write to these publishers for catalogues describing their tests in detail and perhaps to write for specimen sets of the tests that seem most useful in the particular schools.

Bureau of Publications
Teachers College,
Columbia University
New York, N.Y.

California Test Bureau
5916 Hollywood Blvd.
Los Angeles 28, Calif.

Educational Test Bureau
Educational Publishers, Inc.
720 Washington Ave., S.E.
Minneapolis, Minn.

Educational Testing Service
Cooperative Test Division
Princeton, N.J.

Houghton Mifflin Co.
2 Park St.
Boston, Mass.

Personnel Press, Inc.
188 Nassau St.
Princeton, N.J.

Psychological Corp.
522 Fifth Ave.
New York 18, N.Y.

Public School Publishing Co.
Bloomington, Ill.

Science Research Associates, Inc.
57 West Grand Ave.
Chicago 10, Ill.

Steck Co.
P.O. Box 16
Austin, Texas

World Book Co.
South Broadway and
Sunnyside Lane
Tarrytown, N.Y.

Appendix B

The Meaning of Correlation

FREQUENTLY EDUCATORS AND PSYCHOLOGISTS are interested in answering questions like these:

If we have two different forms of the same test of arithmetic fundamentals, how likely is it that these two forms measure exactly the same arithmetic abilities?

If you give pupils a written academic aptitude test today and then give the same test to them again a month from now, will the same children score high on the second testing as did on the first?

How can you most accurately predict a student's success in junior high school: by inspecting his elementary-school grades or by giving him an entrance examination?

Does the Stanford-Binet Intelligence Scale measure the same abilities as the Wechsler Intelligence Scale for Children?

Is there more mental illness among children who have moved frequently from one home to another than among children who have always lived in the same home?

Are children who are skilled in sports also skilled in reading?

Is it true that the higher you have gone in school the more money you will earn?

Do children who become juvenile delinquents read more comic books and see more movies than children who do not become delinquents?

Are children who are skilled in music also skilled in ability to solve mathematics problems?

These questions all have one characteristic in common. They all are concerned with the relationship of one variable and another. That is, they ask about the connection between the Stanford-Binet and the Wechsler examination or between comic books and delinquency or between music and mathematics abilities. They all ask for the *correlation between two variables*. By use of appropriate statistics, we can derive accurate, concise answers to questions like these. There are several types of correlation statistics, each appropriate to different kinds of research problems. The most useful of these types, and the one of most importance to us in this book, is described in this appendix.

The term *correlation coefficient* often frightens the uninitiated person who expects such a phrase to indicate a mathematical concept very difficult to understand. However, the general idea underlying correlation is fairly easy to comprehend. By inspecting a hypothetical situation we can see the logic of the correlation coefficient.

Imagine that we have been asked by a manufacturing firm which employs many machinists to develop a test for selecting the very best candidates from among their many job applicants. In the past the company has found that some men they hired failed to become good workers, whereas other applicants whom they had not hired had later gone to other machine shops and become excellent workers. Our task is to prevent this from happening again. We are to try to develop a test which will separate the good from the mediocre and poor machinists before they are hired.

Our first step in constructing a test will be to estimate what kinds of items would most likely separate the potentially good from the potentially poor machinists. Should we use questions about mathematics? That is, would mathematics questions separate good from poor machinists? Should we test the men in assembling simple puzzles? Should we show them many different tools and ask them to name each tool and tell its use?

Let us say that in trying to develop the test we have come up with many ideas which we think might work out well. From these different ideas we develop four different kinds of tests, each of which can be administered within an hour or so. Our problem now is to determine which of these four tests, if any, can discriminate between the men who will be good and those who will be poor machinists. In other words, we wish to determine the degree of relationship between two variables: (1) test scores and (2) efficiency later as a machinist.

To *validate* our tests (that is, to prove how well each discriminates good from poor machinists) we first develop a method of rating the machinists now working for the manufacturing firm. By considering such factors as speed, accuracy, initiative, and diligence, we construct a rating scale by which foremen rate the machinists whose work they have supervised for the past months or years. On the scale it is possible for the best man to score as high as 40 points. The poorer machinists receive lower scores. We find that in filling out the scale the six foremen show good agreement with each other on where each man in the shop ranks. Thus, we consider our rating scale to be an accurate measure of the efficiency of the men in the shop. This rating of on-the-job effectiveness is called the *criterion* against which we will judge our four tests. (If we were creating a test for determining a child's aptitude for arithmetic we could use as our criterion *school grades* in arithmetic. If we were making a test to measure aptitude for science we could use *school grades* in science or *teachers' ratings* of the students' success in science as criteria.)

A next logical step is to give our four tests to men who want to be employed as machinists in our shop. So we take all applicants and test them. On each of four days they take one of our tests. Then the manager of the shop hires all of them and puts them to work, so that later we can see which of them become good and which become poor machinists.

We now decide to wait nine months, so that the men have a chance to learn their jobs and get a fair trial in their work. After this period we have the foremen rate the men's efficiency on our *job-rating scale,* and we have a record of these ratings along with the test scores from nine months earlier.

Next we compare the test scores and job-efficiency ratings of these twelve men. (If this were a real situation rather than hypothetical, we would try to secure the ratings and scores of many machinists—hundreds of them if possible. Likewise, if we were creating a test to measure children's aptitude for art, we would prefer to use several thousand children in judging the test's worth. The larger the sampling the more likely we are to secure a typical sample of children. However, in our make-believe situation it is easier to see the reasoning behind correlation if the number is small. Consequently, we will use the scores of twelve men who have test results that are typical of the range of machinists.)

Below are the men's on-the-job ratings and their scores on the four tests we are trying out.

Name	*Job Rating*	*Test I*	*Test II*	*Test III*	*Test IV*
Allen	40	98	72	87	53
Bronson	38	93	77	67	58
Cartwell	36	88	90	79	51
Dowden	34	83	83	58	64
Elsworth	32	78	97	48	66
Franks	30	73	78	83	85
Gotich	28	68	64	42	62
Hiller	26	63	88	84	78
Iverson	24	58	73	53	97
Jurgen	22	53	57	65	78
Kent	20	48	42	92	87
Lane	18	43	67	71	85

In order to answer our question "Which test most accurately indicates a machinist's ability?" we can compare the list of job ratings with each test and can estimate the worth of each test. In our example, which contains only twelve cases, this task of estimating is fairly simple. Generally, however, lists of numbers such as these are difficult, if not impossible, to interpret accurately. When hundreds of scores are reported, the numbers merely become a jumble. A better way to observe the relations between the variables (job ratings and test scores) is to plot the numbers on a *scatter diagram* or *correlation diagram*. This gives a clearer picture of the trends, especially when many scores are to be compared.

A scatter diagram for comparing *job ratings* with Test I scores can be constructed by listing job ratings on one axis (vertically) and the Test I scores on the other (horizontally). (Note that in order to keep the scattergram from becoming too large, we have grouped test scores in fives and job ratings in twos.) Next we mark a tally in the square where each man's job rating intersects with his Test I score.

Test I is an amazingly accurate measure of a machinist's job efficiency. The scattergram shows that the men succeeded on the test exactly in the order they succeeded on the job. The scattergram

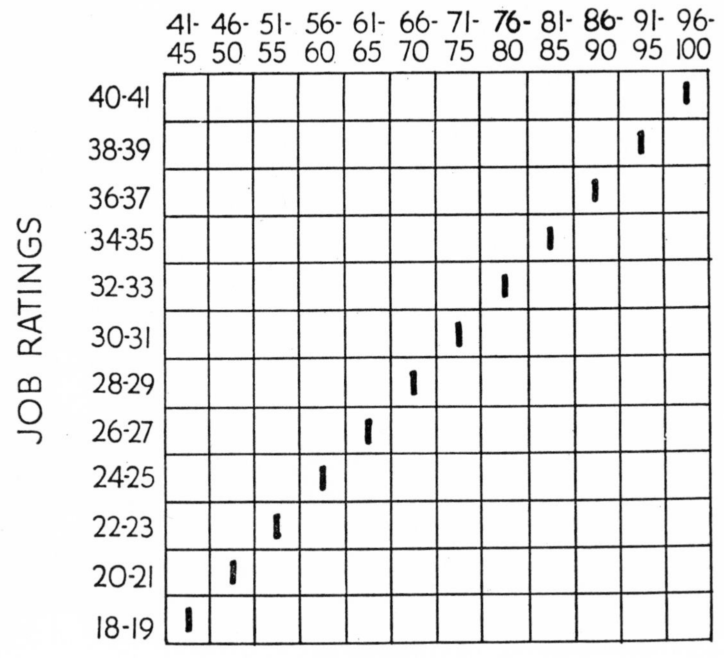

Fig. 49

shows that a regular relationship exists between the two variables being considered here. This is termed *perfect correlation.* Such a test as this hypothetical one probably would never result in real life. It is too good to be true. But when tests are constructed, the goal of the test-makers is to approach as closely as possible such a relationship between the test and its criterion.

With only a dozen pairs of scores to consider here a scattergram has yielded an accurate picture of the efficiency of the test. However, in real-life situations where hundreds or thousands of pairs of scores may be considered, a scattergram can become an extremely unwieldy vehicle for reporting the validity of a test. Consequently, statisticians have determined a way of deriving from all the paired scores a single number which describes accurately the relationship between the two variables, in this case between the test and the criterion. (In other cases, such as when we use correlation to determine the reliability of a test, the two variables may be the scores of the test given one day and the scores of the same test given over again another day.) This single number describing the relationship is called a *correlation coefficient.*

Rarely do elementary or high school teachers find occasion to compute a correlation coefficient. Therefore, the mathematical formula and the process for computation are usually not important to them. *However, all teachers should be able to interpret what a correlation coefficient means; and it is not necessary to know the computation in order to interpret adequately.* Consequently, the present explanation does not treat the actual computation of the coefficient. Instead, it stresses only interpretation and a basic understanding of the relationship between two variables or groups of scores. For those who wish to learn the computational procedure, the fifth part of Appendix C presents the steps in deriving a coefficient of correlation from a scattergram.

Using the job ratings and the Test I scores, we compute a correlation coefficient of +1.00. This number represents the perfect correlation shown on the scattergram. The *plus* means that men who have low scores on the job ratings also have low scores on the test; those who have medium scores on ratings also tend to have medium scores on the test; and those with high ratings also tend to have high scores on the test. A plus in front of the coefficient indicates that high scores on one variable are paired with high scores on the other.

Any time we see a coefficient approaching +1.00 (such as +.93 or +.96) we know that the tally marks on the scattergram form almost a straight diagonal line, lower left to upper right. Such a spread of tallies, which indicates a coefficient approaching +1.00, shows a very high degree of relationship between the two variables considered.

Thus, in judging the four hypothetical tests we constructed for choosing machinists, we have discovered that Test I is phenomenally successful. However, let us see how valid the other three are.

Inspecting the men's scores on Test II is more difficult than with Test I, because the Test II scores do not follow a regular order. By placing these Test II scores on a scattergram along with the job ratings, we are better able to estimate the worth of this second examination.

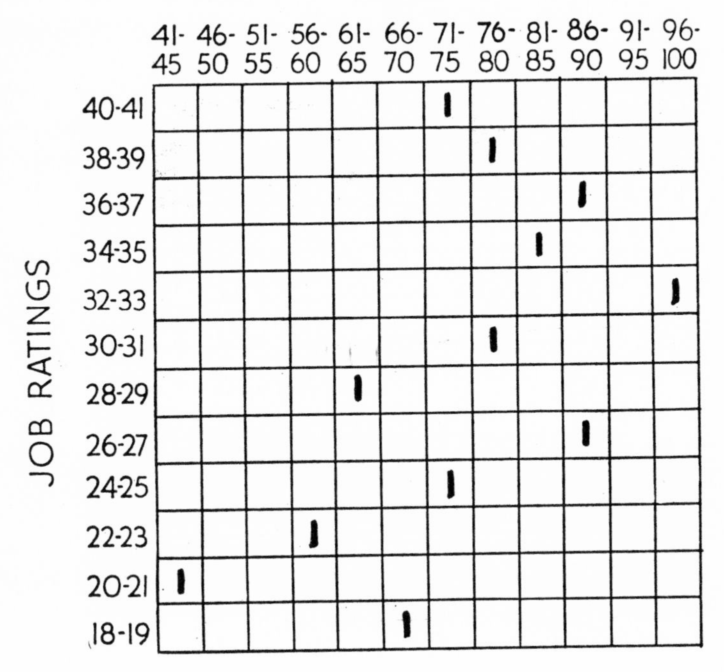

Fig. 50

Test II is not so accurate a measure of machinists' ability as Test I, but it certainly would be a useful test if another were not available. The scattergram for Test II shows that in *general* the better machinists were the ones who did best on the test. At least that is the general trend of their scores, even though there are a number of exceptions. Despite the fact that it is not perfect, this examination would aid in selecting the men who would succeed as machinists.

By the computational technique described in Appendix C, the data on the above scattergram convert into a correlation coefficient of +.56. The *plus* indicates that high scores on one variable tend to pair with high scores on the other. However, the .56 indicates that the relationship is less than perfect.

Test III may be evaluated in the same manner. When the scores are plotted against the job ratings, the scattergram takes the following form.

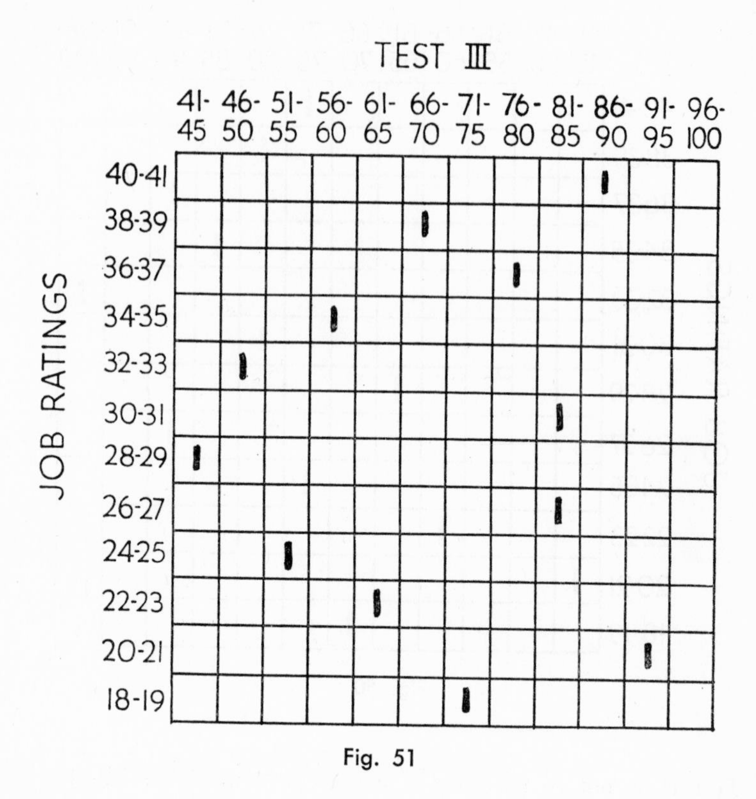

Fig. 51

Merely by inspecting the scattergram we can see that Test III is not a good measure of machinists' ability. The better machinists did not necessarily make better scores than the poorer machinists. How poor this test actually is can be determined more precisely when a correlation coefficient is computed. The coefficient is .oo. This means that there is no relationship between the workmen's proficiencies and their test scores. The personnel manager would be wasting his time using such a test as this in selecting new men.

It is apparent by now that the general trend of the tally marks on a scattergram is somewhat indicative of the magnitude of the correlation coefficient. Psychologists and educators who frequently work with scattergrams become proficient at inspecting the distribu-

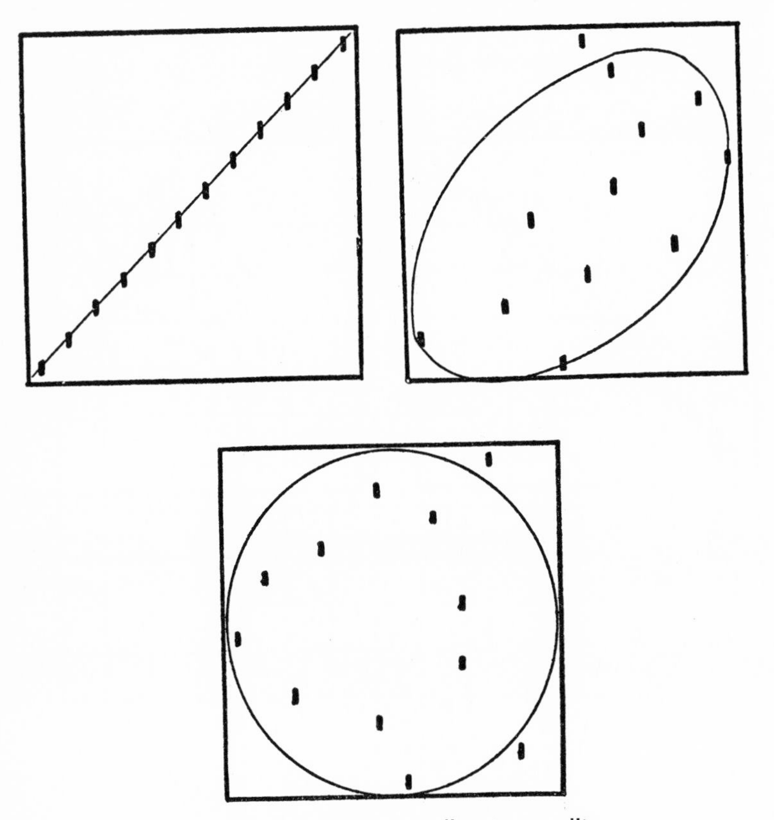

Fig. 52. Encompassing tallies in an ellipse

tion of tallies and guessing rather accurately what the computed correlation coefficient will be. The way they make their estimates can be seen if you *encompass the bulk of the tallies in an ellipse*. When this is done with Tests I, II, III, the foregoing figures are obtained.

Obviously, in Test I the *ellipse* is actually a straight line, for the tallies are in perfect alignment, lower left to upper right. In the scattergram for Test II the ellipse assumes the diagonal direction more than does the ellipse that encompasses the tallies of Test III. As indicated by these and other scattergrams, the closer the group of tallies approaches being a *straight diagonal line*, the higher the correlation coefficient. Below are three scattergrams. One represents a correlation of +.78, another a +.60, and the third +.99. Can you match the coefficients with the scattergrams?

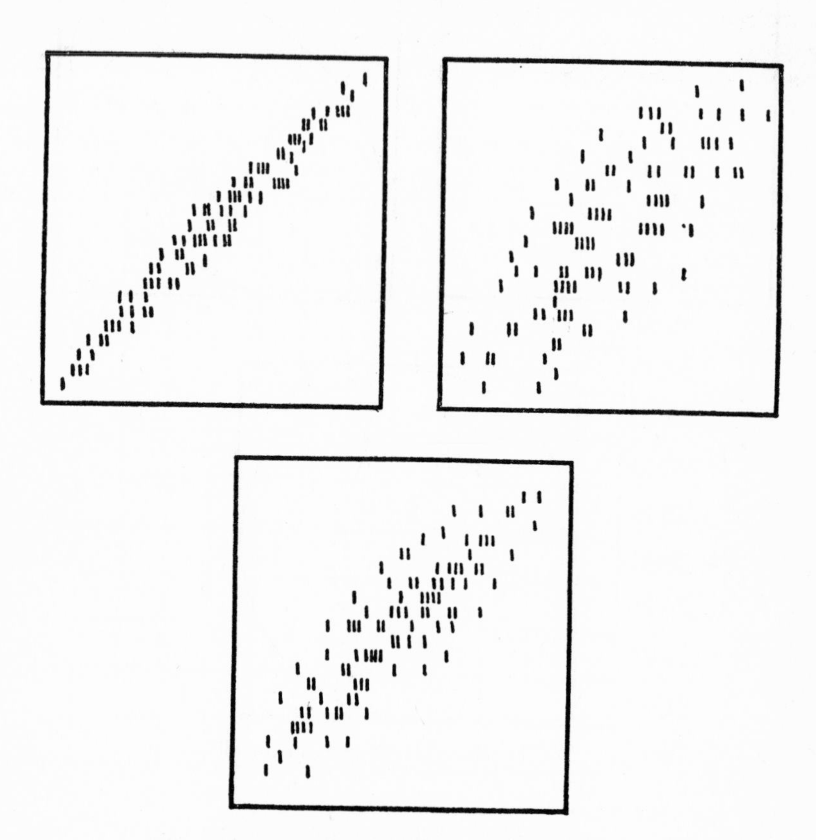

Fig. 53. Estimate these coefficients

Needless to say, this procedure of estimating by sight is not a very accurate way of determining a coefficient. Computation should be performed. However, it often helps a person understand what type of data underlies a coefficient when this estimating procedure is followed. In addition, it also helps him carry out the process in reverse, that is, to see a correlation coefficient (such as +.82 or +.37) in an educational journal and then to estimate in his mind what the array of tallies on the scattergram probably looked like. This sometimes helps us interpret a printed coefficient.

To continue with our machinists' examinations, we can plot the Test IV scores with the job ratings and derive the following scattergram.

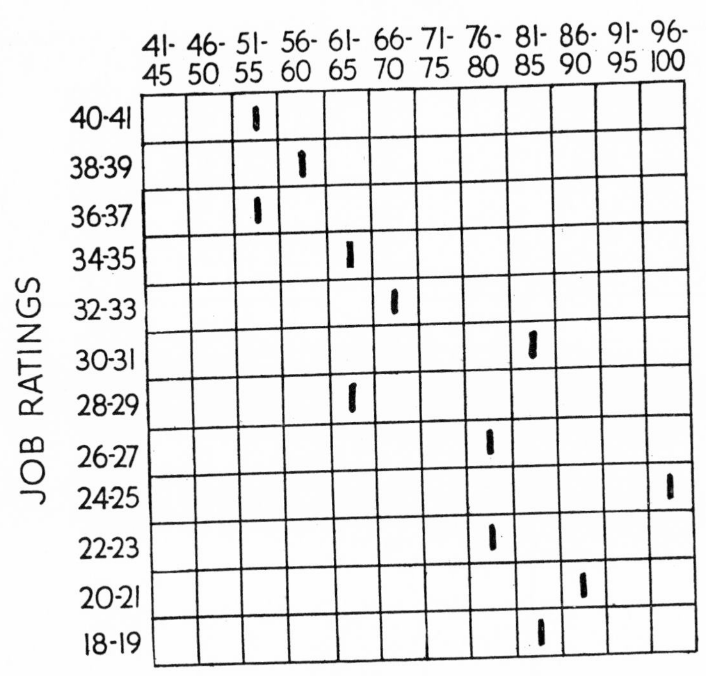

Fig. 54

The Test IV tally marks tend to spread themselves along a diagonal from upper left to lower right. In general, the better machinists made low test scores and the poorer ones made high test scores. We apparently selected strange items for this test, or else we selected unusual answers for it. In any event, Test IV seems to be a *test for poor machinists,* because they are the ones who do well on it. The original question now arises, "How effectively would this test separate good and poor machinists?" Actually, it does the job rather well. There is a definite relationship between test scores and the men's abilities, but the relationship is a *negative* one. By negative we mean that *low scores* on one of the variables *tend to pair up with high scores* on the other variable. Thus, if the personnel manager wishes to use such a test as this, he must be aware that he should hire the men with the low scores. Generally, they will be the good workmen. The correlation coefficient derived from this scattergram is —.83.

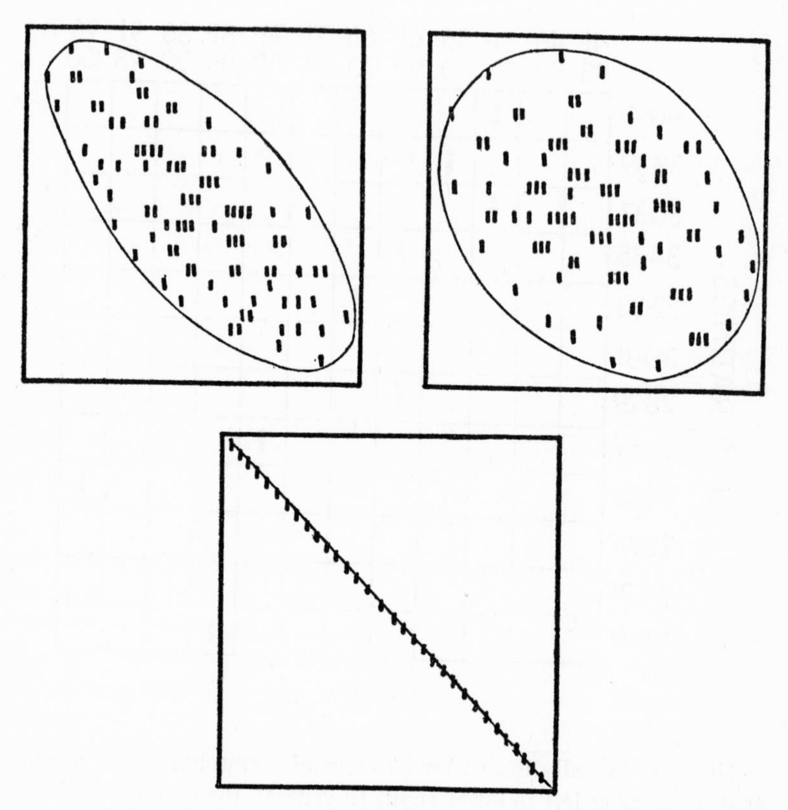

Fig. 55. Negative coefficients .60, .48, and 1.00

It is a common error for teachers who are newly introduced to correlation coefficients to assume that a *negative correlation* means that there is no relationship between two variables. The examples of Tests III and IV should make clear the difference between *no correlation* and *negative correlation.* When there is no relationship between variables, the coefficient is .00. Such a coefficient is useless for selecting machinists. On the other hand, a negative correlation means that a *relationship does exist,* but that the high scores on one variable pair with the low scores on the other. Negative correlations are useful for prediction of a machinist's ability. The test scores must merely be interpreted backwards.

A question commonly asked is: "Which shows a higher relationship between two variables, a positive coefficient or a negative one?" The answer is that the degree of relationship is determined by the magnitude of the coefficient. Thus, a +.85 and a −.85 show *equally high relationships.* They would be equally good for predicting machinists' abilities. However, the positive coefficient indicates that the good machinists score high on the test, whereas the negative one indicates that the good machinists received low scores.

Just as an ellipse encompassing the *main group* of tallies aids in estimating the degree of positive correlation, so the distribution of tallies may also aid in estimating the degree of negative correlation. It is still true that the closer the group of tallies approaches being a *straight diagonal,* the higher the correlation coefficient. However, in the case of negative correlation, the diagonal line is from upper left to lower right. The scattergrams on page 492 may help make these relationships clear.

OTHER USES OF CORRELATION

In the foregoing explanation the term *correlation coefficient* has been used in such a way as to suggest that there is only one type of correlation. This is not true. There are several types of statistics used to show the relationship between variables. However, the type of correlation discussed here is by far the most common one in education and psychology. Generally, it is the only one of importance to the typical teacher. Among educators and psychologists this popular type of correlation is often referred to by a term which distinguishes it from other techniques. Because the term often frightens the student newly introduced to the technique, it was not mentioned earlier. In its entirety it is called the *Pearson product-moment correlation coefficient.* This rather burdensome title is ordinarily abbreviated by a small *r*. (Pearson was an English statistician. *Product-moment* is a mathematical term identifying the basis for the computational formula.)

Pearson's *r* has uses in many areas for describing relationships between two variables. The variables which it has been used to compare include rainfall, crop yield, academic rank in school, scores on all types of achievement and aptitude tests, height, age, population of cities, and many others.

The following correlation coefficients will enable the reader to practice interpreting r and to see some educational contributions this statistic has made. (*1,5*)

Coefficient	*Variable 1*	*Variable 2*
+.94	Form M of Stanford-Binet Intelligence Test	Form L of Stanford-Binet Intelligence Test
+.79	Stanford - Binet Intelligence Test	Tenth Graders' Reading Vocabulary Scores
+.73	Stanford - Binet Intelligence Test	Tenth Graders' Reading Comprehension Scores
+.65	Average School Marks Plus Entrance Exam	Harvard Freshman Marks
+.58	Stanford-Binet Test	Porteus Maze Test, Grade 1
+.41	Stanford-Binet Test	Test in Fundamental Arithmetic Processes
+.27	Pressey Intelligence Test	Burgess Reading Test

The first of the correlations in the chart (+.94) indicates the very high relationship between the two different forms of the 1937 version of the Stanford-Binet Intelligence Test. With few exceptions the children who do well on one form of this test also do well on the other form. Consequently, the r of +.94 has shown us that two forms of the test yield highly consistent (that is, reliable) results. When r is used to describe the consistency of a test it is often referred to as the *reliability coefficient*.

The other coefficients in the above chart indicate different degrees of relationship between a number of variables. Interpreting the correlations, we could conclude that there is a higher relationship between the Stanford-Binet and reading comprehension (+.73) than between the Pressey Intelligence Test and a measure of reading ability, the Burgess Reading Test (+.27). Thus, the Stanford-Binet would be a better predictor of good readers than would the scores on the Pressey Intelligence Test if the children on which these *r*'s were established are similar.

The foregoing explanation of the meaning of correlation has been simplified as an introduction to this statistical procedure. For the student who wishes a more sophisticated and rigorous explanation of *r*, the following readings are recommended.

SUGGESTED READINGS

1. GARRETT, HENRY E. *Statistics in Psychology and Education*. New York: Longmans, Green and Co., 1958.
2. GUILFORD, J. P. *Fundamental Statistics in Psychology and Education*. New York: McGraw-Hill, 1950.
3. LINDQUIST, E. F. *Statistical Analysis in Educational Research*. Boston: Houghton Mifflin Co., 1940.
4. MCNEMAR, QUINN. *Psychological Statistics*. New York: John Wiley and Sons, 1955.
5. TATE, MERLE W. *Statistics in Education*. New York: Macmillan Co., 1955.

Appendix C

Other Statistical Procedures

STATISTICAL PROCEDURES which are of most use to elementary-school teachers have been explained in Chapter 7. Some other procedures for which teachers have only occasional use, or which they may wish to understand, are explained in this appendix. They include: (1) computation of the mean from grouped data, (2) computation of the median from grouped data, (3) computation and interpretation of the standard deviation, (4) use of standard scores, and (5) computation of the product-moment correlation coefficient.

PART I: MEAN OF GROUPED DATA

Sometimes teachers wish to find the average score of a large number of students who have taken a test, such as the reading-test scores of six sections of fifth graders. Because the list of scores is lengthy (143 in all), the task of adding so many large numbers becomes burdensome. In such instances it is often better to place the scores in groups and use a short-cut method rather than adding the long list of raw scores. The following procedure is useful for doing this.

Grouping scores

The teacher, faced with the list of 143 fifth-grade reading scores, must decide how to group them. From their experience with efficient grouping methods, statisticians (*1,3*) have recommended two practices.

First, they suggest that there be no less than 10 and no more than 20 different groups. Usually it is well to have 12 to 15 groups.

Second, they suggest that each of the groups be in one of the following sizes: 2, 3, 5, 10, and 20. These make for easy handling of the data.

The reading scores of our fifth graders seem to lend themselves to 12 groups, each to include 5 points, because the scores cover a total range of 57 points. That is, they extend from 49 to 105, a range that is encompassed within 60 points (12 × 5).

Thus, we create a chart and write these intervals down the left margin, in Column 1. (See Fig. 56.)

Tallying frequencies

In Column 2 on our chart we tally each reading score next to its appropriate interval. The sums of the tallies within each interval are placed in Column 3. This shows the frequency (f) of scores at differ-

(1)	(2)	(3)	(4)	(5)
Intervals	*Tallies*	f	d	fd
101-105	~~////~~	5	+5	+25
96-100	////	4	+4	+16
91-95	~~////~~ ///	8	+3	+24
86-90	~~////~~ ~~////~~ ~~////~~	15	+2	+30
81-85	~~////~~ ~~////~~ ~~////~~ ///	18	+1	+18
76-80	~~////~~ ~~////~~ ~~////~~ ~~////~~ ~~////~~ ~~////~~ /	31	0	0
71-75	~~////~~ ~~////~~ ~~////~~ ~~////~~ ////	24	−1	−24
66-70	~~////~~ ~~////~~ ~~////~~	15	−2	−30
61-65	~~////~~ ///	8	−3	−24
56-60	~~////~~ ~~////~~ /	11	−4	−44
51-55	//	2	−5	−10
46-50	//	2	−6	−12
Totals		143		−31

Fig. 56

ent levels. When the numbers in Column 3 are added, the resulting sum should equal the total number (N) of fifth graders who took the test.

To take the best advantage of short cuts, it is appropriate now to *guess* where the mean probably is. It does not matter how accurate the guess is, because the formula used with this procedure will automatically correct inaccuracies in the guess and will yield the *actual mean*. In the case of these reading scores, we estimate that the mean is in the interval 76-80. Because there is a range of 5 scores within that interval, it is more accurate to say that we guess the mean to be the midpoint of the interval or 78.

In Column 4 we record how much each interval *deviates* (d) *from the interval containing our guessed mean*. The first interval above the guessed mean is given the value +1. The second interval above is +2 and so forth. The intervals below the guessed mean are treated in the same manner except a minus sign is used in front of each of these numbers.

In Column 5 we record the results of multiplying horizontally the frequency (Column 3 number) and the interval deviation (Column 4 number) (fd). We must be sure to include the algebraic signs of these products. The positive products are summed (+113) and the negative products are summed (− 144). The algebraic sum of the entire column is −31.

Using a formula

The above procedure yields numbers which are substituted in the following formula to give the exact mean of the fifth-graders' reading-test scores:

$$M = M' + i\left(\frac{\Sigma fd}{N}\right)$$

The components of this formula are defined as:

M = exact mean
M' = guessed mean = 78
i = interval size = 5
N = total number of students = 143
Σ = sum of
fd = frequencies times deviations-from-guessed-mean

Inserting the appropriate data from the chart, the formula becomes:

$$M = 78 + 5\left(\frac{-31}{143}\right) = 78 + 5\,(-.217) = 78 + (-1.085) = 76.92$$

Consequently, the chart has enabled us to derive the mean of 76.92 for the 143 fifth graders, a task that would have been more difficult if we had attempted to sum all the raw scores and divide by 143 without the use of a calculating machine.

Whether this technique of deriving a mean from grouped data is easier than totaling all scores and dividing by the number of students is a question a teacher must answer for himself in each particular case. Generally, if a calculator is not available, the above process is simpler when many scores (especially those involving large numbers) must be handled.

PART II: MEDIAN OF GROUPED DATA

When we have test scores that are grouped in intervals, we can derive the median by the same general process used in Chapter 7 with ungrouped data. That is, we count up from the bottom to find the halfway point or halfway student. However, in the case of grouped data it is often desirable to determine the median more precisely than just reporting, "The median is one of the scores in the five-point interval 76-80."

Using the arithmetic scores of 42 eighth graders, we find by counting students that the point which divides the upper half of the students from the lower half is within the interval 36 to 40. However, we see that there are also 7 other scores within that in-

Arithmetic Score	*Number of Students*	
56-60	2	
51-55	3	16 cases above interval containing median.
46-50	7	
41-45	4	
36-40	8	—Interval containing median. Exact limits of interval = 35.5 and 40.5.
31-35	9	
26-30	6	
21-25	1	18 cases below interval containing median
16-20	1	
11-15	1	

Fig. 57

terval. How can we determine more precisely just where in that five-point range the median lies? Is it near the top of the interval, near the middle. or at the bottom?

In our process of counting 21 students in order to arrive at the halfway point, we discovered that there are 18 students below the interval containing the median. To secure the desired 21 students, we need 3 of the 8 in the 36-40 interval. In other words, if we go three-eighths of the way up into the interval, we will have arrived at the precise median we desire.

Here is the method for moving three-eighths of the distance into the five-point interval, 36-40, whose *exact* limits are 35.5 and 40.5. Three-eighths of 5 is 1.875. By adding 1.875 to the lower limit of the interval (35.5) we secure 37.375 or 37⅜ as the median of the class. We could have arrived at the same answer by starting at the top of the distribution and moving into the top of the interval containing the median.

PART III: STANDARD DEVIATION AND NORMAL CURVE

Chapter 7 indicated that the mean or median can be used to describe the average or the middle score for a class on a test. But reporting an average is not sufficient to describe accurately the success of a class. A measure of how much the class bunched around the average or scattered away from it is necessary. In Chapter 7 a simple way to describe this spread of scores was shown to be the *distance-between-percentiles*. However, frequently in education and psychology another kind of statistic is used to describe the spread of scores. This is called the *standard deviation*. As its name suggests, it shows to what extent scores *deviate or scatter away from the mean.*

Very few elementary-school teachers ever compute standard deviations. Thus, a common question is: "Why discuss statistical terms we never use?" The answer is that although the classroom teacher rarely has occasion to *compute* standard deviations, he sometimes does find it necessary to *interpret* the meaning of standard deviations. The standard deviation is used in many types of research published in educational journals, and it is cited in manuals for the standardized achievement and aptitude tests commonly used in schools.

From experience we have found that students more readily understand the meaning of standard deviation if they first see how it is computed. Consequently, a brief discussion of computing the standard deviation will be followed by a discussion of its interpretation.

Computing the standard deviation

When a teacher can compute a mean from grouped data, determining a standard deviation is fairly simple, for it entails only a little more computation.

As the following example indicates, the chart used in determining the mean is again followed. (See Figure 58.) However, since an additional step is desired, a sixth column is added to the five used in finding the mean. This sixth column is for listing the *squares of the deviations from the guessed mean* (fd^2). This sixth column is determined merely by multiplying each number in Column 4 (the deviations—d) by the adjacent number in Column 5 (the deviations multiplied by the frequencies—fd). Although positive and negative numbers were found in Columns 4 and 5, *only positive* numbers will result from multiplying these two columns together, since the squaring of numbers always results in positive numbers. Column 6, containing all positive numbers, should then be summed.

Figure 58 provides the numbers necessary to complete the formula for the standard deviation:

$$S.D. = i\sqrt{\frac{\Sigma fd^2}{N} - \left(\frac{\Sigma fd}{N}\right)^2}$$

The components of this formula are defined as:

$S.D.$ = the standard deviation we are determining
i = the interval by which the scores were grouped
Σ = sum of
fd = frequencies multiplied by the deviations from a guessed mean
N = total number of students

The standard deviation for the scores on the test about social-studies facts is computed in this manner:

$$S.D. = 1\sqrt{\frac{466}{50} - \left(\frac{34}{50}\right)^2} = 1\sqrt{9.32 - .46} = 1\sqrt{8.86} = 2.98$$

(1)	(2)	(3)	(4)	(5)	(6)
Score	*Tallies*	*f*	*d*	*fd*	*fd*²
15	/	1	+8	+ 8	64
14	/	1	+7	+ 7	49
13	///	3	+6	+18	108
12	/	1	+5	+ 5	25
11	//	2	+4	+ 8	32
10	////	4	+3	+12	36
9	~~////~~	5	+2	+10	20
8	~~////~~ /	6	+1	+ 6	6
7	~~////~~ ~~////~~	10	0	0	0
6	~~////~~ /	6	−1	− 6	6
5	////	4	−2	− 8	16
4	////	4	−3	−12	36
3	//	2	−4	− 8	32
2		0	−5	0	0
1	/	1	−6	− 6	36
Totals		$N = 50$		$fd = 34$	$fd^2 = 466$

Fig. 58. Scores on test covering social-studies facts

Our standard deviation is 2.98. This statistic could be written a number of ways, for a number of terms or abbreviations are commonly used in textbooks and test manuals in referring to it. It is abbreviated *S.D.*, *SD*, *s*, and *s.d.* It is also called by the Greek letter *sigma* or is indicated by the small Greek symbol for sigma, σ.

Interpreting the standard deviation

The sixth column in Figure 58 may give some insight into the standard deviation's meaning. Note that if in this distribution the social-studies-test scores had been more strung out than they were, with more scores near the top and bottom and fewer near the mean, the squared numbers in Column 6 (and their sum at the bottom) would have been larger. That is, as scores scatter farther away from the average, they cause the squared numbers to increase and consequently the standard deviation is a larger number. Conversely, as scores bunch more around the average, they cause the squared numbers to be smaller and, as a result, the standard deviation is a smaller number.

Therefore, we conclude that a small standard deviation number means more bunching of scores around the average. A larger standard deviation means the scores are more spread out.

It is seen that this general interpretation is similar to the interpretation of the distance-between-percentiles; that is, the larger the number, the more scattered the scores. However, the standard deviation offers additional useful information. In order to understand this, we will inspect briefly the normal distribution curve.

Normal distribution curve

In past years, large numbers of people have been measured to determine their rating on some physical characteristic, such as height, or on an intellectual chracteristic, such as school aptitude. Continual measurements for many different characteristics over a long period has shown that on each such characteristic as those mentioned above the distribution of scores tends to assume about the same shape. Most people measure somewhat alike. That is, the bulk of the group bunch together around an average score or average size. As the scores range farther above this average, the number of people gradually decreases. As scores range farther below the average, the number again decreases. Because so many human characteristics seem to result in such similar tally sheets when scores are recorded, this common curve-shaped arrangement of scores has been called the *normal distribution curve*. (It is also sometimes known as the *bell-shaped curve,* because of its shape when the scores are lined up horizontally rather than vertically.

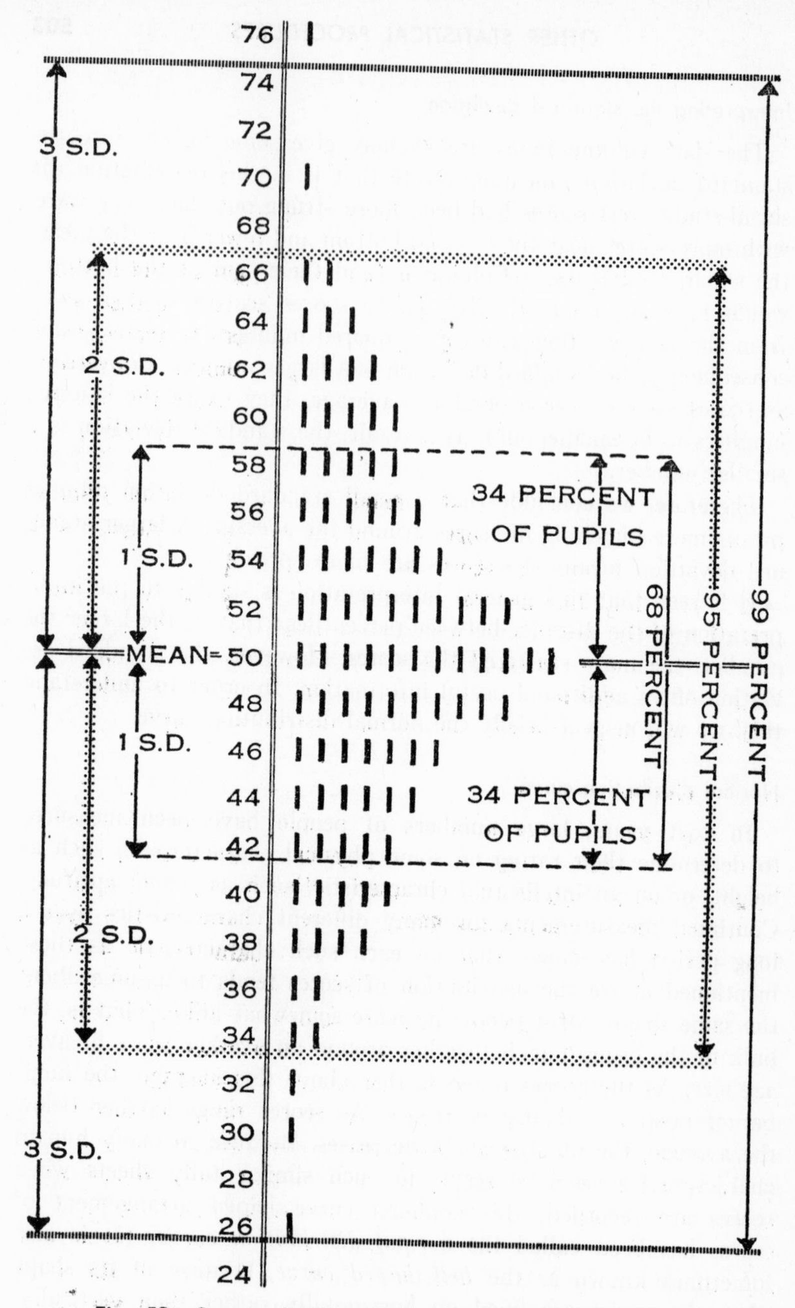

Fig. 59. Scores of 100 normally-distributed nine-year-olds

Or it is called the *Gaussian* curve after Gauss, a German mathematician who developed procedures relating to it.)

The standard deviation formula and its interpretation are based upon the normal curve. This fact provides us with valuable information. For example, say that we test 100 typical nine-year-olds for general intelligence. We find, as we expect, that the distribution of their scores is a normal one (Fig. 59). We compute the mean and find it to be 50. Using the formula introduced earlier, we compute the standard deviation and find it to be 8 points.

Now, if we begin at the mean (50) and add the standard deviation to the mean (50 + 8) we arrive at score 58. Because of the nature of the standard deviation formula, it is true that about *34 per cent* of the students will be found in the area between the mean (50) and one standard deviation (8 points) above the mean (score 58). Likewise, if we begin at the mean (50) and subtract one standard deviation (8 points) we arrive at score 42. And in the area between the mean and one standard deviation below the mean (score 42) we will also find 34 per cent of the students.

From the above explanation it is seen that the *mean* (score 50) *plus* one standard deviation and *minus* one standard deviation defines an area that includes the middle 68 per cent of the children who took the test (34 + 34 = 68). (The percents cited as 34 and 68 are round numbers. Actually the distance of one *S.D.* above the mean includes 34.13 per cent of the cases. Consequently, the distance of one *S.D.* above *and* one *S.D.* below the mean includes 68.26 per cent of the cases.)

The question is often asked, "But any time you compute a standard deviation, will the area between the mean and one standard deviation above it always include 34 per cent of the cases?" The answer is *yes* if the distribution of scores is normal, as it usually is with fairly large numbers of people tested. Therefore, when a teacher is reading about tests for which a standard deviation is reported (such as 8 for Fig. 59 or 2.98 for Fig. 58), he knows that about 68 per cent or slightly more than two-thirds of the students have scored between the point one *s.d. above* the mean and one *s.d. below* the mean.

The nature of the standard deviation also provides us with additional information. If we go *two* standard deviations above the mean in Figure 59 we arrive at score 66 (that is, 50 + (8 × 2) = 66). If we go *two* standard deviations below the mean, we arrive at score 34. Between scores 34 and 66, which is now a total distance of four *S.D.*'s, we have included slightly more than 95 per cent of the students who took the test.

If we move *three* standard deviations above and three below the mean, we have included within this area of six *S.D.*'s slightly more than 99 per cent of all the students. Those who score higher than three *S.D.*'s above the mean are very rare. Students who score more than three *S.D.*'s below the mean are likewise rare on the low end of the scale.

Of what use is this information about the per cent of cases encompassed within a certain number of standard deviations? It has a number of uses. Here are two examples:

1. We are reading the manual that accompanies a standardized reading examination in order to discover how a seventh-grade boy, John Kelly, whom we have tested, stands in relation to other seventh graders. John's score was 147. The test manual does not include a tally sheet with a distribution of scores for all the 1,200 students on whom the test was standardized. Such a tally sheet would be cumbersome. Instead, the manual includes very concise data. It states that among the seventh graders in the standardization group the mean score was 123 and the standard deviation was 21.

   The information we learned about the relationship of the standard deviation to the normal curve will enable us to see about where John stood in relation to other seventh graders. In carrying out a job of interpretation such as this, it is often helpful to picture in our minds or on a piece of paper where the student's score (147) apparently would appear on the distribution curve. We know that 50 per cent of the students are below the mean (123), and John is certainly above that point. If we add one standard deviation (21) to the mean (123) we arrive at score 144. From the information provided earlier we know that 34 per cent of the students will be in this area between the mean (123) and one standard deviation above it (144). Consequently, adding the 50 per cent of cases (area from mean to the bottom of the scores) to this 34 per cent (between mean and score 144) we have 84 per cent of the students. Since John's score of 147 is slightly higher, we know that he scored slightly higher than 84 per cent of seventh graders.

Therefore, knowing the mean and standard deviation we can determine roughly how a student stands in relation to others who took the test.

2. Here is a second example of using the standard deviation. Fifth graders in two different elementary schools took the same test in geography. The following statistics were reported for the schools.

School A	*School B*	
$N = 82$	$N = 73$	N = Number of Students
$M = 76$	$M = 57$	M = Mean
$S.D. = 9$	$S.D. = 14$	$S.D.$ = Standard Deviation

With these data we wish to answer the following questions:

1. Which group did better?
2. Which group achieved scores which bunched together most?
3. Did more than 97 per cent of the students in the better class score higher than the average of the poorer class?
4. In School B, Janice Schmidt received a score of 72. In general, how did she stand in relation to her classmates? If she had received the same score in School A, how would she have compared with the students there?

Either by picturing these distributions in our mind or by sketching them on a sheet of paper, we can readily find the answers to these questions.

1. School A did better in general, for it had the higher average.
2. The School A scores bunched together most, as indicated by the smaller standard deviation.
3. Yes, more than 97 per cent of the students in School A did better than the average of School B. We know this because we realize that when we go two standard deviations above the mean and two below the mean we have encompassed 95 per cent of the cases. This leaves 2½ per cent of the cases at the bottom tip of the distribution and 2½ per cent at the top tip. In School A when we subtract two standard deviations from the mean (75—18=58) we find that we are at score 58, or 1 point above the average of 57 of School B. Consequently, more than 97 per cent of those in School A did better than the average of School B.

4. In School B, Janice Schmidt, with a score of 72, would be among the top 16 per cent of her classmates. However, with the same score in School A she would have been slightly below the mean, or within the bottom half of the group.

PART IV: STANDARD SCORES

The foregoing examples have indicated briefly some uses teachers can make of the standard deviation in interpreting published test results or statistical studies in educational and psychological journals. One further use with which teachers should be acquainted is as a basis for *standard scores.*

For instance, a sixth-grade girl received the following scores on standardized tests:

Arithmetic Problems = 22
Arithmetic Computation = 51
Reading = 72
Science Facts = 26

These numbers are called *raw scores*. Now we want to know what these raw scores mean in telling how adequate the girl is compared to other sixth graders. Upon first glance it might appear that she succeeded best in reading and poorest in arithmetic problems. However, we realize that this assumption is wrong when we learn that the possible scores on the tests were:

Arithmetic Problems = 25
Arithmetic Computation = 60
Reading = 100
Science Facts = 50

As in the cases of these tests, raw scores on different examinations are not usually comparable. Two techniques for making them comparable are in common use. The first, changing students' scores into *percentiles,* was described in Chapter 7. The second, changing raw scores into *standard scores,* is less practical for the teacher to compute but is often used by test publishers and thus should be understood by teachers who interpret standardized test results.

Standard scores are developed in the following manner. The mean and standard deviation for a distribution are computed. Then the distribution is marked off into standard deviations from the mean. The deviations above the mean are marked with plus, the ones below the mean with minus. The distance between each of these standard deviations is called *one standard score.*

Let us return to the tests given to the sixth-grade girl. The means and standard deviations for the four tests are:

Arithmetic Problems	*Arithmetic Computation*	*Reading*	*Science Facts*
$M = 15$	$M = 42$	$M = 50$	$M = 29$
$S.D. = 2.5$	$S.D. = 6$	$S.D. = 10$	$S.D. = 5$

To see how these may be changed into standard scores that can be compared, we can plot them below a normal curve and see how the standard deviation can function as the basic unit for all four tests.

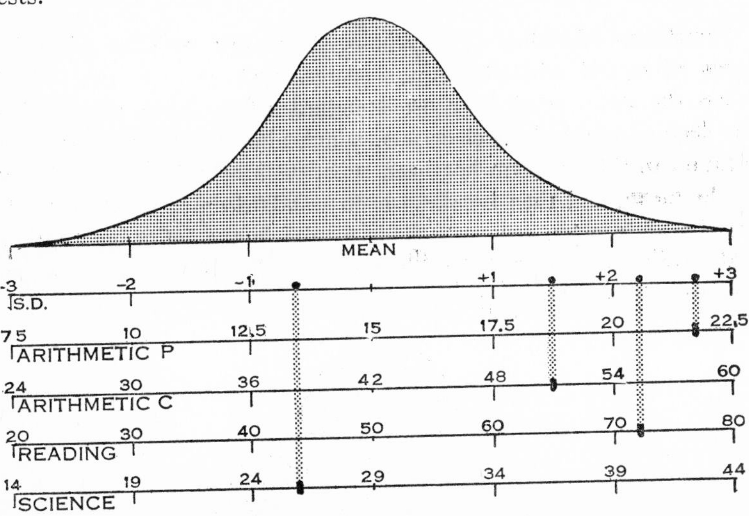

Fig. 60. Standard deviation is basis for standard scores

Here, in order to show the four tests in relation to the normal curve, we have plotted them on scales. And we have placed a dot where the sixth-grade girl succeeded on each. However, in the practical situation it is unnecessary to do such plotting. Instead, we may change the raw scores readily into standard scores by a simple formula:

$$z = \frac{X - M}{s}$$

The terms of the formula are defined as:

z = the standard score we desire
X = the raw score the student received
M = the mean of the distribution
s = the standard deviation of the distribution

Using this formula, we transpose the sixth-grade girl's test results into the following standard scores, which tell us accurately how she succeeded on one test as compared to another.

Arithmetic Problems = 2.8
Arithmetic Computation = 1.5
Reading = 2.2
Science Facts = —.6

Sometimes educators or psychologists dislike working with the mean of 0 and with the minus scores, such as —.6, that occur below the mean when they use standard scores. They also dislike the decimal numbers, such as 2.2, which almost always occur. One solution to this problem has been substituting the number 50 for 0 as the mean, and then breaking each standard deviation (or standard score) into ten segments. This results in the following type of scale, called a *T*-scale, which does not entail minus numbers or so many decimal numbers.

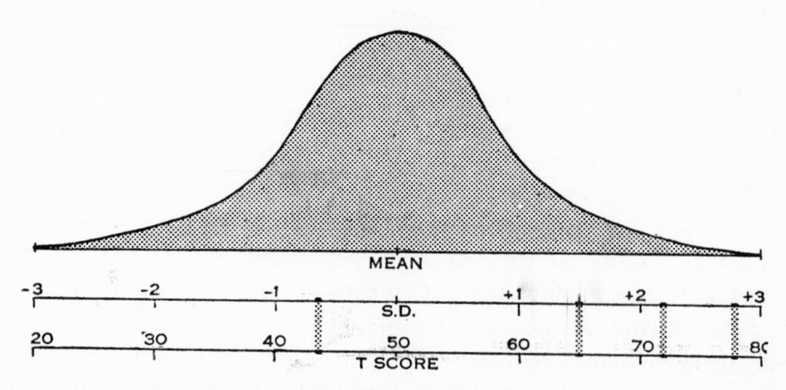

Fig. 61. *T*-scale based on standard deviation

If we used this handier type of *T*-scale for describing the sixth-grade girl's success on the tests, we would report her *T*-scores as being:

Arithmetic Problems = 78
Arithmetic Computation = 65
Reading = 72
Science Facts = 44

PART V: COMPUTING CORRELATION

In Appendix A the meaning of the Pearson correlation coefficient was explained. Although elementary-school teachers usually need to know only the meaning behind correlation so that they can interpret coefficients they read, some may also wish to learn how to compute a coefficient on data gathered from their classes. Consequently, the following section contains a brief explanation of the computation of a coefficient from a scatter diagram.

We begin with the two sets of scores between which we wish to find the relationship. For an example we will use the scores of 50 eighth graders on two tests: one covering facts about local, state, and national government, and the other covering facts of world geography. Our question is: "What is the relationship between the eighth-graders' knowledge of government and their knowledge of world geography?"

On the government test the students' scores extend from 67 to 108. With this rather wide range (42 points) we will wish to put the scores into groups to make computation more convenient. We decide that placing them in groups of fives will be appropriate.

On the geography test the scores extend from 51 to 96. Since this also is an unwieldy range to work with, we decide to group the geography scores also into fives to facilitate computation.

Next we prepare a table with the score intervals of the government test listed up the left side and the intervals for the geography test listed across the top. On this chart we plot the scores received on the tests by each of the 50 students.

The plotting is done in this manner. Dave Smith received 72 on the government test and 65 in geography. Thus, on the government examination (left margin) we see that his score should be within the 70-74 interval. On the geography test (top margin) we see that his score should be in the 65-69 interval. We now locate the *cell* or space where these *two intervals intersect, and we mark a tally in that cell.* Then we proceed to the next student's two scores, locate the cell where his scores on the tests would cross, and mark a tally for him in that cell. We continue this process until all 50 pairs of scores are tallied on the scatter diagram.

The tallies of the cells are summed across to the right margin (Y axis) and down to the bottom margin (X axis) to indicate the total frequencies in the cells. The sum of the f_x row and the sum of the f_y column should equal 50, the number of students tested.

Figure 62 shows how this scatter diagram is further developed in computing a Pearson r. After the frequencies (f_x and f_y) have been computed for each test, we complete the next three columns at the right and three rows at the bottom in the same manner used to compute the mean and standard deviation from grouped data. (See Parts I and III of Appendix C.)

From the foregoing explanation it is seen that the steps so far are the same ones used in computing the mean and standard deviation of a group of scores, with the exception that in developing the scattergram we have placed one distribution of scores across the top (X axis) and the other up the side (Y axis), rather than listing each distribution entirely by itself.

The next step is a new process, that of calculating the cross-products. In doing this we multiply each d_y (which is a deviation from the guessed mean in column at right) by each d_x (deviation from mean found in row at bottom) for *every cell that has a tally in it.* This product for every cell is customarily written in the upper left-hand corner of the cell. Such cross-multiplying should result in every product in the upper-right and lower-left quarters of the scatter diagram being positive numbers and every product in the upper-left and lower-right quarters being negative numbers.

Within each cell we now note how many individuals have received this particular d_xd_y value, that is, how many students scored in this cell. Then within each cell we multiply the cross-product by the number of tallies and write the answer in the lower-right corner of the cell, making sure to include the proper algebraic sign. The next step is to add these resulting products (add the numbers from the lower-right corner of each cell) and put the answers in the last two columns on the right (when adding each row across) and the last two rows at the bottom (when adding each column down). The sums of the positive numbers are to be placed in the first of these final columns, and the sums of the negative numbers in the second. Finally, in the lower-right corner of the chart we write the algebraic sum of the final columns. The algebraic sum of the final two columns on the right should equal the sum of the last two rows at the bottom.

The scatter diagram has now provided the proper information to insert in the following formula, which is commonly used for computing the Pearson r from a scattergram. (3:92–95)

$$r = \frac{N\Sigma d_x d_y - \Sigma d_x \Sigma d_y}{\sqrt{N\Sigma d^2_x - (\Sigma d_x)^2} \quad \sqrt{N\Sigma d^2_y - (\Sigma d_y)^2}}$$

SUGGESTED READINGS

1. GUILFORD, J. P. *Fundamental Statistics in Psychology and Education.* New York: McGraw-Hill, 1950.
2. LINDQUIST, E. F. *Statistical Analysis in Educational Research.* Boston: Houghton Mifflin Co., 1940.
3. MCNEMAR, QUINN. *Psychological Statistics.* New York: John Wiley and Sons, 1955. A more advanced treatment.
4. TATE, MERLE W. *Statistics in Education.* New York: Macmillan Co., 1955.

GEOGRAPHY TEST (X-AXIS)

GOVERNMENT TEST (Y-AXIS)

	50-54	55-59	60-64	65-69	70-74	75-79	80-84	85-89	90-94	95-99	fy	dy	fdy	fd²y	dx dy +	dx dy −
105-109										+16 I +16	1	+4	+4	16	16	
100-104						I		+6 II +12	+9 II +18		5	+3	+15	45	30	
95-99			-6 I -6	-4 I -4	-2 I -2	I	+2 III +6	+4 II +8			9	+2	+18	36	14	12
90-94					-1 II -2	I	+1 IIII/ +5	+2 I +2			9	+1	+9	9	7	2
85-89				II	II	I	III	I	I		10					
80-84			+3 I +3	+2 II +4	+1 III +3	II					8	-1	-8	8	10	
75-79		+8 I +8	+6 II +12	+4 II +8							5	-2	-10	20	28	
70-74	+15 I +15			+6 I +6							2	-3	-6	18	21	
65-69		+16 I +16									1	-4	-4	16	16	
fx	1	2	4	8	8	6	11	6	3	1	50		+18	168	-142	-14
dx	-5	-4	-3	-2	-1		+1	+2	+3	+4						
fdx	-5	-8	-12	-16	-8		+11	+12	+9	+4	-13					
fd²x	25	32	36	32	8		11	24	27	16	211					
dx dy +	15	24	15	18	3		11	22	18	16	+142					
dx dy −			6	4	4						-14					

N = 50; Σdy; Σd²y; Σdxdy = 128; −Σdx; Σd²x; Σdxdy = 128

$$r = \frac{(50)(128) - (-13)(+18)}{\sqrt{(50)(211) - (-13)^2}\ \sqrt{(50)(168) - (18)^2}}$$

$$r = .72$$

Fig. 62. Correlation scattergram

Index